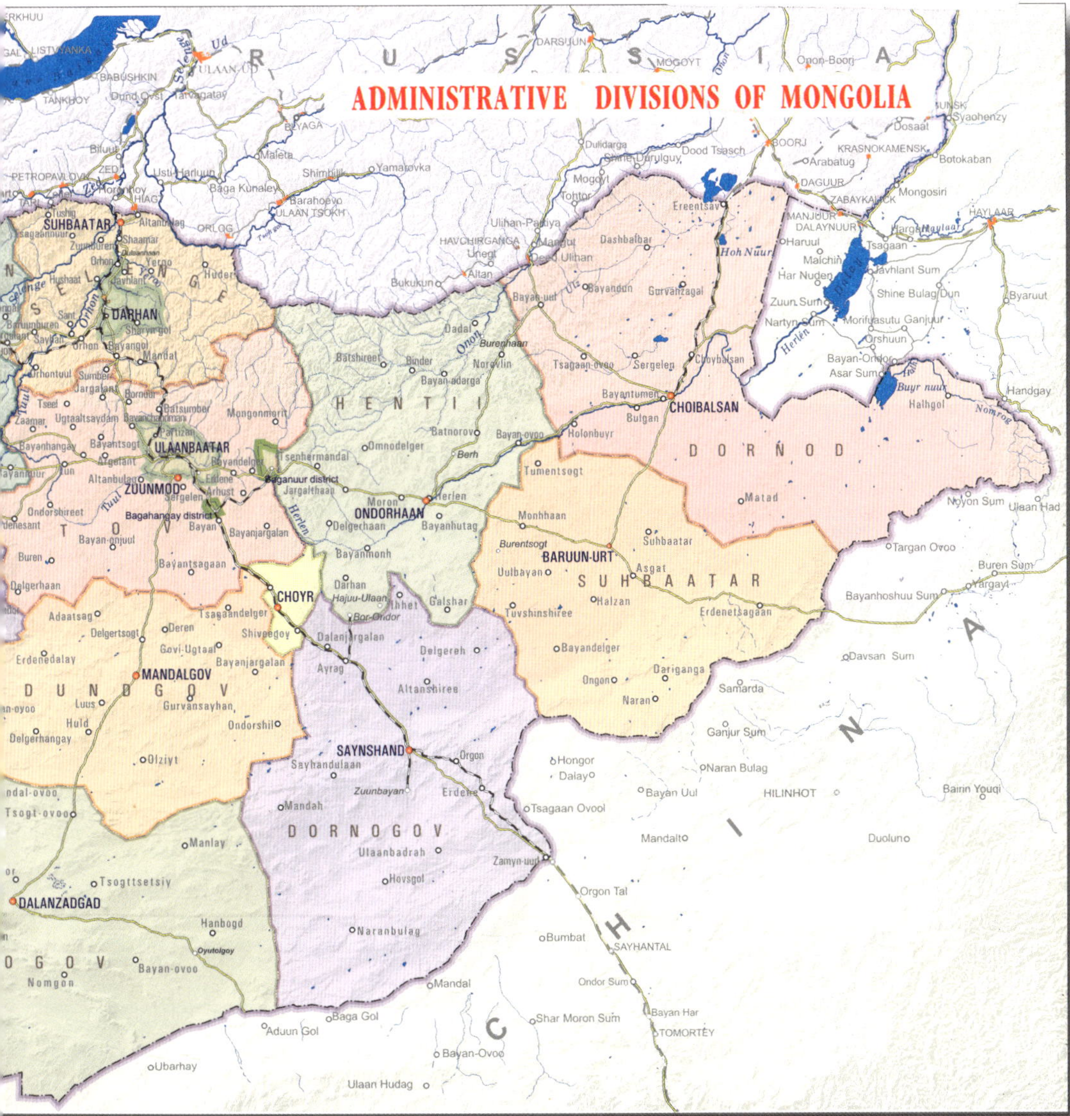

ADMINISTRATIVE DIVISIONS OF MONGOLIA

TENGRI
GROUP

MONGOLIA

NOMAD EMPIRE OF ETERNAL BLUE SKY

CARL ROBINSON

ODYSSEY BOOKS & GUIDES

Odyssey Books & Guides is a division of Airphoto International Ltd.
1401 Chung Ying Building, 20–20A Connaught Road West, Sheung Wan, Hong Kong
Tel: (852) 2856-3896; Fax: (852) 3012-1825
E-mail: magnus@odysseypublications.com; www.odysseypublications.com

Distribution in the USA by W.W. Norton & Company, Inc., 500 Fifth Avenue, New York, NY 10110, USA. Tel: 800-233-4830; Fax: 800-458-6515; www.wwnorton.com

Distribution in the UK and Europe by Cordee Ltd., 11 Jacknell Road, Dodwells Bridge Industrial Estate, Hinckley, Leicestershire LE10 3BS, UK. Tel: 01455-611185; info@cordee.co.uk; www.cordee.co.uk

Distribution in Australia by Tower Books Pty Ltd., a member of the Scribo Group. Unit 18 Rodborough Road, Frenchs Forest, NSW 2086, Australia; www.towerbooks.com.au

Mongolia: Nomad Empire of Eternal Blue Sky
ISBN: 978-962-217-808-3
Library of Congress Catalog Card Number has been requested.

Grateful acknowledgement is made to the following authors and publishers; all materials remain the property of their respective copyright owners as indicated: Professor Thomas J. Barfield for *Mongol Military Organisation* © 2002; Don Croner for *The Abduction of the Eighth Bog Gegeen* © 2008; Pan Macmillan for *Five Months in a Leaky Boat* by Ben Kozel, © 2003 by Ben Kozel; Fredonia Books for *Aross Mongolian Plains* by Roy Chapman Andrews © 2001 (reprinted from a 1921 edition); Kodansha America Inc. for *The Desert Road to Turkestan* by Owen Lattimore © 1995 (first published by Little, Brown and Company in 1929); Gaby Bamana for *On the Tea Road, A Journey into Mongolian Life and Culture* © 2008 by Gaby Bamana; Abacus for *Hearing Birds Fly* by Louisa Waugh © 2003 by Louisa Waugh; Sphere for *Long Way Round* by Ewan McGregor and Charley Boorman © 2004 by Long Way Round Limited; Battulga Tumurdash for *The Sun Eater & Almas: 12 Amazing Snowman Legends* © 2009 (edited by Louisa Waugh).

Managing Editor: Jeremy Tredinnick
Designer: Au Yeung Chui Kwai
Maps: GAZRYN ZURAG Co., Ltd.
Production and printing by Twin Age Ltd., Hong Kong
E-mail: twinage@netvigator.com
Manufactured in Hong Kong

Front cover image: Graham Taylor
Page 4: A deer stone marks a historical site on the open steppe (Carl Robinson).
Right: A test of marksmanship at the Naadam Festival (Elbegzaya Lhagvasuren).

A camel caravan wends its way between Gobi dunes and steppe lake (Gotsbayar Rentsendorj).

Mongolia's vast expanse of lush, flower-strewn meadows have provided superb grazing for horses and other livestock for millennia – a major factor in the rise of its many empire-building tribes (Graham Taylor).

ACKNOWLEDGEMENTS & THANKS

I have many people to thank for their assistance and encouragement. First and foremost is Ivana Grollova, whose translations of large portions of her Czech-language volume *Mongolove* provided me with early and invaluable insights into Mongolian history, culture and society.

In Washington, D.C., Alicia Campi of the Mongolia Society introduced me to Susan Meinheit of the Library of Congress where I spent wonderfully absorbing hours studying its classic works on Mongolia. William Fitzhugh, Director of Arctic Studies at the Smithsonian's National Museum of Natural History, provided insights into Mongolia's deer stones. At the Pennsylvania Museum of Archaeology and Anthropology, Paula L.W. Sabloff gave me valuable assistance while the American Museum of Natural History's Mark Norrell discussed his latest dinosaur-hunting expeditions to the Gobi. In Australia, Karakorum Expeditions' Graham Taylor, Honorary Consul Peter Sloane and Ian Finlayson gave useful practical advice. In Beijing, Khan Orgil and Cui Jingmei of the Mongolia Genco Tour Bureau arranged my Trans-Mongolia Rail journey – and much more.

In Mongolia, profound gratitude goes to Indraa Bold and Erka Erdenechimeg from the Mongolian National Tourism Organisation (MNTO) who arranged my travels and worried constantly about my stamina. Also, special thanks to Khuree Ankhbayar, or Ankhaa, of the Tengrii Group, a long-time supporter of this project and whose advice, wisdom and friendship I value highly. Battulga Tumurdash of Look Mongolia is another special friend who opened his *ger* camp, restaurants and own writings to me. Another great guy, Ulziidelger Batbayar of Battour, got me to the plane on time – even if that promised nightlife tour of UB must await another visit! My drivers and guides were wonderful travelling companions: Khulan in UB; Ogii and Byambaa; Zolbo and Zorgo; and another Byambaa and Davaadorj. A very special thanks to Ulgiibadigan of Mongol Khan Expeditions for showing me the Bayanhongor Gobi, easily my favourite destination in Mongolia. Also special thanks to Gazryn Zurag's hard-working Byambaa on maps.

Others are Tracey Naughton of PACT Mongolia; Rik and Tseren Idema and Peter Oetzmann of Tseren Tours; Zorig Munkhchuluun, MP; historian Baabar; palaeontologist Rinchen Barsbold; the Itgel Foundation's Morgan Keay; Fish Mongolia's Andy Parkinson and Hishge, geologists David Lorge and Mike Lelliott; and Baigal Gongor. For vetting my History and People chapters, I am especially grateful to my Congolese mate in UB, Gaby Bamana. And always with a speedy reply to my many queries, I thank Don Croner for his constant assistance.

In Australia, I am most grateful to Vietnam War colleague and photographer Tim Page for editing photos, and computer wizard Steve Spiers for bringing them together. In Hong Kong, publisher Magnus Bartlett and editor Jeremy Tredinnick have shown tremendous patience as I've struggled to meet deadlines. For putting up with my Mongolian Obsession and neglecting other duties for months, a very special thanks to my dear wife Kim-Dung.

Carl Robinson, 2009

The "manly" sport of wrestling is practised from an early age (Gotsbayar Rentsendorj).

PREFACE

As a long-time American expatriate and former foreign correspondent, I have certainly led a very nomadic life. But while spending much time in Asia, the thought of visiting Mongolia, that legendary home of the world's nomads, had never occurred to me. Sure, I knew about Genghis Khan and the Mongol Empire, the Gobi Desert and dinosaurs, and that Mongolia was the Soviet's first satellite state. My most substantial knowledge concerned Vietnam where I spent many years during the war and am personally fascinated by its long history of repelling foreigners. Back in 1288 in its campaign to conquer southern China, the Mongols were soundly defeated at the Bach Dang River east of today's Hanoi and expelled from the country. Vietnamese General Tran Hung Dao remains a national hero.

So, I welcomed the unexpected opportunity to visit Mongolia for this new guide and discover this faraway link with Vietnam. But unlike the old foreign correspondent who'd so often dropped into exotic places with just a couple of newspaper clippings, I researched heavily, interviewing experts, reading books and articles, and studying photos and maps. But nothing prepared me for the stunning reality of the country, which far exceeded my expectations. Everything was on such a massive scale, including the Mongolians' renowned hospitality. I felt welcomed and was instantly "at home", as if I had fulfilled a personal destiny, even reliving a previous lifetime. (Never mind that most Mongolians are unaware of their history with Vietnam. The only Vietnamese they know today are Ulaanbaatar's expert "panel-beaters", or car body shop repairers.)

With a reporter's eye and historian's ear, what follows is a capsule of today's Mongolia – descriptive, factual and quirkily personal at times. Let me take you to a unique and wonderful corner of the world with hopes that you'll soon follow. I spent two gruelling but wonderful months travelling over 20,000 kilometres around Mongolia in May and June 2008. But returning home, I quickly realised how little I still knew. Further months of research and writing followed but now in a totally different – but understandable – context. I only hope that my friends in Mongolia are pleased with the final result – and I certainly take full responsibility for any errors and misspellings that may have crept in.

Finally, in my English transliterations, I have used a simplified form of Modern Mongolian based on Gazryn Zurag's *Mongolia Road Map*, which uses "h" instead of "kh", but not always consistently. But as visitors soon learn, words are rarely pronounced as they look in Mongolian.

A young Mongol girl sits astride a visitor's mount in front of her family ger (Graham Taylor).

The grand opening ceremony of the annual Naadam Festival in Ulaanbaatar, held over three days and celebrating the "Three Manly Sports" of wrestling, archery and horse racing (Colin Monteath).

A bright flash of green signals the presence of water in the barren rock and semi-desert of the Gobi region (Carl Robinson).

CONTENTS

Kazakh eagle hunters ride out with their birds at the annual eagle hunting festival in far western Mongolia, one of the country's great spectacles (Elbegzaya Lhagvasuren).

MAPS

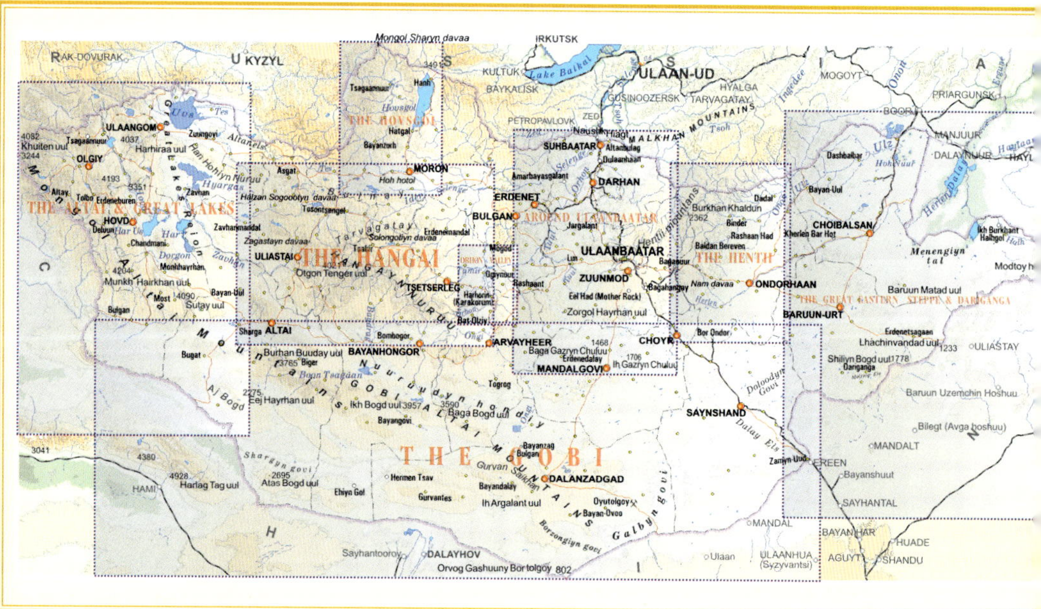
THE ALTAI & GREAT LAKES
THE HOVSGOL
THE HANGAI
AROUND ULAANBAATAR
THE HENTII
THE GREAT EASTERN STEPPE & DARIGANGA
THE GOBI
ORHON VALLEY
IRKUTSK
Lake Baikal
ULAAN-UD
KYZYL
ULAANGOM
OLGIY
HOVD
ULIASTAI
MORON
ERDENET
BULGAN
DARHAN
SUHBAATAR
ULAANBAATAR
ZUUNMOD
TSETSERLEG
ALTAI
BAYANHONGOR
ARVAYHEER
MANDALGOVI
CHOYR
ONDORHAAN
CHOIBALSAN
BARUUN-URT
SAYNSHAND
DALANZADGAD
DALAYHOV
HAMI
Zamyn-Uud
EREEN
ERENHOT
Harhorin (Karakorum)
Otgon Tenger uul
Burkhan Khaldun
MALKHAN MOUNTAINS
Hentii mountains
Tarvagatay
Hangayn Nuruu
Gobi Altai Mountains
Galbyn govi
Borzongiyn govi

INTRODUCTION

Some 800 years ago, people sure didn't need the Mongols when they were brutally forging the world's greatest land empire from the Pacific to Eastern Europe, the Middle East and India. But within 150 years the Mongol Empire had disappeared. Those Mongols not absorbed into distant cultures returned home to their windswept steppes in eastern Central Asia – and were barely heard from again. In today's troubled times, however, the world desperately needs what Mongolia has to offer: an uncrowded and wide-open landscape populated by friendly people where you can be totally cut off from the frustrations, depressions and annoyances of modern life. It's now time to head in the other direction.

Mongolia is a truly amazing place in its magnificent natural environment, mesmerising solitude and ever-hospitable inhabitants and their animals. Here, life is whittled down to its bare essentials, dominated by a languid – and totally comfortable – spirituality based on Nature itself. Mongolia is the ideal destination for crashed-out financiers, getting over a divorce or sorting out a midlife crisis. And even if you are none of the above, be prepared to discover a lot more about yourself. Mongolia is an entirely different world.

With its unique physical setting, bright-blue skies and dramatic climate, Mongolia is an incredibly evocative place. Its ever-changing moods, winds and scenery summon strong personal emotions. Covering its vast distances sets the mind thinking – sometimes a bit too much! But don't get frustrated by your back-home mindset. Keep your eyes, ears and mind open and you'll be amazed what you'll see, a surprise every day and a constant stream of "magical moments".

Almost every time you stop in Mongolia, someone shows up – literally out of nowhere, like that unfortunate nomad over 100 kilometres from home looking for his runaway horses who'd bolted in a storm. Or coming over a ridge and expecting more of the same ahead only to find an entirely new vista spread out far below. And that magnificent and never-tiring vision of shaggy-haired horses – or white-tailed gazelles – pounding across the grassy steppe. The feelings and images stay with you forever.

Mongolia is an eclectic mixture of the ancient and modern. Far out on the steppe, you're more likely to see nomads on motorbikes than horses, but still dressed in traditional tunics, or *deels,* their bike seats covered in heavy wool just like their saddles. Pull up at a *ger,* Mongolia's round, felt-covered yurts, and you'll find a satellite dish, a solar panel for the lights and television, and a mixed fleet of vehicles. But the greetings, food and hospitality remain unchanged. At the same time, with few exceptions, the vast Mongolian landscape is hardly "pristine". This is humankind living with nature for hundreds, if not thousands, of years.

Mongolians are an extremely proud people – all the more since they peacefully abandoned nearly 70 years of Communism as the Soviet Union's first satellite state in 1990. Preceded by 200 years of Manchu and Chinese occupation, Mongolia has effectively been independent barely 20 years. Long suppressed by others, Mongolians have rediscovered their rich history and culture with relish. And while they certainly have many contemporary worries, there is an infectious self-confidence about today's Mongolians. Egalitarianism runs strong and one never judges another simply by what he or she does for a living. No one, for example, is ever "just a driver". Especially after its recent tumultuous history, everyone has a fascinating story – and opinions.

To the surprise of many who travel there, Mongolia offers a tremendous variety of scenery and landscapes, and visitors frequently come away wishing they'd had more time – and vowing to return. As the following chapters will explain in detail, Mongolia has not only grassy steppe and sandy deserts but soaring snow-capped mountains, forested ranges and bare outcrops, plus hundreds of rivers and lakes, including one of the world's largest freshwater lakes. Its rich animal life – wild and domesticated – is totally absorbing.

At the same time, Mongolia's nearly three million inhabitants are remarkably urbanised with over one million in its capital and only major city, Ulaanbaatar, and hundreds of other smaller settlements. Ironically for a people who made their reputation taking on "sedentary cultures", only 40 percent of today's Mongolians are active nomads grazing their domesticated horses, sheep, goat, cattle and camels with the seasons over the sprawling landscape. But the nomadic culture, especially its hospitality, remains strong and the most defining element of the Mongolian character.

Mongolia is a relatively new tourist destination and its infrastructure is still developing. Many visitors pass through on the weeklong Trans-Siberian Railway journey to or from Beijing and Moscow, actually the Trans-Mongolian, spending a couple of days here between trains. Others fly all the way from Europe or closer spots such as Beijing or Seoul for two or three weeks of touring, mostly over rough dirt tracks. At the same time, Mongolia is – quite thankfully, in my opinion – unlikely to ever become a mass tourism destination. In any case, tourism numbers could increase tenfold and hardly anyone would notice in such a sparsely populated land with so much to explore.

But even as things improve with more five-star hotels in the capital, comfortable 4WD vehicles and luxury tourist ger accommodation, Mongolia will always remain a "rustic destination" – and that is precisely its enduring attraction. Mongolia requires a new "mindset"; everything that is familiar disappears or becomes surprisingly irrelevant in this nomadic society. Life is literally "back to basics". Even if there is a signal, you won't need a mobile phone. The Internet is hardly ubiquitous. News is totally unimportant. The food may be unusual but is surprisingly delicious. Toilets are out of doors. And above all, travel here is the journey itself – and at times over the roughest roads you'll ever experience. The reward is the pure satisfaction of accomplishment of distances covered and landscapes traversed. And you won't do a thing without the quietly spoken Mongolians alongside sharing in the wonderful adventure.

Some people visit Mongolia and don't even care where they go – just experiencing the place is joy enough. They hire a driver and guide, point to a spot on the map and head off cross-country. Increasingly, the country's main roads are paved but most are dirt tracks across a totally unfenced countryside. Others are happy at a macro level, travelling just to one spot and riding a horse for days. But the point of this guide, of course, is to educate readers about Mongolia and help them make the most of their travels.

Mongolia: Nomad Empire of Eternal Blue Sky uses a different approach to explaining the country. Instead of the rather meaningless *aimag*-by-*aimag* (province-by-province) approach favoured by others, this guide uses a regional breakdown based on Mongolia's geographical or historical features – such as the homeland of Genghis Khan, the vast Gobi Desert or the mighty Altai Mountains. After explaining Mongolia's geography, climate, history, people, culture and contemporary life, the reader is brought into Ulaanbaatar on the Trans-Mongolian Train from Beijing. Traditionally in Mongolia, every activity – and especially those of a sacred nature – follows the movement of the sun, in a clockwise direction, a habit quickly learned by newcomers. Fortuitously in this book, this is also how readers will discover Mongolia.

Mongolia is a remarkably large country and certainly impossible to see in one simple journey. Its tremendous variety provides another challenge. Unfortunately, a bit of a "tourist circuit" to the same old places has already developed in Mongolia. Quite purposefully, this guide breaks away from that and provides a much wider view to encourage travellers – and tour operators, too – in new directions. There is so much more to explore, so many fresh places to discover. And in today's Mongolia, getting off the track has never been easier.

Following spread: The Bactrian camel is one of Mongolia's "Five Snouts" or livestock animals, domesticated like the horse in millennia past, and most often seen in the southern regions of the country where the steppe transitions to desert (Graham Taylor).

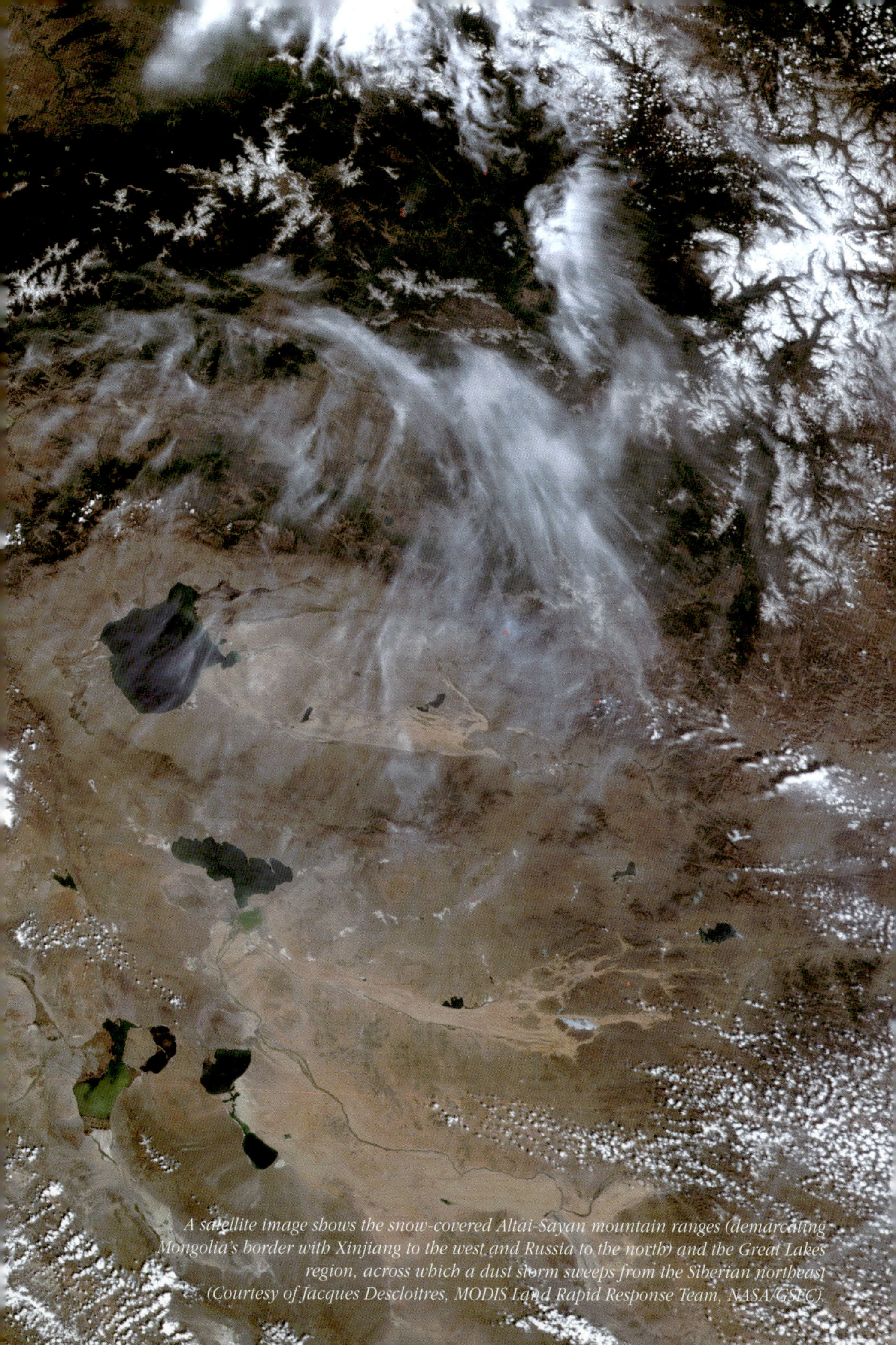

A satellite image shows the snow-covered Altai-Sayan mountain ranges (demarcating Mongolia's border with Xinjiang to the west and Russia to the north) and the Great Lakes region, across which a dust storm sweeps from the Siberian northeast (Courtesy of Jacques Descloitres, MODIS Land Rapid Response Team, NASA/GSFC).

GEOGRAPHY AND NATURE

Encircled by mountains and deserts near the top of the globe, Mongolia stands in a marvellously uncrowded and unique world of its own. Heightened by its clear air and low population, Mongolia offers a breathtaking variety of scenery under its legendary bright blue sky, its people's original deity and their totem colour. With their ubiquitous blue silk scarves, or *hadag*, Mongolians actively worship nature as a part of themselves.

Mongolia – and the people who live here – is a land of constant surprises. Snow-capped peaks soar from grassy, flower-covered steppe and sandy dunes; bare hills, badlands and gorges rise from flat desert floors; and in constant refrain, wide valleys sprawl out into enormous vistas. Waterfalls, lakes, rivers and oases refresh the eye; dense forests and marshy swamps enclose you; and the classic steppe goes on forever. Animals, both wild and domestic, abound, and there is drama too from Mongolia's extremes of climate, especially the blinding dust storms, blizzards and flash floods of spring.

Quite simply, Mongolia is Nature on a massive scale.

Located at the eastern end of the Central Asian Plateau between China and Russia, Mongolia is a landlocked country more than 1,000 kilometres (620 miles) from the nearest ocean and covering an area of 1,566,500 square kilometres (604,829 square miles). This is roughly the size of Western Europe, the US state of Alaska or Australia's Queensland. Mongolia is the seventh largest Asian country and 18th in the world.

Known as Outer Mongolia until the mid-1920s, this independent country stretches about 2,400 kilometres (1,490 miles) from east to west and some 1,260 kilometres (783 miles) from north to south. Mongolia's northern border with Russia's Siberia runs for almost 3,500 kilometres (2,175 miles). Its southern border along the Chinese provinces of Inner Mongolia, Gansu and Xinjiang stretches over 4,600 kilometres (2,860 miles).

Interestingly, Mongolia's overall latitude – 42 to 52 degrees North – is actually lower than Scandinavia, the Russian heartland and even Britain. The country's width would straddle the US-Canadian border and cover northern Japan, including Hokkaido, and Russia's Sakhalin Island. Besides the giant neighbours already mentioned, Mongolia is not that far from Korea, whose border is only 1,000 kilometres (620 miles) to the southeast. (Mongolia's "seaport" is China's Tianjin and the country even has a merchant navy.) With its long-time cultural influence on Mongolia, Tibet lies 1,500 kilometres (930 miles) due south. Immediately to the west lie the now-independent nations of Central Asia with whom Mongolia shares a long – and often tumultuous – history. But for a 60 kilometres (37-mile) strip of Russia and China in the far northwest, Mongolia and Kazakhstan would be able to shake hands.

A rainbow arcs through the sky between summer rain showers, illuminating a nomad home on the forest steppe among mountain foothills (Colin Monteath).

The South Gobi's famous Flaming Cliffs, or Bayanzag, which yielded a treasure trove of fossils in the mid-1920s (Carl Robinson).

Despite its modest latitude, however, Mongolia boasts extremes of climate that stem from its far inland position and high elevation, with any ocean-generated moisture blocked by surrounding mountains. Permafrost, or permanently frozen ground, covers more than 60 percent of the country. Visitors will often read or hear the expression "**extreme continental** climate" which means, quite simply, short hot summers and long, very cold winters. Mongolia also has extreme diurnal temperatures, or wide fluctuations in a single day.

Prevailing winds come from the northwest and the country is remarkably dry with less than 500mm (20 inches) of rainfall annually. Little snow falls and winters are remarkably clear, despite average temperatures of -26°C (-15°F) in January, the coldest month. (With low humidity and no wind chill factor, however, thankfully it rarely feels that cold.) Wind and dust storms come in spring when Arctic winds meet balmy air from the tropical south – and blast away for weeks, often quite dramatically (Mongolia's oldest export is dust to China). Rains fall in the summer months between late July and September. Mongolia's growing season is only 100 days.

Mongolia's location at the junction of the Central Asian Steppe with the **Siberian taiga**, or dense forest, and the **Gobi desert** zone, punctuated by high mountains, gives the country a fascinating diversity that frequently surprises visitors. Simply put, Mongolia passes through several natural zones from north to south. Up along its northern border, the landscape is wet, hilly and forested, turns to grasslands or steppe in the centre, and then semi-desert and finally desert, or gobi, along its entire southern side. Alpine belts mark the summits of Mongolia's highest ranges. These very different regions have also given each its own characteristic plant and animal life – and another one of Mongolia's unique attractions.

Contrary to the popular image, only 30 percent of the country is actually desert, the Gobi or *gov* in Mongolian, and only a small portion of that comprises sandy dunes. In fact, most of the country is mountainous, with snow and glaciers on the highest peaks and dense forests of cedar, larch and pine covering those of central and northern Mongolia. Even the Gobi has soaring mountains, some snow-capped: one notable southern massif harbours alpine meadows and a year-round "glacier" in one of its deep and shady valleys.

In all its sometimes confusing definitions, steppe or grassland covers much of the country and provides the principal grazing land for domesticated animals. The steppe

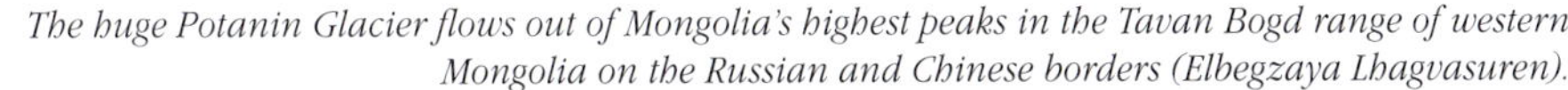

The huge Potanin Glacier flows out of Mongolia's highest peaks in the Tavan Bogd range of western Mongolia on the Russian and Chinese borders (Elbegzaya Lhagvasuren).

spreads out from below the mountain ranges through central Mongolia and into the vast flatlands of eastern Mongolia. (In the other direction, the steppe spreads all the way to Eastern Europe.) There are also hundreds of lakes, both fresh and salty, scattered around the country. Up in the far north, **Lake Hovsgol** is a mini-version and close neighbour of Russia's famous **Lake Baikal**, the deepest lake in the world. Many of these waters contain curative minerals and medicinal salts. Mongolia has an astounding 3,800 rivers, including several tributaries of major ones flowing into the Pacific through China and the Arctic Ocean through Siberia.

From a vast inland sea 200 million years ago, powerful geological forces have lifted Mongolia into one of the highest countries in the world with an average elevation today of 1,580 metres (5,184 feet). (Some 80 percent lies above 1,000 metres.) Although Mongolia is basically a high plateau trending downwards from west to east, these same dynamic forces of nature also created three massive mountain ranges – each with a very different character – that form a major continental watershed between the Pacific and Arctic Oceans and also the dry interior of Central Asia. Mongolia's lowest point is **Hoh Nuur Lake** (560 metres or 1,837 feet) in the grassy steppe of the extreme northeast. Located in a river valley in central Mongolia, the capital of **Ulaanbaatar** stands at 1,380 metres (4,530 feet).

More details follow in the destination chapters ahead, but here is a quick "*tour d'horizon*" of Mongolia. Following local tradition, this journey – as does this guide – takes you clockwise around this marvellous country.

Mongolia's oldest – and most revered – mountains are the gentle **Hentii Range** which runs for 200 kilometres (124 miles) northeast from the capital to the Russian border. Averaging 2,000 metres (6,560 feet) high, the Hentii give rise to three of Mongolia's most significant rivers, two flowing to the Pacific and the other to the Arctic. The range is also a transition zone from the Siberian taiga to what is called "**mountain forest steppe**", where cedar and larch grow only on the sunny northern slopes and the southern sides are covered in grass. Dominated by the mighty bulk of sacred **Burkhan Khaldun**, the Hentii is also the birthplace of Genghis Khan and the Mongolian nation.

To the east sprawls the **Great Eastern Steppe**, including the last untouched grasslands on Earth and their vast herds of white-tailed gazelles, and beyond that rises the bulk of the **Great Hingan Range** of Inner Mongolia, now part of China. More recent volcanic activity has created the fascinating **Dariganga Plateau** with its 200 remnant volcanoes, rich grasslands and spring-fed lakes. Sand dunes here mark the easternmost extension of the vast **Gobi Desert**, actually a semi-desert, which sprawls westwards for nearly 2,000 kilometres (1,240 miles) across the southern third of the country and up to the **Altai Range**, Mongolia's youngest and most majestic range.

Over here in western Mongolia, the landscape has been shaped by more recent geological events, namely the crashing of the Indian subcontinent into Asia some 50 million years ago and its pushing northeast. This mighty confrontation, best known for creating the Himalaya and Pamir ranges, took place only 2,000 kilometres southwest of Mongolia and continues even now at five centimetres (two inches) a year. The process has pushed, cracked, rippled and overlaid the Mongolian landscape up against immovable pre-Cambrian bedrock in Siberia, the so-called **Siberian Craton** west of Lake Baikal.

Fault lines running throughout this region make Mongolia one of the most active seismic regions in the world. Three large earthquakes rumbled through western and northern Mongolia in the 20th century, leaving behind clearly visible fault lines that have barely eroded in the country's cold and dry climate. They are now a fascinating, and most unusual, tourist attraction with some slips up to six metres high (20 feet). (There were no casualties, only a few very rattled nomads and their gers.) Another effect is the numerous hot and mineral springs dotted around the country.

But the most dramatic result of this geological movement is the soaring Mongol Altai Range of western Mongolia where the country's highest peak, snow-capped and glaciated **Mount Huiten** (4,374 metres or 14,350 feet), stands on the border with China and Russia (the Altai extends into Russia, China and Kazakhstan). Running southeast, the mighty bulwark of the Altai's 400 kilometre-long (250-mile) **Tavan Bogd** and **Gobi-Altai** also contain evidence of earliest man in caves and petroglyphs.

Fronted by a massive fault line, this snow-capped, 4,000-metre-high (13,000-feet) range feeds its waters eastwards into the massive **Great Lakes Depression**, a 100,000-square-kilometre (38,610-square-mile) expanse of fresh and salty lakes bordered on the north by another major fault line. The depression is dominated by **Uvs Lake**, located up against the Russian border and Mongolia's largest lake. In summer, the semi-desert landscape turns to marshland and becomes a sojourn for migrating bird life. Continuing as the Gobi-Altai, the range – now fronted by a rift valley dotted with salty lakes – descends over 700 kilometres (435 miles) southeast into the heart of Mongolia's famous Gobi Desert, where snow-capped **Ikh Bogd** (3,957 metres or 12,982 feet) stands like a beacon over the vast desert landscape to the south.

Mongolia's third mountain range, the **Hangai**, rises east and northeast of the entire Altai Range and the lakes. Located in the western part of central Mongolia, the southeast-trending Hangai Range was created by the same geological forces as the Altai but reflects much more volcanic activity with lava flows, ancient volcanoes and hot springs. Older than the Altai, it is also much less dramatic in appearance with more rounded hills, heavily forested with pine and birch, and lush pastures. Many summits have wide meadows. Permafrost stretches far down into this range.

The clear blue water of Hovsgol Lake is flanked by thickly forested hills that invite exploration on horseback or foot (Graham Taylor).

The Hangai Range is also an important watershed for Mongolia's major north-flowing rivers to Lake Baikal and the Arctic Ocean, such as the historic **Orhon** and **Tamir** rivers along which many tribal confederations made their capitals, including the Mongol Empire's **Karakorum**. (Waters from the Hangai's southern slopes flow into a string of "dead-end" lakes.) At its western end, the range's highest peak, **Otgon Tenger** (4,021 metres or 13,192 feet), has a glacier and is permanently covered in ice.

North of the Hangai is the mountainous Hovsgol region – and yet another one of Mongolia's many scenic personalities. Defined by the 3,000-metre-high (9,843-foot) **Sayan Range** along the Russian border, this region has a real taste of Siberia, with densely forested taiga that is home to Mongolia's **Reindeer People** (see Special Topic, page 458.) To the south the landscape turns to wooded steppe, swampland, lakes and increasingly arid landscape. Formed by volcanic activity only 2.5–3.5 million years ago, crystal-clear **Hovsgol Lake** dominates this fascinating region. (The deep lake holds 1–2 percent of the world's fresh water.) Fed by more than 90 rivers, the lake's waters leave from a single outlet at its southern end and flow in a roundabout fashion into Russia's Lake Baikal, less than 300 kilometres (180 miles) to the east.

Farther east, we've now come nearly full circle to the region directly north of the capital, Ulaanbaatar. Here, in a surprisingly broad and lush valley where wheat fields – grown for bread and vodka – have replaced the grassy steppe, all of Mongolia's rivers run north. Within a huge catchment area stretching from the Hentii Range in the east, through the sprawling Hangai across the south and southwest and up into the Hovsgol highlands, the waters of the **Tuul**, **Orhon** and **Selenge** rivers meet, flow across the Russian border into Lake Baikal and eventually make their way to the Arctic Ocean far to the north.

CLIMATE

As noted earlier, Mongolia has a very dry climate with extreme and widely fluctuating inland, or continental, temperatures. Humid air from the Pacific, Indian and Atlantic Oceans is blocked by large mountain chains on all sides. Mongolia has four distinct seasons with long, cold and dry winters and short, warm and wet summers. Cloud cover and precipitation is more pronounced in Mongolia's mountainous and forested north and decreases southwards through rolling steppe and semi-desert.

With an average of 260 sunny days a year, it's hardly surprising that Mongolia is known as "The Land of the Blue Sky". While winter

Right: Two satellite images show central Mongolia in summer and winter – note how Hovsgol Lake and much of the Darhat Valley (west of Lake Baikal) freeze over completely during the winter months (Courtesy of the MODIS Science Team, top, and Jeff Schmaltz, MODIS Rapid Response Team, NASA/GSFC, bottom). Below: The Hovsgol region in the grip of winter (Elbegzaya Lhagvasuren).

temperatures in the north drop as low as -25°C (-13°F), Mongolia's summers – when most tourists visit – are generally pleasant. Spring is notoriously unpredictable and autumn is regarded by Mongolians as the best time of year.

For seven to eight months of the year, Mongolia's mean temperature is actually below freezing. But in the short three months of summer, the weather turns warm and pleasant in most of the country but with temperatures in the Gobi Desert rising to 40°C (104°F). (Night temperatures here can still drop dramatically, however.) Winter lasts from mid-October to April, with January the coldest month averaging -26°C (-15°F). Although a high-pressure ridge over northwest Mongolia provides sunny if freezing days, snow does fall but is relatively light except on mountain peaks. Lakes and rivers are frozen solid up to a metre thick. In some regions, such as the northwest, winter temperatures can drop to -50°C (-58°F). The lowest temperature ever recorded was -58°C (-72.4°F) at Uvs Lake in the Great Lakes region. Even in the Gobi, winter temperatures can drop to -40°C (-40°F). No wonder Mongolia's average annual temperature is barely 1°C (33.8°F).

But the greatest disaster that Mongolian winters can bring is the *zud* when blizzards, fierce winds and record low temperatures combine to freeze grass in a layer of ice which prevents livestock from eating. Usually following unusually dry summers, the zud kills millions of animals and devastates the rural economy. In consecutive winters in 2000 and 2001, more than six million or one-tenth of Mongolia's stock died, prompting massive domestic and foreign aid assistance. Some regions of Mongolia are still recovering from this tragedy.

"Spring is like a woman," goes an old – and obviously very male – Mongolian saying. And the weather certainly is changeable, tempering the joys of the long winter's end and the start of the growing cycle. Starting in March, the air pressure fluctuates madly and constant dust and windstorms blow (it can be difficult just to get out of a vehicle). Even in May, cool days and freezing nights are followed by stifling heat waves. Overnight, blistering winds bring sudden lethal snowstorms – in early June 2008 one such storm killed over 50 herders and thousands of animals on their first post-winter feeding forays on Mongolia's eastern steppe. But as the snow melts, rivers rise, trees sprout and grass reappears, spring is indeed a pleasant time.

By mid-July, Mongolia is in full summer mode. The rains begin. The entire countryside is brightly green and dotted with wildflowers. Rivers flow and waterfalls run. Crops are growing and animals fattening. This is also a time of celebration, especially the *naadam* where everyone competes in the "three manly sports" of horseracing, archery and wrestling. In the mountainous Hangai, daytime temperatures rise to 20°C (68°F) while out on the steppe are comfortable highs of 25°C (77°F). Without any shade, the Gobi's 40°C (104°F) challenges visitors but the heat is dry, not humid (remember to keep up your liquid intake). But the warmth of summer also brings out Mongolia's notorious and pesky flies, especially in its wetter regions and around desert oases (bring "industrial strength" insect repellent).

Mongolia's highest summer rainfalls are in the Hentii, Hovsgol and Altai (up to 600mm or 24 inches) and decrease south across the steppe to the Gobi, which typically receives less than 100mm (4 inches). (Ulaanbaatar averages 310mm, or 12 inches, a year.) At the same time, some parts of the Gobi receive no rainfall for years and are then quite suddenly hit by raging storms and flash floods that literally change the landscape overnight. (Begun in Soviet times, Mongolia uses rockets to seed clouds and create more rain.)

Mongolians rave about their Golden Autumn. Temperatures and rainfall drop off, grain crops are harvested, and the grassy steppe and thick forests turn golden yellow (Mongolia's larch is deciduous, turning colour and carpeting the forest floors in reddish needles). Preparations for winter begin as herders gather fodder and move their animals to winter camps protected from the cold and wind.

Sadly, even remote Mongolia does not appear immune from the effects of global climate change. An internationally funded study in 2005 by the Assessments of Impacts and Adaptations of Climate Change (AIACC), an organisation that assists developing countries deal with this problem, found winter temperatures rising in Mongolia's high mountain regions, generally drier winters and springs, and a drop in annual precipitation in its central region. Summer droughts have also increased, severely aggravating the winter zud episodes in 2000 and 2001. More recent reports from the International Panel on Climate Change (IPCC) blame the phenomena for Mongolia's increased desertification. With world record prices for cashmere, others blame Mongolia's skyrocketing number of goats who, unlike sheep, habitually chew grasses down to the roots.

Mongolians, especially the nomads, live totally in tune with nature and don't rely much on scientific data. But anecdotally, visitors will certainly hear much from them about recent changes in climate (the weather is one of the first topics of conversation after formal greetings). In the spring and early summer of 2008, everyone spoke of the dry winter before and how dreadfully low the rivers and lakes were, even how slow the grass was returning.

FLORA & FAUNA

Mongolia's very different regions provide a rich diversity of flora and fauna. Because of its low population and minimal development, the country also has an amazing amount of plants and animals even though, as in other parts of the world, many are now seriously threatened. Mongolia boasts over 3,000 vascular plants and hundreds of lichens, mosses and fungi; it also has 975 registered medicinal plants. Many species are still being discovered and classified. Some 150 species are endemic to Mongolia and more than 100 plants are considered rare or endangered. Also inhabiting its forests, steppe, desert and mountains are some 136 mammal species, 400 different types of bird, 76 fish species and a mixture of reptiles, amphibians and insects.

Mongolia's flowers are legendary – and literally carpet the landscape at the height of summer. Given the country's high altitude, many are alpine varieties: the edelweiss is prolific and used as a folk medicine; others are lilies, clematis, saxifrage, gentians, even orchids. Caryopteris are a small flowering shrub with white or blue flowers and aromatic leaves. Meadows are covered in a variety of flowers such as anemones, primulas and delphiniums (one particular long-stemmed delphinium, a lovely young lady advised me, is called "do not forget me"), while other flowers include geraniums, rhododendrons and wild roses. One particularly rare species is the snow lotus, or *vansemberuu*, which is

found only at high altitudes and is coveted for its medicinal properties.

Mongolia's forests are an extension of the vast Siberian taiga – the longest continuous forest in the world – and cover over 10 percent of the country, mostly in the north. These are mostly of Siberian larch, a deciduous conifer, with Siberian pine, mosses and lichen at higher altitudes. The north-facing forests of the mountain-steppe zones offer a mixture of larch, aspen, birch and poplar, even currants and blackberries. Unfortunately in recent years, beetle infestations from Siberia have killed off thousands of larch trees in central and northern Mongolia, including in popular Terelj National Park just outside Ulaanbaatar.

Clockwise from top: Wildflowers carpet a meadow in Bulgan aimag; argali sheep populate the rocky mountains and ridges (Gotsbayar Rentsendorj x2); a few species of hedgehog can be found in the steppe and arid scrublands, where they hunt insects; the majestic but elusive snow leopard (R. Enkhbat x2); the pika, a relative of the rabbit (Danny Yee); a pair of demoiselle cranes (Gotsbayar Rentsendorj); a Przewalski's horse, ortakhi, *with her foal (Elbegzaya Lhagvasuren); two buzzard chicks sit atop their ground-built nest crying for a meal in the Middle Gobi (Carl Robinson).*

Mostly uninhabited and difficult to access, these forests are also where Mongolia's wild animals are most prolific, especially musk deer, moose, reindeer, brown bears and squirrels. The bird life is mostly grouse, owls and cuckoos. These forests are also the home of the grey wolf, which proliferates throughout the country and is the biggest threat to domesticated animals, especially sheep and goats. These predators – about whom you'll hear many stories – are why nomads always guard their flocks by day and bring them in around their gers at night, guarded by hulking sheepdogs.

The forests of the mountain-steppe zone cover the lower portions of Mongolia's three main mountain ranges and have a surprising diversity of flora and fauna, often with wide valleys and rivers lined with willow trees. The main mammals here are elk (known here as *maral*), wolf, roe deer and badger, with birds such as partridge, kites and bustards. The forest margin and nearby steppe also support marmots, wild boar, foxes, muskrats, sables, Pallas' cat and a range of rodents such as meadow mice, pikas and kangaroo rats.

Living in burrows, the buck-toothed marmot (*Marmota robusta*) is particularly fascinating, running madly for cover across the rolling steppe at the first sign of man. (Highly prized for their meat and pelts, the fox-sized marmots are also believed to be the origin of Europe's medieval "black plague" and hunting them is banned, theoretically anyway.) The grassy steppe is also where most of Mongolia's domesticated animals graze, although its eastern end is largely uninhabited and is home to many wild animals such as the Mongolian gazelle, gophers and polecats.

Animal species endemic to Central Asia are found in the Gobi Desert and steppe, including a subspecies of the endangered saiga antelope, and several species of jerboa and vole. The desert and steppe are also inhabited by thousands of gazelles, mostly the Mongolian or white-tailed gazelle (*Procapra gutturosa*), with small numbers of the threatened goitered or black-tailed gazelle (*Gazella subgutturosa*) in the western Gobi. Perhaps the rarest animal in the world with only an estimated 25 remaining, the Gobi bear (*Ursus arctos*), or *mazaalai* in Mongolian, is found around the poplar and grass-lined oases of the southwest Gobi. Wild ass (*Equus hemionus luteus*), or *khulan*, and wild Bactrian camels (*Camelus bactrianus ferus*) are also found in this region. The rocky mountains of the Gobi are home to the majestic ibex and the argali sheep, although these can also be spotted in the dry hills of central Mongolia.

The most heartening wildlife story comes from the successful reintroduction from western zoos in recent years of the world's last remaining wild horse, the Przewalski's horse (*Equus przewalskii*), or *takhi*. (A refuge west of the capital is a popular tourist destination while another, in the far southwest, is more difficult to visit.) Several hundred of these horses now graze again on Mongolian lands.

The western Altai Mountains are home to the highly endangered snow leopard (*Uncia uncia*), as well as lynx and the largest of Mongolia's argali and ibex (licensed hunting is permitted). Beavers, muskrats and otters can also be spotted in this region's fast-flowing rivers. As elsewhere, wolves proliferate in the Altai.

Mongolia is a paradise for bird-watchers with eagles, vultures, buzzards, falcons, kites and other birds of prey. Spring can be particularly exciting when buzzard and falcon chicks are easily spotted in central Mongolia. (Black crows and ravens are numerous but barely given a second look by bird fanciers.) Surrounded by distinctive plant life, the country's many lakes, rivers, wetlands and oases attract thousands of water birds such as cranes, ducks, geese, storks, pelicans and even seagulls. The Great Lakes Region and lakes of eastern Mongolia are particularly prolific. Vultures can be seen everywhere and even rare species such as the Altai snowcock and mute swan can be spotted. Strangest of all, however, are seagulls who think there's still a vast inland sea here.

One of the most visible birds throughout Mongolia, even far down in the Gobi Desert, is the lovely and majestic demoiselle crane, often spotted dancing and feeding in pairs. Another is the ruddy sheldrake, a fast-flying reddish-brown and white duck with a distinctive call and usually found in pairs. Other common birds are the crested lapwing and Mongolian skylark.

Traditionally, Mongolians did not eat fish and the country's rivers, especially in the north, are renowned for their unusually large fish, such as the giant taimen, a member of the salmon family, which can reach two metres (six feet) in length. This and other fish resources have brought a growing number of foreign anglers to the country, who travel to remote locations for several days of guaranteed exciting fishing (see Special Topic, page 446).

Despite the richness of the country's flora and fauna, visitors may be disappointed not to see more wild animals in their travels around Mongolia – though they'll certainly see plenty of "free-range" horses, camels, sheep, goats and cows, plus yaks and a crossbreed known as the *hainak*. Mongolia does face some serious conservation issues – and not just with the more obvious snow leopard and Gobi bear. Even the wild ancestors of domesticated animals such as the wild Bactrian camel, wild ass and Przewalski's horse are threatened, despite the latter's encouraging reintroduction. Other animals, birds and plants are also in danger.

Among the many international organisations assisting the Mongolians to manage and conserve their wildlife in recent years is the New York-based Wildlife Conservation Society (WCS), operators of that city's Central Park, Bronx and other zoos. The WCS notes a serious decline in Mongolia's rich fauna since the collapse of the Communist-run economy in 1990 and increasing foreign demand for wildlife and their products. (Previous tight controls on guns were also relaxed and many Mongolians now actively hunt, not always legally. Licensed hunting for foreigners is a strong source of government revenue.)

The world's burgeoning fur trade threatens the marmot, wolf, bear, lynx, Pallas' cat (*Felis manul*), fox and snow leopard. Rampant trapping of marmots over the past five years in the eastern part of Mongolia has seen their numbers halved. Poaching of the rare male saiga antelope for its horn and use in the Chinese medicinal market has been intense, according to the WCS. Further pressure on wildlife comes from the continued expansion of domestic livestock. Sadly, even the graceful white-tailed gazelle – still seen by the thousands in eastern Mongolia – is in danger. (Many say the gazelle's decline began with the construction of the railroad to the Chinese border in the 1950s, which effectively split their habitat.) Among birds, the imperial eagle, white-naped crane, great bustard and saker falcon are also endangered.

Since 1990, the Mongolian government has vastly increased the number of national parks, often called Protected Areas, but often lacks the manpower to adequately patrol them. And, say critics, not all money from licensed hunting goes into conservation programmes. But changing long-entrenched cultural attitudes about hunting, a very long tradition in Mongolia, is the biggest challenge.

Mongolia's legendary flowers carpet entire landscapes in summer when most tourists visit. Many are alpine varieties and used as folk medicine. Left and bottom left: In late spring and summer, both the semi-desert and mountain steppes burst into colourful life as myriad flowers bloom (Leo Murray x2). Opposite top: On mountain slopes edelweiss is prolific (Elbegzaya Lhagvasuren). Below: The saxaul tree is a desert plant much in demand for its excellent burning quality – sadly this means that the huge stands of saxaul that once spread throughout Central and East Asia's desert regions are now drastically reduced (Colin Monteath).

HISTORY

While Mongolia is certainly best known for its vast but short-lived world empire in the 13th century, the present-day nation actually has a much longer history that stretches back to the dawn of humanity. Always remote and harsh, the region's dramatic landscape was home to some of the earliest humans on Earth from the Stone Age, or Palaeolithic Era, which culminated in their domestication and mastery of the horse. Even the memorable **Genghis Khan** (Chinggis Khaan) – today acknowledged as the founder of the Mongolian state over 800 years ago – was not Mongolia's first empire builder. For centuries before, the vast steppe was home to a sweeping succession of other empires, often confederations of nomadic and even sedentary tribes.

When the Mongolian Empire ended in 1368, the nation collapsed inward with its leaders fighting among themselves and eventually opening the way for 200 years of Manchu and Chinese occupation which ended barely a century ago. Ever the proverbial meat in the sandwich between more powerful and populous China and Russia, Mongolia then joined the nascent Soviet Union as its first satellite state in 1921 to play out its own role in the 20th century's epic experiment in World Communism, complete with grisly copycat Stalinist purges, the destruction of religion and collectivised farms. When ideological disputes split the Communist Block in the 1960s and 70s, heavily subsidised Mongolia stayed determinedly loyal to Moscow and was home to 120,000 Soviet troops fiercely staring down the Chinese with jets and missiles. In practical terms, Mongolia only became totally independent with the collapse of the Berlin Wall and the `end of the Cold War in 1990.

During those oppressive decades, the Socialist Era, much of Mongolia's rich and ancient history, both oral and written, was forgotten, sanitised and – in the case of the mighty Genghis Khan himself – actually suppressed. Today, after surviving the tough transition to a "market economy" and with its buoyant multi-party democracy and open society, the intensely proud Mongolians are reclaiming their history – even if most prefer not to dwell too much on the Communist period which ended basically in a whimper.

A statue of Lenin still stands in front of the capital's five-star Ulaanbaatar Hotel. Another statue of Mongolia's very own Stalin, Choibalsan, overlooks a nearby intersection in front of the country's leading university. His name also awkwardly graces the capital of an eastern *aimag*, or province, slated to become Mongolia's economic powerhouse. (For a touch of real kitsch, you can find a Stalin statue on Peace Avenue.) But at least the post-1990 governments removed Choibalsan's mausoleum – a straight copy of the one in Moscow's Red Square – from the front of the national parliament building, or State Hural.

In its place and symbolic of Mongolia's new beginnings stands an impressive statue of Genghis Khan – or a modern sculptor's rendition thereof, as he left no image behind – and his two immediate successors, Ogedei and Kublai Khan.

Mongolia does indeed have a fascinating and vibrant history. Travelling around the country you will most certainly see – and very often simply stumble upon – un-signposted Stone Age cave drawings and **petroglyphs**; Bronze Age and subsequent burial sites, including stunning **deer stelae**; ancient city walls and dwellings; old battlefields; demolished Buddhist monasteries and, from the more recent Communist era, now-abandoned and destroyed collective farms and huge derelict former Soviet military bases and airfields. Sites associated with Genghis Khan, sometimes quite tenuous and even contentious, are ubiquitous, especially in the Hentii Mountains.

But if your Mongolian hosts or guides are sometimes unable to explain everything or are simply wrong, do understand that they are on their own journey of discovery. An early visit to the excellent **National History Museum** in Ulaanbaatar will orient you with the vast time frame and dynamics of Mongolian history and start you on this journey. Adding to the excitement is that Mongolia today has entered its own "Golden Age" of Archaeology, with teams of local and international diggers scouring the country. Thanks to Mongolia's small population and its dry and permafrost conditions, new and remarkably well-preserved discoveries about its past are coming to light all the time. Who knows what they – or even you – will find next?

Prehistory

Mongolia's history, or actually its prehistory, began in the Palaeolithic Era, or the Early Stone Age, which ran from 2.5 million to 12,000 years ago. The oldest evidence in Mongolia dates from the Lower Palaeolithic Period when primitive man, or hominids, were evolving using chopping tools made from rock, bone, horn and teeth. In this region, the entire era was marked by glacial and interglacial periods, and in the latter period the climate was relatively mild. Archaeologists have discovered more than half a dozen sites from this early time around Mongolia, the most significant being 750,000-year-old stone tools at **Tsagaan Agui**, or **White Cave**, in a remote corner of Bayanhongor aimag in south-southwestern Mongolia (see page 322).

During the Middle Period between 100,000 and 40,000 years ago, modern man (*Homo sapiens*) became dominant. He had mastered fire and developed artistic and symbolic skills. But in Mongolia, the climate turned colder and glaciers formed over its western and northern mountains, forcing people into caves and other natural refuges, where they covered themselves in the skins of animals that they hunted with increasingly sophisticated tools.

In the Upper Palaeolithic Period from 40,000 to 10,000 years ago, the ice retreated and Mongolia's climate and geography settled into what we see today. Tools were further developed and the spear became a powerful hunting weapon. Man still lived in caves but now began building structures similar to today's *gers*, or yurts. Artistic skills became more refined; the most remarkable find from this period are the rock paintings of the **Gurvan Senkher Cave** in southwest Mongolia's Hovd Aimag (see page 346). (Reproductions are in the National History Museum and the Hovd Museum.) In addition to wild animals still present today, climate change since that era is vividly illustrated with extinct animals such as bison and mammoths.

Another important Upper Palaeolithic site – all the more so for its continuity into the Genghis Khan Era – is **Rashaan Khad** (or Rock) in eastern Hentii aimag (see page 231), which has rock art showing extinct rhinos and mammoths, and is regarded as a direct link to the next era of the Stone Age.

The Palaeolithic Era came to an end along with the Ice Age – Geology's Pleistocene Epoch – about 12,000 years ago. This ushered in the Middle Stone Age, or **Mesolithic Era**, which lasted until 7,000 years ago and was characterised most dramatically by the Great Migrations out of the Central Asian region to North Asia and then across to Alaska and into the Americas. Bows and arrows appeared at this time, but archaeology from this period is rare anywhere in the world and less than a handful of sites have been found in Mongolia. The most significant find is at **Moojoo** in Uvs aimag up in Mongolia's northwest, where rock art, or petroglyphs, show people had domesticated cows, one of the "five snouted animals" which Mongolians raise to this day (the others are the camel, horse, sheep and goat).

Top: A huge statue of Genghis Khan sits in front of the Ceremonial Hall facing onto Suhbaatar Square in the capital Ulaanbaatar (Leo Murray). Above: An ancient portrait of Genghis by an unknown artist, this is a common image of the "world conqueror". Right: A rich collection of Bronze Age petroglyphs cover the steep valley walls of Bichigt Khad, or the Valley of the Writings, in South Gobi's Bayanhongor (Carl Robinson).

By the Late Stone Age, or **Neolithic Era**, from 7,000 to 3,000 years ago, people in Mongolia were living in dwellings, often on rivers and lakes where food was plentiful. They had domesticated more animals, including the horse for the first time, were growing cereal crops and hunted. Archaeology from this period shows higher-quality stone tools such as hoes and grain-grinding devices, improved by using other tools and harder rocks. There are also earthen pots, accessories of bone and simple decorations. People believed in an afterlife and buried their dead underground in a seated position such as at sites on **Mount Tamsagbulag** and **Norovlin** in eastern Dornod aimag. The oldest anthropomorphic representation discovered in Mongolia, in this case an amulet with a carved face, comes from this period.

What is particularly fascinating about the Neolithic Period is how sedentary or settled communities appear to have coexisted with nomadic pastoralism – and even preceded it. But the rapid shift to nomadism, where animals are moved over vast distances on a seasonal basis for the best grazing, would simply not have been possible without the domestication of the horse, including the development of the riding bit, which took place at this time. Also, let us not forget that neighbouring China was going through its own early development at this same time. There is little doubt that contact was taking place then between these late Stone Age peoples and the sedentary Chinese to the southeast. At this stage in history, however, the nomads were still divided between "proto-Mongols" in the east and "proto-Turks" in the west.

About 3,000 years ago – or roughly 1000 BCE – Mongolia's **Bronze Age** began, ushering in a period when stone tools and other implements were replaced by bronze, an alloy of copper and tin. Animal husbandry developed and heavily influenced the economy, social structure and culture. The horse predominated and encouraged the rapid development from a sedentary to nomadic society. Influenced by advances in China, metal-working became widespread and contributed to **Karasuk-style art** which made extensive use of realistic animal images, particularly on bronze knives and daggers.

Mongolia has a remarkably rich Bronze Age legacy. The first are its gravesites, including the country's majestic Deer Stones (see Special Topic, page 396), and secondly an incredible amount of rock art, both pictographs and petroglyphs. There are also large collections of weapons such as arrowheads, knives and swords, along with household objects and personal ornaments, including jewellery.

The graves differ in style and reflect an anthropological, cultural and even topographical division of the period. In the mountainous western part of present-day Mongolia, proto-Turks built burial mounds called "*kurgan*" or "*khirigsuur*", while proto-Mongols to the

east favoured "square tombs", often with fences of rocks around them (not all graves are from the Bronze Age, of course, but later ones do differ in style). Mongolia's collection of Deer Stones – often remarkably well preserved – is even more dramatic. Found singly or in groups of up to 20, Mongolia has over 500 of these tall, monumental sculptures featuring stylised deer and other animals, mainly in western Mongolia. Another 200 are located in neighbouring countries (see Special Topic, page 396). Widely regarded as the world's most advanced nomadic art, they date from the second millennium to the third century BCE.

At the same time, Mongolia's collection of rock art is so prolific that discoveries are still taking place and detailed surveys conducted. The country has a small number of pictographs, or coloured paintings on walls and usually in caves, such as **Gachuurt Valley** outside Ulaanbaatar. But Mongolia's number of petroglyphs, where percussive blows are used to pound an image onto a rock surface in the open air, is truly amazing. Typically, these show scenes of hunting, herding, individual animals and human figures, even wheeled vehicles or abstract masks. While the earliest found so far date from the **Eneolithic Period** – the transition from the Stone to Bronze Age in the South Gobi – most petroglyphs date from that age and into the early Iron Age. The most elaborate find is along the **Upper Tsagaan River** in mountainous Bayan-Olgii aimag in Mongolia's mountainous far west.

Archaeologists date Mongolia's **Iron Age** from the seventh century BCE, from an extensive site found at **Chandmani Mountain** in Uvs aimag in the country's northwest. As the Bronze Age melded into this new age, nomadic pastoralism became the dominant way of life. A "horse culture" developed which survives passionately to the present day. But as Mongolian historian Baabar astutely points out about the horse: "Whether nomadism necessitated the domestication of the animal or whether its domestication gave rise to nomadism, no one knows."

The taming of the Eurasian Steppe's semi-wild horse, the *equus gmelini* or *tarpan*, was certainly a stroke of genius. Adapted to the tough climate and scarcity of food, the shaggy-haired horse allowed people to move their huge flocks and herds over vast distances while also providing sustenance. The extremes of weather could barely support sedentary

Above: An artist's rendering of some of Mongolia's rich vein of rock art (N. Bat-Erdene).

communities, and the "mounted lifestyle" lent itself well to the constant migration required to find the best pasture throughout the year, sheltering from fierce winter winds and cold in protected valleys, and then taking to the lush open grasslands in summer. (Even today, nomads have a minimum of four camps, one for each season.) But as pastures were exhausted or climate changed, conflicts between family groups and tribes emerged.

By around 500 BCE, the first nomadic confederations began to form. They invented the stirrup so archers could fire backwards, and sleighs to pull their cargo. When they were not going after another group of neighbours, these horse-mounted nomads raided sedentary Chinese communities far to the south for the supplementary goods their own lifestyle could not provide – such as grains, silk and tools. The pattern of relations between Mongolia and China was established very early. Rarely peaceful for very long, the relationship manifests the world's most enduring "culture clash" between totally opposite lifestyles and mutual disdain. It's worth remembering that China's Great Wall was put up essentially to stop horses – not man – and that nomads were nothing without their horses.

In discussing "horse culture" this is also an appropriate time to discuss who exactly these early Mongolians were – and even how they looked. Over the following centuries, the great migrations provided by the horse saw them pushed and scattered – like a huge conveyor belt – over the vast steppe westwards into the rest of Central Asia, Russia and eastern Europe. Other waves moved into the Middle East, Persia (Iran) and even the Indian subcontinent. At the same time, Mongolia was a huge "melting pot" of different races and tribes.

In fact, one of the founding legends of Genghis Khan's own ancestry – as told in the *Secret History of the Mongols* – speaks of a tribal girl impregnated by a "mysterious fair-headed man who descended to her on a moonbeam through the open roof-top of her *ger*". And there is evidence, most dramatically of a Scythian warrior discovered in the western Altai Mountains in 2006, indicating the presence of Indo-Europeans in the region in the early Iron Age. But by the time historical records begin, the three main ethnic groups in what is now Mongolia were the Turks, Mongols and Tungus (Manchurians) from the same Altaic linguistic family. Over the centuries, each group successively ruled the others and the racial pot mixed even more.

THE ANCIENT STATES PERIOD

THE HUNNU OR XIONGNU EMPIRE (3RD CENTURY BCE–1ST CENTURY CE)

From their earliest historical records, the Chinese spoke of the nomads in modern-day Mongolia and referred to them as **Hu**, or primitive tribes, and others as **Xiongnu**, or northern slaves, who regularly raided and looted its northern kingdoms. When the Qin Dynasty emerged in 221 BCE to unify the sedentary Chinese, one of the first moves by Emperor Qin Shi Huangdi – most famous as the creator of the Terracotta Army – was to merge a smaller series of walls into a major new defence line, the predecessor of today's Great Wall of China. The nomads fought back by creating the first powerful Central Asian state of **Hunnu** under the legendary **Modu Shanyu**, who murdered his own father to usurp the throne in 209 BCE. Also known as the Xiongnu, these Turkic-speaking nomads from the southwest of today's Mongolia created a vast empire stretching from Manchuria and Lake Baikal in the east and north to today's Inner Mongolia and northwestern China.

Recognising that only a massive transformation would unite his independent-minded nomads, Modu Shanyu introduced a decimal system of military organisation that would serve the Mongolians well for centuries. Each *tumen* of 10,000 men was subdivided into units of 1,000, 100 and 10 with each leader accountable to the leader above. Each soldier answered to everyone in his unit. With an army of 240,000 men, this iron discipline allowed him to conquer other nomadic tribes and eventually force the collapse of the Qin Dynasty and its replacement by the Han with whom Modu signed a peace treaty, including the provision of a Chinese princess – not for the last time in forthcoming history. But before long, the agreement collapsed over who would control the trade routes now known as the "Silk Road", which by then had become China's link with the rest of the world.

With its capital in the Orhon Valley, the Hunnu Empire lasted for another 100 years after Modu's death in 147 BCE, dominating Central Asia and leaving behind a rich legacy of royal cemeteries and city-fortresses in the Mongolian heartland. They show a mixed sedentary and nomadic society and a high level of prosperity. Archaeologists have excavated and studied a vast city, including a cemetery, at **Tamiryn Ulaan Khoshuu** along the Tamir River, a tributary of the Orhon. But best known is the large burial site of **Noyon-Uul** north of Ulaanbaatar, where archaeologists first discovered evidence of trade along the Silk Road. In 2007, a joint Mongolian-South Korean team discovered bronze and iron artefacts, a gold necklace and silver spoon in a tomb complex at **Duulga Uul** in Hentii aimag east of the capital. Remains of other city-fortresses from this period also exist around the country, although often complicated by later construction, such as the **Herlen Bars** complex along the Herlen River in eastern Dornod aimag.

Finally crushed and then split, the southern Hunnu became vassals and joined the Han Chinese in attacking their northern relatives around the year 90 CE. The defeated northerners eventually fled westward to present-day Hungary, from where in the fourth century CE they terrorised Rome and Constantinople under the infamous **Attila the Hun**.

THE XIANBEI EMPIRE (2ND–5TH CENTURIES CE)

As the Hunnu weakened, a nomadic tribe from eastern Mongolia and Manchuria whom they had conquered early in their 400-year rule rebelled. Known as the **Xianbei**, they quickly gained control over former Hunnu lands and resumed assaults on Chinese territory, eventually forcing the collapse of the Han Dynasty – and a unified China – in 220 CE. In the disintegration that followed, the southern branch of the Xianbei, known as the Toba, eventually turned sedentary themselves and became sinicized, adopting Chinese ways. They established the Northern Wei Dynasty (386–533 CE), one of the Three Kingdoms in this tumultuous period of Chinese history. The dynasty controlled a vast region of northern China south to the Yangtze River, and most of today's Xinjiang Uygur Autonomous Region. And in the ultimate irony for these one-time nomads, when remnants of the northern Xianbei, now known as **Rouran**, gained control of the Mongolian heartland and attacked their southern cousins, they were forced to follow Chinese custom and reconstruct the Great Wall.

THE ROURAN EMPIRE (5TH–6TH CENTURIES CE)

Also known as the Joujian, Ruan-Ruan or Ruruan (Chinese for "wriggling insect"), this empire was formed around 400 CE by the northern Xianbei in confederation with other nomadic tribes in the Mongolian heartland. Driving the Xiongnu farther west to the Ural Mountains and Caspian Sea, the Rouran established a vast and powerful empire generally north of the Northern Wei and stretching from Korea to Central Asia, including the eastern part of present-day Kazakhstan.

The Rouran are credited as the first Mongolians to use the title "*khan*" for their leaders, previously a title used by the Xianbei nobles. But the confederation, spread over such a vast area and with a mixture of tribes, was always a tenuous one. Early on, the legendary **Ephthalites** split off at the western end on a campaign of conquest all the way to Persia and India. The Chinese fomented several rebellions against the Rouran, finally forcing the empire's collapse to the Turks in 552 CE. (The Rouran disappeared as an entity, prompting speculation that they fled westwards to become the Eurasian Avars of Central and Eastern Europe in the sixth century.)

The Turkic Khanate (6th–8th centuries CE)

Nothing better illustrates the dynamics of repeated migrations out of this part of the world over the centuries than the Turks – an Altaic-language people whose ancestral home is in the mighty Altai Mountains of western Mongolia. For newcomers to Mongolia and its history, the concept of their movement thousands of kilometres to present-day Turkey is a bit hard to grasp. But in successive waves over the centuries that is precisely what happened, peaking with the modern Ottoman Empire which lasted until the end of World War I.

For some 200 years, starting around 552 CE when Turkic iron miners in the Altai revolted against the Rouran, the so-called **Turkic Khanatc** was Asia's largest and most powerful nomadic empire prior to the rise of Genghis Khan nearly 700 years later in the early 13th century. Known as the *Tujue* by the Chinese, they were also referred to as *Gokturks*, and were the first to use "Turks" as their political designation. Their empire quickly stretched over the vast Eurasian steppe from the Great Wall of China to the Black Sea and south through formidable mountain passes into Persia and India.

Although still nomads, the Turks quickly recognised the strategic importance of the Silk Road. In return for keeping this lucrative trade link between China and the West open, they – and their successors – profited by levying tributes and taxes. The move not only promoted trade and the creation of urban centres, but also propagated the exchange of ideas and beliefs, such as Buddhism, Manichaeism, Nestorian Christianity and eventually Islam. Importantly, the trade routes also brought the Mongolians their own written language, a runic script based on Aramaic and Sogdian.

Within 50 years, however, the meteoric rise of what is called the **First Khanate** was succumbing to the same perennial internal divisions over successions and the fragility of tribe-based confederations that always afflicted Mongolia's empires. The Turks fell into a civil war and split into eastern and western wings, which the now-reunified Chinese were quick to exploit. In the east, the Turks appealed to the Chinese for protection. But when they boldly resumed attacks over the Great Wall, the Turkic capital in the Orhon Valley was attacked and occupied by China. The new **Tang Dynasty** also launched a massive foray for control far to the west, even clashing with Arab armies coming into the chaotic region from the other direction. By 659, the Chinese had regained control of the Silk Road and now enlisted the Turks to guard this vital link.

But the Turks were certainly not vanquished. Starting around 680, they revived as the **Second Khanate** which lasted for another 60 years and was divided into two independent

Following spread: The ruins of Manzshir Monastery on the southern side of Bogd Khaan Mountain, destroyed during the Communist religious purges of the 1930s (Carl Robinson).

parts. The **Western Turks** out of the Altai focused on Central Asia, extending their power and influence to the Aral Sea and down to Transoxiana near Persia. The **Eastern Turks** ruled much of today's Mongolia out of the historic Orhon Valley and extending up into the Tuul and Selenge river systems to the north and northeast.

Interestingly, all Turkic remains in today's Mongolia are from this second period with over 40 stelae, many with inscriptions, plus stone statues and grave stones, or *balbal*, still visible. The most famous are the two monumental stelae – with Chinese inscriptions on one side and runic symbols on the other – inside the black-walled ruins of an ancient Turkic fortress at **Khooshoo-Tsaidam** in the Orhon Valley about 400 kilometres west-southwest of Ulaanbaatar. Carved in 732 and 735, they honour Turkic prince **Kutlug Tigin** (685-731) and his brother **Emperor Bilge Khan** who ruled over a brief "golden age". Known as Orhon Script, these and inscriptions scattered around the area are the oldest examples of Turkic writing and describe their legendary history, including battles with the Chinese and their liberation under the Bilge Khan.

The importance of these and other monuments to the world's Turkic heritage is evident in close archaeological, cultural and economic relations between today's Mongolia and Turkey. (Much work has been done at the site and the paved 40-kilometre road to the site from the later Mongol Empire capital at Harhorin, or then-Karakorum, was a recent aid project from Turkey.) After the Bilge Khan died in 734, the Second Khanate quickly collapsed.

The Uyghur Khaganate (mid-8th to mid-9th centuries)

In 741, the **Uyghur** tribe from the Orhon and Selenge River valleys, who had been part of the Turkic Khanate confederation, took over. Also Turks, they set up their capital at Har Balgas or **Ordu Baliq** further up the Orhon Valley. They brought a period of peace by actively allying themselves with the Chinese Tang Dynasty and contributed further to the region's cultural development by refining the Turko-Sogdian alphabet.

They translated numerous Chinese texts and also created the first indigenous Mongolian literature. (The **Uyghur script** was later adopted by Genghis Khan's Empire and survives today as **Old Mongolian**.) While Buddhism had already made strong inroads, Manichaeism – a third century Gnostic religion positing that Man is both good and evil – became the official state religion, introducing a strong Persian element into the culture. The Uyghurs also staged a campaign of lopping the heads off stone statues left behind by the Turks.

The Uyghur Khaganate controlled roughly the same territory as today's Mongolia. But during this same period, the burgeoning Tibetan Empire, which already controlled much of southeastern China, was pushing northwards and threatening China's western flank, including control of the Silk Road, its riches crucial to both the Chinese and Uyghurs who had jointly established trading posts along the route.

In an ironic turn of history – in view of Mongolia's later extremely close religious and political links with the mountain kingdom – the Uyghurs agreed early on to help the Chinese defeat the Tibetans. They also put down several rebellions against the nascent Tang Dynasty inside China. In return, the Chinese paid tribute to the Uyghurs, including the gift of a princess to the ruling khan.

Emboldened, the Uyghurs then launched a vicious military campaign against a rival steppe tribe in the Yenisei River Basin to the northwest, the Kyrgyz. Through the late 700s and early 800s, the khaganate prospered and built its capital, today 46 kilometres (28.5 miles) northwest of Harhorin, into a mighty trading centre with a fortress surrounded by walls and a canal. They also continued military campaigns against the Tibetans and Kyrgyz. But in 840, the Kyrgyz wrought their revenge by invading with a force of 80,000 horsemen, sacking and burning down the Uyghur capital and executing the khan. Other cities were also destroyed.

The defeated Uyghurs fled into Central Asia, including today's Xinjiang region in western China – eventually this area was given the name Turkestan. When Arab armies to the west defeated the Tibetans, Islam became the new religion of the Uyghurs. With their strong commercial and literary expertise, the Uyghurs would later become crucial to the administration of the Mongol Empire, especially because of their written language.

THE KYRGYZ PERIOD (MID-9TH TO MID-11TH CENTURIES)

Originally from the headwaters of the Yenisei River, which flows north to the Arctic Ocean from southern Siberia due west of Mongolia's Lake Hovsgol region, the Kyrgyz were a pastoral people of Turkic origin who also engaged in hunting and fishing. They were particularly well known for their metallurgy. But as a small tribe, they were always subject to larger confederations from the Xiongnu period onwards. When they revolted against the constant depredations of the Uyghurs in 840, they rapidly expanded southwards through the western part of today's Mongolia to the Tien Shan mountains of Xinjiang and eastern Turkestan, which they dominated for 200 years.

Although they'd successfully overthrown the Uyghurs, they exercised only nominal control over their former empire, especially in the east. What power and influence they held was eventually crushed by the expanding Khitan, who were pushing west from eastern Mongolia. Today, many of their descendants live in Tuva, an autonomous Russian republic across Mongolia's northwestern border. Others, driven by the Mongol Empire, migrated southwards where they now form the majority of Kyrgyzstan's population.

THE KHITAN EMPIRE (EARLY 10TH–12TH CENTURIES)

In the chaotic period of destruction and dispersions that followed the end of the Uyghur Khaganate, the balance of power now shifted to the so-called "proto-Mongols" far to the east. The Khitan (also Kitan) were a nomadic people from the eastern end of today's Mongolia and Manchuria who'd once been part of the Xianbei confederation in the second century CE.

When the Wei Dynasty was formed, the Khitan refused to join their now sedentary cousins and, over successive centuries, paid a heavy price. With their own distinct identity, including a written language, the Khitan were under constant attack and any attempt to assert their power was crushed by the Turks to the west and Chinese from the south. Even the Koreans from the east, the Goguryeo, had a go at controlling them.

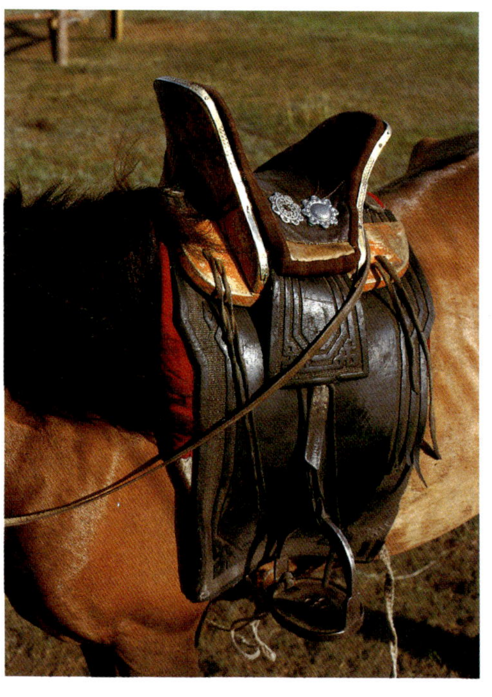

Under such constant domination and oppression, any attempts at gaining their own independence were constantly crushed. Renowned as warriors, the Khitan joined in alliances only to find themselves betrayed, most dramatically during the Li-Shun Rebellion in 696 CE when the Turkic Khanate encouraged a revolt against the Tang, only to attack them from the rear, a decisive move for the revival of the Second Khanate. They suffered further blows from the subsequent cosy alliance between the Uyghur and the Tang.

The moment for the Khitan finally came with the routing of the Uyghur in the west and then the collapse of the 300-year-long Tang Dynasty in the early 10th century. Acting quickly, the Khitan established the Liao Dynasty in 947 and asserted their power over the northern China plain. They moved into eastern and central Mongolia, including the important Orhon Valley, which like others before them became their capital. Moving west and south, they gained control of the Silk Road and the movement of salt and iron. Diplomatic and commercial relations reached all the way to the Arab Caliphate and Persia.

The high lines of the traditional Mongol saddle allowed for the development of superb military horsemanship and gave the nomadic "hordes" superiority on the battlefield (Graham Taylor).

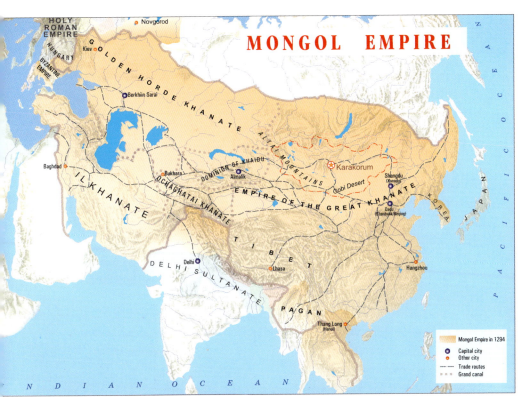

MONGOL EMPIRE

A modern-day reenactment of Mongolia's martial past, the armed and helmeted participants sweep across the steppe with silken banners flying in the wind (Elbegzaya Lhagvasuren).

Inspired by its contacts with the Chinese, the Khitan brought another feature to Mongolia's nomadic society with the creation of over 150 cities, the ruins of more than a dozen of which are still visible today, especially in the eastern Herlen River valleys. The most notable are the ruined walls of twin cities west of Ondorhaan in Hentii aimag (see page 238). And 100 kilometres (62 miles) northwest of Ulaanbaatar at Chin Tolgoyn Balgas, or Kedun, in Bulgan aimag are the ruins of a significant fortress that include a stupa believed to be one of the oldest Buddhist monuments in Mongolia. These Khitan cities were religious, commercial and agricultural centres, including the cultivation of silk. Its military power weakened the tradition of tribal confederations with the empire divided into two parts, one based on nomadic traditions and the other on the Chinese model.

Fearful of losing their hard-won ethnic identity, the Khitan fiercely maintained their own traditions, refusing to use the Chinese language. They devised their own writing system, which is still difficult to decipher. Buddhism became the state religion but, as always in nomadic society – including the Mongol Empire – they accepted other sedentary religions, most importantly Manichaeism and Nestorian Christianity. Confucianism and Taoism also became part of the Khitan culture. Today's Mongolian culture was heavily influenced by the Khitan.

While their empire lasted over 200 years, internal struggles around 1125 led to their conquest by the **Jurchen**, a pastoral and hunting tribe of Tunjusic background and ancestors of the Manchu from the far north of Manchuria, who established the Jin Dynasty. While some stayed on to help fight the southern Song Empire, some 100,000 Khitan, including its leaders, migrated westwards through the Altai Mountains where they established the sizable **Kara Khitai Khanate**, or Western Liao, in Central Asia. Still living as nomads, they conquered the mostly sedentary Muslim tribes of the region, turning their mosques into Buddhist or Nestorian Christian churches. When word of Kara Khitan leader **Gur Khan**'s deeds reached Rome, who'd just lost control of Jerusalem to the Muslims, this gave rise to the legend of **Prester John** and a saviour of Christianity from the east.

From their capital at Balasagun in today's Kyrgyzstan, they ruled for nearly 100 years before the empire's diversity of tribes led to rebellion. When Genghis Khan moved on the Naimans, a powerful Turkic tribe then controlling western Mongolia, many fled to the khanate, briefly usurping power there before Kara Khitai's final destruction by the Mongol Empire in 1218. Interestingly, considering their dispersal and virtual disappearance from history, the Khitan's name survives in today's words for China in Russian ("*Kitay*"), and the classic English "Cathay", Portuguese "*Catai*" and Spanish "*Catay*".

With the Jurchen preoccupied as they extended their power over eastern China and Korea as the Jin Dynasty, the steppes of the Mongolian heartland returned to a state of disorganised nomadic tribes in an almost constant state of war. But they also faced threats from more organised outsiders. They feared not only what the Jurchens might do next, but the Song Chinese Dynasty south of the Yangtze River and the **Tangut Khanate**, a Tibetan-related people controlling western China as the **Western Xia** (1038–1227.) With five or six tribal confederations vying for power and influence, this was the tenuous situation inside Mongolia at the end of the 12th century.

GENGHIS AND THE GOLDEN AGE

THE MONGOL EMPIRE (EARLY 13TH TO MID-14TH CENTURIES)

At its height in 1279, the **Mongol Empire** was the largest land empire the world has ever seen. Stretching along the Asian coastline all the way to Vietnam and Burma and across the Eurasian continent to Persia, Iraq and up through Turkey and the Caucacus to the Russian and Ukrainian heartland, the empire covered over 33 million square kilometres (12.7 million square miles) and encompassed over 100 million people. This vast empire literally changed the world.

Created on the blood of millions, the Mongol Empire left behind a mixed legacy debated to this day. At home, particularly in the post-Communist period, **Genghis Khan** is proudly honoured and revered as the founder of the Mongol state. Elsewhere, and particularly in the Middle East and Central Asia, memories still linger over the brutalities of the Mongol invasion, the massacres, destruction and occupation. When Mongolia volunteered a small contingent of troops for the Iraq War in 2003, they were kept out of Baghdad neighbourhoods who still vividly remember the 500,000 killed when Mongols sacked the fabled Mesopotamian city in 1258.

Unlike earlier empires and khanates that came out of the fringes of today's Mongolia, the Mongol Empire was born in its nomadic heartland – the people who led a traditional lifestyle of hunting, fishing and herding, and who moved their animals with the seasons along with their round, felt, moveable homes, or gers. Scattered and independent, they worshipped Eternal Heaven, or Tengri, and followed the wisdom of the shamans who had their own links into the great unknown. Although organised into family clans and even tribes, they were often at the mercy of more sedentary-minded outsiders who came in, built their now-ruined cities and then – influenced by faraway dynamics – moved along, always bit players in the greater scheme of things. On their own after the departure of the Khitan in the early 12th century, attempts by the Mongols at creating their own unity inevitably collapsed to tribal rivalries and their fiercely jealous aristocracies.

Genghis Khan was born from one of those failed attempts at Mongol unity. His own great-great-grandfather, **Habul**, was khan of the **Hamag Tribe** in the northeastern Hentii, which was demoted and the family lineage usurped by other aristocrats. The epic story is told in *The Secret History of the Mongols* – "secret" because it was meant only for the Mongol court. When Habul's great-grandson and unproclaimed khan, **Yesuhei**, was poisoned by the Tatars in 1171, his wife and sons were banished from the tribe in the hope they would soon perish out on the steppe on their own. For Yesuhei's second-born son Temujin, then only nine, this betrayal and rejection kindled a fierce determination for survival and power that turned him into a world conqueror.

Early on, Temujin learned the value of loyal friends and forming alliances. He enlisted the help of his father's *anda*, or blood brother, **Toghrul Khan**, from the neighbouring **Kereit Tribe** around today's Ulaanbaatar to rescue his kidnapped wife **Borte** from the Merkits further north along the Selenge River. But Temujin's success aroused the jealousy of his own anda and childhood friend, **Jamuha**, who also had leadership ambitions. They split, each with his own followers. When Temujin was elected khan of the Borjigin, Jamuha attacked Temujin and defeated him. Several years passed before he recovered, re-formed his alliance with the stronger Kereits and, now with a subsidy from the Jin, defeated the Tatars. (For Temujin, this was also sweet revenge for his father's death.) Overcoming repeated intrigues and double-crosses, Temujin eventually prevailed, first over the Kereits, the Merkits and the Naimans where Jamuha had sought final refuge. According to tradition, his childhood friend was then wrapped in a carpet and trampled to death by horses, an "honourable death" not to shed any blood on the earth.

By 1206, Temujin was firmly in control of all tribes and lands between the eastern Khingan and western Altai mountains and from Lake Baikal to the Great Wall. Without any reference to previous tribal or confederation names, he gave this entity the new name of **Mongol Uls**, for state or people, the official beginning of the nation now called Mongolia. A great gathering or *kuriltai* of tribal chiefs – believed to have taken place at Hoh Nuur Lake (see page 229) – endorsed Temujin as Genghis Khan, the "ruler of the sea" or "universal ruler".

Quite deliberately, Genghis Khan broke away from traditional – and inherently divisive – tribal structures and created a centralised and autocratic state backed by a code of law, the *Yasa* (also spelt *Yassa* or *Yasaq*), its own written language and even a communications system. Most importantly, of course, was his creation of a powerful non-tribal military structure and a tactical doctrine, including using sieges and winter campaigns, that changed the face of warfare and conquered most of the known world. Instead of simply slaughtering or enslaving his conquered foes, Genghis Khan brought them into his own military where they joined mixed units based on the decimal system, units of 10 up to 10,000, or *tumen*, the size of modern division. (A "horde" was made up of several tumen.)

Using only a small nucleus of Mongols with a clear chain of command, Genghis Khan quickly built up a vast and well-disciplined military machine using horses and engineering units. Highly mobile, well armed and trained, and experts at marksmanship and horsemanship, the units were backed by an intelligence-gathering system, psychological, even bacteriological warfare, and a rapid communications system based on horse relays. Clearly, the world had never seen anything like it before (see Special Topic, page 68).

Even before launching his first outside military campaigns, Genghis Khan was joined peacefully by tribal groups on the western fringe of Mongolia, such as the Oirads (Oirats), Kyrgyz and Uyghurs (the Kara Khitan would doubtless have joined too had the fleeing Naimans not usurped their power). Although now being converted to Islam, the Uyghurs played an important role in the growth and administration of the empire, including a written language. Religious and racial tolerance and promotion on merit and skills were early trademarks of the Mongol Empire.

With such unity behind him, Genghis Khan began his massive military campaigns, first against the Tanguts of the Western Xia to the southwest, where he developed new siege tactics against their fortified cities and forced them into vassalage by 1209. He then pushed southeast over the Gobi Desert and the Great Wall against the more powerful Jin Dynasty, capturing their capital of Yanjing (today's Beijing) in 1215. The Jin ruler escaped south of the Yellow River to Kaifeng, where he held out for another 20 years. The Mongol leader then moved west on Kara Khitai in 1218, easily overrunning its capital with only two tumen and executing the fleeing Naiman leader Kuchlug who had usurped the throne.

Then came the campaign that earned Genghis Khan his reputation for bloody ruthlessness. With the defeat of the Kara Khitai, he now overlooked the powerful **Khwarezmid Empire** encompassing a large part of Central Asia, in what is now Uzbekistan, Tajikistan, Turkmenistan, Afghanistan and most of Iran. Mostly Turkic and Muslim, the region was an important section of the Silk Road. When Genghis Khan sent some 200 merchant-ambassadors to establish trade links in 1218, the Shah executed them as spies. He did the same when diplomats arrived demanding an apology.

Vowing vengeance, Genghis Khan brought 200,000 troops into Khwarezmia the following year, splitting them into three groups in a massive pincer movement. The city of **Otrar** was overrun and destroyed after a month-long siege and the city governor famously killed by pouring molten gold into his mouth. The capital of **Samarkand** and city of

MONGOL MILITARY ORGANISATION

In many ways the Mongol army was similar to its Xiongnu and Turkish [Turkic] predecessors. It consisted almost exclusively of cavalry: mounted archers armed with short and long-range arrows, sabers, lances, and maces. They wore steel cap helmets and armor consisting either of lacquered hide or overlapping iron scales. Organized around decimal units of 10, 100, 1,000, the largest Mongol tactical division was the tümen *of 10,000 men. Although the decimal system had been employed by the Xiongnu, in an imperial confederacy unit commanders were also tribal chiefs in their own right and so often decided on their own what orders to accept. The Mongol armies had no autonomous tribal base so its commanders could expect absolute obedience down the whole chain of command. Like most nomad armies the total number of Mongol troops was surprisingly small. At the time of Chinggis Khaan's death in 1227 it consisted of only about 138,000 effectives, and even at the height of the empire a generation later it had about twice that number.*

What distinguished the Mongol military from its predecessors, however, was its iron discipline and central control, a model of organization first developed by the Manchurian Khitan who had conquered northeastern China three centuries earlier, but never previously employed in Mongolia. Xiongnu and Turkish [Turkic] cavalry armies had tended to be disorganized in battle, with each individual fighting for his own gain. The Mongol army was trained to fight as a coordinated group following signals from flags or horns. Those individuals who broke ranks either to advance or retreat, those who engaged in personal combat without regard to orders, or those who stopped to loot, were severely punished. Nobody, under pain of death, was allowed to move to another unit without permission. Because his trusted military commanders were not rivals for political power, Chinggis Khaan gave them a great deal of autonomy to carry out his overall strategy. And he was a brilliant talent spotter, for out of the Mongol ranks rose a series of world-class generals who led his armies to victory across Eurasia.

But perhaps Chinggis Khaan's unique innovation was his incorporation of military engineers, Chinese and later Muslim, into the Mongol army after his first campaigns in China. These specialists provided the Mongols with thousands of siege engines that could be used to take fortified cities: catapults for hurling stones, ballistae for throwing javelins, and other machines for throwing fire. They also provided him with the ability to bridge rivers or even divert them to wash away enemy fortifications. All other steppe cavalry armies had been stymied by walled cities. They could attack around them and lay waste to the countryside but they could not take them by direct assault. Without this ability, no nomadic group could ever expect to conquer well-defended sedentary lands. The Mongol army could and did. It became so efficient that none of the great walled cities of Central Asia were able to withstand their power when Chinggis Khaan launched his war there against the Khwarazm Khan in 1218.

These innovations gave Chinggis Khaan a military machine that was completely under his control, that fought according to a coordinated plan, and that had the ability not only to strike deeply into enemy countries but (unlike any nomads before or since) to engage in effective siegecraft that rendered walled cities vulnerable to a steppe army. It was an army of conquest, not a grand raiding force like those of the Huns in Europe or the Xiongnu against China. And conquer it did.

Professor Thomas J. Barfield, Boston University, excerpted from a longer text titled "Something New Under the Sun: The Mongol Empire's Innovations in Steppe Political Organization and Military Strategy", prepared for the 8th International Congress of Mongolists, held in Ulaanbaatar in 2002.

Bukhara were sacked and then destroyed after longer sieges. The physical damage and human casualties were simply horrendous. The only people spared were skilled tradesmen who became slaves of the empire.

While the killing of the Mongol merchants and diplomats may simply have been just a pretext for Genghis Khan's attack, the clear message to his adversaries after this particularly brutal campaign was that surrender and cooperation, basically vassal status, was a better option. With the defeat of the Khwarezmians in 1220, the Mongols then set off on two massive reconnaissance operations. With a small contingent, Genghis Khan ventured down into Afghanistan and northern India while another 20,000 under **General Subetei** headed west around the Caspian Sea and then on a devastating swing up through the Caucasus, the Crimea and into the Ukraine, where he defeated the Slavic princes of Kiev at the **Battle of Kalka River** in 1223. They returned to Mongolia the following year around the northern side of the Caspian Sea. It wasn't long before they were back.

Genghis Khan returned home to find that his Western Xia vassals, who had refused to join the campaign against the Khwarezmid Empire, were now in alliance with the remnants of the Jin Dynasty and hoping he'd be too weak to respond. In 1226, Genghis Khan retaliated with a massive offensive through Tangut territory, sacking cities and engaging in several set-piece battles against superior forces. The capital of Ningxia on the banks of the Yellow River was totally obliterated – turned into a cemetery, the annals say. When the emperor finally surrendered, Genghis Khan ordered the entire imperial family executed to leave no heirs. He died shortly afterwards.

Just how Genghis Khan died is still debated. But the likely explanation is that it happened in battle. A more intriguing story claims he was killed while making love to a vengeful Tangut princess he'd taken as a war prize. Mystery, too, surrounds where Genghis Khan was actually buried – it is said there is even a *DaVinci Code*-like "secret society" that knows *exactly* where his grave is! The accepted legend is that his body was returned home and buried atop sacred **Burkhan Khaldun Mountain** in the Hentii in an unmarked grave according to his own tribe's customs. The site was then trampled over with horses and all who participated executed. A Japanese archaeological team touched off a huge controversy in 2004 when they launched a high-tech effort to find Genghis Khan's grave and were forced to back down, although they did find traces of an old palace and other graves. Most Mongolians prefer the simple mystery.

Before his death, Genghis Khan appointed his third son **Ogedei** as his successor, a decision approved by a kuriltai in 1228 at Avarga. With Ogedei as Great Khan, the empire was divided between the founder's four sons. Oldest son **Jochi** had died on the long reconnaissance up into the Ukraine and Russia and his son **Batu** was given that region, starting the lineage that became the **Golden Horde**. Genghis Khan's second son **Chagadai** took the southwest down into Afghanistan and Persia. Ogedei received China and the rest of Asia. By custom, youngest son **Tului** inherited the central Mongolian homeland. The same kuriltai also approved a military offensive against the Turkic **Bulghars** in the middle Volga region of Russia, a task completed by Batu the following year, and also to wrap up the conquest of the Western Xia. After occupying Korea in 1231, Ogedei then resumed the war against China's Jin Dynasty south of the Yellow River. The Great Khan also began construction of the Mongol Empire's capital in the Orhon Valley at **Karakorum**, today's Harhorin.

Forming an alliance with the Southern Song Dynasty, Ogedei sent Tului south with a large army, but his younger brother died the following year and his command was taken over by Subetei, who continued the long siege of Kaifeng. Despite strong resistance, including the first recorded use of missile-rockets, the Jin capital fell in 1233. Many Jurchens were driven back to their Manchurian homeland (as the Manchu, they would revive in the mid-17th century as China's last imperial dynasty, the Qing, which lasted until 1911 – a period which also included their occupation of Mongolia). Other Jurchens were absorbed into the Mongol military. When the Song attacked the Mongols for not sharing their conquest, Ogedei declared a war against the rest of China that would last another 45 years.

Let us stop here for a moment to consider the sheer audacity of what the Mongols were now doing. Genghis Khan's chosen successor and son, Ogedei, was committing his nation of barely one million people to an offensive war against the most populous country in the world, China, roughly 100 million people. At the same time, other Mongol-led armies were invading Persia, the Caucasus and the steppes of western Siberia and Russia. Smaller invasions were running elsewhere, such as in Korea and Tibet. At the beginning of the 13th century, the Mongolian state had 44 tumen (that is, 44 x 10,000) of military capable men aged 13 to 60 and their families at its disposal. This represented some 700,000 to one million people, of whom only about 130,000 were constantly ready-to-fight troops. (In comparison, the population of Europe was 30–40 million around the year 1000 and by 1300 was already about 80 million.) So, ethnic Mongols were a minority in their own armies. The remainder were outsiders, such as Turks, Tatars, Tanguts, Jurchens, Chinese, Cumans, Bulghars and other Inner Asian tribes who were recruited or drafted into the highly disciplined tumen structure. The self-confidence of the Mongol leadership, to say nothing of its subsequent success, was truly remarkable. In short, the Mongols would never have succeeded without a lot of help from other peoples.

Of course, on the negative side, the population drain on the Mongolian heartland was devastating – to say nothing of the huge casualties the Mongol armies inflicted on the populations they encountered. Barely 100 years later, there were barely 100,000 people in Mongolia as many troops died on these far-flung operations. Others were assimilated into the local population, adopting new cultures, faith and languages, a fate that ultimately befell even the ruling Mongol elite of this sprawling empire. Another step towards economic and ethnic stagnation in the Mongolian heartland came when **Kublai Khan** moved the Empire's capital from Karakorum to Beijing in 1267 (see below).

With the defeat of the Jin Dynasty and his eastern flank now secure, Ogedei turned to Europe – a massive operation that would have catastrophic effects on its Medieval peoples and ensure the Mongols' lasting reputation. Nominally under Batu, actual command was under the ageing but still brilliant General Subetei, the most gifted Mongol military leader after Genghis himself, who had conducted that massive reconnaissance up into southern Russia 15 years before and then defeated the Jin. The long campaign set off in 1236 with some 600,000 men, quickly defeating the Bulghars. Then, operating even in winter, they swept a path of blood and destruction through Russia and the Ukraine, capturing **Kiev** by late 1240.

The year of 1241 was critical to Europe's very survival. Pushing farther west in three columns, the Mongols swept through Lithuania and Poland, destroying the Polish army at **Cracow** in March and then decisively defeating a superior combined force of Europeans at the **Battle of Leignitz** in April. Meanwhile, another column swept southwards through Transylvania in today's Romania, across the western steppe and up the Danube into central Hungary where King Bela IV was annihilated at the **Battle of the Sajo River**, also in April. Gathering their forces, the Mongols spent the summer months recuperating and consolidating the eastern bank of the Danube while planning another winter campaign.

The Mongols crossed over the frozen Danube in December 1241, with scouting parties raiding northern Italy around Venice and Treviso and up the Danube towards **Vienna**. Suddenly, however, everything stopped. The Mongols' renowned horse messenger service had brought word of Ogedei's death back in Karakorum on 11 December. Under the Yasa promulgated by Genghis Khan, all offspring had to return to elect their new khan. The hordes turned east with one last foray through the Balkans and Bulgaria. Advances by Chagadai down into India also halted.

Fortunately for Europe, the kuriltai to replace Ogedei was delayed by five years, mostly by Batu's stalling on the Volga River while he established the Golden Horde at Kipchak, and political manoeuvrings by other relatives. After a regency by his widow, Teregene, who was herself a Nestorian Christian, their son Kuyuk was selected in a meeting witnessed by papal envoy **John de Plano Carpini**, who was there to ascertain the Mongols' intentions after their devastating attacks on eastern Europe (he also provided the first European eyewitness account from the Mongolian homeland and capital of Karakorum). But Kuyuk was undecided between military campaigns in China and Europe and died after only three years, perhaps poisoned. By now firmly established on the Volga, Batu opted out, giving his support to **Mengke**, the oldest son of Tului, Genghis Khan's youngest who'd died in the earlier campaign against the Jin Dynasty in 1233.

Confirmed as Great Khan in 1251, Mengke chose to leave Europe for later and made his first priority the long-neglected conquest of China with the Southern Song now stronger than ever. But the succession had badly split the family. Another contentious issue – as in today's Mongolia – was the power and influence of the Chinese and the Mongol fear of losing their own identity, or becoming "sinicised". The ever-pragmatic Genghis Khan and his sons had always used Han Chinese extensively to administer their far-flung empire, such as **Chancellor Yeh-Lu Ch'u-Tsai**'s running its treasury and tax system. Chinese also helped run the vast military machine.

In a foretaste of Mongolia's Communist-era purges of the 1930s, Mengke ordered massive executions of his enemies, including Ogedei's own sons, their mother Toregene and her infamous Muslim advisor Fatima, who'd undermined the Chinese courtiers. Mengke and his brother **Kublai** took over Ogedei's realm in East Asia. The writ of Chagadai was now limited to Central Asia's Oxus River and the Hindu Kush. Brother **Hulegu** was given the rich and vast lands beyond in the southwest. He would become the first of the **Ilkhans** (subservient khans) and Mongol rulers of Persia, today's Iran. Mengke also urged Batu to resume his attacks on Europe. But without sufficient manpower, his forays were limited to the Baltic and the Balkans. Western Europe was finally off the hook.

Mengke resumed the campaign against the Song Dynasty in southern China, appointing Kublai as viceroy in the north. From their now well-fortified and provisioned cities, the Song put up determined resistance. The Mongols staged a massive flanking manoeuvre through southwestern China when Kublai conquered **Namchao** in modern Yunnan Province. He then swept across through **Tonkin**, or northern Vietnam, to the South China Sea, taking **Hanoi** in 1257. Inside this vast encirclement, the Chinese began to crumble to a series of brilliantly executed campaigns personally directed by Mengke. Then in 1259 – and at a critical time once again – everything changed when the Mongol leader died of dysentery.

When the kuriltai was called to choose Mengke's successor, Kublai claimed he was too busy fighting in southern China to return. He quickly called his own council in the field to declare himself the new Great Khan. His actions confirmed growing suspicions that Kublai was drifting too far from his Mongolian roots and becoming too sinicised. Instead, the main kuriltai chose his younger and more traditional brother **Arik-Buka**. The two-year war between the two brothers that followed this disputed accession effectively ended the unity of the Mongol Empire. By 1261, just over 50 years after its creation – and now only into its third generation – the vast empire was falling apart.

While Mengke and Kublai were in China, their brother Hulegu was extending his Persian-based fiefdom up into Mesopotamia. In 1257, after the sultan of the Abbasid Caliphate refused help in crushing the Assassins, a terrorist sect headquartered in the remote Persian mountains near the Caspian Sea, Hulegu moved his forces on ancient and gloriously rich **Baghdad** – one of Islam's most important centres of culture. By now swollen to over 150,000 with reinforcements from the Golden Horde and Chagadai, their 8,000-kilometre (5,000-mile) trek from Karakorum had taken three years. The force included 1,000 "families" of skilled Chinese artillerists to conduct sieges, and Hulegu's deputy was the famous Chinese general **Guo Kan**. Also included were a large contingent of Christian allies from Georgia and Armenia.

When the sultan in Baghdad refused to surrender, the city was besieged and quickly fell, touching off an orgy of massacre, rape, looting and destruction that some records claim left 800,000 dead. Mosques were turned into Christian churches; with help from local Christian vassals, the horde then swept into **Damascus**, destroying the **Ayyubid Dynasty**, and was rapidly moving on the last seat of Islamic power in Cairo when word came of Mengke's death. Hulegu departed with most of his troops, leaving only a skeleton force behind.

By the time Hulegu returned from the accession of his brother Kublai in 1262, the situation in the Middle East had changed dramatically. Allowed through their territory by European Crusaders who'd decided they feared the Mongols more than the Muslims, the **Egyptian Mamluks** had inflicted the first-ever military defeat on the Mongol Empire at the **Battle of Ain Jalut** in Palestine. When Hulegu sought revenge for the loss, he was attacked from the rear by **Berke Khan**, who'd succeeded Batu as head of the Golden Horde to the northeast. His uncle was now a convert to Islam pledged to protect its holy sites.

Different parts of the Mongol Empire were now at war with each other. Despite repeated attempts, Hulegu was unable to forge an alliance with the Pope, France or England to crush the Mamluks and regain Palestine. The Ilkhan withdrew back to Iran where he focused on expanding trade along the Silk Road and the genteel life, while Turkic viziers ran the country. His successor invaded Palestine and Syria but the **Ilkhanate** was now under attack from the **Chagadai khanate**, and its troops returned home. (The Ilkhanate ended in 1335 when the viziers took control.)

Kublai was now the Grand Khan, but the massive Mongol Empire was already falling into pieces, torn apart not only by family quarrels at the top. "Genghis had divided his empire into four parts, not only because he had four sons, but also because the empire was made up of four radically different ethnic, cultural and religious worlds," explains historian Baabar. So few in numbers and dependent on outsiders for control, the Mongols were assimilating into these respective cultures and would eventually disappear. Berke's attack on Hulegu was just the start as more quarrels broke out over succeeding generations. Three became Muslim. After 1260, they would have little to do with Mongolia – and their fascinating histories are unfortunately beyond the space available here. But from the **Great Moguls of India** to the **Ottoman Empire**, even Tsarist Russia itself, the Mongols left behind a lasting legacy, most notably as Baabar explains, "a whole school of a unitary state administration that was to last until the 20th century". The world certainly had changed forever.

For one last glorious period – as immortalised by **Marco Polo** – the Mongol Empire endured but far from its nomadic roots on the steppes. Highly educated and hardly averse to the sedentary life, Kublai soon turned his back on the Mongolian heartland and moved his capital out of Karakorum – and a further two-week horse relay away – to **Dadu**, today's **Beijing**. (Dadu, or "great capital", was also called **Khanbalik** or Marco Polo's **Cambaluc**.) In summer, the capital shifted north of the Great Wall to **Shangdu** – popularised as **Xanadu** – in today's Inner Mongolia.

In 1268, Kublai resumed the conquest of China, finally capturing the Song capital of **Hangzhou** in 1276, and three years later bringing the outlying provinces fully under Mongol control. In 1279, Kublai declared himself the emperor of a now-united China and heralded the start of the **Yuan** ("first") **Dynasty**, which lasted until 1368. Mongol rulers quickly developed a reputation for opulence and luxury.

Kublai Khan's rule also marked the zenith of the period that historians call "**Pax Mongolia**", a golden age of commerce and cultural exchange between East and West. Certainly, the Mongol wars of conquest were absolutely devastating, with for example 30 percent of the Song Chinese population, or 29 million people, killed and equally staggering figures from elsewhere. But within remarkably little time, especially where submission came early and without resistance, local economies recovered and prospered.

With roads now safe, trade flourished from one end of the Mongol Empire to the other, giving rise to the oft-repeated line from a Turkic historian that "a young virgin with a tray of gold on her head" could travel unmolested from the Pacific to the Mediterranean. Persian, Arab, Greek and Venetian merchants traded goods along the Silk Road in deals backed by paper money, a Mongol innovation. Another was the passport guaranteeing safe passage. Moveable type used by the Chinese reached Europe and saw the printing of the Gutenberg Bible in the 14th century. Other ideas in the arts, architecture, shipbuilding, navigation, literature, foods and medicine were swapped between East and West. The visits by Marco Polo and other Europeans led to the great period of sea explorations, including the discovery of the New World. Let us not forget that Christopher Columbus was, after all, sailing westwards to find Cathay!

The exchange of religious ideas also flourished – especially in the empire's early days before the ultimate religious "winners" emerged – and then helped destroy it. Tolerance ruled. Missionaries from near and far came to Karakorum where the ruler encouraged them into religious debates that sometimes turned to farce. **Nestorianism**, dismissed as heresy by the early **Christian Church**, had already made strong inroads when Genghis Khan chose Christian wives for his own sons (the mother of Kublai, Mengke, Hulegu and Arik-Buka was also Christian). **Islam**, **Buddhism** and **Taoism** were also heard in this marketplace; after first destroying mosques in the Khwarezmid Campaign, Genghis Khan had soon reversed his policy to allow religious freedom.

But as the empire expanded, tolerance gave way to the viciousness of the Baghdad Campaign and its aftermath. For a brief moment, Islam was on the defensive but was then fervently embraced by most of Genghis Khan's descendants. In China and the east, Kublai Khan briefly tolerated Nestorian Christianity and even Roman Catholicism. But eventually, and in return for the mountain kingdom's accepting vassal status, Kublai embraced **Tibetan Buddhism** as his empire's official religion and appointed **Phagspa** of the **Sakya Sect** as his "Imperial Preceptor", or advisor. (This brilliant monk also created a universal script known as the Phagspa Script for the Mongol Empire that was never widely adopted.)

On the military front, Kublai had reached his limits. Thanks to fortuitous typhoons – dubbed *kamikaze* or "divine wind" – on each occasion, massive invasions of **Japan** failed in 1274 and 1281 and military campaigns down into **Burma**, **Vietnam** and **Champa** later in the decade stalled. More puzzling was an attempt by Kublai to occupy far-off **Java** in today's Indonesia even later in his reign in 1293.

But most of his energies went into establishing a strong centralised government for China using traditional institutions, including examinations to choose its civil servants. The Mongols also engaged in massive public works projects, such as completing the **Grand Canal** into Dadu. Artificial lakes, hills and palaces were also built in the new capital

– their shapes still evident today. Travel and trade flourished, as did cultural life with the popularisation of drama, music and the written vernacular.

But ultimately the Mongol experiment failed, largely through a heavily discriminatory system against the Chinese and a bias for employing non-Chinese from other parts of the empire, such as Marco Polo. As Kublai Khan's successors became more sinicised, they also lost further influence back in the Mongolian heartland without gaining anything among the Chinese. Divided by political intrigue and uninterested in governing, with the country torn apart by dissension and banditry, the last Mongol emperor was driven out of China by the incoming **Ming Dynasty** in 1368.

Post-Mongol Empire Period (mid-14th to mid-17th centuries)

While Kublai Khan and his successors were relishing their luxurious sedentary lifestyle in Beijing, resentment constantly simmered back in the Mongolian heartland, first over Kublai's controversial accession as Great Khan and then his shift of the Mongol capital from Karakorum into China, a move seen as abandoning his own heritage.

Mongol warriors openly rebelled against Kublai. From farther west, Ogedei's grandson **Kaidu**, angry at losing his heritage, started a rebellion that briefly occupied the old capital at Karakorum. Ordinary people also frequently revolted as the homeland was depleted and demoralised. With the collapse of the empire a tragic sequence of spilled blood and shattered hopes ensued, and things would barely improve over the coming centuries.

With the fall of the Yuan Dynasty in 1368, Mongolia reverted to a lengthy period of feudal separatism and rivalry for control of the khan's throne. Some 60,000 Mongols fled north with **Emperor Tongoontomor**, while many stayed behind to serve the Ming Dynasty, often in military units. (Others were actually prevented from leaving China, such as a small community of Mongols whose descendants remain in Yunnan Province to this day.)

Now rebadged as the **Northern Yuan Dynasty**, the Mongols staggered on with an increasingly acrimonious succession of leaders, all claiming links back to Genghis Khan himself – and the right to recreate the empire. The Ming Chinese had attacked from the south, sending the last Yuan Emperor and his followers fleeing north into a Mongolia that, in those days, began just over the Great Wall in today's Inner Mongolia region of China. It wasn't long before the new Chinese dynasty launched a series of brutal invasions into the Mongolian heartland, culminating in the sacking of Karakorum in 1388 and the capture of 70,000 troops. Other cities were also destroyed.

Rather than outright occupation, the Ming Dynasty's objective was to batter and weaken the Mongols and prevent their resurgence, a policy that also included "economic warfare". Aware of the nomadic Mongols' long-time reliance on sedentary societies for certain goods, such as silk, iron and grains, the new dynasty in Beijing imposed a trade embargo.

Increasingly, the Mongols retreated back into subsistence-level herding and built up their military strength for raids on China's sedentary populations for the goods they needed. The more peaceful alternative, of course, was trade. But here, the Mongols were at the total mercy of the Chinese, not only on costs but their divide-and-rule tactics. And, as we shall see, the ultimate price for the Mongols in this endless game would be face-losing "vassal status" – one chunk at a time – to its more powerful neighbour.

The endless battles continued. The Ming never got a foothold and the Mongols always expelled them, even staging the odd raid – including famously kidnapping one Ming Emperor – back into their old stomping grounds. The Ming would find little peace from the scrappy Mongols for the entire duration of their dynasty. It's no wonder the Great Wall underwent its grandest renovations – including its present brick and stone façade – during this period. (And when the Ming did fall, someone simply opened the gate to the Manchu from the northeast.)

Among what we'll now call the **Mongolians** (rather than Mongols, given the diversity of the region's tribal groups), the most disturbing – and ultimately self-defeating – development was their rapid reversion to the tribal divisions of the past (it certainly sanctifies the sheer genius of Genghis Khan in having surmounted these to create his empire). By the early 15th century, a civil war had broken out between the **Halh** of central and eastern Mongolia and the **Oirads** of the western Altai Mountains. The battle was also between what are called the **Genghisids**, those claiming links back to the Great Khan, and the non-Genghisids.

The Oirads had sat out the Yuan Dynasty, even supported the anti-Kublai rebels, and were in a strong economic position from their strategic location along the Silk Road. They now renounced the Mongol Empire's khans, whose remnants ruled the Halh, and the struggle for power between the two parts of Mongolia began. With the Chinese – and later the Russians – contributing their divide-and-rule tactics, the struggle between the country's east and west would continue for centuries and remains very much in the public memory today.

In the first half of the 15th century, the Oirads were clearly in the ascendancy and brought most of greater Mongolia under their control. In 1449, after attempts to establish normal trading relations failed, **Esen Taishi** invaded China and in a battle against a superior Chinese force actually captured the young Ming **Emperor Zhengtong** and held him hostage. But any hopes the Oirad leader had of a ransom – much less normal relations – collapsed when his brother took over as emperor and refused to negotiate. Zhengtong was held for another four years, regained the throne and heavily purged Mongols still serving in Chinese units. Esen Taishi was soon overthrown by his own supporters.

Power now switched eastwards to the Halh with the legendary story of Mongolia's own Joan of Arc, **Queen Manduhai the Wise**, a khan's widow who adopted and later married Kublai's last surviving descendant, five-year-old **Batu Mongke**, to keep the lineage alive. Acting as regent, she then defeated the Oirads and reunified a Mongolia that spread into Central Asia. Also known as **Dayan Khan**, her now-husband ruled from 1470 to 1543 and was one of the longest ruling post-Empire khans. But after his death, the country again fell into disarray, now a land of many khans.

Among the warring factions was Batu Mongke's grandson, **Altan Khan**, who ruled over the **Tumed** in today's Inner Mongolia and was best known for introducing the now-dominant **Yellow Hat** form of Tibetan Buddhism into Mongolia in 1578 (see page 127). Then still a minority sect back home, Altan Khan coined the title "**Dalai Lama**" – or "ocean lama" – for its leader and in return was conveniently recognised as the reincarnation of Kublai Khan. With other local rulers soon scrambling to convert and also gain similar recognition, Altan Khan's move re-established Buddhism and created a path that would lead to the religion dominating Mongolia's political, social and economic life.

(In fact, the Yellow Hat Sect gained such fervent support in those early days that Mongolian troops invaded Tibet to overthrow the dominant **Red Hats**. Today's Dalai Lama, also deeply revered in Mongolia, clearly owes his lineage to these 16th century Mongolians.)

At the same time, after a small incursion towards Beijing, Altan Khan was finally able to secure peace and normal trade with the Ming, who also allowed him to make Tibet a Mongolian sphere of influence. He established the city of **Hohhot**, or Blue City, the capital of today's Inner Mongolia, and drove the Oirads out of Karakorum.

By the early 17th century, Mongolia had dozens of khanates and princedoms, each running their own agenda and obsessed with titles, first, from China and later from Tibet. The Dalai Lama also gave Altan's brother the title of **Tusheet Khan** over Mongolia's sacred heartland in the Orhon Valley, where he would soon establish the **Erdene Zuu Monastery** on the ruins of the Mongol Empire's capital city. Not long after this in 1635 his grandson was born; the Dalai Lama proclaimed him the Buddhist reincarnation of Javzandamba, who would become **First Bogd Javzandamba**, or spiritual leader of Mongolia, but he was best remembered as **Zanabazar**.

In the Tibetan Buddhist hierarchy, Mongolia's theocratic leader was the third-highest ranking incarnation after the Dalai Lama and Panchen Lama. Quite conveniently, Mongolia's own imperial family – that of Genghis Khan – was now tied into the highest ranks of the Buddhist hierarchy. The feudal lords hoped, as in Tibet, that this combination of the political and spiritual, or theocracy, would unify their country. The Ming and then the **Manchu (Qing)** saw the tie-up as a means of weakening and controlling the Mongolians. In the end, the consequences would be catastrophic and would last into modern times.

THE MANCHU (QING) PERIOD (17TH–EARLY 20TH CENTURIES)

The nearly 300-year-long control of the country – many say "occupation" – by the Chinese Qing Dynasty remains the stuff of much public anger and bitterness in today's Mongolia. Anti-Chinese prejudice is strong and the visceral hatred expressed by some Mongolians towards Chinese – even the mere sight of them – can shock visitors. Adding to these sentiments is Mongolia's dependence on China – as over the centuries – for consumables and food, even for skilled labour to build its infrastructure and operate mines and oilfields. The Chinese can certainly be blamed for running a pretty tough operation back then, but the popular telling heard by many tourists does overlook some quite serious failings among the Mongolians themselves. Unfortunately, and as we've heard so many times already, they were once again their own worst enemies.

The main factors to keep in mind about this admittedly grim period of Mongolia's history was that it was actually the Manchu – and not Chinese – who were involved... and they also had many willing Mongolian accomplices. The only group that comes out well for their persistent resistance were the Oirads, also known as the **Dzungars** or **Junggars**.

The Manchus started off as the Jurchens, a Tunjisic but also Altaic-language group of nomads based farther east and northeast of the Mongolians. As already mentioned, there was certainly no love lost between them, especially after the Jurchens formed the Jin Dynasty in the early 12th century. Genghis Khan went after them early on, capturing their capital in today's Beijing, and his son Ogedei brutally finished them off in 1233. From their northeastern lair, they'd nursed their wounds through the Mongol Empire and then the Ming Dynasty until, now known as the Manchu, they started flexing their muscles again in the early 17th century.

Labelling themselves the **Late Jin Dynasty**, the Manchu moved on the Ming, now severely destabilised by peasant revolts around China. Heading southwest towards the Great Wall, they encountered the Mongolian tribes of today's Inner Mongolia. Divided as ever, some quickly joined the Manchu. But **Ligdan Khan** of the **Chahars** – the Great Khan in name only – determinedly resisted until forced to flee westwards with 100,000 followers. Resistance in southern Mongolia collapsed.

At a now-infamous kuriltai of the 16 eastern khans in 1636, these Mongolians became willing vassals of the Manchu, even handing over the jade "imperial seal" of the Yuan Dynasty to legitimise the new rulers. Mongol troops from this region then helped the Manchu conquer the Ming and take over **Beijing** and its newly built **Forbidden City**. Six years later in 1644, the Manchu renamed themselves the **Qing Dynasty** and would become totally sinicised by the time of their collapse in 1911. This Mongolian surrender also marked the permanent partition of its people into **Inner** and **Outer Mongolia**, with the former now part of China.

As the Manchu consolidated their power in southeastern Mongolia and inside China, the Oirads in western Mongolia were growing in a huge power base known as **Dzungaria**. In a particularly fascinating development from this relatively late period, one tribe (the **Torguts**) who refused to join in this new confederation simply packed up and migrated west – some 250,000 of them – to the Volga River where they became the **Kalmyks**, today a significant Russian minority of over 500,000 people.

Securing their hold over Tibet, including beating off an attempt by the Red Hat sect to regain power, the Dzungars actively pushed Yellow Hat Buddhism and Lamaism throughout Mongolia, including building palaces and monasteries, to strengthen their overall position. When **Galdan Khan** – widely regarded as the greatest of all the Mongolian princes – came to power in 1671, he quickly expanded Dzungar rule over today's western Xinjiang and into Central Asia. Trade expanded along the Silk Road and also into **Russia**, now starting its own eastward imperial drive.

In 1678, Qing **Emperor Kangxi** – who had already devoted so much time to defeating the Mongolians – formally recognised Galdan as Khan of Dzungaria. But for the astute Manchu emperor, his entitling of Galdan was simply another tactic designed to bring all of Mongolia and Tibet under his control, in which everything, including Tibetan Buddhism, was fair game. The Halh of eastern Mongolia were never that supportive of Galdan Khan who was, after all, an Oirad, and the Manchu were quick to pick up on the old Chinese game of divide-and-rule. A growing number of Halh princes became vassals of the Qing Dynasty and were rewarded with presents, titles and princesses. When war broke out between the Oirads and the Halh in 1688, Galdan Khan won a quick victory and united east and west into a nation the same size as today's Mongolia. For the Mongolians, this was their last opportunity to unite against the Qing – and they failed. Once again, the Mongolians were their own worst enemies.

By this time, the Halh nobles had fervently embraced Tibetan Buddhism and quickly rallied around the young man whom the Dalai Lama had proclaimed head of the Buddhist church in Mongolia when he was only four, the First Bogdgegeen Javzandamba. **Zanabazar**, as he was popularly known, had been educated in Tibet and formally converted to the Yellow Hat, or **Gelugpa**, sect. He was also an extremely gifted artist, a Mongolian Michelangelo, and renowned Buddhist architect. Clearly, many Mongolians today prefer remembering Zanabazar for his artistic genius, including his creation of the **Soyombo** symbol (see Special Topic, page 159), than what happened next.

Extending his authority into the political realm, Zanabazar convoked and conferred titles on the Halh nobles. He placated both the Ming Emperor and Galdan Khan with gold statues, artworks, sacred texts and even temples. He also sought to reconcile his nobles with the Oirads. But when Galdan Khan invaded in 1688, Zanabazar and many other Halh nobles and followers fled in panic to Inner Mongolia, where they threw themselves at the mercy of the Manchus. In a ceremony at **Dolonnur** – not far from Kublai Khan's Xanadu – in 1691, personally attended by Emperor Kangxi, they became vassals of the Qing Dynasty.

Fifty years after the capitulation of Inner Mongolia, Outer Mongolia also lost its independence. Explains historian Baabar somewhat bitterly: "These Halh people decided that submitting themselves to the alien Chinese was better than being ruled by the hated Oirad khan Galdan."

Zanabazar headed off to China, where under Kangxi's patronage he would spend most of the rest of his life, dying there in 1723. But back home in Mongolia and down in Tibet too, the stage was now set for a final bloodletting. In 1696, the emperor personally led a 50,000-man force equipped with cannons into the Mongolian heartland and inflicted a fatal blow to Galdan Khan at **Zuunmod** near today's Ulaanbaatar. Of the khan's force of 30,000, some 5,000 were killed, including his own wife, and another 3,000 taken prisoner. Galdan fled westwards with his survivors – a handful of whom settled in Arkhangai aimag – and committed suicide the following year. The battle for control of Tibet dragged on for 20 years before falling to a huge Chinese-led force in 1716.

Despite the Dzungar defeat in eastern Mongolia, Galdan Khan's descendants held on to its western region and Central Asia. For a while, they were able to play off the now-expansionist Russians against the Chinese. But when these two nations signed treaties clarifying their borders and spheres of influence, the Dzungars came under renewed pressure, including increasingly one-sided battles against musketry. Still, bringing the Oirads/Dzungars under Chinese domination was an epic struggle that dragged on for decades with all the intrigues of divide-and-rule, crosses and double-crosses – even the odd uprising back in Halh Mongolia.

After one last stand, the legendary **Amarsanaa** – honoured with a statue in the capital of Hovd aimag – was finally defeated in 1757 and he fled into Russia. So many Oirads were executed in retaliation – at least 500,000 – that the Chinese emperor invited the Kalmyks to return and resettle their former lands. (Only some returned.) It had taken the Manchus 130 years, but Mongolia was finally under their control. And just to make sure, the western town of **Uliastai** became their all-important military headquarters. (The rest of Dzungaria on the other side of the Altai Mountains became Xinjiang in China, and farther west into Central Asia part of Tsarist Russia's new territory.)

Even before it had completed its conquest of Mongolia, the Qing Dynasty had already established an administrative, military and economic structure to run the country. Mongolia was not only divided into four aimags, or provinces, but into scores of smaller civilian and military fiefdoms that reinforced the feudal system. Under the banner system, each entity owed its loyalty directly to the emperor. Overlapping all these were the serfs and herds of the tax-exempt Buddhist church and its growing number of monasteries.

Under the treaty of vassalage at Dolonnur in 1691, Chinese-Mongolian relations were tightly controlled. Intermarriage was forbidden, although Mongolians who married Manchus were granted a special title. Chinese were not allowed to stay overnight with a Mongolian family and needed special permission, renewable annually, to trade in Mongolia. Soon, Buddhist monasteries became powerful commercial centres, trading and storing goods for the Chinese who also lent money to the clergy and nobility. Taxes and duties were harsh.

After the second Bogd Javzandamba was implicated in the Oirads' last campaign, the Qing court ordered that all future reincarnations come from Tibet, ending the theocracy's links back to Genghis Khan. But that hardly slowed the Buddhist church which, now with active Manchu encouragement, became even more powerful. Mongolia's indigenous culture also underwent a dramatic change. Warriors no more, Mongolians fervently embraced a religion which absorbed many of their traditional superstitions. Religious festivals kept everyone occupied from spring to autumn. Out of poverty or piety, families gave up their sons to monastic life. The use of Tibetan in teaching and liturgy saw the near-disappearance of Mongolian script (ironically, the script survived in Inner Mongolia).

By the beginning of the 20th century, Mongolia had 700 monasteries and so many monks that the country was literally unable to feed itself. Some 100,000 of its 700,000 males were in monasteries. Well-off Mongolians spent their fortunes to make elaborate pilgrimages to Tibet, further weakening the economy. The hierarchy of the Buddhist church, including the Bogd Javzandamba of the day, was increasingly corrupt and indulged in opulent and immoral lifestyles. Voices for reform were lost in the morass.

Isolated and cut off from the world, Mongolia was stagnating. But by the mid-19th century, turmoil inside China from internal rebellions and Western intrusions saw the first cracks in Qing control over Mongolia. Taxes rose and were now demanded in silver, not animals. Poverty grew as usury by Chinese traders became rampant. Except as a buffer zone between itself and Russia, Mongolia held little real interest for the Qing. But now its policies became increasingly colonial as it relaxed earlier restrictions and allowed more traders and even colonists into Mongolia.

Just as in Inner Mongolia, the Mongolians now worried that they would become a minority in their own land. The end of the 19th century saw riots against the Chinese and the destruction of shops, mutinies by Mongolian troops and increasing anti-Chinese incidents. Dissatisfied Mongolians vainly sought Russian help in 1900. Some reforms were already taking place – including a secular revival – when the Manchu Qing Dynasty staggered to a dramatic close in 1911 and Mongolia declared its independence. But the road ahead would hardly be easy.

MODERN MONGOLIA (20TH CENTURY)

All through the 20th century, Mongolia sat at the Table of History, as it were. Unacknowledged by anyone, not even its neighbours, Mongolia was a constantly abused guest – its feet trampled upon, its opinions unsought and mind twisted. It's amazing that Mongolia survived the monstrous historical feast that was the 20th century. And yet Mongolia was served up every course – and right on its own dinner plate, like it or not. The collapse of centuries of Imperial Chinese rule and the warlords who followed; the fall of Tsarist Russia and the civil war between the Whites and Reds; the Soviet Union's expansionism; Stalinist purges and collectivisation; Japanese imperialism and World War II; the Cold War and Sino-Soviet split; a Brezhnevian interlude; and finally through Gorbachev's *glasnost* and *perestroika* and out into the blazing sun. But, first up after that, a cold shower to a market economy and globalisation. Mongolia has seen it all.

THE BOGD KHAAN PERIOD (1911–1924)

The **Chinese Revolution** which overthrew the Qing Dynasty – and 2,000 years of imperial rule – was still playing itself out when Mongolia proclaimed its independence on 1 December 1911. The Manchu *amban*, or representative, was sent packing back to Beijing. Elsewhere, particularly in the western region, Mongolians took up arms against the Manchus and Chinese, most dramatically around Uliastai, their military headquarters, and Hovd, an important commercial centre, in battles lasting into the following year. The head of Mongolian Buddhism, the **Eighth Javzandamba Hutagt**, was named the **Bogd Khaan**, or "Holy Leader". (Although a Tibetan, his wife was Mongolian and he was strongly anti-

Manchu.) Now formally a theocracy, the state's new ministers were secular nobles who answered directly to the Bogd Khaan.

From the start, there were attempts to create a **pan-Mongol state** to include Inner Mongolia, Urianhai in the northwest and other nearby regions. The Mongolians argued they'd been vassals of the Manchus and did not owe any allegiance to the new regime in China. Ironically, their only diplomatic recognition came from Tibet, in turmoil itself as it sought – ultimately in vain, of course – to make the same argument.

The change began. Most of Mongolia's then 600,000 population lived in a pre-20th century "time warp", running livestock and living a nomadic lifestyle. With its heavy overlay of superstitious beliefs, **Buddhist Lamaism** was deeply entrenched. Some 100,000 men and boys were lamas living in 700 temples and monasteries around the country. Apart from Hovd and Uliastai, the only town was **Ih Huree**, or **Urga** (Orgoo) as the Russians called it, which was the seat of the theocratic leader and home to over 60,000 lamas. Known today as **Ulaanbaatar**, this monastery town had only developed in 1779 after drifting its way east over two centuries from Karakorum. In the 19th century, Ih Huree/ Urga grew into an important trading centre on the **Tea Road** between China and Russia, with several thousand residents from those two countries.

Secular life was very limited, however, with reforms frequently opposed by high-ranking lamas jealous of losing their power and privileges. Despite this, Mongolia did progress quickly toward a modern army, local industry, secular education and journalism, plus creation of the country's first parliament. Russian and European influences were strong, especially from the **Buriat Mongolians** of Siberia. Those first involved in these reforms would drive the period ahead.

But any hopes of full independence for Mongolia – much less a Greater Mongolia – were quickly dashed by its stronger neighbours. In addition to China and Russia, Japan was the third important player back then, especially after the **Russo-Japanese War** of 1904–05 when the defeated Russians secretly granted them Inner Mongolia as their "sphere of influence". Russia wanted Mongolia and China – the whole lot. As we shall see, this three-sided game would continue for decades. But the end result was the permanent splintering of the Mongolian people. At the **Treaty of Hiagt** in 1915 between Russia, China and Mongolia, the latter was forced to accept a rather tortured status of "autonomy under Chinese suzerainty".

With post-revolutionary China now torn apart by warlords vying for control, little happened until Russia's **Bolshevik Revolution** of 1917 sent violent ripples eastwards through Siberia to the Far East of the Tsarist empire. As the **Communists**, or **Reds**, fought against pro-Tsar remnants, or **Whites**, hostilities flared all along the northern borders of Mongolia and China. (Japan, too, was involved in supporting the White forces in Siberia, occupying Vladivostok and providing sanctuary in Manchuria.)

Ostensibly to protect Mongolia from Bolshevik intrusions, three divisions of Chinese troops led by a notorious soldier-adventurer named "Little Xu", or **Wu Shuzeng**, occupied Ih Huree in November 1919. But his real agenda was to abolish Mongolia's autonomy, which he did by publicly forcing the Bogd Khaan and his ministers to prostate themselves repeatedly before a portrait of the Chinese President. Little Xu then locked up the government, disbanded the local army and took power. Backed by Russian Communist agents, underground resistance networks of middle-class intellectuals formed, including what would become the **Mongolian People's Revolutionary Party** (**MPRP**), the country's Communist Party, in June 1920. They approached the Soviets for help in defeating the occupying Chinese but were stalled.

Then came one of the more fascinating episodes in modern Mongolian history with the appearance of the "**Mad Baron**", a renegade Tsarist officer named **Baron Roman von Ungern-Sternberg** (see Special Topic, page 88). On the run from the Reds now rapidly consolidating Siberia, the Baron and 800 men of his well-armed "Asian Cavalry Division" slipped into Mongolia in October 1920. The Mongolians welcomed the Whites as their saviour from the Chinese, provided supplies and joined up in droves. Pledging to expel the Chinese and restore the Bogd Khaan, Ungern attacked Ih Huree but was turned back after a fierce battle. He embraced Buddhism, donned a traditional *deel* with general's insignia and vowed to restore the empire of Genghis Khan.

In early 1921, Ungern staged a surprise attack on the capital, freed the Bogd Khaan and sent the Chinese troops fleeing to the northern border. After installing a new government, his megalomania soon earned him the name "Bloody Baron". Helped by a sadistic colonel, he launched a ruthless reign of terror, singling out Bolsheviks and Jews, and sending thousands of foreigners and Mongolians fleeing. When "Little Xu" moved a relief force up from the Great Wall, the Baron's force slaughtered thousands of Chinese troops in the southeast, their bleached bones and tattered uniforms visible on the desolate steppe for decades.

Quite perversely, this Russian madman had now rid Mongolia of the Chinese, a move Moscow had been reluctant to take out of respect for Peking's "suzerainty". But with Mongolia now a dangerous sanctuary for the White Russians, the Bolsheviks began moves which determined Mongolia's future for the remainder of the 20th century. A "provisional government" of Mongolian sympathisers was formed. Then, a large Red Army force crossed the northern border where they joined a small Mongolian military force headed by

Damdiny Suhbaatar and advanced on Ih Huree, where they installed a new government on 11 July, now celebrated as Mongolia's **National Day**. (Although Suhbaatar is still hailed as a national hero with a statue and square in downtown Ulaanbaatar, the role of his forces was minor, only the expulsion of demoralised Chinese troops around Hiagt on the northern border and whom the Soviets soon repatriated to China. The bulk of the fighting was by Red Army troops.)

Meanwhile, Ungern and his forces had already fled the capital. Eventually turned over by his own Mongolian troops, the Mad Baron was tried and executed in Siberia a couple of months later. The Chinese allowed more Red Army troops to transit through western Xinjiang Province and fierce fighting between the two Russian sides continued all over western and northern Mongolia until early 1922, when the Whites were finally defeated. (Tales and locations of those battles are still heard of today.) Now, and still somewhat reluctantly, the Soviets were the new power brokers in Mongolia.

A power struggle broke out inside the new **People's Government** between moderates and Communists. At first, the Soviets were prepared to allow a nationalist government, even paying lip service to Chinese suzerainty, but that soon changed. Once again, the now-blind Bogd Khaan was head of state but was quickly undermined by Soviet-backed radicals who arrested and executed his 50-man bodyguard. Tacitly backed by the Soviets and a notorious Buriat Mongolian named **Rinchino**, Mongolia's long years of "red terror" began. By the end of 1922, the moderate **Prime Minister Bodoo**, 15 of his ministers and many nobles were executed for allegedly conspiring to reinstate an autocratic government. Commander Suhbaatar, then aged only 30, died mysteriously in February 1923.

Soviet advisors – including many Buriats from Siberia – took on an increasingly powerful role in running the government. At the same time, any hopes for a Greater Mongolia were dashed as the Soviets annexed **Urianhai** in the northwest, renaming it **Tannu Tuva**. Interestingly, the only concession was the **Darhad** (Darhat) region west of Lake Hovsgol, home of Mongolia's Reindeer People. (The status of Buriata east of Lake Baikal was not even discussed and Inner Mongolia remained under Japanese hegemony.)

In May 1924, the Bogd Khaan died and orders were issued banning the reincarnation of a Javzandamba to lead Mongolian Buddhism. Following the signing of a **Treaty of Friendship**, Mongolia on 26 November 1924 officially declared itself a Soviet-style republic and became Moscow's first "satellite state". Outer Mongolia ceased to exist. One of the first acts of the new **Mongolian People's Republic** was the execution of another prime minister, **Danzan**. The capital was renamed **Ulaanbaatar**, or Red Hero, after Suhbaatar. Mongolia's 70-year-long "Communist Nightmare" was under way.

THE BLOODY BARON'S ABDUCTION OF THE EIGHTH BOGD GEGEEN

I recently visited the former monastery and now museum at Mandshir Khiid, on the south side of Bogd Khan Uul, the huge massif which looms over the southern horizon of Ulaan Baatar. Among the dozen or so ruins scattered around the Mandshir Khiid area are the remains of the so-called Shar Süm, *or Yellow Temple, built in 1770 to serve as a secondary residence and retreat for the Bogd Gegeens, who usually dwelt in Örgöö, now Ulaan Baatar.*

It was here at the Yellow Temple of Mandshir Khiid that the 8th Bogd Gegeen was housed after he was abducted by Roman "the Bloody Baron" von Ungern-Sternberg in 1921. Ungern-Sternberg, at the head of the grandly styled Asiatic Cavalry Division, hoped to expel the Chinese overlords who then occupied the country and set up his own Pan-Mongolian Buddhist empire. The Baron claimed to be a Buddhist, the self-styled leader of an "Order of Buddhist Warriors", and reportedly the 13th Dalai Lama had declared that he was an emanation of Mahakala. It was also averred that he was an incarnation of Chingis Khan and/or Tamurlane.

The Bogd Khan's Winter Palace in Ulaanbaatar – now a museum (Don Croner).

The ruins of Mandshir Khiid on the south side of Bogd Khan Mountain (Don Croner).

Despite his extremely checkered past the Baron was at first welcomed into Mongolia. According to Joseph Geleta, a Hungarian living in Örgöö at the time:

> *He [Ungern-Sternberg] made speeches to the inhabitants of the frontier villages, declaring that he had come to the country in order to liberate it and drive out all foreigners, and calling upon the people to join him as a patriotic duty. He also promised again and again that once the liberation of the Mongolia people were [sic] accomplished he would organize a mighty Mongolian army, lead it into China, and after restoring the Emperor to his throne, attack Europe with a combined Sino-Mongolian army and "wipe out the revolution-mongers among the white races."*

When he first entered Mongolia the Baron's army consisted of a ragtag assortment of White Russian soldiers-of-fortune and refugees, displaced Cossacks, desperados, criminals and psychopaths of various hues, along with a leavening of Central Asian riffraff, including a detachment of Bashkir Moslems. By means of his pro-independence propaganda the Baron quickly attracted an ever-larger following of Mongolians. D.P. Pershin, a White Russian also living in Örgöö at the time, reported:

> *Mongols who had secretly slipped through into Urga said that everywhere along the way the Mongols assisted the Baron in whatever way they could; particularly in recruiting young men, and requisitioning horses and furnishing provisions. The Baron always paid in gold coin for whatever he took from the population and he did not permit his soldiers to be violent towards or outrage the peaceful inhabitants. The population looked upon the Baron with great favor, while one wealthy Mongolian, Taiban-Teregun, gave his considerable support. Many Mongols joined the general as volunteers . . .*

Ungern-Sternberg's first attempt to take Örgöö was launched on September 24, 1920. His 2,700–3,000 troops were unable to dislodge the entrenched Chinese garrison of 10,000 and finally on November 7 he admitted defeat and withdrew his troops to Dalai Nuur in what is now Inner Mongolia in China.

While his army set up camp here, the Baron traveled west into Mongolia itself to meet with delegations of Mongolian nobles, included the Setsen Khan, ruler of the Setsen khanate, which at that time occupied much of eastern Mongolia and the territory around Dalai Nuur. Soon a plot was hatched to make another attempt on Örgöö, with the ultimate goal of expelling the Chinese from the territory of Mongolia and the creation of an independent country. The 8th Bogd Gegeen, already the nominal leader of the Mongolian people, was to be declared the king of this newly independent Mongolia.

The 8th Bogd Gegeen resided at that time in Chinese-occupied Örgöö, held under virtual house arrest by the Chinese authorities. During the winter of 1920 – apparently after the Baron's first assault on Örgöö, although the chronology remains uncertain – he had been forcibly removed from his palace and placed under guard in a residence in the Polovinka quarter of town. "This was, for the Urga population, thunder out of a clear blue sky, and now all awaited extraordinary events," noted Pershin, who was in Örgöö at the time. He continued:

> *No one understood the grounds for his arrest. It was believed the Chinese generals wished to show the people their power and their importance and that they could do anything with impunity. It was also believed that the generals intended this to be a lesson to all who expressed discontent with the Chinese authorities: if the Bogdo [the 8th Bogd Gegeen] could be treated without*

> *ceremony, there could be no question of the others. And the garrison was to be convinced that the deity Himself remained helpless before military force and that consequently there was nothing to fear in either the incantations of the lamas or their moaning and roaring horns . . .*

After fifty days in detention the Bogd Gegeen was allowed to return to his Winter Palace, but it was clear to all that he was still under house arrest, a hostage to the demands of the Chinese administration in Örgöö. Inside the Winter Palace the Bogd Gegeen was surrounded by his own retinue of lamas and bodyguards, but outside a Chinese detachment of 350 soldiers remained constantly on guard.

In preparation for the assault on Örgöö the Baron moved his army to near the present-day town of Nailakh, some 15 miles to the east of the city. The first order of business, he concluded, was to secure the Living Person of the 8th Bogd Gegeen so that the Chinese could not use him as a bargaining chip in the upcoming battle for Örgöö. As Dmitri Alioshin, a White Russian soldier-of-fortune in Ungern-Sternberg's army who later wrote a highly colored account of the ensuing events, noted, "It was imperative to have the Buddha among us, for then, we expected, all of Mongolia would back us to the limit of its resources." Pershin sounded a similar note:

> *It was extremely necessary for Ungern to kidnap lest the latter become a hostage in the hands of the Chinese authorities. If that were the case the Chinese would be in a position to demand many things from the Mongols, knowing full well in advance for the sake of the Bogdo the Mongols would make all sorts of concessions.*

With the assistance of Setsen Khan the Baron managed to infiltrate into Örgöö secret emissaries who were finally able to arrange a meeting with the Bogd Gegeen. The details of this operation remain vague, but apparently the agents were either lamas or men posing as lamas who were able to bypass the Chinese guards by claiming that they needed to talk to the Bogd Gegeen about religious matters. In any case, they obtained the Bogd Gegeen's agreement to play a passive role in his own kidnapping and, perhaps more importantly, were able to convince the entourage of Mongolian lamas and bodyguards surrounding him to assist in the plot.

The Bogd Gegeen had to be seized before the actual attack on Örgöö began, and for this Ungern-Sternberg needed confederates within the town itself. His network of agents within Örgöö soon managed to recruit a Buryat named Tubanov, according to Pershin "a local desperado of unsavory reputation and repulsive exterior." Tubanov in turn recruited cohorts from the so-called Tubuty, *a colony of Tibetans who lived by themselves in a special quarter near the Zakhadyr market and subsisted by trading in Tibetan goods and money-lending. Pershin relates:*

> *Of these* tubuts *Tubanov selected a gang of about sixty of the hardiest and bravest men who since childhood were accustomed to climbing their native Tibetan mountains and, what was more important, were fanatical lamaists: for the sake of serving the faith – in this case rescuing Bogdo – they would go against any odds and perform miracles of bravery. The selection was undoubtedly correct, as no one could have carried out this task better than these Tibetans; the more so as they hated the Chinese as oppressors of Tibet and outragers of the Dalai-lam [Dalai Lama] . . . The Tibetans*

A 19th century artist's view of Orgoo, located at the entrance of the Choiijin Lama Temple Museum (Don Croner).

> *were particularly inspired by the thought that they were not only performing a feat of godliness and devotion, but were also helping their national cause, as the Bogdo-GegenJebusan-damba-Khutukhtu was of Tibetan origin and consequently a countryman of theirs . . .*

An original painting of the Bogd Gegeen in the Zanabazar Museum (Don Croner).

Once recruited into the kidnapping plot, the Tibetans, who according to Pershin "knew how to keep their tongues between their teeth," maintained absolute secrecy, sneaking out of their quarter "to investigate at night all the nooks and crannies, trails, paths, and projections of the Bogdo-ula along the route which they later used to carry the kidnapped Bogdo-Gegen in their arms, from the palace to the monastery of Manchushry-lam [Mandshir Khiid] on the other side of the range."

Meanwhile, the Baron instituted a regime of psychological warfare against the Chinese garrison in the city. Pershin describes in detail one of his first gambits:

> *In broad daylight the town, which had been declared to be under martial arrest and even under a state of siege, and in any case supposedly under reinforced guard and teeming with soldiers, was visited personally by none other than his Excellency Baron Ungern. He called on the manor of the main representative of authority, Chen-Yi, and thereupon returned to his own camp . . . Baron Ungern wore, as usual, a bright cherry colored Mongolian robe with a tall white fur* papakha *[Russian hat] and carried a* tashur *[long bamboo riding stick]. He rode his speedy white mare at a middling trot, along the main street of the Polovinka towards Chen-Yi's residence. In the courtyard, the Baron dismounted leisurely, motioned to a soldier of the ever present guard to come to him and ordered him to hold his horse by the bridle. He then quietly walked around the house, returned to his horse, glanced carefully at the entire surroundings, tightened the*

> *saddle-girth, mounted and rode unhurriedly out of the yard in the direction of the Consular settlement and his camp. On his way back he noticed a sentry asleep at the gates of the prison. Such a breach of discipline revolted the Baron and, without dismounting, he rewarded the sleeping soldier with several blows of his* tashur. *The frightened soldier could not collect his wits and stood perplexed, whereupon Ungern (who knew a little Chinese) explained to him that a sentry must not sleep at his post and that for such a breach of discipline, he, Baron Ungern, had punished him personally. The scared sentry raised an alarm, but by that time the Baron was far away.*

Word of this incredible stunt soon spread all over town and the superstitious soldiers in the Chinese garrison quickly concluded that the Baron must possess supernatural powers.

This was just one of the Baron's ploys intended to demoralize the Chinese forces before his attack on the city. He also dispatched his men in groups of three to build campfires on the side of Bogd Khan Uul. Soon the mountainside was ablaze with hundred of campfires, creating the impression that a much larger army was camped above the city. In addition to this, according to Pershin, the fires "were given a grave and mysterious meaning: the Baron up there was offering sacrifices to the host spirits of the mountain so that they might send various calamities upon those who had insulted Bogdo, the exalted protector and lord of all the surrounding country."

By now the Chinese garrison was thoroughly rattled. Still, the Chinese generals did not suspect that the 8th Bogd Gegeen could be snatched away from under their very noses. As Pershin noted:

> *The whole Tola [Tuul] valley was open on every side, with not a single shrub or structure in sight. The valley nowhere afforded any protected approach to the palaces of the Bogdo, while the steep, stony fastnesses of the Bogdo-ula seemingly excluded the possibility of approaching from that side . . . Under such topographical conditions to kidnap the Bogdo from his palace was an exploit of great difficulty if not entirely impossible . . . But Ungern was a warrior to the marrow of his bones, and a gifted military chieftain at that. The harder the problem, the more zest he had for tackling it . . .*

The abduction was scheduled for February 1. This date had been arrived upon by the concerted prognostications of the whole passel of fortune-tellers, clairvoyants, mystics, and mental cases which the Baron retained in his entourage. Special importance was given to the pronouncements of lamas skilled in the art of divining the future from the scorched shoulder blades of sheep. Alioshin noted, "According to Mongolian fortune-telling and learned prophesies, the Living Buddha was supposed to be liberated from the Chinese on the first day of the battle, February 1, and we had to make the prophecy a reality at all costs."

At the appointed hour the Tibetans appeared at the Winter Palace in monks' dress, appearing at first to be lamas seeking an audience with the Bogd Gegeen. Monks in the entourage of the Bogd Gegeen who were already inside the palace and who had secretly been supplied with weapons quickly disarmed and tied up the Chinese guards. The Tibetans rushed into the palace and grabbed the blind Bogd Gegeen, who was waiting for them warmly dressed and equipped for a trip over the mountains. Two monks held the Bogd Gegeen under each arm and helped him onto a horse. One group of Tibetans led the Bogd Gegeen up Zaisan Valley to the ridgeline of Bogd Khan Uul. "Another group of Tibetans, armed to the teeth, waited until the Bogdo was out of the palace, when they opened fire with automatic rifles upon the exterior guard of the palace to prevent them from pursuing the kidnappers . . ." The Chinese soldiers, "lacking all incentive to climb the steep, unblazed hillside," as Pershin put it, made no real attempt to pursue the Tibetans and the Bogd Gegeen. Alioshin claims that Tubanov and his men captured several machine guns from the Chinese and turned them on the Chinese themselves, killing over a thousand, although this sounds like an exaggeration.

Pershin continues:

> *By chance, at about four o'clock on the afternoon of the kidnapping, the author of these memoirs [Pershin writing about himself here], was looking out of his window through his Zeiss binoculars, and observed some movement on the Bogdo-ula mountainside. He did not pay much attention to this, believing that the dots moving up the hillside were Mongol guards patrolling the mountain. Besides, these dots could be observed only when they were in the snow-covered clearings. Later it transpired that they were the kidnappers of the Bogdo-Gegen.*

The Bogd Gegeen, meanwhile, was handed off to a succession of relays who escorted him to Mandshir Khiid on the south side of Bogd Khan Mountain, a distance of 9.2 miles south of the Winter Palace. There he was deposited in the Yellow Temple, which had been built as a residence for the Bogd Gegeens in 1770. He resided here while the Baron secured the city.

Although the abduction was a carefully planned and executed commando raid, in the minds of the populace of Örgöö the episode soon came to resemble, as Pershin pointed out, "a magic tale rather than reality." People opined that the kidnapping was "not accomplished without the intervention of some supernatural force." Pershin elaborates:

> *"Of course," someone would say and others repeat, "Don't you know that the kidnappers penetrated in broad daylight the palace which is in plain view of everyone, disarmed or, when necessary, killed outside and inside guards, took Bogdo and carried him in their arms out of the palace and across a high, steep and nearly inaccessible mountain, while most of the guard either remained inactive or ran away – is it not a miracle? No, no, this never could have happened without the intervention of some special force! They used sorcery to divert all eyes, there is no other explanation." Such reasoning could be heard among the Russians, Chinese, and Mongols and evoked a feeling of wonderment mixed with fear.*

An early photograph of Baron Roman von Ungern-Sternberg.

Indeed, the seizure of the Bogd Gegeen seems to have completely demoralized the Chinese garrison. The next day a diversionary attack by units of Ungern-Sternberg's army was launched on the Chinese district of Maimaicheng out near Uliastai Gol, on what is now the eastern edge of Ulaan Baatar. That same day the now totally unnerved Chinese officers and civil authorities fled the city, leaving the troops to fend for themselves. The next day, February 3, the main body of the Baron's army attacked Örgöö proper and quickly overran what remained of the Chinese garrison, most of which had fled in the night. A three-day orgy of pillage, plunder and murder commenced against rich Chinese, Russian, and other foreign traders; suspected Bolsheviks; and especially Jews, toward whom the Baron had a diabolical hatred. Alioshin, an eyewitness to the pogrom – he is a bit coy about the degree of his own participation – describes with all too much relish the horrific atrocities visited on the victims. This gruesome catalog of crimes need not be recounted at length here; one detail reported by Alioshin will suffice: "The humiliation of the women was so awful that I saw one of the officers run inside a house with a razor and offer to let the girl commit suicide before she was attacked. With tears of gratitude she said a simple thanks and then slashed her throat."

After three days the Baron called an abrupt halt to the pogrom and any of his soldiers who disobeyed his order met much the same fate as their victims a few days earlier. Having satisfied his own bloodlust on his perceived enemies the Baron allowed the Mongolians to organize a new government. On March 21, 1921 the independent country of Mongolia was reborn, and the Bogd Gegeen was proclaimed ruler with the title of the Bogd Khan. "The actual coronation of the Living Buddha was an intricate religious ceremony requiring many hours to complete," historian Thomas Allsen tells us. The Bogd Gegeen granted Ungern-Sternberg and Rezukhin, one of the General's chief officers, the princely title of Gün *as a reward for their services. As Allsen points outs, "The Living Buddha was delegated supreme secular and religious powers. However, as supreme military commander of the Mongol armies, Ungern decided all matters major or minor. The Living Buddha's addiction to heavy drinking and his total blindness further enhanced the Baron's position." Ungern-Sternberg would remain the real ruler of Mongolia until dislodged from the country by the Bolsheviks, who in the end executed the Bloody Baron. One of the Baron's riding boots, apparently stripped from his body when he was captured, can now be seen in the National Museum of Mongolian History in Ulaan Baatar.*

Don Croner, The Abduction of the Eighth Bogd Gegeen, *2008*

THE COMMUNIST PERIOD (1925–1990)

In the midst of today's bustling and modernising Mongolia, it is easy for visitors to overlook – perhaps not even know about – the country's grim history during the 20th century. Cut off from most of the world, Mongolia suffered nearly seven decades of Communist rule. But Mongolians have certainly not forgotten, even if many prefer to remember those days as "the socialist period" and the purges and destruction of monasteries as "Stalinist". More vividly – and always great conversation starters – they personally remember the dramatic end of the Communist Era in 1990 and the hard adjustments that followed. But do not expect any deep or nuanced introspection. Many say quite simply that the agony, pain and loss of those days were the harsh price that Mongolia had to pay for today's cherished independence. Like their cousins next door in Inner Mongolia, they could have well ended up as part of today's China.

The early days of the Mongolian People's Republic were marked by continued power struggles between the right and left wings of the Communist **Mongolian People's Revolutionary Party (MPRP)**. But the Soviets ran every aspect of Mongolian life.

Soviet-equipped Mongolian troops in Ulaanbaatar's main square at the height of the Communist period (Photomon Agency).

Following the Stalinist model, the deeply entrenched feudal system and Buddhist Lamaist church were early targets. The Moscow-dictated **1928 Party Congress** expelled thousands of rightists and executed its leaders. Hundreds of feudal and religious properties were seized, with 700 killed or imprisoned. Nomadic herders were collectivised, private enterprise abolished and trade turned into a state monopoly. One-third of Mongolia's adult males were lamas and the crackdown on Buddhism was particularly fierce. Lower-ranking lamas were forced into the army or economy, middle-rankings to prison and the highest simply executed. Thousands fled into China and Manchuria. Forced collectivisation caused widespread food shortages.

A spring flood inundates the capital in the 1920s (Photomon Agency).

In 1932, public resistance exploded into a full-scale and bloody revolt – some say civil war – which quickly spread throughout Mongolia. Beginning at a Hovsgol monastery in April, its hundreds of lamas were soon joined by nobles, ordinary civilians and even party officials. Armed with antiquated or captured weapons, the so-called **Yellow Soldiers** went on an angry and often vicious rampage across the country, destroying schools, cooperatives and killing government workers. Both sides engaged in harsh brutalities; the government crackdown was fierce with Soviet-operated aircraft, tanks, artillery and even soldiers used against the rebels. Thousands were killed and any captives executed. By October, the rebellion was crushed.

Mongolian troops rally during World War II (Photomon Agency).

The first attempt by the Communists to radically transform Mongolian society and economy had clearly failed. Now, Stalin and the Politburo imposed a more relaxed regime allowing a "capitalist democratic society". Seemingly unaware of the tragedy that followed Lenin's similar

New Economic Policy in the Soviet Union in the 1920s, Prime Minister **Butachiin Genden** fervently reversed policies on private enterprise, collectivisation and religion, even releasing falsely accused lamas and openly declaring his own religious beliefs. Refugees returned and were granted herds and land. Livestock production rose. Enterprise flourished with new power stations and other industries. For the only time in the entire Communist Era, government was more important than the party.

But the Soviets had other motives, of course. Japan was now a serious worry after declaring its puppet state of **Manchukuo** in 1931. At the same time, the Japanese were making a special point of treating the Inner Mongolians sympathetically, accepting refugees and promoting pan-Mongolianism. (Inner Mongolia would later become the puppet state of Mengkukuo, recognised only by Japan and Manchukuo.) More than ever, Mongolia was an important buffer state for the Russians. To preoccupy the Japanese and keep them away from the Soviet Far East, Stalin provided the Nationalist Chinese with massive shipments of arms and equipment which arrived through western Xinjiang province.

But Stalin's relaxing of his grip on the Mongolian people was just a ploy while he planned his next move. In a foretaste of what was to come, the **Lhumbe Affair** of 1934 exposed a supposed pro-Japanese "plot" in which hundreds were executed, imprisoned or exiled. Then came Genden's turn. After refusing to follow Stalin's instructions to "destroy the lamas" and famously insulting the Soviet dictator at a Moscow reception, the popular prime minister was stripped of his power in 1936. The next year, Genden was forced to the Soviet Union for "medical treatment" where he "admitted" being a Japanese spy and counter-revolutionary, and was then executed.

The time was now ripe for Mongolia's very own Stalin: **Horoloogiin Choibalsan** was a docile time-server of peasant background who had trained as a lama and been around since the early revolutionary days of Bodoo, Suhbaatar and Danzan. Never destined for much, he'd headed the commission to confiscate feudal property in the late 1920s, and was then Minister of Livestock and Agriculture under Genden. In 1934, he was picked from obscurity by Stalin himself and made Deputy Prime Minister. Two years later, the now Marshal Choibalsan was named head of the newly created **Ministry for Internal Affairs**, Mongolia's KGB or secret police. In an oft-heard story, Stalin then sent Choibalsan a gift of four rifles and 30,000 bullets. Mongolia's **Great Purge** would now begin – and close to that same number would be killed.

Planned and directed by the Soviets, the Great Purge – coinciding with a similar one in the Soviet Union – would last from 1937 to 1939 and leave an indelible stain on Mongolian society, with some estimates of the dead as high as 100,000 (a more widely accepted estimate ranges between 22,000 and 35,000, or three to four percent of the population). The common accusation was spying for Japan and began with the arrest, show trial and public execution in downtown Ulaanbaatar of a group of Buddhist lamas. Next came the death by poisoning of Mongolia's popular Minister of Defence, Demid, by Soviet agents while en route to Moscow. In this deliberately created atmosphere of crisis and tension some 30,000 Soviet troops arrived, supposedly to protect the country from Japanese invasion. Purges and executions then swept through government ranks, the army and party, with Choibalsan the only surviving member of the Presidium.

Horoloogiin Choibalsan was Stalin's puppet leader in Mongolia (Photomon Agency).

But the main thrust of the purge was against the Buddhist clergy and their monasteries. With Soviet help, over 15,000 lamas were persecuted, mostly shot. In an orgy of looting and destruction, including the burning of ancient texts and religious art, all but a handful of Mongolia's 700 monasteries and temples were totally destroyed – their battered-down walls and foundations now grim tourist attractions. Kazakhs and Buriats who'd fled the Soviet Union into Mongolia were tracked down and killed. The notorious **Rinchino**, the Buriat who'd helped the Communists to power in the 1920s, was taken to Moscow and executed. Not trustful enough of Choibalsan and his cronies to conduct a show trial in Mongolia, the independent-minded Prime Minister **Anandiin Amar** was taken to Moscow in March 1939, tortured and finally killed in 1941.

By 1939, Choibalsan was fully in charge and would rule Mongolia until his death in 1952. Never charismatic, he'd proved the perfect "yes-man" for Stalin. Minor purges would continue, but the last act of the Great Purge was the elimination of the purgers themselves, with Choibalsan elevated into a national hero who stopped the excesses of his underlings. Frightened and docile, the population was now easy to control, manipulate and regiment, such as the 100,000 men – out of a population of only 900,000 – press-ganged into the massively expanded, Soviet-equipped and trained Mongolian Army.

The extent of pro-Japanese "plotting" among Mongolians was clearly exaggerated for the Great Purge. But Japan was indeed a looming military threat all through the 1930s, with Stalin's worst nightmare an invasion of Mongolia to cut the Trans-Siberian Railway to the north, necessitating a two-front war. Just how far Japan was prepared to go is questionable, but with World War II looming, both sides were certainly testing each other out.

Starting in 1935, a string of border skirmishes – including along the Manchurian-Siberian border – took place between the Soviets and Japanese and culminated in the massive but little-known **Battle of Halhgol** (also Khalkhin Gol) along the Manchurian-Mongolian border in 1939 (see The Great Eastern Steppe, page 261.) The Soviets came out decisive and devastating winners in the five-month-long battle on Mongolia's eastern steppe. Japan signed a non-aggression pact that allowed Moscow to focus on its western front, and Japan to shift its own towards Southeast Asia – and the United States.

When World War II broke out shortly afterwards, patriotism ran high and Mongolia became part of the Soviet Union's all-important rear, providing constant shipments of meat, sheepskin, clothing and other supplies. Public contributions funded a Revolutionary Tank brigade including a couple of T-34 tanks that took part in the Battle of Berlin (one of the tanks is now on a monument on the south side of UB). An air squadron was also formed. The Soviet-Japanese non-aggression pact held up until near war's end, when Moscow finally declared war against Japan and launched a massive invasion of Manchuria and Korea. To assert its own independence from China, Mongolia also declared war and under Soviet command its 80,000 troops invaded Inner Mongolia where, at the **Battle of Janchuugijn**, they lost 10 men.

During the war, Mongolia's independence was always on the table at allied conferences in which China also took part, such as the one in Teheran in November 1943. Finally, to guarantee the Soviets would join in the attack on Japan and return Manchuria, the Chinese Government of **President Chiang Kai-shek** abandoned its long-held suzerainty claims and accepted Mongolia's full and legal independence, but subject to a face-saving referendum. In October 1945, Mongolia voted overwhelmingly in favour and was finally – *de facto* and *de jure* – an independent country.

In the post-war period, Mongolia moved rapidly to modernise its economy – including massive industrialisation – with economic assistance from the Soviet Union and, after the Communists won power in 1949, from China as well. Using gulag labour, including German POWs from the Battle of Stalingrad, a railway link – today's **Trans-Mongolian Railway** – was connected from the Soviet Union to Ulaanbaatar in 1949 and extended to the Chinese border in 1956. Collectivisation was resumed and completed in 1959 with

390 cooperatives, or *negdels*. Virgin lands were opened up for broad-scale agriculture, including self-sufficiency in wheat. New educational institutions were created, and a simplified Cyrillic version of Mongolian saw literacy improve markedly. Hospitals and other health programmes were established, including veterinary programmes for herders.

Choibalsan was now the object of a Cult of Personality and fêted by Moscow and Beijing alike. When he died on 26 January 1952, the nation mourned and a Kremlin-style mausoleum overlooking Ulaanbaatar's main square was built for his remains. His body was joined by that of Suhbaatar, now elevated to national hero status. Choibalsan was replaced by **Yumjaagiyn Tsedenbal** who, just as Nikita Khrushchev did with Stalin in the Soviet Union, launched a similar denunciation of Choibalsan's excesses in 1956. The move was followed by a smaller purge of his supporters.

Relations with China were smooth and Mongolia played off Beijing's burgeoning rivalry with Moscow to boost aid. China also provided generous assistance, built power stations and even imported workers to build public housing in Ulaanbaatar. Mongolia joined the **Non-Aligned Movement** in 1956 and the **United Nations** in 1961. But as the Sino-Soviet rivalry intensified in the 1960s, Mongolia stayed firmly at Moscow's side and relations with China froze, including the departure of over 12,000 workers. The Soviets moved troops into Mongolia, building a string of massive military bases, missile sites and airfields along the Chinese border, peaking at 120,000 men in 1979. (Now abandoned, these too make an interesting tourist sight in eastern Mongolia.)

But the huge subsidies required for Mongolia's "socialist modernisation" and the simple cost of running the country were a constant source of friction between the Soviets and their Eastern European satellites. By 1984 and with Moscow now working toward a rapprochement with Beijing, Tsedenbal's continued anti-Chinese rhetoric had become increasingly embarrassing, while at home the constant interventions of his Russian-born wife were deeply resented. He was ousted by the Kremlin and replaced with **Jambyn Batmonh**. With the coming winds of change now blowing through Eastern Europe and the Soviet Union, Batmonh would be Mongolia's last Communist leader.

The Post-Communist Period (1990–present)

By the 1980s, Mongolia had become a totally transformed society. Its population had mushroomed to over two million and was also heavily urbanised, not just the capital but the new industrial centres of Darhan and Erdenet north of Ulaanbaatar and Choibalsan in eastern Dornod aimag. The level of education had also grown, in rural areas as well as urban centres, creating a growing intelligentsia. Interestingly, the dramatic crackdown on pro-democracy demonstrators in Beijing's Tiananmen Square in 1989 barely caused a ripple in

Mongolia. Instead, change came from the West and when perestroika was introduced in the Soviet Union, the ripples swept into Mongolia. Batmonh's new communist leadership had tried unsuccessfully to implement economic change, but a new generation of Mongolians – mostly educated in the Soviet Union and Eastern Europe – demanded similar changes. Thankfully, the central role of the secret police and army had also diminished.

In contrast to other communist states of the time, Mongolia's democratic revolution was remarkably peaceful and began with a series of popular demonstrations in late 1989 and early 1990. In a heady time frequently recalled by Mongolians today, mass demonstrations filled Ulaanbaatar's Suhbaatar Square demanding an end to one-party rule and free elections. Opposition parties were formed and hunger strikes called.

By March 1990, the Politburo of the long-ruling Mongolian Revolutionary People's Party (MPRP) resigned and massive constitutional and legislative reforms were implemented. After re-registering itself, the MPRP was joined by five new democratic parties. In Mongolia's first free election in July 1990, the former Communist Party won a majority but agreed to share both the presidency and the government leadership with the opposition. A new constitution was drafted declaring Mongolia a parliamentary democracy with an elected president exercising limited powers, guarantees of individual and property rights and freedoms, the separation of powers and a single 76-seat national assembly called the **State Great Khural**, elected every four years. For most of the time since, the MPRP – with its strong rural base – has controlled government.

Mongolia's embrace of democracy has produced unprecedented freedoms – but also frequently acrimonious debates on a range of political, social and economic issues. And the excitement of those early days soon gave way to a downright tortuous and painful transition as the heavily subsidised and command-led Soviet-style economy gave way to one based on the free market. The painful years of severe shortages, rationing and unemployment between 1990 and 1992 are still vividly recalled. Mongolians have survived much, and their resilience is now moulded by a rediscovery of their traditional culture – and its long and gloriously agonising history.

Historical Amnesia in Mongolia

By *Christopher Kaplonski*

With the collapse of socialism in 1990, Mongolians were finally free to rediscover the truth about their own history. Topics that had been strictly forbidden under socialism could now be freely discussed, and those falsely revered could be taken off their pedestals. So runs the standard account. The story behind retelling history is in actuality much more complex. It is indeed a case of the forgotten remembered, and the already known rethought. But it seldom plays out how a visitor to Mongolia might expect. Mongolians' relationship with their own history, both under socialism and after it, are much less straightforward, and much more interesting. What we might think are dual forms of historical amnesia are taking place. On one level, there is an apparent forgetting or glossing over of certain aspects of the socialist past. On another level, there is a misremembering of other aspects of history, including how history was presented under socialism. Both are worth thinking about.

Perhaps the best-known example of the latter historical amnesia is the case of Chinggis Khaan (Genghis Khan). Best known to those outside Mongolia as a conqueror, in Mongolia today he is better thought of as the father of the Mongolian nation who also gave them their first set of codified laws. Many people will tell you it was forbidden to talk about Chinggis Khaan during the 70 years of socialism. We should be clear: people could, and did, get in trouble for talking about him. Yet if we actually go back and look at the socialist period, it is hard to miss the fact that Chinggis did not disappear from the history books of the period. There was even official interest in studying him in the early days of socialism and even after, and books and articles were published about him. The first strident critiques only came in the late 1940s, when a textbook was recalled for not being sufficiently critical of Chinggis Khaan's feudal nature. It was only after this that Chinggis Khaan became a much more sensitive topic to talk and write about, and this was part of a broader trend to instil a more Marxist perspective on literature and education.

People will sometimes point to what happened in 1962 as proof of Chinggis's despised nature under socialism. That year, a number of events to commemorate the 800th anniversary of Chinggis's birth were planned. While some took place, others ended up being cancelled when the leadership of the Soviet Union took issue with the plans, particularly in light of deteriorating Sino-Soviet relationships, which Mongolia was caught in the middle of both literally and metaphorically. Various people, prominent and not, lost their jobs, were exiled or had to publish self-critical articles as a result of their roles. What is often overlooked, however, is that the commemorations, the conference and other events were all planned with government approval. It was not, as the implication seems to be, that a band of dissidents tried to celebrate Chinggis Khaan, only to be squashed by the government. Rather, the government itself approved the plans, only to change its mind later on.

But such a story does not make for as interesting press as the received wisdom. As the 19th century French philosopher Ernst Renan once observed, one characteristic of a nation is getting its history wrong. This is what has happened in the case of Chinggis Khaan. Since portrayals of him were indeed subject to limitations under late socialism, he served as a convenient marker on which to hang a new understanding and rejection of socialist Mongolia. The reading back and exaggeration of late socialist strictures on Chinggis Khaan to cover the entire period is relatively easy to understand. It allows people to put a distance between themselves and the now undesirable aspects of the socialist past. It is not so much that Chinggis was completely forbidden under socialism as it was useful to think him so. This allowed people to rethink what it meant to be Mongolian amidst the economic and social collapse of the early post-socialist period, and still helps draw a line between Then and Now. This tendency is taken to its logical extreme in the idea that Chinggis was actually a democrat. Although unsupportable, it nicely sidesteps the problems of the socialist period, and draws a direct link between a key historical figure and the present.

Yet we must not make the mistake of extending this tendency too far. Mongolians' relationship with the socialist past is not a simple inversion of good for bad or sharpening grey areas into black and white. People and events foreigners might reasonably expect to be excoriated have in fact not been. Perhaps the most striking example of this is the case of H. Choibalsan, generally, and not completely inaccurately, glossed as Mongolia's Stalin.

Choibalsan is probably best known for ruling Mongolia during the repressions of the late 1930s, when around 35,000 people were killed, and almost every last monastery – out of over 700 – was destroyed, along with many other cultural artefacts. Yet his statue remains in front of the main building of the national university, and, among other things, the provincial capital of Dornod remains named after him.

The reasons why this should be so are actually quite complex and many, but a few points can be highlighted. It is often claimed that Choibalsan kept Mongolia independent from the Soviet Union after World War II, when Stalin is said to have played with the idea of incorporating Mongolia as the 16th republic. He can thus be presented as someone who had Mongolia's best interests at heart, and stood up to the domineering northern neighbour. Yet this alleged ability to stare down Stalin was absent less than 10 years previously, during the repressions. Then, it is common to hear, Choibalsan, and by extension all Mongolians, are not really to blame. There was no choice. The repressions were forced upon Mongolia by Stalin and the Soviets. One person told me – as if to underline his essential humanity and decency – that Choibalsan took to drinking heavily after the repressions.

This unresolved tension in the image of Choibalsan nicely illustrates the complexity of history in post-socialist Mongolia, and in particular, the history of the socialist period. On the one hand, Mongolia was effectively a Soviet colony. Independent, it was nonetheless bound more tightly to the Soviet Union than the Eastern European countries were. On the other hand, the socialist period did see the spread of education and health care, among other things, throughout the country. There is room for competing valuations of the period.

The treatment of Choibalsan reflects this ambiguity towards the socialist period. While the killings of the 1930s may ultimately be traced back to Stalin's policy decisions, most of what actually took place was carried out by Mongolians, acting for a variety of reasons, some honourable, some less so, but most of whom apparently believed at some level in what they were doing, as interviews have revealed. By saying Choibalsan, and by extension all Mongolians, had no choice, Mongolians can avoid the need to examine too closely the actions of their own relatives. Yet this view is troubling on another level, as it threatens to render all Mongolians into passive victims of the Soviets, a disempowered underclass writ large. (To be sure, at least under late socialism, Soviets in Mongolia did often enjoy privileges Mongolians did not, including among other things special shops.)

It has always struck me as highly unlikely that, had Stalin been bent on making Mongolia part of the Soviet Union, Choibalsan's stand would actually have had much effect. Yet the story is an important one, since it works to counter the potential image of Mongolians as powerless to determine their own fate. Choibalsan is thus nicely emblematic of a past that cannot be forgotten, yet raises troubling questions if examined in too sharp a light.

Chinggis Khaan and Choibalsan are not the only two figures to be subject to such forms of rethinking and amnesia. In a similar vein, although on a smaller scale, Tsedenbal, who ruled Mongolia from the 1950s to the mid-1980s, has experienced something of a resurgence and at times is portrayed as a victim of political repression himself, as he was removed from power in 1984 by the Soviets, and had various titles and honours stripped in 1990, which were later restored. Early socialist revolutionaries, such as Danzan and Bodoo, who had been repressed and then written out of the history books, were brought back as early democrats and capitalists (largely accurately) who did symbolic service as embodying the potential that the revolution of 1921 – now often called a National Democratic Revolution, rather than a socialist one – was never able to manifest because of the influence of the Soviet Union. All these historical personages, then, are not so much the subjects of historical amnesia as a complex grappling with a complicated past that continues even today.

Chris Kaplonski is a Senior Research Associate at the Mongolia and Inner Asia Studies Unit, Department of Social Anthropology, University of Cambridge. He edited the English edition of Baabar's History of Mongolia *(1999) and authored* Truth, History and Politics in Mongolia: The Memory of Heroes *(RoutledgeCurzon 2004) and numerous academic publications viewable at www.chriskaplonski.com. With David Sneath, he is compiling articles by Western and Mongolian scholars, plus translated source materials, for* The History of Mongolia *(Global Oriental, 2009).*

LIFE ON THE STEPPE

Based on text by *Ivana Grollova*

Anyone Who Abandons Nature Dies.

This rule has applied to Mongolian society for ages. Even now, like it or not, this truth has to be appreciated by anyone who spends any time in Mongolia. Any modern attempt to change the traditional "easy-going" attitude towards time or a daily schedule usually fails. The only time such attempts might succeed is among urban dwellers as part of wider changes they've undergone – but the conflict between technological progress and tradition has always been an undercurrent in Mongolian history. All pluses and minuses in the Mongolian temperament, superstitions and habits – with the notable exception of those characteristics of the "Homo Sovieticus" period such as irresponsibility, passivity or malevolence – have their very rational roots, even if long forgotten, in the natural conditions around them.

The most glorious example of a "natural tradition" is hospitality, which in Mongolia is still expressed at any hour of the day or night. It derives from the vastness of these lands: if a host does not provide a visitor with shelter, he or she might very well have died by the following morning. The nearest alternative household might be dozens of miles away, and the journey there could be through ice-cold and windy plains full of wolves. A host also has to keep in mind that he might as often find himself in a similar role as a visitor.

Besides this solidarity, the newcomer has always been welcomed for the news brought from distant places, always a local topic of conversation for weeks. Nowadays, the situation has slightly changed; most families have TVs and they can quickly update a "pilgrim" on the latest episodes in an imported soap opera series. But a visitor to another person's *ger*, at whatever time and with no warning, will still receive a hot meal and cup of tea.

Mongolia's nomads and their urban descendants are often criticised as lazy. But once you've made it through a winter and spring in landlocked Mongolia, you'll certainly be more tolerant. At an altitude of 5,000 feet (1,500 metres), the air is thin and the frost very severe. Temperatures of minus 20°C last for at least three winter months, and often fall below minus 45°C. People and animals hit the depths of their energy supplies, and the strain brought by spring is then even more drastic for them. Compared to the Mongolian version, what Westerners call a "spring fatigue" is a piece of cake. Spring in Mongolia is often as cold as winter; unceasing icy winds bring swirling, omnipresent dust and sand from the eroded steppes. The ground is frozen and hard as stone, and don't forget the snow.

The first grass only appears at the end of May. Planting of young trees or bushes is possible only after fertile soil is brought in, layered on top of the permafrost ground and then massively irrigated. In bad years, this might not be possible until mid-June. Then, if the summer is fine, two months of blazing heat come suddenly as if by magic, moderated only by a cooling, but at the same time constantly dehumidifying, breeze. However, in the Gobi Desert even daytime temperatures of 40°C don't prevent overnight temperatures from falling to 0°C before dawn. The most pleasant of the seasons is the so-called "golden autumn", which lasts from August to October. Afterwards, the morning nip starts again, and the end of November can already bring on severe, freezing winter weather.

The lifestyle and daily regime of Mongolia's nomads have adapted to all of these conditions. Care of the herds and flocks, housework and other activities proceed fitfully, and to an uninformed observer appear unsystematic, even illogical. On the other hand, Mongolians in action are highly agile and skilled. Putting up a ger can take a mere half-hour, and a vast camp can be set up or disappear without a trace overnight. The vegetative period of plants is short and relatively dry. On average, crops are sparser than in other regions, but thanks to the dry air wheat is usually of good quality. Cattle have to graze quickly in the short summer period. The human body quickly cleans out cholesterol accumulated from the meat and fat of the winter diet, though the summer's dairy products mean that through autumn it bulks up again with a protective, energy-rich layer of fat for the coming winter.

Traditionally, the dependency of nomadic society on nature extended to its protection as well. Litter, dirt or blood must never pollute the water in rivers or lakes, and the ground should not be kicked – an alleged reason why the toes of Mongolian boots curl up. Mongolians wash themselves and their dishes carefully in a small bowl of water right next to a full-flowing river. (The majority, by the way, may not know how to swim.) In modern times, some paradoxes have arisen from these habits, particularly with respect to mining and urbanisation. While apartments in towns, as with gers, are impeccably clean and carefully arranged, the corridors and streets outside are littered with garbage – traditionally there was no comprehension of altering or damaging the steppes around gers, since nomadic households used to live a "zero waste" lifestyle.

In fact, the circular ger long ago proved the most suitable and practical kind of shelter for a nomadic way of life, developing from Palaeolithic times and used by various ethnic groups long before the Mongolians themselves. (Archaeological evidence shows that the Hun versions were constructed on a base with wheels and even the North American Inuit "igloo" is an ice variation of the same type of shelter.) The wooden lattice, or wall, is easy to fold and move and a number of them can enlarge the ger to dozens of square metres.

An artist's drawing of nomadic life on the steppe (N. Bat-Erdene).

For centuries, too, nomadic households covered their gers with felt produced by rolling sheep's wool. (Canvas was only introduced by trading with China as Mongolians traditionally did not weave.) In summer, the bottom margins of the felt and canvas over the ger are lifted to provide ventilation. In winter, more layers of felt are placed on and the ger can also be protected from the cold and winds by being based in a natural or manmade hole. Ropes slung over the ger are weighed down with heavy rocks or discarded machinery as further protection from the winds. Finally, the ger's base can be further layered up with dried cow or camel dung (*argal*) that provide extraordinary insulation. At the same time, argal serves as an excellent non-scented and highly calorific fuel, especially valuable in areas with no forested vegetation.

Smoke from a small fireplace or stove in the middle of the circular "room" of the ger leaves through a hole in the roof, the so-called *toono*. The fire keeps the temperature inside at a pleasant 20°C for the entire night. Only before dawn does the temperature drop towards zero, and the housekeeper has to get up and light the fire again. The ventilating hole serves also as a kitchen clock and a calendar: the sunlight, falling at different angles through the toono during the day, reaches accurately calculated points on the ground and thus measures the hours, even quarter-hours. Given the strict condition that a ger entrance must always face south, Mongolians can also read the months of the year from the length of the sunbeam.

The traditional Mongolian outfit, or *deel*, is also primarily practical. It warms a horse rider's back and the long coat protects the rider's legs and knees from the cold. It is tied with a long silk girdle, which strengthens the stomach and protects the body's innards from constant jolts. The doubled cloth of the chest creates a large pocket, and the long sleeves cover and protect the hands up to the tips of the fingers. The winter deel is usually underlaid with fur, while summer ones are thinner, most likely made of leather and rough canvas in earlier times. Later on, as trade with the Chinese flourished, a tradition of using silk deels became popular among the Mongolians, too. (Silk cools the skin but, at the same time, does not let the wind blow through. The tight weave of silk also repels fleas, and it is said that a typical arrow could not penetrate the fabric and the silk would follow the arrowhead into the wound if it did, making it easier to pull out.) The deel's collar is, in fact, a more modern style from the Manchu period, having replaced one that simply hung down across the chest, as in historical portraits of Mongolian khans and their wives. Similarly, the head covers, especially the robust ceremonial "horns" for the braids of married women, date only to the post-Empire "Khalkha" times, while medieval women once wore tight-fitting caps elongated at the top into a plume-shaped box.

With relationships and customs originating from such tough natural conditions, some may appear to be downright cruel, while others are quite touching. A sheep is very handily killed, for example, by breaking its aorta inside the chest. Such a butchering might seem cruel but, in actual fact, the animal has no time to sense any pain before its death. In this way, its blood is also collected inside the ribcage for further use, instead of gushing out as when the carotid artery is cut during slaughters performed by Muslims, for instance by Mongolia's Kazakhs. (We need only mention in passing the horrible stress of Western-style industrialised slaughters.) Muslims consider meat impure if the blood has not visibly drained out; Mongolians, on the other hand, not only avoid any waste of what nature has provided, but even consider it an act of honour. This understanding of honour has traditionally been applied to the souls of animals as well as people – and in *The Secret History of the Mongols*, we read about esteemed enemy warriors being executed "without shedding their blood".

Another good example of the sometimes quite complex and even mysterious mixture of cruelty and deep humanity can be seen in the Mongolian relationship towards children. Children are, without doubt, deeply treasured; if you therefore see a toddler in a ger bound to the foot of a bed, don't automatically think the child is being mistreated or punished. Limiting its movements is just a necessary precaution by the busy mother, who often has nobody else around, to prevent the child from getting to the fireplace and scorching itself. At the same time, a baby's hair is traditionally left uncut until the child is two years old, or three years old by Mongolian reckoning. Thus, even boys wear pigtails and ribbons. No child is addressed by a name. Instead, they are called various pejorative nicknames, such as "ugly" or even "piece of shit". This strange habit reflects traditionally high infant mortality rates, with people believing babies are taken away by evil spirits, who also specialise in stealing things and causing illness. Calling a baby a bad name makes it appear worthless, and this tricks the evil spirit from drawing away the child's soul – which is still only getting used to its new body – into the underworld. The care of younger children by older siblings is quite extraordinary and there is remarkably little jealousy among brothers and sisters in Mongolian families. When children grow up, they care for their parents as a matter of course. Retirement homes are still largely unknown in today's Mongolia. The father's household, or "the hearth and home", along with responsibility for the elderly parents, is passed to the youngest child.

The Mongolian love of children is only equalled by their love of horses. At the "three manly games" festival, or *Naadam*, one can only imagine the mixed feelings of a proud herdsman sending his best horse out for a race mounted by a "jockey" aged between four and 12. The horse and its owner are the real winners. In the old days, the straight race across the steppe was 40 kilometres (over 24 miles) long, and nowadays is still a mighty 28 kilometres (17 miles). The accidents that do occasionally occur during these races were always attributed to fate. For nomads, the Naadam – and hunting too – were first of all hard training for life's many challenges. Mastery of horse riding, archery and wrestling were crucial to their very existence. The training might seem cruel – but leaving the tribe unprepared would be much more so.

The attitude towards women is rather pragmatic in Mongolian society, and women have traditionally held quite strong positions. Women were protected by Genghis Khan's legal code, or *Yasa*, because in the nomadic lifestyle each member of the household has his or her set of tasks and is indispensable for the life of the family. There is also a pragmatic attitude towards virginity and marital infidelity that has its own logic and wisdom. Girls ride horses from a very young age and sometimes their hymens are broken even before starting their sexual life. From the age of three, children become useful helpers and that is why families are very large in rural areas. (Traditionally, high mortality rate played its role too.) When a husband leaves home for weeks in late spring to take his cattle – grazing slowly on the way to keep up their weight – and sell them at the end of the journey, he may return home several months later to find his wife pregnant. He might argue but most probably he will not divorce or repudiate the newborn child. The child, after all, is innocent and welcomed as a future hand in the household. (And, let us be frank about what the man was up to on his trip, too.) In the struggle for survival, pragmatism wins out over prudery in the nomadic approach to family relations.

Similarly, traditional polygamy was primarily based on economic and social survival. The brother of a dead man took care of his wife and children. An old wife, unable to bear any more children, often picked out and brought her husband a fresh young wife. A husband, a tribal elder, even the *khan* for the whole nation, was fully responsible for the wellbeing and safety of his children, relatives and subjects. Only during the Soviet-imposed Communist era were Mongolian men deprived of fulfilling these responsibilities,

Moving perennially with the seasons, constant practice and familiarity make the raising and dismantling of a ger an amazingly quick affair for Mongolia's nomads (Carl Robinson).

losing the opportunity to gain wealth and keep individual property. Under this irrational economic and social system, men were unable to sustain their own families. Frustrated and unable to stand up against the regime, men often reacted with rage against their closest ones – and only then were Mongolian women more discriminated against than ever before. Ironically today, nearly two decades after the end of the Soviet system, Mongolian women dominate Mongolia's entrepreneurial class, running their own businesses and often feeding the entire family. Many are single mothers or divorced from their still passive and hard-drinking husbands.

Czech-born Ivana Grollova graduated in Mongolian Studies and Linguistics at Prague's Charles University and later worked with the Czech Academy of Sciences. First visiting Mongolia in 1983, she is the author of Mongolove*, a major Czech-language book on the country published in 2001. She has also produced documentary films and staged photo and art exhibitions on Mongolia.*

Top left: Camels are one of the Mongolian nomad's main beasts of burden, able to carry heavy loads – including satellite dishes – from one camp site to the next (Leo Murray). Bottom left: A camel waits patiently while its load is securely fastened for the trek ahead (Graham Taylor).

THE PEOPLE AND THEIR CULTURE

Mongolia's population numbers just over three million, scattered over the country's 1.5 million square kilometres (605,000 square miles). Half the population is aged under 30. The country's population density is one of the lowest in the world at 1.7 persons per square kilometre (4.7 per square mile). Its people are vastly outnumbered by vast holdings of the traditional "five snouts" – horses, cattle, sheep, goats and camels, or 42 million head in early 2009. (Even larger numbers of Mongols – 3.4 million – live next door in China's Inner Mongolia, where they are now outnumbered by Han Chinese settlers, while smaller communities live in parts of Russia, principally Buriatia, Tuva and Kalmykia, and in southwestern China and Afghanistan.) An estimated 20,000–30,000 Mongolians, mostly young men, work and live in other parts of Asia, Europe and the United States. Thousands more study abroad.

While Mongolians are fiercely proud of their traditional nomadic lifestyle, most actually live in cities or towns. Mongolia's capital – and single largest city – of **Ulaanbaatar** has a population of over one million, half of whom have moved in or were born there since the end of the Communist Era in 1990. Other major cities are **Erdenet** (120,000), **Darhan** (63,000) and **Choibalsan** (45,000) in eastern Dornod *aimag*, or province. Mongolia also has scores of provincial and district townships, called aimag and *sum* (district) centres respectively. Only 40 percent of Mongolians actually live as nomads, in solitary family groups moving seasonally with their herds and flocks. For a people who made their reputation over the centuries waging wars on "sedentary societies" such as the Chinese, the Mongolians have become remarkably so themselves.

Most Mongolians – some 90 percent – consider themselves **Halh**, while the remainder identify with one of about 20 smaller Mongol or Turkic ethnic groups, such as the **Dorvot**, **Buriat**, **Myangat**, **Uriankhai**, **Zakhchin**, **Torguud** and **Uzemchin**. The **Tsaatan**, or Reindeer People, in the remote northwest number only a few hundred. The largest non-Mongolian minority, at five percent of the country's population, are the Muslim **Kazakhs** of the western Altai region, who first came as refugees from China's neighbouring Xinjiang province only in the late 19th century. There are also small numbers of Chinese and Russians and their mixed descendants.

Not necessarily ethnic, the Halh – which means "shield" – originated under the protection of the Great Khans in the Mongolian heartland. Subgroups or clans of Halh speak the same language but other ethnic groups speak with a different vocabulary and accent. With the growth of media and centralised government in modern times, Halh Mongolian became the national language and forged a sense of national unity.

In appearance, Mongolians look very much like other Asians but, in general, are taller and more heavily set with more pronounced eyelids. The classic ideal of female beauty is rounded cheekbones, a large bosom and a tall physique. But as should be expected in a country that's been a veritable melting pot of different racial and ethnic groups over millennia, Mongolians are also amazingly diverse. (Kazakhs, however, are instantly recognisable.) Perhaps from all those Chinese and other princesses presented to khans and nobles over the centuries, Mongolian women are particularly attractive and certainly among the most beautiful in the world. Men can be quite stocky and, given it's a national sport, many do indeed look like wrestlers.

Culture

Despite the country's now heavy urbanisation, Mongolia's nomadic heritage and lifestyle remain the strongest influence on its culture. Unless actually born in the capital, most Mongolians identify with a "home country" and maintain their links through mutual visits to family and friends, especially at the **Lunar New Year**, or ***Tsagaan Sar***. Mongolians are inveterate travellers and there is a busy two-way street between city and country. Traditional values are strong; as in their oldest literature, Mongolia's modern pop songs speak of love of mothers and nostalgia for a time and place gone by. Everyone loves the horse, which is the object of countless sayings, proverbs and songs, even musical instruments and car ornaments. And then there is Mongolia's legendary hospitality, where no one is turned away and tea is always offered.

The nomad's worship of nature – Mongolia's first religion – is another aspect of traditional culture, even if sorely challenged by today's rapid unplanned urbanisation and plastic bags flying everywhere. Nomads experience first-hand the blessings and curses of a vast natural world and have created numerous traditions, customs and teachings to protect it, such as banning the pollution of rivers, destroying forests or the unnecessary killing of animals. Greetings, blessings and well-wishes centre on how a person is relating to the natural world, even in the city.

Travelling around Mongolia, visitors soon become familiar with the slow and melodious refrain as strangers meet, even when you're lost and in a terrible hurry. Greetings of "hello" are always followed by enquiries on the season, weather and herds. And the reply, even in the worst of circumstances for the nomads, is always positive, for one must never greet a newcomer with bad news. There will be plenty of time later for those "marauding wolf" stories – and they are certainly no joke in many rural areas.

In fact, the whole languid pace of Mongolia owes much to its nomadic origins. There is a different sense of time, even attitude to work, which frequently frustrates expatriates and

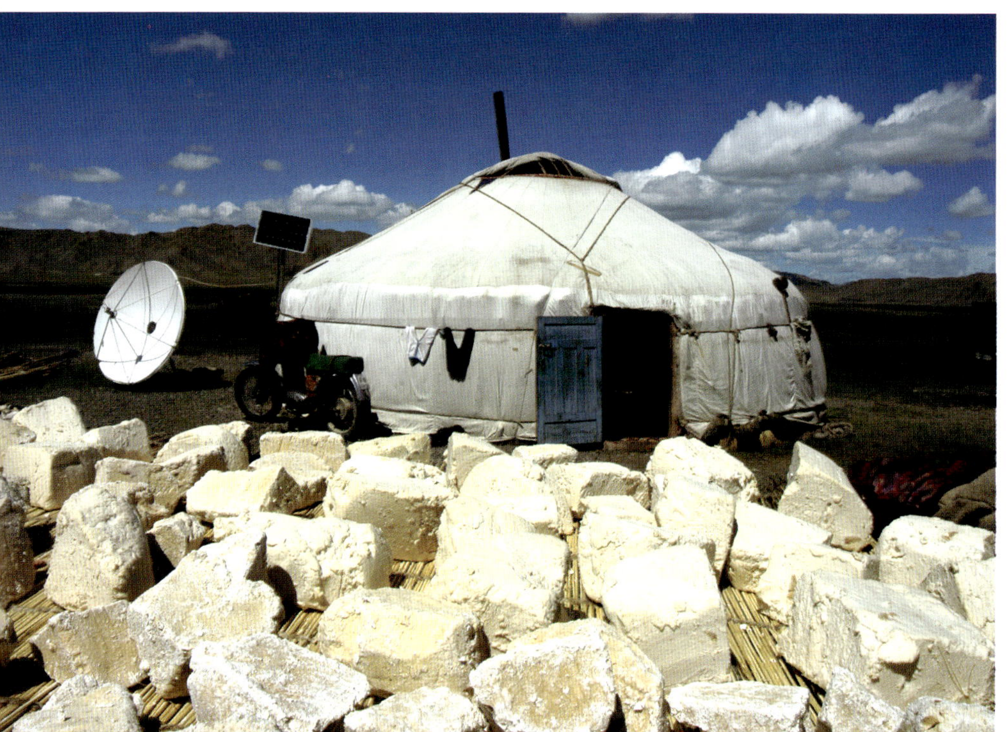

Chunks of curd, or aarul, *are laid out to dry in front of the ger (Elbegzaya Lhagvasuren).*

visitors. And it's not that nomadism isn't hard work – far from it. But everything happens at a different pace and impatience simply isn't on the agenda, even if you're still milking your goats and sheep at 9pm on a summer night. And any excuse is used to party and socialise. Who knows when you'll see your guests again?

In Ulaanbaatar and country towns, the social scene is amazingly frenetic. Even if your hosts haven't been out partying, they love a good sleep-in. It's not easy getting an early start in Mongolia. During my visit, I often wondered how Genghis Khan ever got his troops out of bed in the morning to invade the next country down the road!

Another unique aspect of Mongolian culture is the powerful role of women. Traditionally, women ran the home or *ger*, raised the children, cared for the health of the herds, processed the milk, meat and other products, and even decided when to move on to new pastures. Even if the man was not off fighting wars, the marriage was a partnership

Right: Faces of the steppe – life can be hard but the bonds are strong (Leo Murray x4).

of equals. Genghis Khan's mother was widowed, exiled from her clan and forced to raise her children on her own. Mongolia has its own Joan of Arc figure. On several occasions in history, women ruled as regents for younger male heirs.

The Communist period glorified gender equality even more but also at the cost of crushing men's self-esteem. And in recent times, women have pushed even further ahead as boys were kept home for herding and girls completed higher education and entered the modern workforce. Some 80 percent of college and university graduates are women; male resentment, even misogyny, is now a serious problem – as is the high divorce rate, often initiated by the woman.

While Mongolians are normally not very demonstrative, the physical affection shown towards their own children is wonderful to see. The elderly receive great respect and remain an active part of extended families. When the old regime collapsed in 1990, many middle-aged parents – especially fathers – were thrown, quite literally, onto the scrap heap of history as their jobs and positions were eliminated. Their children saw them through and care for them even now. Today's government and business leaders and entrepreneurs are incredibly young compared to other countries. Most are in their mid-30s and early 40s.

Mongolians certainly are hospitable. But beyond the bonhomie and bowl of tea, there is often a certain reticence, even abruptness, with outsiders. It's not unusual, for example, for Mongolians to engage in lively conversation and totally ignore you. Sometimes, they'll excuse themselves beforehand or even brief you on the conversation later. But do not expect to be the centre of attention. At the same time, don't be overly profuse in proffering gifts – or even your thanks – at risk of seeming insincere. Offering money is totally insulting. Be sensitive to your body language.

Surprisingly, Mongolian men can also be incredibly shy. Vehicles passing each other in the middle of nowhere rarely acknowledge each other. And farewells – typically with tossed milk into the air or glasses of vodka – are so formal and elaborate that you don't dare leave anything behind that might require an embarrassing return.

Another aspect of nomadic thinking – and certainly worth touching upon briefly in view of Mongolia's tortured history – is the fatalism, even stoicism, that constant struggles with extreme nature have bred. Nomads accept that bad things – drought, ice storms and floods – happen and do not question them. That is the key to survival. Mongolians pride themselves on their individuality, certainly essential for the nomadic lifestyle, but are also quick to defer to authority, especially with their traditional worship of the state. According to historian Baabar, this attitude goes a long way to explaining how they not only accepted but even supported the Stalinist excesses of the Communist period (see Special Topic

"Historical Amnesia", page 105.) But this also illustrates how radically the culture has changed since Mongolia's peaceful revolution of 1990.

Old traditions certainly took a beating during Mongolia's nearly 70-year-long attempt at creating a new Soviet Man. The traditional silk tunic, or *deel*, first had its long sleeves, which also act as gloves and carry-all, trimmed back and then fell into disfavour as stodgy utilitarian Soviet-style clothing was adopted. Elaborate hairpieces worn by women were banned and men's hair was cut short. Buddhism was brutally crushed and lamas murdered, and the even more ancient Shamanism, which communicates with the spirit world, was banned along with other traditions labelled as "superstitions".

Many of Mongolia's *ovoo*, piles of rocks at sacred spots all around the country, were levelled. Today, they've been rebuilt and the tradition of walking around them three times in a clockwise direction and adding more rocks or gifts to the pile has been passionately revived. Typically, this ceremony takes place at the first ovoo on your day's travels and more selectively after that. But each one has a great view. With few exceptions, drivers always pass around the left of an ovoo, sometimes honking their horns as a sign of respect.

The revival of old traditions and customs adds a certain piquancy to modern life in Mongolia. Everyone is re-learning the past and they love sharing this knowledge with newcomers. Snuff bottles are elaborately exchanged. The deel – always with a long silk girdle-like belt to hold the gut in during long horse rides – is worn with tremendous pride by both men and women, even in dusty and drab sum centres, and for both work and leisure. (The classic Mongolian pointed hat, or trilby, less so in preference to baseball caps and cowboy hats.)

Do everything in a clockwise direction. One hand under the elbow when accepting a drink. Shake hands if you accidentally brush your foot against another's leg. Don't point with your finger. Never begin a journey on a Tuesday. And, believe me, that one's true!

Of course, Mongolia's festivals never died out but have certainly become bigger and more elaborate in recent years. Ironically, the day Communist-led troops liberated the capital in 1921 is still celebrated as Mongolia's National Day on 11 July – and with it the traditional three-day *Naadam* or Games Festival. (Smaller ones also take place at aimag and sum levels.) The games involve horse racing, wrestling and archery and attract thousands of participants and spectators, including overseas tourists.

Focused more on family reunions, Tsagaan Sar takes place at the Lunar New Year in January or February. Family and friends visit each other, exchange presents – especially the sky-blue *hadag* (ceremonial blue scarves) – and eat huge quantities of *buzz*, or meat dumplings, and other delicacies. Once-banned Buddhist festivals (see below) have been

revived. Interestingly, and despite their long antagonism towards the Chinese, Mongolians have long used the Chinese lunar calendar with its 12-year cycle of animal years.

Other influences on Mongolian culture have come from Tibet, principally through its form of Buddhism, and also China, Russia and Europe. Today's Mongolians frequently describe themselves as more European than Asian. In reality, they occupy a very special world of their own between the two.

LANGUAGE

Mongolian forms part of the Altaic family of languages which originated in the country's western Altai Mountains and spread over a vast area of Eurasia but are clustered principally around Central Asia. Over 60 Altaic languages are spoken by about 250 million people from the Persian Gulf to Siberia and the Baltic to China. The main families are Turkic, Mongolic, Tungusic and – somewhat controversially among linguists – Korean and Japanese. Theories over the language are complicated by the relatively late development of written scripts. Arguments also persist over whether the language comes from a common ancestor or through massive borrowings from human contact over the centuries – such as through the Mongol Empire and constant migrations.

With its various dialects, Mongolian is spoken by an estimated six million people in Mongolia, China, Russia and even a small part of Afghanistan. The language is polysyllabic and non-tonal, unlike Chinese, and at first hearing sounds like Korean (but of course that's only one outsider's first impression). The language has lots of French "r's" and Germanic "kh's", short and long vowel sounds, and words ending in both vowels and consonants. Mastering that, pronunciation is relatively easy.

Mongolian has an "agglutive nature" which does not recognise gender, and grammar categories are expressed by various suffixes attached to a core word. (For example, *aav* means "father", *aavtai* means "with father", *aavtaigaa* means "with your own father".)

Verbs sit at the end of sentences. The vocabulary includes many words of Persian, Chinese, Tibetan, Russian and now English origin. And vice versa, Mongolians gave the word Kremlin, or fortress, and other familiar words to the Russians dating back to the days of the Golden Horde.

In its earliest form during the Mongol Empire, Mongolian was written in a Uighur-developed script of Turko-Sogdian, or Aramaic from Palestine, originally known as Old Mongolian. In the early 20th century, a Latinised form of the language was introduced but was formally replaced by a Soviet-imposed simplified-Cyrillic in 1946.

As part of a resurgent nationalism after the Communist period in 1990, Old Mongolian was reintroduced into the entire school curriculum but then quietly dropped, largely because of the vast expense and trouble involved. But many young people can read the script, which takes particular pride of place on monuments and statuary. Learning the Cyrillic-based alphabet is relatively easy and certainly helps getting around. Of course, it's also useful to learn a few expressions (see Language, page 512).

Below: These days the motorbike is a common alternative to horses for getting around. Left: The yak cart is an ancient but still popular mode of travel in the remote countryside (Leo Murray x2).

With universal education since the 1950s, Mongolians have an extremely high literacy rate of 83 percent and are voracious readers. The post-Communist period saw a rapid explosion in newspaper, magazine and book publishing. Although considered of medium difficulty – alongside Finnish, Hungarian and Vietnamese – and taking up to one year to learn fluently, many long-term foreign residents master both spoken and written Mongolian. Mongolians themselves are quite skilled in languages and, even those in their 30s can speak and read Russian. Just as easily, many now embrace English. Latinised words present no problems.

TRADITIONAL RELIGION

Although **Tibetan Buddhism** is Mongolia's dominant religion, this was a relatively late cultural development. From its legendary past, Mongolians always had a very deep religious and spiritual sense. Their predecessors worshipped the spirits of nature and practised an ancestor cult that gave early rise to **Shamanism**, or the ability of healing and communicating with the spirits of the dead.

Much later on, many of these original beliefs were incorporated into what's called the "Outer Faith" of **Mongolian Buddhism** to draw public support. In fact, for those familiar with Buddhism, the Mongolian – and Tibetan – variants have quite a confusing addition of local traditions, customs and rituals. Even Genghis Khan makes an appearance in the pantheon.

Many relics remain in Mongolia from a time when people worshipped trees, rocks and animals that provided them with sustenance or caused them fear. The first nomads of the **Scythian Era** in 2000–1000 BCE left their famous deer steles showing stags and other totem animals prancing upwards towards the sun. Later tribes within Mongolian territory, such as the Hun, took over this ancient symbol, and this helps explain the "creation legend" from *The Secret History of the Mongols* of the arrival of the mother figure, the Beautiful Doe (*Goa maral*) across a sea from the west. With her came the father figure of the Grey Wolf (*Borte Chino*), an important totem animal of the prevailing Huns and widely regarded as the ancestor of today's Mongolians, even if not directly and genetically related. Interestingly, the word for wolf, *chono*, remains taboo and is replaced with more oblique references such as "the steppe animal" or "the forest animal".

Another persistent symbol of the pre-Buddhist tradition is milk, which in a nomadic society represents a source of life. Even today, before someone sets out on a long journey, milk is sprayed to the four winds as an oblation to the deities. The expression for the Mongolian New Year, Tsagaan Sar, actually means "White Month" and, before shifting to the lunar calendar, took place in midsummer when a new life cycle began for both livestock and their herders. Milk is certainly the dominant gift from the thousands of pilgrims who flock to mysterious Mother Rock southeast of Ulaanbaatar (see page 204).

On a more abstract level, the early nomads who lived under Mongolia's renowned clear blue skies also developed their own belief in a supreme god, known as **Tengriism**, or Eternal Heaven. There were no formal symbols other than the so-called World Tree and four cardinal points. But the core beings were Father Heaven, or *Tengri*, and Mother Earth, or *Eje*. When he headed out to conquer the world, Genghis Khan claimed a personal mandate from Tengri and typically started his declarations with the words, "by the will of Eternal Blue Heaven".

Father Heaven was an abstraction – the timeless and infinite blue sky – and was not a figure, although he had at least two sons. Tengriism's greatest hero is **Gesar of the Kingdom of Ling**, sent down from heaven as a shaman to save the world. With special singers accompanied by horse-head fiddles and lasting several days, *The Story of King Gesar* is widely celebrated in Tibet, Mongolia and Central Asia in what is reputedly the world's longest epic poem.

Under Tengriism, sacrifices and offerings were made to the Earth, or Mother, typically at a pile of rocks known as an *ovoo* located on hilltops and in mountain passes. In traditions continuing to this day, people make offerings to the "lord" – more accurately the "lady" – of the location and leave money, sweets, a symbolic gift like a ceremonial blue scarf (hadag), horsehair or a spare part from the car, or add at least one more rock. Traditionally, those who don't stop at an ovoo can expect punishment by the lord or lady of the mountain.

When climbing a mountain on horseback, one must not say "mountain" or "pass" out loud and only use the most respectful appellation, or *khairkhan*. Interestingly, Buddhist ceremonies at today's ovoos make offerings to patrons of the faith, or *dharmapalas*, who were once local deities and protectors of specific natural locations under Tengriism. The ancient rituals and spirits certainly live on.

A fascinating influence on Tengriism – and certainly indicative of vast movements in commerce and ideas through this diverse region – was the ancient Persian religion of **Mazdaism**, which gave the world the expression "magic". This religion originated around the 10th century BCE when today's Iranians were still nomads, and explains how the herders of Mongolia and Central Asia could easily relate to a belief system explaining creation, truth and goodness. Evolving into **Zoroastrianism** from the sixth century BCE, the religion emphasised the role of a solar deity, Mithra, and the gods of water and fire, respectively Anahita and Atara. By the third century CE, Zoroastrianism had spread among merchants and the soldiers of the Roman Empire, and was a serious rival to Christianity.

An ovoo *stands completely covered by devotional blue scarves, or* hadag *(Leo Murray).*

Over this same period, the religion also headed northeast along trade routes into Tibet and Mongolia, where it differentiated the more abstract Tengrii into the material world of the "blue sky" and into its more spiritual "eternal heaven". With their own worship of nature, the nomads also identified with the religion's emphasis on the purity of the elements – earth, fire and water – and accepted its "dualism", or the struggle between good versus evil and the balance of opposites. From this, a demonology emerged – later incorporated into **Tibetan Buddhism** – with its cosmology of Sky, Earth and Underworld.

Out of bold self-confidence in their blue sky-based belief system or simple wide-eyed curiosity, Mongolian society was traditionally very tolerant toward religion – at least up until Tibetan Buddhism became the state religion in the 16th century. Polytheistic Shamanism easily coexisted alongside other religions for centuries. From the sixth century onwards, **Manichaeism**, a Gnostic cult also from Persia, and later **Nestorian Christianity** made inroads through the steppes and into China itself. But when Han Chinese dynasties reasserted control and expelled these religions, including Buddhism, many followers sought refuge among the Mongolians and other tribes on the steppes.

By the 12th century, many Mongolians – including Genghis Khan's own family – had adopted Nestorianism from missionaries expelled from China. Visitors to Karakorum in the early days of the Mongol Empire noted the presence of Christian churches, Islamic mosques and Buddhist temples.

Modern Religion

The tumultuous and tragic story of Mongolian Buddhism has been discussed extensively in this guide's History section. In brief, Buddhism arrived from Tibet during the Mongol Empire but disappeared after its collapse in 1368 as people re-embraced ancient Shamanism. Some 200 years later, the reformist but still minority **Gelugpa Branch** of Tibetan Buddhism – also known as the **Yellow Hats** – was championed by Mongolian princes anxious for a unifying secular and religious element in their now-fractured nation, even coining and invoking the original title of **Dalai Lama**, or Ocean Lama. In an evangelical-style revival complete with missionaries and aristocrats competing for "merit" by building temples and monasteries, Tibetan Buddhism soon overwhelmed Mongolian society – even as civil war raged between its east and west.

As the Manchus became China's Qing Dynasty in the 1640s, they too embraced Tibetan Buddhism as their official religion but for very pragmatic purposes. By doing so, they easily ingratiated themselves with the theocratic-minded leaders of Tibet and Mongolia and eased the way to grab political control. Granted special privileges, Buddhism became a powerful, privileged and even corrupt "state within a state", controlling vast numbers of people, animals and real estate but also holding back modernisation.

The entrance to the Tsogchin Temple, the main temple at Amarbayasgalant Monastery in the Even River Valley (Don Croner).

When the Qing Dynasty collapsed in 1911 and Mongolia declared its independence, one-third of males were Buddhist lamas living in over 700 monasteries. In one of the grimmest chapters of modern Mongolian history, as part of its drive to modernise the country, Soviet-style Communism brutally crushed Buddhism, killing thousands of lamas and leaving only a handful of "showcase monasteries" and a few ageing clergy.

The end of Mongolia's Communist period in 1990 saw a dramatic revival in Buddhism – at least as a tradition. But how deeply or devoutly a now-modernised Mongolia embraces Buddhism is open to question. While most are quick to call themselves Buddhists, one is as likely to find – especially among the young – those who don't follow any religion at all. Statistics claim 90 percent of Mongolians are Buddhists, but a more realistic figure would be 50–60 percent.

At the same time, various forms of Christianity have made highly visible inroads in recent years, even if numbers remain low at four percent. More localised to the western aimags of Bayan-Olgiy and Hovd, Mongolia's minority Kazakh population (about five percent of the population) are **Muslims**. And Mongolia's oldest religion, Shamanism, is showing fascinating signs of revival (see Special Topic, page 458).

Visits to Mongolia's few surviving Buddhist monasteries are a tourist staple and one is easily awed by their understated – and often weatherworn – beauty and majesty. On the other hand, the ruins of monasteries from the Stalinist 1930s leave one with a feeling of profound sadness, so massive and total was their destruction. Typically, simple wooden temples with corrugated iron roofs and "prayer wheels" made from discarded oil drums mark first attempts at reviving these once huge monasteries. More substantial new Buddhist temples are cropping up literally everywhere.

Of the old Buddhist monasteries that survive, most are in serious need of repair and not all, or only part of them, are actually used for worship, such as the **Erdene Zuu** in Karakorum, today's Harhorin. Walking into one of these monasteries – and I'd recommend a guided tour of the pocket-sized **Choiijin Lama Temple** in Ulaanbaatar – is truly a step back in time. A slow visit certainly helps to understand the religion.

Of all the branches of Buddhism, the Tibetan version is certainly the most elaborate and complicated, even incomprehensible. Combining the Mahayana, or Greater Vehicle, tradition which predominates in East Asia and Vietnam, with elements of the Tantric School, renowned for its chanting, Tibetan Buddhism also incorporated many ancient native traditions, or *bon*. This continued when the religion came to Mongolia in the 17th century, with the absorption of rituals and natural deities of Shamanism, such as the *tsam* dance (see Special Topic, page 131.) However, strict vegetarian rules were waived for the meat-eating Mongolians.

Ovoos became Buddhist sites, sometimes with stupas added, and animal sacrifices were replaced with religious objects. Monasteries were often built at the junction of trade and migration routes or at summer pastures where nomads traditionally gathered for shamanistic rites and sacrifices. Many of the shamans' functions as healers and diviners were taken over by the Buddhist church. Increasingly, shamans were pushed further to the fringes of Mongolian culture and religion, such as around Lake Hovsgol in the northwest.

In Buddhism, life is suffering and the individual's goal is to reach *nirvana*, or enlightenment, and end the constant cycle of rebirth, or reincarnation. Tibetan Buddhism places a key role on selfless and enlightened individuals who've stopped short of that goal to help others, known as Bodhisattvas. Others are so-called Living Buddhas, or reincarnations of previous leaders, often from noble families, who played a secular role.

Together, this huge cast of characters joins a vast and incredibly diverse world of gods and demons, wandering ghosts, inhabitants of heaven and hell – most from old folk religions – alongside more familiar and traditional statues of Buddha. Ancient Tengriism makes an appearance as the gods of sun and moon. Genghis Khan is honoured. The founder of the Yellow Hat Sect, **Tsongkhapa**, and the First Bogd Janzandamba known as Zanabazar (see page 82) are regularly honoured. It is quite a full plate – and not easy to absorb.

Mongolia's older monasteries and temples are so ornate and detailed in their architecture, décor and statuary that one easily understands how those thousands of lamas were kept busy in the church's heyday. The worksmanship is exquisite. The structures are also rich repositories of art works and relics, including ornate tsam masks and costumes used in religious dances. Holy texts are preserved on parchment wrapped in silk. Some objects were preserved by the authorities when the monasteries were closed down, but much more has reappeared in recent years from secret stashes around the country, or been recreated.

Among the more macabre but typical relics are flutes made from the leg bone of a 17-year-old virgin, and a drinking cup made from the skull of a high-ranking lama. More ubiquitous – and obviously quite indestructible to the purges – are huge and heavy brass cauldrons once used to feed hundreds of Buddhist lamas and their followers.

The revival of Buddhism has, of course, also seen a rise in the **Lamaist Tradition** as hundreds of boys and young men now devote their lives to the church. At the **Gandan Seminary** in Ulaanbaatar (see page 191) and other monasteries, the timeless and colourful rites continue. Row upon row of prayer wheels – spun clockwise to generate a mantra and gain merit – surround the buildings. From a high point, young shaven-headed novices in their red and yellow robes whine out the call to prayer over conch shells. The service inside begins with the drone of chanting monks facing each other across rows of wooden desks and supervised by a more senior lama.

Visitors can sit down and marvel at the scene or walk quietly clockwise around the room taking in the rich details of this ancient religious tradition. At one special altar, as at many gers and homes around the country, there is a picture of the current Dalai Lama – bringing home the links that began right here in Mongolia over 400 years ago. Highly revered, the Dalai Lama has visited the country on two occasions, the last in August 2006, but always touching off angry reactions from neighbouring China.

With **Christianity**, we've noted earlier Mongolia's long history with Nestorianism, which was embraced by the nobility in the days of Genghis Khan. However, always dismissed as a heresy by the rest of the Christianity, the sect eventually died away. During the Manchu period, **Roman Catholicism** and **Russian Orthodoxy** appeared but virtually disappeared during Mongolia's Communist Period.

Since 1990, Christianity has boomed, largely due to a heavy influx of foreign missionaries, mainly from South Korea and the United States. (Their more generous funding has also led to frequent tensions with the more numerous but much poorer Buddhist hierarchy.) Travelling around Mongolia, you'll frequently spot Christian missionaries or the occasional Protestant church. Many Christian groups are involved in social outreach projects and soup kitchens for the poor.

Today, an estimated four percent of Mongolians are Christians, with some 30,000 in the capital. The city's Roman Catholic Cathedral was recently completed and its old Russian Orthodox church refurbished. Other Christian groups include Lutherans, Presbyterians, Seventh-Day Adventists, The Church of Jesus Christ of Latter-Day Saints (Mormons), Jehovah's Witnesses, the Unification Church (Moonies) and several Evangelical groups. The latter run a radio and television station in Ulaanbaatar. While religious freedom is guaranteed, laws require registration and limit proselytising, especially in combination with language or other training.

Islam had a long history with the Mongol Empire, with three of its four khanates later becoming Muslim. Only the Mongolian heartland held on to its traditional beliefs and, as we've seen, later embraced Tibetan Buddhism. Today's Muslims come from the historically more recent migration of Kazakhs into western Mongolia in the 19th and early 20th centuries from the neighbouring Chinese province of Xinjiang and make up five percent of the country's population. While most are in the western aimags of Bayan-Olgii and Hovd, many other Kazakhs – who are heavily employed in mining, especially coal – live around Ulaanbaatar and in the northern industrial towns of Erdenet and Darhan. With private contributions, and some assistance from the Turkish and Kazakhstan governments, they have built a network of modest mosques and schools in their communities.

THE TSAM CEREMONY

Visitors to Ulaanbaatar's Zanabazar Museum of Fine Arts and the Choiijin Lama Temple cannot help but be impressed with the colourful and giant *tsam* masks on display. Made on a backing of papier mâché, they are wonderful examples of Mongolia's classical Buddhist artistic tradition and were used in elaborate religious dancing ceremonies. Usually performed around the New Year or at the end of summer, these *tsam* ceremonies were "morality plays" to exorcise evil and incorporated a vast pantheon of terrifying deities and

Above: Elaborate clothing and fantastically fashioned masks make the Tsam Ceremony a visual feast for visitors (Gotsbayar Rentsendorj). Top: Tsam dances are often performed in hotels for tourists (Leo Murray).

stories from Tibetan Buddhism and traditional Shamanism. Thousands of devout nomads gathered to watch and participate. At one time, over 500 of Mongolia's 700 temples and monasteries staged their own performances. Suppressed in the brutal anti-Buddhist purges of the 1930s, tsam ceremonies have revived in today's Mongolia with regular performances in the country and overseas.

Known as *cham* in Tibetan, tsam arrived relatively late to Mongolia with the first performance in Ih Huree, or present-day Ulaanbaatar, only in 1811. But the Mongolians developed and refined their masks, costumes and choreography to an unmatched artistic level. The masks were unusually large with added height gained from performers looking out through the character's mouth. By this time, elements of traditional Shamanism were already heavily incorporated into Mongolian Buddhism and this added further layers, particularly dance, to the harmonious and colourful ritual, which could include a couple of hundred performers. Western travellers found the grotesque masks and exorcistic atmosphere so forceful they dubbed them "devil's dances".

The largest and most popular was the Ih Huree Tsam, which culminated in a vast procession through the streets with an elephant pulling a huge carriage containing the Maitreya, or Buddha of the Future. Like all such ceremonies, this tsam was clearly designed to instil awe and reverence, even fear, in the audience. On a large square decorated with a huge *tangka* and shrine of Vajrapani, the Supreme Diety, at one end, the actual dance took place in concentric circles around a skull-topped pyramid, or *zor*, with a doll of dough, or *lingka*, at its feet. To the sound of cymbals, wind and percussion instruments of a 20-person orchestra, the dance begins with two skull-masked characters, or *khokhimoi*, representing death, circling and chanting mantras. Other characters join in, such as the White Old Man, a comical Shamanistic character representing Fertility, and Khashin Khan, or the Ruler who invites in more demonic characters – such as the God of War, Guardian of Religion and God of Wealth – whose role is to banish evil into the lingka, which is actually made of fast-rising flour and swells massively as the tempo builds. (Interestingly, the coral-encrusted God of War, or *Jamsran*, usually accompanied by the Carrier of the Sword, is unique to Mongolia and most likely a pre-Buddhist deity to whom human sacrifices were once made.) Several animals also play a role.

Finally, a lama wearing a stag mask, or *shava*, yet another traditional symbol of fertility, tears into the swollen doll with his sword and cuts it into pieces, in effect cleansing the world of evil. The only characters not wearing masks are the black hats, or *shanag*, who represent Tibet's own shamanistic influences, or *bon*, on its own form of Buddhism. The final masked character to appear is the distinctive and menacing God of the Dead and Defender of the Faith known as *Yama* or *Tshoijoo*, sporting a shiny black buffalo head, and wielding a lasso for catching souls in one hand, and a skeleton-shaped sceptre in the other.

The modern tsam revival began as a tourist attraction in the early 1990s with the recreation of masks and costumes and ensemble companies performing excerpts locally and overseas. With help from surviving monks, complete ceremonies were then reembraced by Buddhist temples with the Ih Huree Tsam now performed annually in the capital. In 2002, the lovely and remote Amarbayasgalant Monastery performed its own famous tsam, the Dharmaraja, for the first time in 65 years.

Above and opposite: Two archival images of tsam dances taken in the early 20th century, before the repression by the Communist regime (Photomon Agency x2).

FINE ARTS

Until the early 20th century, Mongolian art was mostly of a religious nature. While this tended to repetitiveness and lack of originality, some quite exquisite works of art were produced, using techniques unique to Mongolia. Many were destroyed during the anti-Buddhist purges of the 1930s, but a remarkable number of these treasures survived. The best collection is at the **Zanabazar Museum of Fine Arts** in Ulaanbaatar, but smaller exhibitions are found at many monasteries and temples, even just as reproductions. The most numerous objects are *tangkas*, woodblock prints and *tsam* masks. Others of importance are the amazingly fine religious bronzes of Zanabazar and his school of disciples. The three-dimensional *mandala* at the Museum is particularly impressive.

From the 19th and early 20th centuries, there are virtual "aerial view" paintings of Chinese, Tibetan and Mongolian monasteries, often drawn by artists on pilgrimages. The famous and even cheeky *One Day in Mongolia* by Marzan Sharav (1869–1939) moved arts into the secular. Mongolians are amazingly talented artists and even through their own Socialist Realism period produced great works. Since 1990, just as religious art revived at one end of the spectrum, contemporary works have mushroomed in all mediums. In its modern art, Mongolia straddles an interesting line between Asia and Europe.

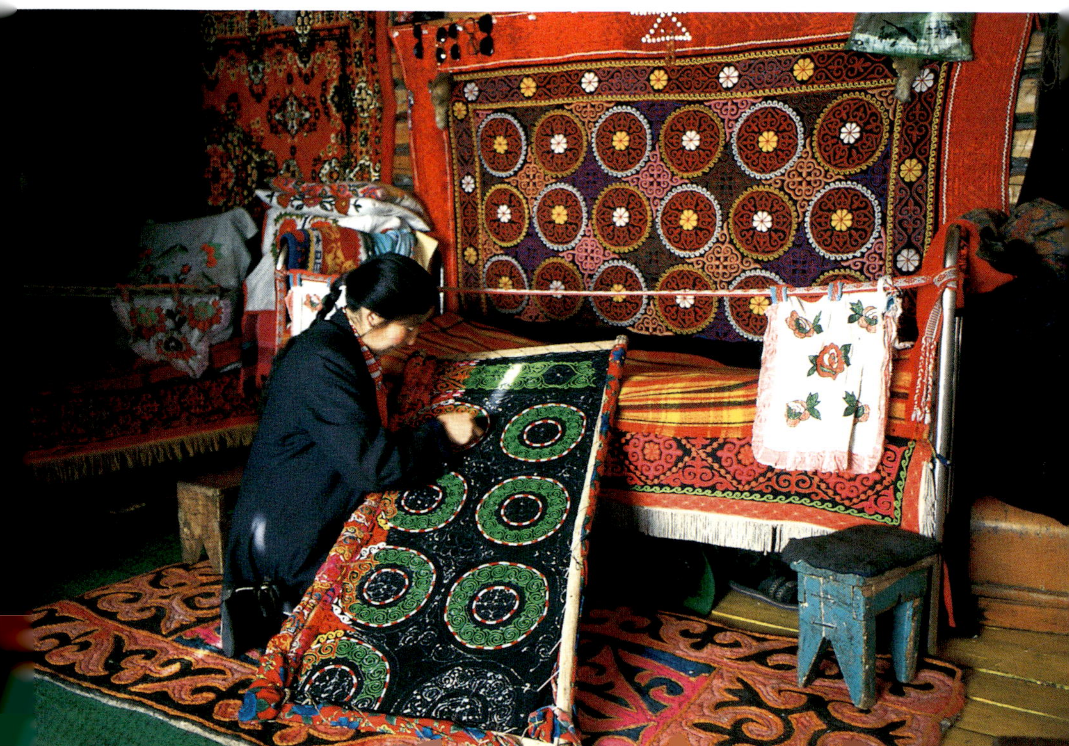

Mongolia has an extremely rich heritage in tangkas, cloth scrolls of widely varying size that perfectly suit the nomadic lifestyle – easy to roll up and move on. Using special techniques, Mongolians have created these scrolls as paintings, appliqué and embroidery, all on a backing of canvas. They vary in size from miniatures only a few centimetres square to giants over two metres high, but traditionally most were of poster size.

Purposefully aimed at visual stimulation and extremely detailed, tangkas told important religious stories and were often used as teaching tools for travelling lamas and at ceremonies such as the tsam. The viewer is literally drawn into these intricately drawn tales. The scrolls used paint mixed with alcohol and glue and covered in gauze or silk for protection.

Mongolia's textile appliqué tangkas are regarded as the most advanced in the world, surpassing those of Tibet and Manchuria. While the technique was in use since the Hun period and also used in Chinese handicrafts, Mongolian artists in the 17th century applied it to more monumental works. Following an artist's design, pieces of cloth were glued and sewn on canvas and the outlines accentuated with gold or silver threads or thicker coloured strands. (The most notable tangkas at the Zanabazar Museum are the fabulous *Kalachakra Mandala* and an enormous one depicting *Lama Tsongkhapa and the Thirty-Five Buddhas of Purification*.) Others are detailed embroidery.

Less grand but quite ubiquitous, woodprints – both old and new – have always been a popular art form at monasteries and sold to pilgrims. With simple or complex designs, some are also coloured in with paints. Tsam masks, made of lacquered papier maché and used in a special religious ceremony (see page 131), qualify as works of art and can be seen at several locations. Made from bright-orange coral (although so far from the sea), the God of War, or *Jamsran*, is certainly the most spectacular.

No discussion of the Mongolian arts is complete without mentioning the incomparable Zanabazar (1635–1723), whose life, actions and works had a profound – and controversial – effect on modern history. As explained in the History chapter (see page 82), he was spotted early as an imperial reincarnation or *hutagt*. After his religious education in Tibet and formal conversion to the Yellow Hat, or Gelugpa, Sect, he became Mongolia's First Bogdgegeen Javzandamba, or theocratic leader. Later, and to his everlasting discredit, Zanabazar signed over eastern Mongolia to the Manchus in 1691 and opened the way to over 200 years of Chinese occupation. But at the same time, he was an extremely gifted artist and a renowned architect of Buddhist temples and monasteries, many destroyed in the Communist era.

A Kazakh woman hard at work – Kazakh embroidery is of very high quality, rich in colour and symbolism, and is one of the most popular souvenirs bought by visitors (Graham Taylor).

destroyed as central planners moved nomads into new provincial and district settlements, the aimag and sum centres of today. (In fact, 60 percent of Mongolians are now urbanised.) Built around one or more heavily subsidized industries, workers lived in typical concrete apartment blocks with nearby offices, schools and shops, all centrally heated from the town's coal-fired power station.

Today, most towns are littered with the tattered and rusty remnants of a bygone era – a post-industrial wasteland of abandoned factories and power plants, but quite a curiosity too. Away from their commercial centres, many residents have reverted to traditional gers, staking off a block of land as their very own space. (Everyone is entitled to a free block of land.) All are in transition and growing in number, and you sense a certain civic pride and surprising prosperity as new timber and brick homes, hotels and businesses go up, parks are beautified and monuments erected. The most devastated remnants of the past, however, are the old collective farms, or *bag*, which lie almost universally in total ruin – roofing, timber and bricks carted away for new lives.

Pit stops: You'll see plenty of men openly urinating – and always downwind. The needs of women are respected: everyone else stays in the car! Then, everyone out for another stretch. Typically, in outhouses most toilets are squatters – or what Australians call "thunderboxes" or "long drops"; there are Western-style ones in some sum and aimag centres, and tourist ger camps offer generally good facilities. Bring toilet paper and wipes, but never go to the toilet near an ovoo – you must go somewhere out of sight. No one goes to the toilet to read in Mongolia!

The language barrier: One day's "Magic Moment" occurred when we stopped at a cliff face overlooking Mongolia's little-known but vast Ulz River Valley (see The Great Eastern Steppe, page 246). Two nomads, herding 200 horses and almost home from a three-day forage, galloped up and were soon joined by a friend. They chattered away happily, ignoring us and only bumming our smokes. I asked Byambaa, my guide, what they were talking about – and he just laughed. "Man, I can only understand 70 percent of what these guys are saying! They're Buriats." This happens a lot and you'll even pick up the odd non-conventional Mongolian accent. Mongolia is full of tribes! The Kazakhs of western Mongolia are certainly the most distinctive. Do practise reading Cyrillic – a little effort will be rewarded when you can walk into the right place!

Ger life: Mongolia seems to go on forever like no other country – you top a ridge and an entirely new landscape sprawls out before you. Way off in the distance are little white dots that, driving closer, turn into gers surrounded by flocks and herds grazing on the surrounding summer pasture. Gers are everywhere and always face south for protection from the prevailing winds (this serves as a convenient compass when you're wondering in

Mongolia has millions of free-range animals, here high-quality cashmere goats who've made this nomad family in the South Gobi's Bayanhongor very prosperous (Carl Robinson).

what direction you're heading). Closer in, you'll typically see a solar panel, a satellite dish, a jeep, motorcycle and even a couple of horses.

Not quite sure if you're on the right track? Your 4WD will drive right up to the ger, its dogs restrained, greetings will be elaborately exchanged and then the nomads will point the right way. Even 12-year-old kids always know where they are. Not that there's ever a problem with getting lost in Mongolia, but if you are in trouble, head for the nearest ger. This is Mongolia's own "GPS" system, otherwise known as Ger Positioning System.

Quite spontaneously, you'll often enter and share these nomads' lives . . . and food. At one, I was treated in quick succession to warm goat's milk, a vodka shot of camel's milk, a nibble of cheese and a yoghurt – all proud homemade recipes. "And from the ger roof, do help yourself to the dry yoghurt for your trip ahead." A great trail mix that's also good for teeth.

"Tie up your dogs!": Coming in for a "Mongolian GPS" reading requires some deftness regarding the nomad's traditional guardian, the dog. "Four-eyed dog" is what they call this hardy, dark-haired Mongolian breed with a big chest and two yellow spots above its eyes. And no, dog lovers, just let them be – they're working dogs and up all night chasing away wolves. (Only cats enter gers – and you'll need ear plugs if the cat's on heat with no mate anywhere across the steppe.) Fiercely protective, the dogs bound right up to your vehicle – or even just give you a good chase passing by. The traditional cry of the approaching stranger is, "Tie Up Your Dogs!" Only then do formal greetings follow. Speaking of man's best friend, out in the middle of nowhere, no flocks in sight, you'll occasionally spot a solitary dog out walking or running across the vast countryside. What's his story?

Dust & wind: Every visitor to Mongolia has a Dust Storm story. Dust is Mongolia's biggest export, just ask China. The storms create quite a drama, chasing you across the steppe or hitting you full on from any direction, making you grind to a blinded halt (the worst is heavy rain mixed with dust). Mongolia's legendary wind can never be overemphasized, but you'll soon understand its many moods and manifestations. Wind is a defining element to Mongolia's character; it's always there, and when Mongolians go overseas, they miss their winds the most.

The smell of a cow dung fire: This is a pleasant and memorable odour, almost an incense. You'll see grandma far out on the steppe, big plastic bag on her back, picking up dried "cow paddies" or *argul*, used to compensate for the lack of trees. They light and burn like charcoal, requiring regular feeding in the iron stove you'll spot on entry, its chimney sticking out of the roof, but warming up the ger very nicely. A big metal box contains plenty more fuel – it's the enduring smell of Mongolia. At the other end of the heating scale, the South Gobi's saxaul bush burns and roars quickly like a turbo jet, while in northern climes, it's the smell of burning pine from the surrounding forests.

Ger camp "sweeties": They'll be bounding up to your vehicle at the tourist ger camp from the moment you arrive. Full of broad smiles and happy greetings – and just "so cute" – they'll hurriedly carry your bags to your very own ger and help settle you in, book a shower and arrange dinner time. Most are young women studying tourism at university or colleges in UB, who spend the summer months working in the camps (they heavily outnumber their male schoolmates). All study English – but they can sure use lots more practice. They are always pleased to have a chat, providing a fascinating insight into contemporary Mongolia with stories about their families, lives and dreams. So, encourage them into a new language – many also study Japanese, Spanish, French, German and Chinese – and you'll leave with a fond milk-tossing farewell indeed. Stories abound about "ger girls" who slip in for more than just relighting the fire during the night. But these girls make a virtue of innocence – and that's to be respected.

Western-style toilets didn't quite work out at this tourist ger camp and were replaced with old-fashioned squatters, or "long drops", behind (Carl Robinson).

RIDING THE TRANS-MONGOLIAN EXPRESS

In my brief stopover in Beijing, I hadn't the time for the obligatory dash up to the Great Wall – after all, the Chinese built the barrier to stop the folks I was heading off to visit in Mongolia. But as our 18-car train headed out of busy Beijing East Railway Station right on time at 7:45am, I already pictured a suitably dramatic view of the famous wall running along the ridgeline high above. We were soon in rugged hills of steeply uplifted sedimentary rock, steep canyons with swiftly running streams and the odd reservoir with ancient and modern roads heading ever northwards.

But there was absolutely no sign of the Great Wall as we passed on through endless tunnels, some quite long, and soon popped out onto a vast plain that reminded me of the semi-desert of South Australia's near-Outback or Southern California with blue-tinged mountain ranges far in the distance. Grapes grew on trellises and flocks of sheep scampered about. Lines of poplar trees – always a sign of Chinese civilisation – served as windbreaks.

This vast and once sparsely populated frontier region is now a collection of crowded cities, many with new multistorey buildings, and China's modern-day mix of factories, steel and chemical plants. Massive power stations are fed by a constant stream of trains and trucks hauling ratty-looking brown coal mined throughout the region. Alongside new expressways sweeping over the rail line, horse- and ox-drawn ploughs work the hardscrabble countryside in fields of rice and vegetables.

Big Ben tolled 11 o'clock as we stopped at the old fortress town of **Zhangjiakou**, long-known as **Kalgan** where camel caravans once headed 1,500 kilometres (932 miles) up the legendary Tea Road to Urga, today's Ulaanbaatar, and then far into Russia. The Great Border Gate, **Dajiangmen**, through the Great Wall lies in those hills just to the north with the great Mongolian Steppe beyond. We were close. But instead, we headed southwest and I scrambled for the only map I had – inside Charles Gallenkamp's *Dragon Hunter*, the story of Roy Chapman Andrews' epic dinosaur-hunting "Central Asiatic Expeditions" from 1922 onwards. Sure enough, there was a railroad back then and we were heading southwest with now the odd glimpse of the Great Wall in the hills. Arriving at Datong about 2pm, we finally turned north. But hardly anyone in the restaurant car noticed when – tipped off by my old map – we finally passed through China's Great Wall, here not much more than disappointing broken-down earthen ramparts across a wide valley floor. (From Datong, another rail line continues west to Inner Mongolia's capital **Hohhot** near the northern bend of the Yellow River.)

We were now in **Inner Mongolia**, an autonomous province of China that has more Mongols (3.5 million) than its neighbouring independent country. It is also obvious just how outnumbered they now are by Chinese settlers. Only late in the afternoon did the countryside open up into wide, almost empty valleys – some growing wheat and vegetables – with buttes and volcanic outcrops in the near-distance. Vast coal mining operations appeared, even an old iron ore mine.

And then the first real sign of Mongols with the odd *ger*, and flocks of sheep and goats. In a preview of what lay ahead, the steppe was littered with discarded multicoloured plastic bags blown along by those notorious winds and dirt off the vast Mongolian interior. More environmentally friendly, a modern wind farm throbbed away nearby. The train's comfortable restaurant car filled up for Chinese-style meals with a mixture of Europeans, Russians and Australians. But most of the Chinese passengers preferred to tap into the acrid-smelling, coal-fired hot water heaters at the end of each carriage to make their instant noodles. The wine on offer, Great Wall Red, was running dangerously low as the Trans-Mongolian pulled into the border town of **Erenhot** about 8:30pm.

The international border crossing between China and Mongolia, located 843 kilometres (524 miles) from Beijing and 676 kilometres (420 miles) from Ulaanbaatar, is hardly a simple matter – and I'd certainly been warned about it. The problem – and it's quite a daunting one as far as developing international trade and commerce is concerned – is that China and Mongolia have different railway gauges. In a legacy from its long decades as a Soviet satellite, Mongolia operates its trains on a Russian "broad gauge" (1,520mm or 4ft 11 7/8 inches), while China uses the more universal "standard gauge" (1,435mm or 4ft 8 1/2 inches). So, with the exception of our wonderful restaurant car (as I'd discover later), every carriage has its "bogies" or wheels changed for the onward journey, a lift and drop process that seems to take forever. Handing over our passports and visa papers, most passengers disembarked and wandered into an oversized and surprisingly modern terminal with escalators leading upstairs to a duty-free shop and lots of seats. Everyone settled into the wait, one couple even catching a taxi into town to an ATM. Starting off pleasantly enough, even with my book and jovial passengers all around, the wait soon became interminable.

The **Trans-Mongolian Railway** was certainly a long time coming too. The Mongol Empire prided itself on its amazing horse-relay postal system, which, in just a matter of days, could shuttle a confidential message – or the announcement of a Great Khan's demise – to its farthest reaches in Persia, Russia and Egypt. (Similar systems in Manchu China and Russia continued up into the first part of the 20th century.) Some 1,200 postal relay stations, each with horses half-on and half-off duty and spaced between five and 50

Near journey's end, the Trans-Mongolian's Russian-made diesel locomotives kick up into the mighty Hentii range before the final run down into the capital of Ulaanbaatar (Carl Robinson).

kilometres (3–30 miles) apart, were on constant duty, the arrival of a messenger – each wearing a seal around his neck – often signalled by horns. In a rush, four messengers could travel 500 kilometres (310 miles) in only 24 hours.

A network of carriage, horse and walking trails became the basis of Mongolia's transportation system using carts and camel caravans for imported flour, cloth, silk and tea, with the most important linking Dadu, today's Beijing, with the ancient capital of Karakorum (Harhorin). Interestingly, trees were planted along both sides of many of these primitive roads for protection from sun and wind. Where the railway now runs was once an exclusive military road that passed through the Great Wall at Zhangjiakou. When the Manchus occupied Mongolia in the 17th century, the link grew into the so-called **Tea Road to Russia**. But attempts to push a railway through to Urga met tremendous resistance from the so-called Outer Mongolians and collapsed along with the Qing Dynasty in 1911.

Even after Mongolia joined the Soviet Union as its first satellite state in 1921, railway construction made little progress. (Roads are an even more dismal story – don't expect to see any asphalt alongside the line until you're almost in UB.) The only railway built before World War II was a 268-kilometre (167-mile) link in eastern Mongolia between Ereentstav on the Trans-Siberian Railway and the aimag capital of Choibalsan – and that was mostly for defence against a pre-war Japanese invasion from Manchuria (see The Great Eastern Steppe, page 246).

When construction finally began on the Trans-Mongolian from Suhbaatar on the Soviet border to the capital, the workforce came from the infamous Gulag 505 near Darhan, including soldiers who'd joined General Andrey Vlasov's Russian Liberation Army to fight alongside the Nazis. That end of the railway was completed to Ulaanbaatar in 1949 and the link to the Chinese border at Zaamin Uud only in 1959. Then, for nearly two decades during the Sino-Soviet split, the border was sealed as troops from both sides squared off against each other, only reopening again in 1989.

Today, this Chinese-Mongolian border "port" is a Free Economic Zone (FEZ) and two-way traffic is thriving, mostly raw products coming out and finished goods and food heading inwards. One of Mongolia's more fascinating exports to China is crude oil – by rail and road – with the country receiving all its own needs from Russia. There is even ambitious talk of a "rail bridge" between Asia and Europe cutting through Mongolia, cutting weeks off sea shipments. But the gauge change remains a serious obstacle, even with machinery to shift containerised cargo. (Of course, there's another gauge change at the western European end, which is also on "standard gauge".)

The Chinese-run Trans-Mongolian runs from Beijing to Ulaanbaatar – and doesn't use much English: the bottom lines are the cities in Cyrillic Mongolian (Carl Robinson).

Our own obstacles were finally overcome when, close to midnight and now very sleepy-eyed, we reboarded our "re-wheeled" Trans-Mongolian. Shunting barely five kilometres (three miles) up the track and into Mongolia, we came to another halt at **Zaminn Uul** for visa and customs formalities – and another hour's delay. Finally, a stunningly beautiful and statuesque female immigration officer in full Soviet-style uniform, high boots and long hair tucked into her cap, handed back our passports – and we were officially into a very dark Mongolia (as exhausted as I was, I could hardly wait to see the place in daylight).

Before that, sleep certainly came quickly in the Trans-Mongolian's comfortable four-berth first-class cabin. Clean and comfortable and designed more for lounging or lying down than sitting up, there was a small tray table for food, drinks and writing. Toilets, one Western and the other Asian, were at either end of the carriage. (Old-fashioned, they are always locked at stops along the way.) My roommates were two young Chinese men who spoke little English but constantly shared food bought at stations along the way. Just why they – and most other Chinese on board – were travelling to Mongolia wasn't clear, but the pair had two very heavy suitcases, perhaps filled with goods for some unofficial trading or tools to work illegally on the capital's many new construction sites, both serious problems for authorities. My other roommate was a young French woman at the end of a six-month break, travelling through Asia and now heading into Mongolia for a bit of horse-trekking.

Using two diesel locomotives from Datong onwards, the Trans-Mongolian is Chinese-operated and runs twice a week from Beijing. Ours terminated in Ulaanbaatar but a second runs all the way to Moscow, another five days away. The uniformed staff, mostly men, are courteous but speak little English. (For coffee, bring along your own mug and powder, or wander up to the pleasant restaurant car where the views on both sides are certainly better.) Many foreigners were disembarking for a couple days of touring before resuming their journey to Moscow.

In mid-May at this latitude, the sun rises at 5am, and I was quickly out for my first look at Mongolia. We were at the eastern end of the vast **Gobi Desert.** Gazing out through the dusty doors at the end of the carriage, I saw a desolately flat, windswept landscape and flocks of black crows, then horses and camels. In a bit of a race, a half-dozen new orange-coloured dump trucks – no doubt heading for a mining operation somewhere – trundled alongside on no visible track, my first look at a do-it-yourself Mongolian road. There were low sand dunes and a touch of green, with telephone poles and broken down barbed-wire fence by the track. The impression was of endless emptiness – I was immediately entranced and mumbled aloud, "I'm going to love this place!"

Then, in the first sign of human settlement up ahead, those dreadful windblown plastic bags reappeared. We stopped briefly at **Saynshand**, a small ramshackle provincial centre, where a bright-green restaurant sat right by the station with rows of Russian-style, single-storey buildings on the ridge behind, the streets all dirt. A dog or two wandered about but no one was up. On the adjoining track, containers sat on flatbed carriages secured from the winds by vertical steel bars. We continued, now spotting small herds of white-tailed gazelles, and moved onto the Mongolian steppe, the land gradually rising and distant ridgelines appearing, along with the odd ger too. In early spring, everything was still brown and little vegetation grew. I wandered up to find they'd switched the restaurant car during the night to something now totally Mongolian – its walls ornately decorated with a bow and arrows plus a sword and shield, polished timber tables and benches with carpeted seats and a low ceiling. And my first lesson too in how slow Mongolians are to rise in the morning. I was rudely chased away and told to return at 8am.

I was first up for that cup of coffee, catching the surprised look of other passengers as they joined me in that warm and cosy restaurant car. Lilting Mongolian music played and the vast Mongolian landscape lazily slid past. We passed the occasional mine and railway settlement, but mostly the vista offered just entrancing emptiness. For the first time – and then repeatedly during my entire visit – I was humbled at how all my reading and research had barely prepared me for the sheer reality of Mongolia: bright-blue skies; endless horizons; wide-open nature; the sheer sweep of the place; huge herds and flocks . . . and few people.

We stopped at the industrial town of **Choyr** (pronounced nothing like it) and made our first steps onto Mongolian soil outside the cake icing-style railway station, its name in Cyrillic, chatting amiably with English-speaking Mongolians delirious just to be home (the Chinese were now noticeably much more withdrawn). We were definitely in a new zone. Just outside the town on the left – and this I had researched – I spotted the forlorn remnants of what was once the largest Soviet base in Mongolia. Across the undulating steppe were abandoned four-storey concrete buildings, power plants and old storage bunkers, a spur rail line, even an old airstrip. As I'd discover, these modern ruins now litter the landscape of eastern Mongolia – abandoned by the Russians in the early 1990s and, some early looting aside, of absolutely no use to the Mongolians. (Who knows? The way Mongolia is going, they may well revive as bases for mining companies, or even as five-star resorts.)

Soon, the undulating steppe gave way to gentle hills, the southwestern reach of Mongolia's **Hentii Range**, and the rugged-looking, Russian-made diesel locomotives poured out clouds of black smoke as we wound ever upwards with new and distant landscapes appearing far below. Then finally, over a crest with forested peaks higher above, we swung in a long, wide, circling descent into the narrow east-west running valley of the **Tuul River.** Crossing over a bridge, we had our first glimpse of the Mongolian capital not far ahead through the slightly hazy midday sun, its downtown skyline marked by a couple of high-rise buildings that would soon become very familiar. Ulaanbaatar has its own suburbia, with single homes and then increasing numbers of new apartment blocks as we finally pulled past shopfronts and into the Russian-style railway station.

The station's clock read just past 1pm. For me, it had been an unforgettable 30 hours up the old Tea Road. And what an entrance to Mongolia!

ULAANBAATAR

After all that vast emptiness coming up the railway – or if you're flying into Mongolia's only international airport – the bustling capital of **Ulaanbaatar** can't help but come as a surprise. Located in a long east-west running river valley with a sharply rising pine-crested mountain range right to its south and more gentle hills in other directions, the Mongolian capital is a compact and busily modernising metropolis. Truly gone are the days when UB – as expats call it – could be described as a "drab Soviet-style provincial city". The city today is one vast construction site with cranes everywhere. Two huge towers, one quite futuristic, now dominate the downtown skyline.

Although certainly designed along Soviet lines, sporting wide boulevards with overhead trolley-bus lines, even ring roads, the traffic – vehicles drive on the right – is in an almost constant snarl, a fascinating mix of old Russian trolley buses, jeeps and trucks, South Korean-made buses including a large mixture of right- and left-hand-drive vehicles, many cheap second-hand imports from Korea and Japan. But there's lots of obvious prosperity, too, with flashy brand-new Japanese-made 4WDs, even the odd massive Hummer and Cadillac 4WD Escalade. Horses are banned from the city and everyone jokes that Mongolians drive like they ride – "all over the place". And, yes, "road rage" is a serious problem among these normally mild-mannered folks.

Somehow, there is a very European feel to the capital. Every bit of signage – including huge flashing overhead light boxes, television screens and billboards – is in Cyrillic letters. Old colonnaded government buildings and banks sit alongside four-storey apartment buildings from the Communist era, many repainted and with ground floors turned into shops and restaurants. Long limited to that height by a lack of elevators, tall glass-fronted office buildings, new apartment blocks and hotels now rise above them. Shopping centres with brand-name shops have appeared. The tree-lined sidewalks dotted with kiosks are wide and full of Mongolians in Western-style clothing with the women quite stylish indeed, especially in spring and summer. There are also many parks, their flowerbeds carefully replanted every short summer season as lawns struggle to return. And if there is a certain drabness around, blame the harsh climate and blustering winds of winter and spring that would ruin any paint job. In Mongolia, you quickly learn to never judge a building by its exterior. Inside is a very different, and often quite cosy, world indeed.

Ulaanbaatar – with the stress on the double-a's – has certainly grown by leaps and bounds in the years following the fall of Mongolia's Communist system in 1990, and

Previous spread: The city of Ulaanbaatar fills the Tuul River Valley, watched over by the Megjid Janraiseg Statue (Gotsbayar Rentsendorj).

now has over one million inhabitants, or one-third of the country's entire population. The creation of a market economy and collapse of the collectivised rural economy, plus several devastating late-winter storms called *zug* in recent years, have seen massive internal migration. So-called *ger* districts have cropped up on the city's outskirts and up into the surrounding hills with no infrastructure to match. Unemployment, poverty, crime and disease are serious problems out here, even just keeping warm in winter when temperatures drop to -20°C (-4°F).

Giant, smoky, coal-fired power stations on the city's western outskirts generate electricity and also pour steam down huge drab-green pipes – quite visible coming in from the airport – to centrally heat office buildings and residences in built-up areas. But up in the gers, the newcomers burn anything they can, including old tyres, just to warm up. Roughly 30 kilometres (18 miles) long and barely 15 kilometres (nine miles) wide, the city's narrow valley, prevailing winds and temperature inversions do make for some serious pollution problems – but not all the time. With the massive increase in water consumption, old-timers bemoan how much the city's famous willow-lined **Tuul River**, and its tributaries, have dwindled in recent years.

Ulaanbaatar, located at an elevation of 1,350 metres (4,430 feet), has a comfortable average temperature of around 22°C (72°F) in summer (June, July and August) when most tourists visit and also when most rain falls. But in winter, still very much a developing tourist market, overnight temperatures drop to -26°C (-15°F) in January, the coldest month. Spring can be extremely variable – even day-to-day – with highs in the high teens and low 20s. As I personally discovered in the Mongolian spring, you get everything from frosts to heat waves, even the odd dust storm and blizzard. (But hardly off-putting, I must add, and certainly part of the adventure.) Everyone positively glows about the Golden Autumn as winter slowly sets in. Because of its continental climate – the result of its land-locked location far from the sea – Mongolia experiences extremely low humidity (look out for static electricity, especially when changing clothes or taking off your coat).

Ulaanbaatar, a separate administrative area surrounded by Tov *aimag* (province), is clearly a city on the move with a very distinctive hustle and bustle, plus a lively night scene, so don't be put off by first impressions and rush straight out of town. Understanding UB takes time – the city's charming side is easiest to appreciate on returning from Mongolia's wide-open countryside with new friends, or by making friends among the city's residents. UB has a wide variety of accommodation – from luxurious and comfortable hotels, backpacker hostels and tourist gers, even short-term apartment rentals – and a rich mixture of restaurants, cafés, shops and boutiques. (Also, you no longer need worry about bringing in travel essentials such as batteries, film, insect spray and even extra computer memory. It's all here.)

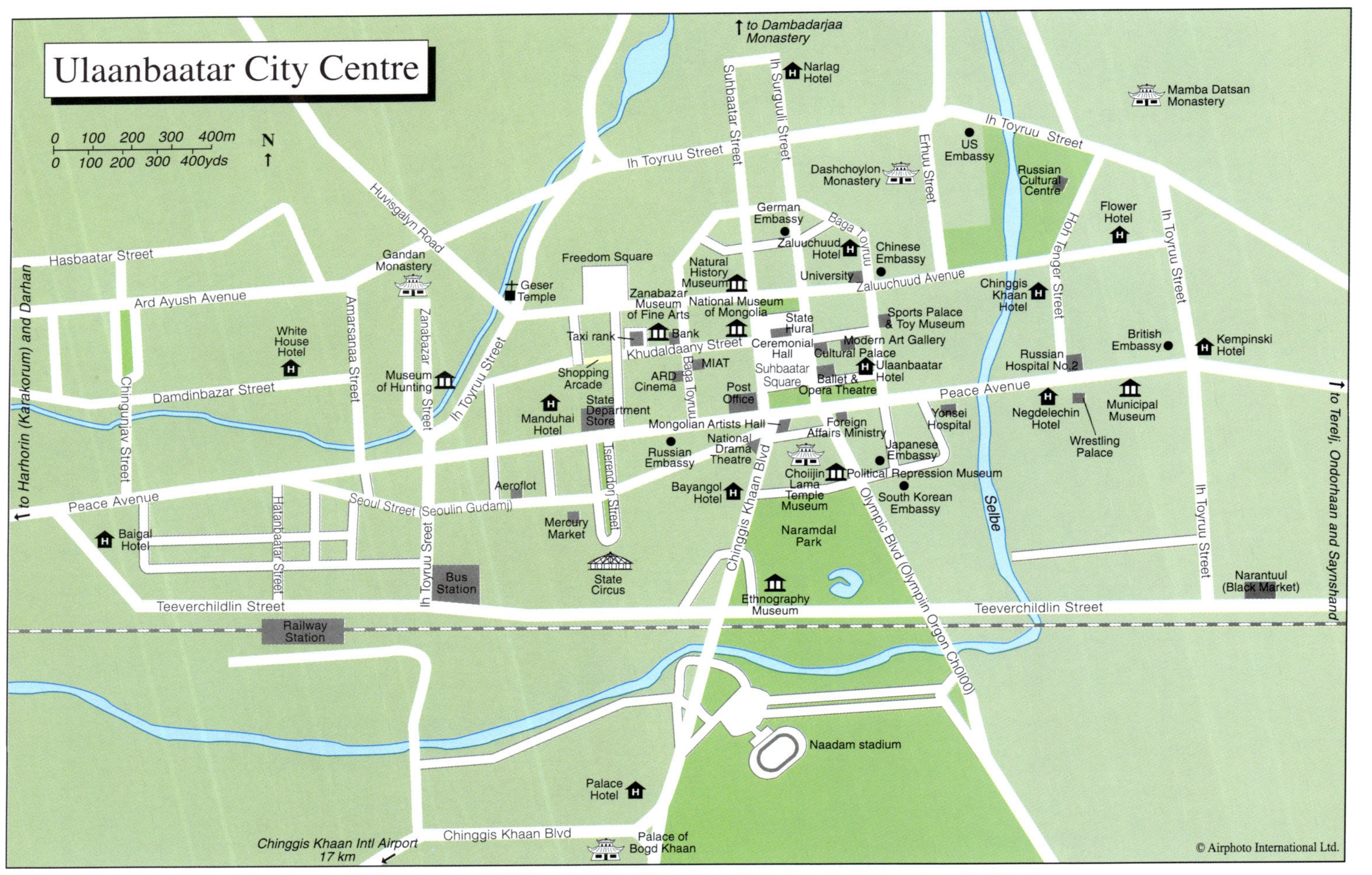

Ulaanbaatar City Centre
0 100 200 300 400m
0 100 200 300 400yds
N
to Dambadarjaa Monastery
Narlag Hotel
Mamba Datsan Monastery
Ih Toyruu Street
US Embassy
Dashchoylon Monastery
Erhuu Street
Russian Cultural Centre
Flower Hotel
Huvisgalyn Road
German Embassy
Baga Toyruu
Zaluuchuud Hotel
Chinese Embassy
Hoh Tenger Street
Hasbaatar Street
Gandan Monastery
Freedom Square
Natural History Museum
University
Zaluuchuud Avenue
Chinggis Khaan Hotel
Geser Temple
Zanabazar Museum of Fine Arts
National Museum of Mongolia
State Hural
Sports Palace & Toy Museum
Ard Ayush Avenue
Suhbaatar Street
Ih Surguuli Street
White House Hotel
Amarsanaa Street
Zanabazar Street
Taxi rank
Bank
Khudaldaany Street
Ceremonial Hall
Modern Art Gallery
Cultural Palace
British Embassy
Kempinski Hotel
Russian Hospital No.2
Museum of Hunting
Ih Toyruu Street
Shopping Arcade
MIAT
ARD Cinema
Suhbaatar Square
Ulaanbaatar Hotel
Ballet & Opera Theatre
Damdinbazar Street
Post Office
Peace Avenue
Negdelechin Hotel
Municipal Museum
Manduhai Hotel
State Department Store
Baga Toyruu
Mongolian Artists Hall
Foreign Affairs Ministry
Yonsei Hospital
Chingunjav Street
Russian Embassy
National Drama Theatre
Japanese Embassy
Wrestling Palace
Tserendorj Street
Choijiin Lama Temple Museum
Political Repression Museum
Aeroflot
Bayangol Hotel
South Korean Embassy
Peace Avenue
Seoul Street (Seoulin Gudamj)
Chinggis Khaan Blvd
Selbe
to Harhorin (Karakorum) and Darhan
Mercury Market
Naramdal Park
Baigal Hotel
Ih Toyruu Street
Bus Station
State Circus
Olympic Blvd (Olympiin Orgon Ch0l00)
Ih Toyruu Street
Narantuul (Black Market)
Hatanbaatar Street
Ethnography Museum
Teeverchildlin Street
Teeverchildlin Street
to Terelj, Ondorhaan and Saynshand
Railway Station
Naadam stadium
Palace Hotel
Chinggis Khaan Intl Airport 17 km
Chinggis Khaan Blvd
Palace of Bogd Khaan

With the summer sun come balmy days, plenty of smiles – as well as fresh fruit and soft drinks mostly imported from China, here awaiting the crowd rush at Naadam (Graham Taylor).

Road linking the two countries. A large Chinese settlement named **Mai Mai Cheng** grew on its eastern edge while smaller numbers of other foreigners, mostly Russians, also lived in the town. By the end of the 19th century, the town had over 60,000 lamas. When Qing rule ended in 1911, the town was first renamed **Niislel Huree**, or "capital camp", and then **Ulaanbaatar,** or "Red Hero", in 1924 upon the death of the last theocratic leader Bogd Gegeen and the declaration of the Communist-led Mongolian People's Republic. Ulaanbaatar is named after national hero Damdin Suhbaatar, whose Red Army-backed troops "liberated" the city from the White Russian Ungern von Sternberg, known as the Mad Baron, in 1921 (see History, page 86 and Special Topic, page 88).

Up until the early 1930s, Ulaanbaatar's population was only 50,000 and its skyline was still dominated by steep-roofed temples and monasteries, and gers surrounded by wooden walls. But that soon changed as the Communist government cracked down on the power and lands of the Buddhist church, killing and imprisoning thousands of lamas and destroying and looting most of the country's 700 temples and monasteries. Little remains of the old Urga; with the exception of the **Gandan Monastery**, which lived on as a showcase to supposed religious freedom, only a handful of temples and palaces survived and were turned into museums. Today, these survivors – and the treasures within – are the highlights of any visit to UB.

Right: Suhbaatar Square, with its eponymous statue centrally placed and the Ceremonial Hall behind (Carl Robinson). Top right: An Irish pub regularly pulls in the crowds – UB's night life can be very lively (Gotsbayar Rentsendorj).

CITY SIGHTS

The best place to start a tour is **Suhbaatar Square** at the centre of the city, the location where *tsam* ceremonies (see Special Topic, page 131) once took place and are now revived. Dominated by an ochre-coloured statue of the young Mongolian revolutionary on horseback, erected on the 25th anniversary of the revolution in 1946, the vast concrete and marbled square is a favourite meeting spot for locals – and visitors from outside the city – at any time of the day or night. People wait for friends, kids ride roller blades, hawkers sell ice cream and souvenirs, and professional photographers wait for customers. (Others simply walk hurriedly across chatting away on their mobile phones.) Surrounded by a heavy chain fence held up by stone lions and on a plinth illustrating various revolutionary scenes, the traditionally dressed Suhbaatar faces east – towards China – with hand upraised and vows in an inscription below: "If we, an entire people, unite in common effort and common will, there is nothing in the world that we cannot achieve, learn and succeed in."

During the Communist period, the square and its surrounding Soviet-style buildings – built by Japanese POWs – was the venue for grand military parades and was dominated at its northern end by a Red Square-style mausoleum to Suhbaatar and the Stalinist dictator Choibalsan. In 1990, the square became the focus of popular demonstrations, even a hunger strike, which led to the peaceful collapse of the old regime and the introduction of parliamentary democracy. (Political protests gather, too, most dramatically in July 2008 when a crowd protesting election results rallied here before attacking, looting and burning down the nearby ruling ex-Communist Party headquarters. Five were killed, hundreds arrested and a State of Emergency declared.)

In the early 2000s, the mausoleum was demolished and, in keeping with the Mongolians' rediscovery of their past, replaced with an ornate but tasteful colonnaded concrete-and-glass structure called the **Ceremonial Hall**, or *Yoslolyn Ordon*. Out front and facing the square is a large statue of a seated Genghis Khan – known in Mongolia as **Chinggis Khaan** – at the centre, with his son Ogedei and grandson Kublai on either side. From this point forward, we will switch over to the Mongolian spelling of Chinggis – which is also closer to its pronunciation.

Many Mongolians gather here to pay their respects. Two oversized Mongol warriors on horseback form a Guard of Honour – but real soldiers and police do show up when demonstrators get out of hand.

Behind this façade – and the actual object of the odd protest – is Mongolia's new **State Palace**, or *Toriin Ordon*, which houses the popularly elected national parliament, the **State Hural**, or *Ih Hural.* High-level security surrounds this building and, after some earlier rowdy demonstrations inside, the public can no longer witness proceedings. (It's best to give this area a wide berth as you stroll around downtown.)

Suhbaatar Square is very much the political, cultural and economic heart of modern Mongolia. (In fact, all roads – such as they are in Mongolia – begin at a marker on its southwestern corner.) On the eastern side are the modern multistorey **Cultural Palace** and the salmon-coloured, colonnaded **Opera and Ballet House** – both worth checking out for musical performances – along with the **Democratic Party Headquarters** and a new 18-floor office block. To the west are the dark-green colonnaded **Stock Exchange**, a converted movie theatre; the **Central Post Office** with its clock tower, and various banks and shops. UB's main east-west boulevard, known as **Peace Avenue**, or *Enkh Talvan Orgon Choloo*, and a park with a bell tower form the square's southern edge, now dominated on the other side by a curved 25-storey office building known as **Blue Sky** that is the city's latest landmark.

Across the street from the Post Office, and easy to miss, is the **Monument to S. Zorig,** the bespectacled young leader of the peaceful 1990 revolution and later member of parliament who was cruelly assassinated in 1998, his killers never found and still the stuff of much speculation. Because of the square's sheer size, traffic jams frequently build up on the surrounding streets, particularly at rush hour.

Suhbaatar Square is also a good place to get your bearings. Constrained by its geography, Ulaanbaatar is actually a fairly easy place to find your way around. Taxis are easily available and inexpensive, and once you've built up your confidence, you can even do like the locals and flag down the unofficial ones. (But do know where you're going and roughly what it'll cost beforehand.) The **Ulaanbaatar Railway Station** is located one kilometre (half a mile) southwest of the square on a street roughly parallel to **Peace Avenue**, or *Teeverchildlin Gudam.* There is also a great display of old locomotives at the **Railway Museum** just east of the station.

Chinggis Khaan International Airport, formerly Buyant Ukhaa Airport, is 18 kilometres (11 miles), or roughly a half-hour drive, southwest of the city on the northern side of Bogd Khan Uul Mountain which dominates the city's southern edge. (Because of its proximity to the mountains, a new airport is planned much farther away at Zuunmod on the mountain range's southern side.) Travellers typically come into the city from the airport on **Chinggis Khaan Boulevard**, or *Chingislin Orgon Choloo,* and over the **Peace & Friendship Bridge** with its distinctive colonnaded towers and railway line underneath, then right into Suhbaatar Square.

From the square, there are several attractions within easy walking distance. But be warned that blocks along the main boulevards are long and taking shortcuts off side streets, as many motorists certainly do, opens up a fascinating and perhaps unwanted look into the city's underbelly. Typically, the inside of these vast blocks are full of Soviet-era apartment blocks and newer commercial and residential buildings, also crisscrossed by sidewalks (pavements) and parks, and you're never quite sure where – even if – you'll come out the other side. They can also be quite muddy and treacherous after rain but are otherwise safe. The condition of sidewalks varies everywhere, no doubt affected by the freeze of winter, so don't get too distracted. Also, wherever you walk in UB, even along the main streets, do keep an eye out for missing manhole covers which are regularly stolen and sold for scrap.

Just to the northwest of the square is the two-storey **National Museum of Mongolian History**, well worth an early stop (most tours certainly do). Once known as the Revolutionary Museum, and still evident from the large socialist-realism mural on its side wall, Mongolia's

modern transformation is illustrated by a huge and moving bronze memorial outside its entrance to the many victims of communist-era political repression. Inside, the refurbished museum has a series of informative and attractive exhibits starting with Mongolia's earliest beginnings in Palaeolithic times and Stone Age up to the present day. The pre-Mongol period is well covered, including exhibits of tools, ceramics, weapons and statuary (some are copies), including photographs from various archaeological digs and their findings. The Turkic Period is particularly good. Another room includes traditional clothing from all of Mongolia's diverse ethnic groups, including the minority Kazakhs in the west.

The Museum's exhibit on the Mongol Empire is like entering a shrine with a large seated statue of Chinggis Khaan flanked by his distinctive horsehair banners, black for war and white for peace, at one end of the large room. There is a rich collection of paintings, maps, scale-models of Karakorum (Harhorin) in its heyday and many other objects of war, helmets and armour, and from daily life. The Manchu period is grim and includes objects of torture, including a large wooden box for prisoners, used during their 200 years of occupation up until 1911.

But more grim still is the nearly 70-year Communist period which followed, accentuated by grainy black-and-white photos including images of those executed in the purges of the 1930s. The post-war period focuses on massive industrialisation and developments in transport, education and health. By design or not, the lighting

Left: A firework display lights up the night sky in Suhbaatar Square (Elbegzaya Lhagvasuren). Right: UB's newest landmark – the Blue Sky – towers over charming Choiijin Lama Temple. Above: An old couple wear the traditional deel *at a university graduation ceremony (Carl Robinson x2).*

on these last two exhibits is dark – as those times certainly were – and the captions are not always translated. Then, up a narrow staircase, visitors suddenly enter a brightly lit exhibition on the 1990 Revolution which brings you up to the present-day. The museum certainly has much to absorb, and those with time may wish to return at the end of their stay in Mongolia. There is also an excellent book shop and small café to refresh yourself.

By contrast, the nearby **Natural History Museum** a bit farther north comes as a real disappointment, especially considering how synonymous Mongolia is with dinosaurs. Located in a decrepit Soviet-era building with creaky linoleum-covered floors and dangerously cracked staircases, the exhibits and dioramas are dusty, tired and poorly captioned. In the gloomy light, I almost walked past the famous Fighting Dinosaurs discovered in the Gobi Desert in 1971. Other palaeontology exhibits include dinosaur eggs, nests and bones, including material from Roy Chapman Andrews' Central Asiatic Expeditions in the 1920s (see Gobi Chapter, page 302 & Special Topic, page 304). The most complete specimen is the skeleton of a Tarbosaurus dinosaur (related to America's Tyrannosaurus Rex) discovered in 1948.

Other exhibits deal with Mongolia's geology, botany, fauna and anthropology. The only recent addition is the museum's "Golden Camel Museum". With the millions spent by international teams discovering these ancient dinosaurs and other ancient creatures, especially in recent years, one can only hope that Mongolia receives a more modern facility in the near future. With its rich natural history, the country certainly deserves much better.

One block further east from the Natural History Museum, and also accessed more directly north from Suhbaatar Square, the **Statue of Choibalsan**, Mongolia's diminutive and uniformed Stalinist dictator, stands somewhat incongruously outside what's now the leading **National University of Mongolia**, previously named after him. Since 1990, Mongolia has seen a boom in public and private universities with more than 20 now in Ulaanbaatar. (Some aimag centres also have universities.) Many are located north and east of here and attract thousands of students from around Mongolia, many of them young women; the result is that UB has turned into something of a "university town". (As you'll discover, many study tourism and spend their summer break working in tourist ger camps around the country.)

A couple of blocks to the west – a gentle tiptoe past the former Ministry of Internal Affairs or Mongolia's former KGB and now FBI, so they say – is the **Zanabazar Museum of Fine Arts.** Located in a flaky green, two-storey Russian-style building with a colonnaded entrance, this museum was actually founded in 1966 by the former Communist regime to preserve what was left of Mongolia's rich tradition of fine arts. A visit to the museum – despite its tattered outside appearance – is a real highlight with a large collection of artworks, sculptures and paintings, even back to Palaeolithic times. The best sections are on traditional religious art such as *tangkas*, embroideries and tsam masks and, of course, the 17th century bronzeworks and paintings of the famous Zanabazar, Mongolia's first theocratic leader.

Back at Suhbaatar Square and looking east, a short stroll down a side street at the back end of the Cultural Palace, you'll make another great find, the **Mongolian National Modern Art Gallery** which contains a wonderful collection of 20th century artworks – paintings, silk appliqués, woodblocks, engravings and sculpture. The woodcarvings are particularly impressive. As an indication of Mongolia's lively arts scene, there are also regular exhibitions by up-and-coming artists, some still students. (Sadly, in the July 2008 riots, the gallery was damaged and some works stolen, while a fire destroyed the Mongolian Philharmonic Orchestra's musical instruments next door.) Do make the time to visit these last two galleries. (For those interested, the Cultural Palace also has a **Theatre and Cinema Museum** on its third floor.)

Also on the eastern side, down a walkway between the Opera and Ballet House and a new 18-storey, glass-fronted office building once planned as a new Shangri-La Hotel, is the **Mongolian Revolutionary People's Party Headquarters** (MPRP), the former Communist party that has ruled Mongolia for most of the post-1990 period. (The squat five-storey building was looted and burned by angry rioters in July 2008 over parliamentary election results.) Right next door is the famous **Ulaanbaatar Hotel** – where travelling chroniclers in Communist times often stayed – and now refurbished into a luxury five-star hotel. Another survivor is the **Lenin Statue** in a park just in front of the hotel facing Peace Avenue. Nearly 20 years after the end of Communist-run Mongolia, no one has bothered to tear it down – even during the 2008 riots.

A couple of blocks down from the hotel across Peace Avenue and down **Olympic Boulevard**, or *Olympiin Orgon Choloo*, is the **Museum to the Victims of Political Repression**, a post-1990 tribute to those killed and persecuted during the Communist period. Located in an old wooden house surrounded by a chain-link fence, exactly why I'm not sure, this was once the home of Prime Minister Butachiin Genden, whose brief period of liberalisation brutally ended in his execution in the Soviet Union in 1936. Founded by his daughter, the museum chronicles the Stalinist purges of the 1930s and also takes a critical view of long-time dictator Choibalsan.

In a room on the ground floor, there is a memorial with the names of the victims – estimated between 30,000 and 100,000 – while upstairs are grim exhibits documenting that period of arbitrary arrests followed by interrogation, prosecution, death and burial. A glass-enclosed case contains many human skulls, each with a bullet hole, disinterred

A sobering display in the Museum to the Victims of Political Repression (Carl Robinson).

outside the capital in the early 1990s. Like a time capsule, Genden's office is duplicated in one room. Unfortunately, few tourists visit and little is translated, but museum guides are pleased to assist. One can't help leaving without a strong feeling of sadness.

Down a side street from here is the modernistic **Wedding Palace,** a leftover from the Communist era and still used for civil marriages; with its ornately decorated interior with grand wooden staircase it's certainly worth a quick look (you might even catch a wedding). By this stage, you are directly behind the towering 25-storey Blue Sky office building. Straight ahead, with a lovely old temple garden out front is one of the real gems of Ulaanbaatar, the **Choiijin Lama Temple Museum.** Although only built in 1904–08, this small temple complex is a classic example of Buddhist architecture with its blend of Tibetan and Chinese influences.

This was the home of **Luvsan Haidav Choiijin Lama**, the brother of Mongolia's last theocratic leader, the Eighth Bogd Gegeen, and also the official State Oracle, or soothsayer. Now a museum and recently restored, the temple has lovely curved archways and five halls or temples with many art and religious objects on exhibit, including a rich collection of ancient texts, tsam masks, tangkas, sculptures and embroideries. Among the paintings in the **Main Temple**, or **Temple of Spreading Compassion,** are those showing in detail all the torments of Hell – even more sobering if you have just come from the Museum to the Victims of Political Repression. (At least this wonderful complex was saved from destruction.) The next room is where, on important occasions, the State Oracle would enter a trance and pronounce the path ahead.

The temple's guides are well informed and certainly essential, especially to unlock the large wooden doors of the other halls, each so full of objects and spread out that the entire grounds suddenly appear much larger. (For some reason, unusually, the tour goes anticlockwise.) The highlight of the **Amgalan Temple,** or **Ondor-Gegeen Temple,** is Zanabazar's famous **Green Tara**, or Siamatara, the female Buddha. (For a basic understanding of Tibetan Buddhism, see page 124.) This temple also includes paintings of Mongolia's own 16 bodhisattvas – those who put off Nirvana to help others. Directly

The delicately painted entryway into the main temple at the Bogd Khaan Palace (Carl Robinson).

behind the main hall, the spooky **Hall of Yiddam** was once forbidden to ordinary people; this is where secret Tantric rituals took place, sometimes involving sex. The **Hall of Zuu**, west of the main temple, is a more conventional temple dedicated to the Buddhas of Past, Present and Future. Don't be rushed, as a visit makes quite a fascinating insight into the Mongolian version of Tibetan Buddhism.

Leaving the temple in a westerly direction, across a narrow street is the **Marco Polo Plaza** where, on the ground floor, you'll find a relaxing Cuban-run coffee shop, **Millies Espresso**, a private art gallery and the **Xanadu Bookshop**, UB's best book store, which also sells a great selection of imported wines, a great spot to pick up both, including detailed guides and maps around Mongolia. Heading north, you'll pass one of UB's most popular restaurants, the upstairs **Verandah Restaurant**, with comfortable couch-style seating inside, and a covered conventional sitting area on the wide balcony – a great spot for lunch or dinner.

Winding up to another small street, turn left and you'll shortly be on busy Chinggis Khaan Boulevard, just southwest of Suhbaatar Square, and the main – and very busy – thoroughfare to the southern part of the city. Just to the left past the **Mongolian Artists Exhibition Hall** (with its works by local artists) and a restaurant is the yellow-coloured **National Library**, where a statue of Stalin stood until 1990 and is now replaced with the

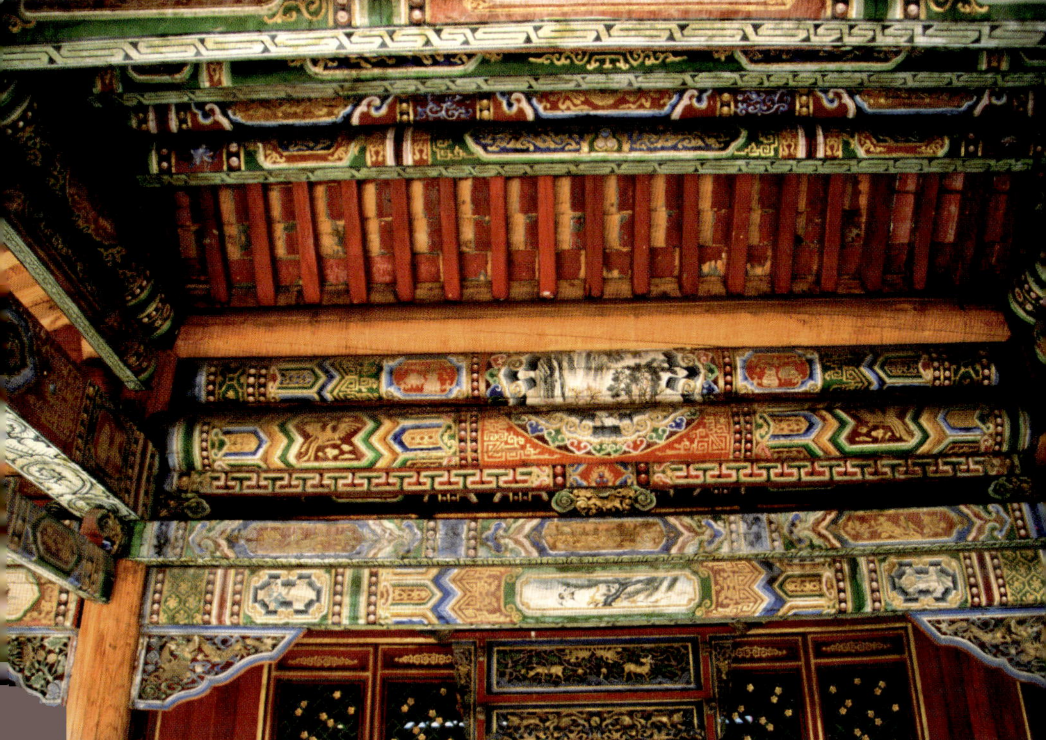

Rinchen Statue, a prominent intellectual. (For those keen to see him, Stalin now sits beside the dance floor at the Ismuss Nightclub up Peace Avenue near the Wrestling Stadium.)

Directly across the busy boulevard – which takes some real choreography to cross – is the imposing pink-coloured and colonnaded **National Drama Theatre**, which overlooks a tiny square containing the controversial **Tsendenbal Statue** – the Communist leader who followed Choibalsan – erected by the MPRP government only recently. Another small monument here marks the start of **Seoul Street**, or *Seulin Gudami,* named for one of Ulaanbaatar's Sister Cities. Running diagonally to Peace Avenue, this is UB's "eat street" with a wide choice of restaurants and a lively nightlife of bars, discos and clubs. Halfway along, just past the massive **Russian Embassy**, the street intersects with a divided street, *Tserendorjiin Gudami,* with the huge ger-like **National Circus of Mongolia** at its southern end. (Created in 1940, the Russian-style circus is world famous for its contortionist, acrobatic and weightlifting performances, and also includes tightrope walking, animals, clowns and magic acts.)

Across from the street's northern end at Peace Avenue is the imposing glass-fronted **State Department Store**, a six-storey relic from the Soviet days but now well stocked with modern clothing and goods, including a souvenir and bookshop. Everyone is warned not to use the cumbersome elevator, and watch out especially for pickpockets; those dangers aside, it's a great one-stop place to pick up any last-minute gear.

Walking south along Chinggis Khaan Boulevard on its western side – just past a "ger on wheels" souvenir shop – is the twin-towered **Bayangol Hotel**, one of UB's original hotels where many tourists and business people stay. Across the street is a large shopping centre and **Naramdal Park**, a vast children's park of lawns and trees. (The **Ethnography Museum** is on its southwest corner.) But you'll need a taxi to visit sights farther south across the modernistic Peace & Friendship Bridge which crosses over the railway and the **Dund Gol**, a tributary of the Tuul.

Unsightly steam pipes once on the left are now buried underground, opening up a vast parkland leading up to the **National Sports Stadium**, the focus of the colourful Naadam Festival of the "Three Manly Sports" every July (see page 420). The festival's horse races, the longest covering 28 kilometres (17 miles), take place on the city's far western outskirts. Reflecting Mongolia's newfound prosperity, the district south of the bridge is full of soaring modern apartment buildings and shopping centres. With its large round restaurant with Greco-Roman façade and an expanisve outdoor drinking area on a large wooden cart, the **Palace Hotel** on the right is another popular tourist hotel. The boulevard heads west towards the airport, while directly across the roundabout is another one of the capital's major attractions.

BOGD KHAAN PALACE MUSEUM

The **Bogd Khaan Palace Museum** is another old survivor, although only completed in 1903, with a triumphal arch added in 1912 to celebrate the end of Manchu rule. Also known as the **Winter Palace,** this large complex of seven halls and a two-storey Russian-style house was the winter home of Mongolia's last theocratic leader and third in line in the Tibetan Buddhist hierarchy after the Dalai Lama and Panchen Rimpoche. The Tibetan-born Eighth Bogd Gegeen – the last in the line starting with Zanabazar – was named Khaan, or "Holy Leader", when Mongolia declared its independence in 1911 (see History, page 84).

The Winter Palace was also where Chinese troops – who'd brutally occupied the capital in 1919 – held him hostage before he was sensationally freed by the White Russian Mad Baron in early 1921 (see Special Topic, page 88) and taken into hiding in a remote monastery on the other side of the looming Bogd Khan Mountain. When Mongolian revolutionaries (backed by Red troops) freed the city in July 1921, the blind and supposedly syphilitic leader was made titular head of state but quickly lost all power to the Communists, his own bodyguard among the early casualties. When he died in 1924, Mongolia was declared a People's Republic and the complex became a museum in 1961.

For obvious reasons, visitors are immediately drawn to the two-storey European-style – and very incongruous – **Winter Palace of the Bogd Khaan.** (It is certainly a perennial illustration in brochures and guidebooks.) Tucked away on the right-hand side of the vast temple complex, the whitewashed building's floor-to-ceiling windows are surrounded with ornately carved wooden decorations with a green corrugated iron roof and several chimneys leading from the many fireplaces inside (see the image on page 88). A tin-roofed awning with its front slightly raised and a stone lion on one side mark the entrance. Built as a gift from Russia's Tsar Nicolas II in 1905 to assert his country's influence over Mongolia, even though he'd turned down an earlier request to help overthrow the Manchus, the interior of this large wooden mansion reflects the sumptuous lifestyle of the theocratic leader in the midst of the grinding poverty around him.

There are precious clothes of silk inlaid with fur and precious stones, opulent beds, furniture, crystal, porcelain and silver utensils, and – occupying an entire room – a huge ger covered in leopard skins. The walls are painted yellow, indicating the Dalai Lama had stayed there, as he did after the British invaded Tibet in 1904. An eclectic mixture of gifts from foreign leaders is on display, along with early technological wonders such as an old gramophone and typewriter. But perhaps strangest of all was his zoo, now lifelessly preserved, mostly inside dusty glass cabinets. There is a stuffed giraffe, its neck trimmed to fit the ceiling, a polar bear, a giant turtle, a sloth, a boa constrictor and several seals. No one knows what happened to his elephants, who somehow survived the harsh Mongolian winters. The museum also includes several sculptures from Zanabazar and his followers.

The contrast to the adjoining green-tiled, Chinese-style temple complex could hardly be more dramatic, with the recently refurbished **Triple Gate** and **Peace Gate** and lovely landscaped park at its entrance particularly impressive. (But as visitors enter the grounds next to the Palace, do take time to walk around for a look.) Spread over a fairly large area and known as **Sharavpeljiilin Sum**, or Monastery Spreading Wisdom, the complex is a regal one and its six temples and halls encompass the symbolism, activities and ceremonies of the theocratic ruler. The first is devoted to Buddhist cosmology, another three to music, paintings and library, a ceremonial temple and a main temple known as the **Nogoon Laviran.**

Particularly fascinating in the middle one, the Temple of Apostles, or **Naidan**,

With its ornate, newly refurbished Triple, or Peace, Gate in a landscaped garden outside (below), the entry into the Bogd Khaan Palace's main temple complex (right) is quaintly understated (Carl Robinson x2).

is a long white rope that the Bogd dangled out of the window of his Winter Palace to bless the faithful. He apparently had a cheeky sense of humour, too; American explorer Roy Chapman Andrews tells how the Buddhist leader wired up a car battery to the rope to give these pilgrims some extra-special "divine energy" – and then roared with laughter as they jumped at the shock.

Gandan Monastery and Other Suburban Sights

Heading south from the Palace on Zaisan Street, a bridge crosses over the gravel-strewn Tuul River, its banks covered in willow trees, to **Zaisan Hill** at the base of **Bogd Khan Uul** (Mountain). On two adjoining grass-covered foothills – visible from some distance away, including the downtown square – are a rendition of Chinggis Khaan made of whitewashed rocks, and the Soyombo, Mongolia's national symbol. The nearby valleys were once a favourite location for the ruling elite's weekend *dachas* (cottages). Now, being some distance away from the city's growing pollution, this is UB's most prestigious neighbourhood with fenced-in mansions and villas. The large, gold-coloured **Megjid Janraiseg Statue**, or Avalokiteshvara-Janraiseg, a Buddhist deity, was erected in 2005 and looks north towards its more famous twin at the Gandan Monastery across the wide valley floor.

Above: The Megjid Janraiseg Statue stands on a hillside in UB's southern suburbs (Leo Murray). Below: Another suburban sight – an image of Chinggis Khaan created out of whitewashed rocks (Vidor).

Nearby is the landmark **Zaisan Memorial**, erected on the 50th anniversary of the Communist revolution in 1971, which honours Soviet and Mongolian troops who died fighting Nazi Germany. At its base, the old Soviet-made tank atop a white plinth is the **Revolutionary Tank Brigade Monument,** a unit funded by public donations in World War II and which, as the map on its side illustrates, pushed all the way to Berlin. Steep steps lead up to a concrete statue of a helmeted soldier holding a stylised flag with the Hammer and Sickle on one side and the Soyombo on the other. A large circular mosaic illustrates the everlasting friendship between the two peoples, but – quite symbolically – the **Eternal Flame** no longer burns. While a bit of a hike up, the view out over the sprawling capital is superb.

From here, one can clearly spot the **Four Sacred Mountains** that surround Ulaanbaatar, and appreciate its magnificent physical setting. Some 28 kilometres (17 miles) to the right, or east, is **Bayanzurkh Uul** (Mountain); just north of the city not far from the Gandan Monastery is **Chingelt Khairkhan Uul**; and off to west, clearly visible on landing at the airport, is **Songino Uul.** These mountains give their names to the nearest suburb and are traditionally worshipped by their residents with *ovoos* at their summits. But everyone worships massive **Bogd Khan Uul**, which rises sharply 1,000 metres (3,280 feet) from the valley floor behind you to the south. In pre-Communist days, elaborate ceremonies were held twice a year to the mountain and its protective deity, the Garuda bird, which is on the city crest and flag. (Each mountain has its own protector, whose masked images were part of the Tsam Ceremony, see page 131.) Since 1778, Bogd Khan Uul's pine and larch-covered summit and wildlife-filled slopes have been a large national park (see below). Many old-timers still remember when deer wandered into the city from the park.

Another popular destination – and often first-up on the tourist itinerary to observe the 10am Call to Prayer and Service – is the **Gandantegtechilin Monastery**, or the Mahayana Monastery of Complete Joy, and the reason for the city's original existence. Located on a hill in the capital's northwest and abbreviated as **Gandan**, this is Mongolia's largest and most significant monastery, and the only one that continued to function throughout the Communist period, with the closely watched monks on the government payroll. The monks, however, were among the first to publicly support the anti-regime protestors in 1990.

Today, the monastery is at the heart of Mongolia's Buddhist revival, has rebuilt many of its schools, and helps fund both new construction and the rebuilding of destroyed temples around the country. As a vast centre of learning, Gandan attracted the best lamas and its library contains some 60,000 rare volumes of Buddhist texts in both Tibetan and

Mongolian. Once at the centre of a Great Circle of gers around a dozen temples and stupas dedicated to past Bogd Gegeens and others, much was still razed as the Communists crushed Buddhism and modernised the city. Unlike many other Buddhist sites around Mongolia, Gandan is a fully active and functioning centre, including the Mongolian Buddhist University, and visitors need to respect that.

Gandan Monastery has four main temples: the **Temple of Vajradara,** or Ochirdara, built in 1838 of brick and stone with a tiled roof, is where the main religious ceremonies take place before a Buddha of the same name sculpted by the ever-prolific Zanabazar. The **Temple of Zuu,** or Jewel Temple, dates from 1869 and houses the relics of the Seventh Bogd Gegeen – who died at only 19 – and also a wooden statue of the goddess Lkhamo. The **Temple of Didan-Lavran** is a two-storey, glazed-roof structure originally built as a library, now moved elsewhere on the grounds; this is where the 13th Dalai Lama stayed after fleeing Tibet in 1904. Its halls are a vast gallery of tangkas, the tombs of past Bogd Gegeens, a bronze statue of Zanabazar and a silver one of Tsongkhapa, the founder of the Yellow Hat Sect of Tibetan Buddhism. More modern donated Buddhas are also on display, including one presented by India in 1957.

But the highlight of a visit to Gandan is the Chinese and Tibetan-style **Temple of Megjid Janraiseg**, or Avalokiteshvara, a landmark still visible from many parts of the capital. Built in 1911–12 to commemorate the end of Manchu occupation, legend says the temple was also built to cure the Bogd Khaan of his blindness. Its massive height was to house an immense 25-metre (82-foot) standing statue of the deity, similar to one at the base of Zaisan Hill. Much controversy surrounds what happened after the statue was torn apart and trucked into the Soviet Union in the 1930s – no one believes the statue was simply melted down for bullets, and supposed sightings of its bits and pieces around Russia perpetuate the intrigue. With donations from Japan and Nepal, plus local contributions, a new statue was consecrated in 1996 and remains one of the best-known works of religious art in Mongolia. The interior of the 20-ton statue is hollow and is used for storing precious items.

At the risk of becoming "templed out" – and don't forget you'll see many more on your travels – Ulaanbaatar has nearly a dozen other functioning Buddhist temples and monasteries, some only opened after 1990. Among the older ones is the **Dambadarjaa Monastery**, or Temple for the Propagation of the Faith, on the city's northern outskirts, built by the Qing Emperor Qianglong in 1765 for the remains of the Second Bogd Gegeen, which were later transferred to another monastery. (Regarded as complicit in a rebellion, all his successors were chosen in Tibet.)

Clockwise from above: The Zaisan Mural boasts impressive views towards the city (Yaan, licensed under Creative Commons Attribution ShareAlike 3.0); the 25-metre statue of Janraiseg within Gandan Monastery is a masterpiece of religious art (Elbegzaya Lhagvasuren); devotional passion remains strong among older Mongolians (Gotsbayar Rentsendorj); within the Gandan Monastery complex (Leo Murray); a rural suburb of Ulaanbaatar gets a light dusting of snow in winter (Gotsbayar Rentsendorj).

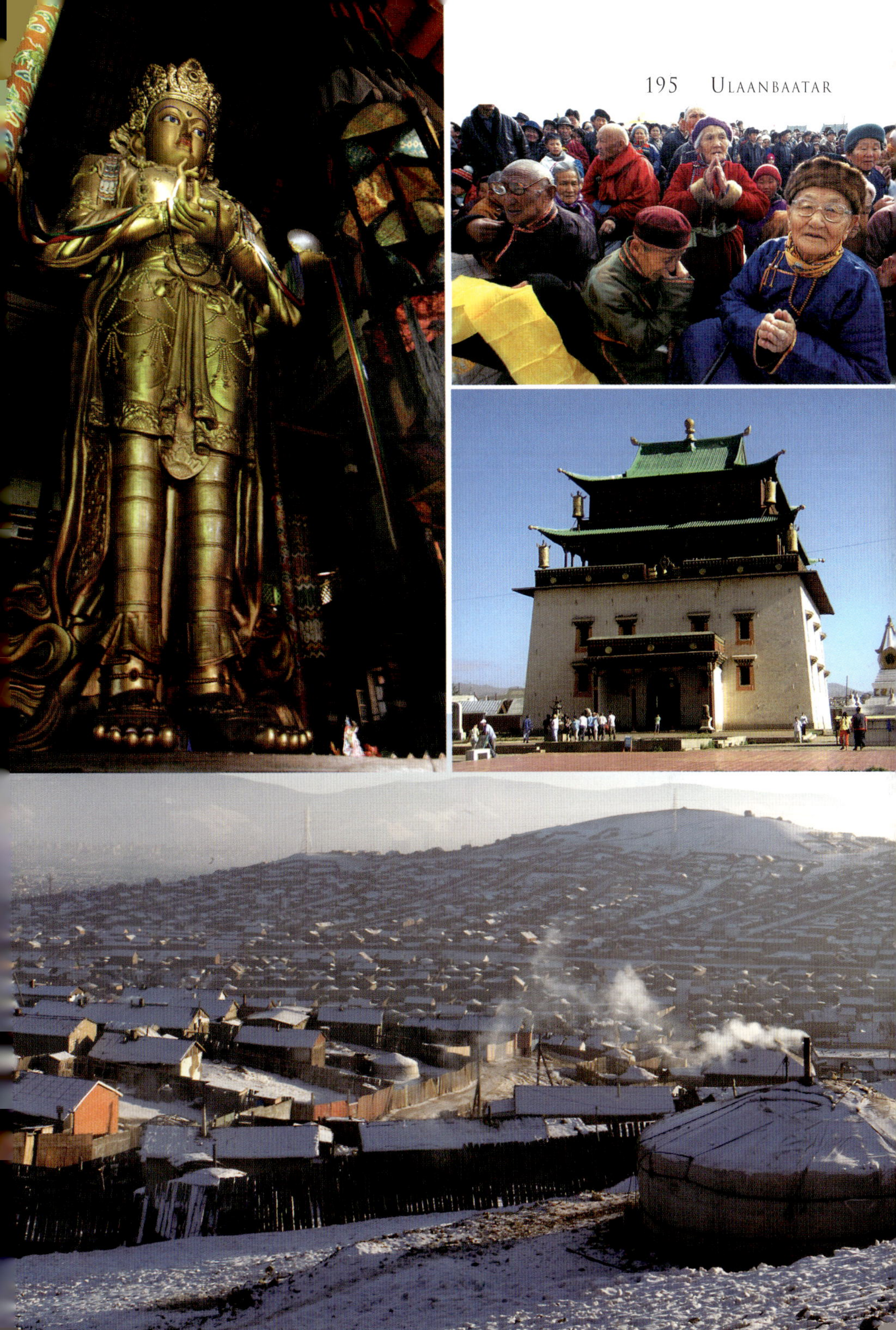

On Elephant Head Hill near Gandan Monastery, the **Geser Temple** honours the legendary Tibetan king – and the subject of the world's longest epic. Others include the **Temple of Vajrayogini**, run by nuns and dedicated to Indian master Padmasambhava, who introduced Tantrism and the Red Hat sect to Tibet. Another Red Hat temple is the ger-shaped **Dashchoilon Monastery**, while **Betub Monastery** was founded by former Indian Ambassador and Buddhist scholar Bakula Rimpoche, and is where the Old Mongolian script is taught. The **Mamba Datsan** in the northeast of the city teaches Buddhist medicine.

Similarly with museums, there are always a few more specialised ones to explore – if you have the time. For those wanting a more detailed look at the capital's history, visit the **Ulaanbaatar City Museum** located in an old Russian-style building in Blue Sky Street (*Khoh Tengeriin Gudami*), with its collection of archival photographs, paintings and tapestries, including an old map of the city carved on an elephant's tusk. The recently renovated **Military History Museum** on *Lkhagvasurengiin Gudami* relates Mongolia's martial history from the Stone Age to the present day, including the 1921 Battle of Kyakhta on the Russian border where Suhbaatar routed remnants of the Chinese Army. (Tanks and artillery pieces are on display outside.) Other museums of possible interest are the **Mongolian Hunting Museum**, near Gandan Monastery, the **Mongolian Toy Museum** near the UB Hotel, and the **Museum of Geology and Mineral Resources** at the Mongolian Technical University.

Although most sights of interest are in the downtown area around Suhbaatar Square, Ulaanbaatar's nine districts sprawl out in both directions and you'll certainly catch these areas on your way out of town. What is generally called **East UB** is more upmarket with Peace Avenue turning into a divided boulevard with many government and educational institutions, plus the city's **Russian Orthodox Church** and **Roman Catholic Cathedral.** The five-star **Kempinski Hotel** is also in this area. Once Urga's Russian quarter, this district has also seen a boom in new high-rise apartment buildings. Heading east on the avenue parallel to the railway, *Namy Gudami*, is the city's so-called **Black Market**, actually a free-enterprise collection of huge sheds specialising in everything imaginable, from fresh vegetables and live animals to hardware and hard-to-get spare parts.

Towards **West UB**, **District Three** is a California-style shopping district, which also has great restaurants, bars and discos frequented by locals. It is so popular that weekend traffic jams are a real problem. Just beyond and dominated by a huge Soviet-built flour mill is the city's vast and busy industrial district – an eclectic mix of railway freight yards, truck depots, oil storage tanks, warehouses, factories and – just in case you're wondering about those missing manhole covers – some mighty busy scrap-iron dealers. Either way, Mongolia's vast and open landscape is just a short drive away.

DAY TRIPS FROM THE CITY

Surrounded by **Tov aimag**, the capital offers several quick getaway destinations, either as one-day or overnight trips, especially if you're passing through to the Trans-Siberian Railway or on a break between longer tours. They'll certainly give you a taste of the surrounding countryside and all are very different.

Although the northern edge of **Bogd Khan Uul National Park** is clearly visible from the city and certainly approachable by determined hikers, its main entrance is 46 kilometres (29 miles) around the mountain's southern side, and a visit is easily combined with a stop at the remnants of a famous Buddhist monastery. Except for the last section, the trip is on a sealed road and takes about one hour. Driving out of UB, the road passes through outlying suburbs around the airport and then east through a valley at the base of the mountain. Several roads lead off into the edges of the park to holiday homes, tourist ger camps, a deer farm and even a racing horse stud farm.

By the roadside, nomads living in gers tend flocks of fat-tailed sheep and cashmere goats – sometimes a bit of a traffic hazard – and herds of horses and cattle graze the grasslands. You'll notice how trees, which include the odd forest of white-barked birch, only grow on the northern-facing slopes, the southern sides being covered in grassy steppe. Especially on weekends, the traffic can be surprisingly busy as city folk take a break.

Zuunmod is the aimag centre (provincial capital) of **Tov**, and typical of others around the country – a rather drab mixture of Communist-era administrative buildings, apartment blocks, schools, cinema, theatre, single-storey shops and restaurants, with a bus station set around a central park and a grid of concrete streets and curbing but few sidewalks. Typical of the post-1990 market economy and an end to state subsidies, such industry as once existed lies rusting or derelict, such as the old power plant and a multistorey clothing factory. A mobile phone tower sits atop a nearby ridge above a suburb of fenced-off wooden houses and the odd ger.

The town of 20,000 people is a microcosm of modern Mongolia with its heavy urbanisation and underemployment. Perhaps the capital's proposed new international airport near here will help. Historically, Zuunmod was the scene of a frenzied battle in 1696 when 50,000 Manchu troops equipped with cannon devastated some 30,000 Mongolians from the west who'd refused to join the empire (see History, page 82).

From the town, a dirt road leads north up a valley to the park's entrance, and the number of pine trees increases along the rock-strewn creek and thickens up into the looming hills ahead. You are in a new world. Regarded as sacred from the time when Chinggis Khaan's early allies, the **Kereit**, inhabited the region, and protected as a national park since 1778, Bogd Khan Uul remains mostly untouched – even with the odd intrusion by poachers and illegal loggers. The **Strictly Protected Area**, as it's called, covers 41,000 hectares (101,000 acres) of which 18,000 are forest – mostly pine, larch, cedar and birch – and marks the southernmost extension of the Siberian taiga. Wildlife, among them deer, *maral* (elk), wild boar, sable, wolf and fox, proliferate along with numerous birds and reptiles. The slopes below comprise steppe, which extends far south and eventually turns into the sands of the Gobi Desert.

The park is a popular destination, especially in summer when the lush meadows between the woods, watered by several springs and streams, are covered in flowers such as the ever-popular edelweiss. Strewn with large granite boulders, the top of the range – which runs roughly 32 kilometres (20 miles) by 16 kilometres (10 miles) builds up to its highest point at **Tsetseeguun Uul** (2,256 metres, or 7,377 feet) which is barely visible to Ulaanbaatar's southeast. Annual ceremonies once took place here. Even just a short stroll up into the mountains is rewarding. For keen hikers, the walk to or from the capital takes about 10 hours and is best done as an overnight camping trip. (Maps, a compass and even GPS are essential along with gear to handle any weather, even in summer.)

Located near the park entrance is the **Manzshir Monastery**, which once rivalled the one in today's Ulaanbaatar in importance and number of followers, particularly at its annual autumn tsam ceremony. When the Mad Baron freed the Bogd Khaan from the Winter Palace

The aptly named Turtle Rock in the Gorkhi Terelj National Park northeast of UB (Carl Robinson).

in early 1921, the leader was secretly brought up and over the mountain here for his safety. Unlike the Gandan Monastery, however, this large monastery was completely destroyed in 1937 during the Communist purges, and today evokes a melancholy sadness. Only the thick mud-brick walls of its main Tibetan-style temple remain. Built in 1733 in the Manchu era and named after their patron saint, the Buddha of Wisdom, its setting was – and still is – magnificent, a southward-facing valley with pine forests, bubbling streams and faraway vistas to the flat steppe beyond. In its glory, there was even a large artificial lake, its shape still visible today.

Above: A rebuilt temple marks the modern revival of the Manzshir Monastery, destroyed in the 1930 purges.
Below: Great food and hospitality make Terelj Lodge a wonderfully relaxing break (Carl Robinson x2).

Bare earthen platforms with stone walls sprawl all across the valley and give some idea of the monastery's former size. A new temple serves as a museum with old pictures, paintings and relics. On the steep hillside above are several rock carvings and paintings of Buddhist images and shelters where lamas once meditated. Another survivor is a huge bronze cauldron that supposedly could feed 1,000 monks at once. There is another museum, mostly of stuffed animals, with a few stone relics, some with Chinese characters, on the grounds outside. But two Turkic era "man stones" draped in sky-blue *hadag* (votive scarves) do seem of more modern vintage. The grounds offer tourist facilities, including overnight ger accommodation and a restaurant, and horses can be rented for trips up into the surrounding forests.

Only an hour northeast of Ulaanbaatar, or 60 kilometres (37 miles), the **Gorkhi Terelj National Park** is certainly one of Mongolia's most popular destinations. Referred to more commonly simply as **Terelj**, the park is at the southwestern extremity of the **Hentii Range**, one of the country's three principal mountain ranges which runs northeast into Russia's eastern Siberia. Terelj is renowned for its lovely natural scenery of stunning rock formations, larch forests, sweeping grasslands and swiftly flowing streams.

Although now highly developed with numerous tourist ger camps and cabins, some nomadic life of horses and yaks continues. Many facilities offer excellent restaurants and accommodation, and are open year-round. The park offers great hiking, rock climbing, horse riding and rafting down the nearby **Tuul River**, plus cross-country skiing and skating in winter. Returning from another intense trip into the Mongolian Outback, I found the simple peace and quiet – plus the great food and hospitality – of the **Terelj Lodge** wonderfully relaxing. Hardly surprisingly, Terelj figures high on most tourist itineraries, including those on train stopovers, and is a very popular weekend destination for stressed-out city-dwellers.

The drive on the paved road east from the capital – part of the **Millennium Road** – follows the Tuul River and passes newly built outer suburbs, including the turn-off to the flashy **Hotel Mongolia.** With the Hentii range on the left and Bogd Khan Uul fading away on the right, the valley opens up onto rolling steppe with views far into the distance. At the compact former coal mining town of **Nalayh**, actually part of UB and housing mostly Kazakhs from western Mongolia, there is a turnoff for the main road southeast to the Chinese border, paved only to Choyr. Turning off just past a former Soviet Army base, supposedly with vast bombproof underground facilities, the road travels up a ridge and then sharply down into the **Terelj River Valley** and the park entrance at a small creekside settlement of cabins and weekend homes. The atmosphere is immediately entrancing, and only grows the further north you travel.

In late spring and summer, the small valley is a flower-covered meadow dotted with pine-covered hills and dissected by a swift-flowing creek. Its sharply rising walls of heavily eroded, sandy-coloured rock are dotted with individual larch trees, which have gained a foothold and thicken into forests on the peaks high above. Small side valleys thick with other vegetation are camps for nomads, who hire out their horses to visitors.

Nearing the Hentii Mountains, the valley widens and is scattered with freestanding rock formations with **Turtle Rock,** or *Melkhii Khad*, certainly the most fascinating. Nearby at the head of the valley and across a long footbridge is the newly built **Aryaval Temple** with a smaller second one dedicated to Kalachakra, including a tangka of the mythical city of Shambhala. Its **Gallery of Buddhist Philosophy** has over 200 modern paintings by artist Bayantsagaan illustrating the religion's beliefs and philosophy. From its elevated position, the view back down the Terelj Valley stretches out to the flat steppe beyond.

Most only see this easily accessible resort section of the park. But for those with time and energy, hiking and horse trails run into its rugged and forested heartland, including its main peak, **Altan Olgii Uul.** Another site of interest, particularly for those interested in history, is the remote **Gunjiin Sum**, or **Temple of the Peaceful Princess.** (The temple is also accessible by a rough 4WD track.) The story involves Manchu manoeuvrings to assure a loyal successor to Zanabazar, the first Bogd Gegeen, who'd accepted eastern Mongolia's suzerainty in 1691, through the marriage of an imperial princess to a leading khan. The most popularly told legend plays well to deeply entrenched anti-Chinese prejudice. When her son – deemed Zanabazar's reincarnation – was born, he was murdered and replaced by the son of the khan's Mongolian concubine, who then became the Second Bogd Gegeen. When she discovered the deception years later, the princess died of a broken heart.

A more prosaic story comes from resident Mongolist Don Croner's study of written records. The princess gave her newborn son to the Mongolian wife to raise as her own, an act of generosity praised in a tangka in the Zanabazar Museum. In this telling, the Manchu princess loved Mongolia so deeply that she wanted to be buried here. In any case, the temple was built in her honour by the second Qing emperor Qianglong in 1740. The setting in a tranquil larch forest – a deciduous pine that covers the ground in orange-coloured needles – is magnificent. The temple complex was heavily damaged in the purges of the 1930s, but a guardhouse, entrance and part of its walls remain. Also visible is the princess's tomb, looted by grave robbers.

Farther to the northeast – and overlapping into neighbouring Selenge and Hentii aimags – is the even more remote **Khanhentii Strictly Protected Area**. This vast 1.2-million-hectare (nearly three-million-acre) national park gives rise to three of Mongolia's main rivers, including the Tuul, and is the homeland of Chinggis Khaan (see The Hentii, page 219.)

Another popular destination outside UB and, like Terelj, worth an overnight stay in a tourist ger camp, is the **Hustain Nuruu Reserve** 110 kilometres (68 miles) to the west. The reserve's forested steppe is home to the last true wild horse in the world, the **Przewalski's horse** or *takhi*. It disappeared in the Gobi in 1960 but has now been successfully reintroduced here – and in another reserve in southwest Mongolia – from zoos in Holland, Germany and Australia. There are now over 400 horses in the reserve, which is a perfect spot for hiking and horse riding. The grassy steppe is home to a wide variety of wildlife, including gazelle, deer, wild boar, wildcat and wolf, which are best seen late in the day. The nearby **Enhiin and Tavangiin Els** are the closest sand dune formations to the capital. For those pressed for time, the reserve provides a pleasant taster of the vast Mongolian wilderness.

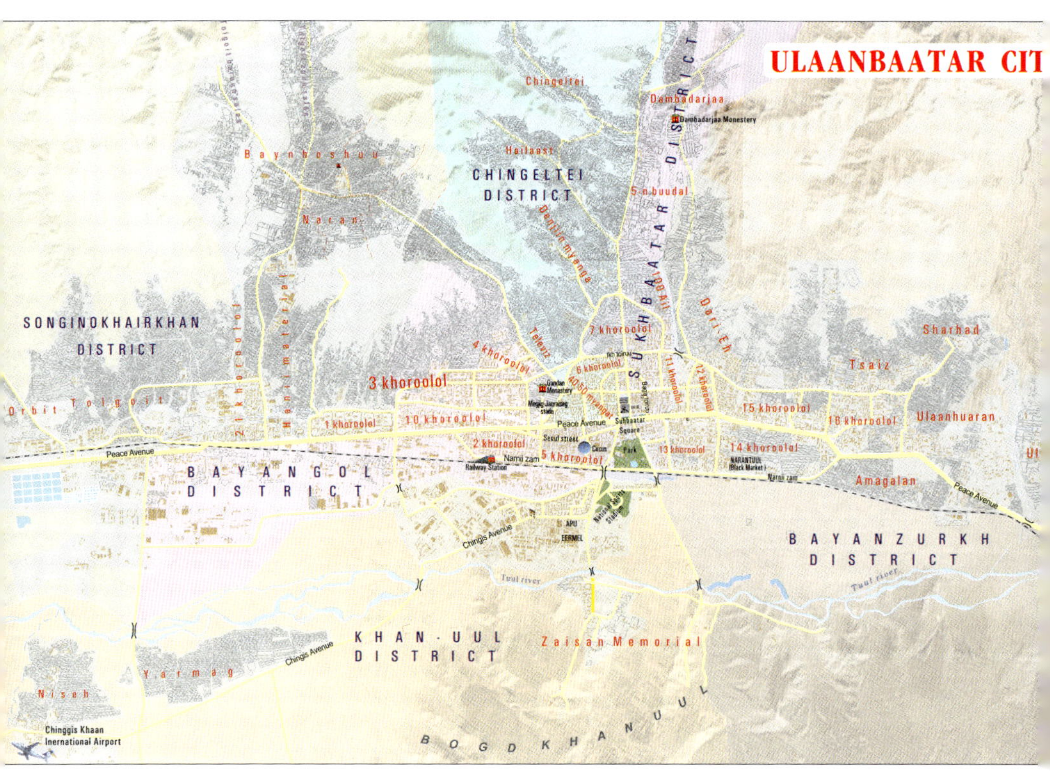

AROUND ULAANBAATAR

Mention has already been made of three popular destinations immediately outside the capital, but throw the net even further out, perhaps another two or three hundred kilometres, and a number of other destinations fall within your grasp. Most are stopovers on the way to other places, but for time-pressed travellers looking for something more off-the-beaten-track, or those looking for just one more trip out of UB, these present some interesting alternatives –best visited as part of an overnight trip.

Looking southwards, the alternate road to the South Gobi (see The Gobi, page 292) travels southwest past UB's international airport and through the mountain-steppe country and valleys of Tov aimag which surrounds the capital. Near its southern boundary, after about 100 kilometres (62 miles), are some of the closest sand dunes to UB, the **Ar Burdiin Els.** Set up against a low mountain range, the white-coloured dunes make a fascinating stop before travelling to nearby **Zorgol Khayrkhan Uul** (1,668 metres or 5,472 feet), a spectacular pyramid-shaped mountain rising sharply from the flat valley floor.

The same winds that created the dunes have blasted and swirled the mountain's face bare, which at first glance looks like a stark black-and-white photograph. A small lake sits at its base along with a couple of nomadic gers. Out of the wind on the other side,

Pilgrims seek comfort and advice from the naturally shaped Mother Rock south of UB (Carl Robinson).

the mountain's character is completely different, its sandstone ramparts rising sharply and dotted with trees and other vegetation. From the range a short distance away, a small creek descends through thick trees into a lush green valley where horses graze. An ideally placed tourist ger camp sits beside the creek and there are also places to camp. The hills just beg to be explored.

Farther east and about 50 kilometres (30 miles) southeast of the aimag centre of **Zuunmod** (see Ulaanbaatar, page 197) is one of Mongolia's most unusual attractions, **Eej Khad** or **Mother Rock.** Travelling east of the main highway to the South Gobi, the road passes through wide valleys and then rises high up into a grass-covered range of unusual granite outcrops with spectacular views out over the flat steppe beyond. In a shallow, spring-fed valley on its southern side are a couple of buildings and a parking area which, especially at weekends, are full of hundreds of pilgrims who drive down from the capital. Protected by a high, circular concrete-block structure is a two-metre-high (six-foot) block of granite eroded by nature into the shape of a woman and now clothed in colourful robes and blue *hadag*, or scarves.

Long revered as sacred, its worship was suppressed by the Communists who even tried to bulldoze it away. Today, Mongolians actively worship Mother Rock again and come seeking comfort and advice. After walking around the rock three times, pilgrims burn incense and offer milk, vodka and sweets. They then line up quietly to embrace and make three wishes to the armless statue. (They must also make three separate visits.) Outside are several other sacred rocks on which pilgrims lie or sit. At **Dog Rock**, they rub against it to cure physical ailments. (There is even a Money Rock a bit up the track.) Gifts of brick tea form low walls around the complex. The feeling is of witnessing a very ancient ritual, from a time when nature was actively worshipped. Given its isolated setting, the scene is most incongruous, especially if one approaches from the southwest returning from the South Gobi. Coming from this direction, the granite outcrops are even more spectacular and monumental, some appearing as ancient fortresses, before suddenly coming upon that crowded scene in the valley below.

Further cross-country and southwest of Mother Rock is the granite country of **Dundgov**, or **Middle Gobi**, aimag. The landscape enroute is a mixture of rocky outcrops and rolling steppe with distant vistas, a pleasant microcosm of Mongolia. Rising out of the desolate-looking and dusty plains some 60 kilometres (37 miles) northwest of the aimag centre of **Mandalgov** is **Baga Gazriyn Chuluu**, a fascinating granite formation with legends dating back to Chinggis Khaan's day, when he supposedly grazed his horses here. (Zanabazar also hid out here during the war with the western Oirads.) Argali sheep live up in the scrub-covered rugged hills.

The range's highest peak, **Baga Gazriyn Uul**, (1,768 metres or 5,800 feet) takes about five hours to climb. Surrounded by unusual rock formations is a cave with an underground lake. There are also mineral springs and several pleasant ger camps nearby. The sacred nature of these mountains is clear from the many *ovoo* dotting its high points. Hidden away in a tiny valley are the remains of a lovely Buddhist monastery, its protective wall still standing and the ruins inside shaded by poplar trees. (The area also makes a pleasant stop returning to UB on the main road from the South Gobi.)

West of Ulaanbaatar and past the Przewalski's horses (*takhi*) of Hustain Nuruu Reserve (see Ulaanbaatar, page 202), the all-paved **Millennium Road** heads southwest across the wide, lush valley of the Tuul River and up into low hill country. Past the small *sum* (district) centre of **Rashaant**, the valley ahead is crossed by a massive line of sand dunes known as the **Bayangobi**. This pocket-sized region offers a rare combination of forested mountains and desert landscape, even nature and religion, within a very small area. On the southern side of the valley is a large red granite massif known as **Hogno Han Uul**, or **Hungnukhaan**, which rises sharply above the surrounding steppe. Hidden among the rocky ridges and cliffs of its southern slope are the ruins of two temples built by Mongolia's first theocratic leader Zanabazar in the late 17th century and later destroyed in the war with the Oirads when the eastern Mongolians turned to the Manchus for protection (see History, page 82).

Known as the **Hogno Tarnyn Khiid**, also Uvgun Temple, the complex included a lower monastery on the valley floor and a second, more important one higher up the valley, supposedly a scaled-down version of the famous Potala Palace in Tibet's capital of Lhasa. Only the lower one was rebuilt but was itself demolished by the Communists in the 1930s and only reopened in 1994. Many legends surround the site, including a portal into the fabled realm of Shambhala where everyone lives in peace. (Don Croner's *Guidebook to Locales Connected with the Life of Zanabazar*, widely available in UB, is an excellent travelling companion for this and other locations in the region, including the Amarbayasgalant Monastery described below.)

Not far away is **Bat Khan Uul**, or Mt Batkhaan, which is a 218-square-kilometre (84-square-mile) nature reserve protecting wildlife, sand dunes and historic relics. Interestingly in this semi-desert region, the mountain includes remnants of once more lush forests which are home to wolves, deer and lynx, and its springs feed into streams both north and south of the mountain.

Following spread: Only three hours west of the capital, a climb up the Mongol Els provides spectacular views of the surrounding rugged and largely empty landscape (Carl Robinson).

There are several tourist ger camps in the area, which is also called **Mongol Els** (Dunes). Located only 270 kilometres (168 miles) west of the capital, an early arrival assures plenty of time for lunch and an afternoon scamper up into the dunes with spectacular views out over the landscape with more exploration the next morning. The area is a pleasant stopover enroute to the ancient capital of Harhorin, or Karakorum (see The Orhon Valley, page 428), which lies only another 50 kilometres (30 miles) to the west, or for those travelling to the Bayanhongor Gobi (see The Gobi, page 318).

To the north of Ulaanbaatar up towards the Russian border is a fascinatingly different region. As incongruous as it sounds, this is Mongolia's industrial and agricultural heartland. After wandering around more remote parts of the country, entering this landscape of all-paved roads, modern cities, busy rail lines, billowing smokestacks and huge open-cut mines can be a bit of a "culture shock". Many visitors pass through this region on the Trans-Mongolian train. Local trains also run from the capital.

Coming from the south through deserted desert and steppe and through UB, train travellers will certainly notice the dramatic contrast. But from the other direction, the region must look like an extension of Russia itself. The dominant feature here is the watershed for all rivers heading north into Russia and its famous **Lake Baikal**, only 150 kilometres (93 miles) from the border.

Travelling by road out past Ulaanbaatar's outer suburbs, the landscape is "mountain steppe" with larch and birch growing on northern slopes and grassland on southern slopes and in river valleys, actually the western foothills of the Hentii range (see page 219). Secondary roads lead to a string of tourist ger camps and many well-to-do Mongolians also have weekend homes here. East of the road, though not visible from it, lies the massive open-pit **Boroo Gold Mine**, a big revenue earner for Mongolia.

After clearing a pass through the range, the road descends into a valley, crosses the **Haraa River** at **Bayangol** and meets up with the rail line, which follows a lower route up from UB. Instantly noticeable are the number of solid masonry buildings – in quite varied condition – and very few gers. The valley soon broadens into rolling steppe, but instead of the familiar grassland seen elsewhere in Mongolia, vast fields of wheat stretch to the horizon. With such a short growing season, early summer is a busy time as solitary Russian-built tractors plough up vast fields for planting, dwarfed by the surrounding vastness. The bright green fields look amazingly lush.

A legacy from Soviet days, when Stalin ordered the Mongolians to boost their wheat production to an impossible 200 million tons a year, the region now produces a more modest 40 percent of the country's grain, its former collective farms now run as private enterprises. Huge grain silos dot the countryside and several distilleries produce vodka, including the popular Haraa Brand named after the river. (Written *Xapaa* in Cyrillic, it'll certainly "zap 'ya" after a few too many!)

This northern region encompasses the main aimag of **Selenge,** named after the major river from the Hovsgol region which flows on into Russia, and also includes the two smaller aimags hived off to create the large industrial and mining towns of Darhan and Erdenet and their immediate surrounds. Sited on the eastern bank of the Haraa River and 220 kilometres (137 miles) from the capital, Darhan's skyline of billowing smokestacks can be seen for miles, but on closer inspection is a surprisingly neat and modern town with office buildings, hotels, restaurants and shops.

Once the site of the infamous Soviet-run **Gulag 505**, which held Russians who'd fought alongside the Nazis during World War II, and who were later used to build the Trans-Mongolian Railway, **Darhan** is Mongolia's third largest city with a population of 63,000 residents. Created in 1967, the city is a large industrial centre for steel processing, building materials, carpet manufacturing, and leather and food processing. A rail line connects the city to a coalmine at Sharyn Gol to the southeast. The best view is from the stupa-topped hill that separates the town into residential and industrial districts. Past the busy rail line, a wide valley stretches west to the famous **Orhon River** and a mountain range beyond. From here, the crossing point of **Altanbulag** on the Russian border, closed to foreign tourists, is only 122 kilometres (76 miles) to the north, just past the frontier agricultural town of **Suhbaatar,** named after the 1921 hero who, with Soviet help, led his troops south to liberate the capital. The Orhon River, its waters swollen by those of UB's Tuul, the Haraa and many others, joins the **Selenge River** just below the border and flows north into Lake Baikal.

Located another 170 kilometres (106 miles) across this valley to the west-southwest of Darhan, **Erdenet** is Mongolia's second largest city (population 120,000) and the site of the country's largest copper mine and smelter, a development dating back to Soviet days. (Today, the mine's Russian share is privatised but not that of the Mongolian government, an interesting twist.) Established in 1973, Erdenet is a well laid out and modern city with all the usual amenities, plus Mongolia's largest indoor sports arena – a source of much local pride. With a joint workforce of Russians and Mongolians and a modernised smelter, the town exudes a real air of prosperity. Most of its 15 million tons of ore is shipped to Russia. A paved road and separate rail line link the town with Darhan.

But unless you're keen to do a bit of religious conversion (such as the intense group of Mormon missionaries we met in a restaurant in Darhan), these industrial centres are

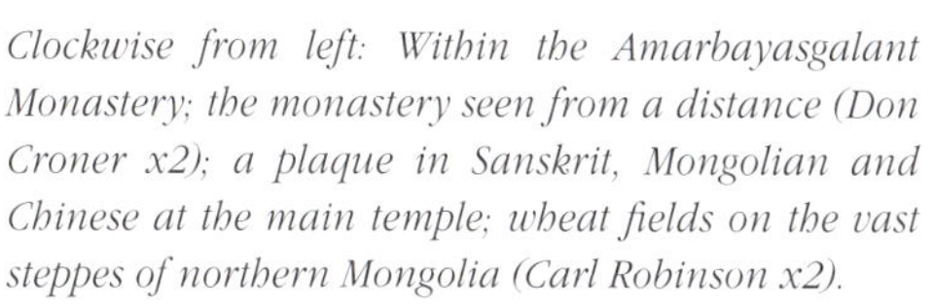

Clockwise from left: Within the Amarbayasgalant Monastery; the monastery seen from a distance (Don Croner x2); a plaque in Sanskrit, Mongolian and Chinese at the main temple; wheat fields on the vast steppes of northern Mongolia (Carl Robinson x2).

barely worth the trip. However, the surrounding countryside of broad river valleys, low hills and distant ranges – all lushly green in early summer – is certainly lovely. Even the extent and method of wheat cultivation is fascinating (unusually, this is steppe with no domesticated animals).

Just west of Darhan, the historic Orhon River nears the end of its long journey from the Hangai Mountains in the southwest, passing the ancient Mongol capital of Harhorin (Karakorum) on the way. At a stall next to the modern concrete bridge over the river, entrepreneurial locals sell an assortment of smoked fish, while others fish in the waters below. (It makes a refreshing change to cross a river without having to ford it.) West of the river, the countryside turns more mountainous but the valley floors are still planted with wheat.

The main destination up here – and the reason why most people visit this region – is the famous **Amarbayasgalant Monastery**, regarded as one of the four most important such Buddhist institutions in Mongolia. In both its setting and architecture, this remote monastery is arguably the loveliest in the country. About one hour up a dirt track off the main road to Erdenet, past lovely flower-drenched, grass-covered hills, the monastery is set hard up against a tree-covered range with streams flowing down into the wide **Even River Valley,** home to dozens of nomad families and their herds, as well as several tourist ger camps. The monastery is a favourite overnight stop for travellers heading west through Bulgan aimag to Lake Hovsgol. Unfortunately, the paved road ends at Erdenet and the run to Moron is widely regarded as the worst road in the country.

Amarbayasgalant – which translates as "peaceful happiness" – was built by the second Qing Emperor Yongzheng to house the remains of Mongolia's First Bogd Gegeen or theocratic leader, Zanabazar, who had capitulated eastern Mongolia to Yongzheng's father in 1636 and later died in exile in Beijing (see History, page 82). Built in Chinese style in the early 1730s using imported craftsmen, the monastery is certainly different and more unitary than any other in Mongolia (the main temple was built without using a single nail). There is a particularly nice view from the hilltop just north of the monastery.

Surrounded by a wall, the buildings are set in a north-south axis around the main two-storey **Tsogchin Dugan**, or main temple. Pavilions, courtyards and smaller temples are set methodically around the grounds. Zanabazar's remains were moved into one of the temples in 1779, 56 years after his death, and were later joined by those of the Fourth Bogd Gegeen in 1813. By the early 1890s, Amarbayasgalant was one of the most important pilgrimage sites in Mongolia, visited by the ruling Buddhist leaders of the day. In the early 1900s, over 8,000 monks lived at the monastery.

Rowing to the Arctic Ocean

Looking for a new challenge after rafting down South America's mighty Amazon River from source to sea, Australian adventurer Ben Kozel chose Siberia's Yenisey (Yenisei) River, which begins in Mongolia's remote Hangai Mountains and flows north 5,540 kilometres (3,442 miles) to the Arctic Ocean. This little-known river is the second longest in Asia, after China's mighty Yangtze, and the fifth longest in the world. Travelling in 2001 with two Canadians, his partner from the Amazon trip Colin Angus and newcomer Remy Quinter, they were joined in Russia by Australian Tim Cope, who later rode a horse from Mongolia to Hungary. As told in *Five Months in a Leaky Boat*, here are some of his impressions floating through north-central Mongolia down the Yenisey's source and major tributary, the Ider River, shortly before near-disaster struck the crew.

Carcass Canyon harboured more than just rapids. A stupendous spectacle greeted our eyes when we emerged from the tents next morning, a backdrop that deserved partial credit for the recent surge in my heart rate. Pale and bright green mosses and lichens were scattered over the volcano-born rock, resulting in a range of colour from beige to charcoal black. Grass tussocks, herbs and wildflowers sprouted from the numerous nooks and crannies as fissures, cracks and gullies carved downwards from the tortured heights. All along the canyon's rim, spires merged with contorted protrusions, their silhouettes lending the canyon an enchanted air.

Not all the beauty was out of reach, however. Our beach campsite ranked on a par with the prettiest and cosiest I'd known on the Apurimac River in the upper Amazon. As in South America, much of my delight stemmed from an awareness that few, if any, other human feet had trodden there before us. The beach was reminiscent of an amphitheatre, comprising tiered levels of sand, fringed by boulders and rocky outcrops. Waves lapped at the shore incessantly, sourced from the mayhem at the base of a nearby cascade.

Past the boulders a modestly angled slope led up to the base of an escarpment; some of it wooded with birch and a variety of pine bearing brilliant foliage, the rest a lush green meadow sprinkled with wildflowers. Over the past few

Top: Above the entrance to Tsogchin Dugan in the Amarbayasgalant Monastery, young novice monks issue the call to prayer with conch shells. Bottom: Summer flowers carpet the steppe nearby (Carl Robinson x2).

days, the temperature had increased dramatically. The night just gone had been the warmest in Mongolia so far and now it seemed that this riverland had woken fully after many months of torpor.

Though the rapids we tackled that morning were the biggest to date by far, the raft and I rode them all without incident. Similarly, neither kayaker experienced any difficulty.

After a half-day's travel from Carcass Canyon, the landscape reverted to the way it had been upstream of Orgil. The shift back occurred just as abruptly, highlighting the canyon's status as a geological anomaly, a violent blip on an otherwise gracefully curving expanse of steppe. I felt privileged to have witnessed something so different from the bulk of the Mongolian landscape. None of us had expected to encounter anything like the spectacular Carcass Canyon, not before arrival in the country and especially not after travelling so long through terrain that had not given the vaguest hint of the canyon's existence.

After the confines of Carcass Canyon, Mongolia's great open spaces overwhelmed me more than ever. My purest impression of Mongolia was of a vastness, remote and partially forgotten by time. Combined with what I'd already known about the place, it struck me now as like an enormous unfenced grazing paddock, a land of animal herds and men on horseback, living a lifestyle so ancient that the country's cultural traditions are considered to be the least changed out of any country over the past millennium. There aren't any boundaries to speak of, at least not until you travel far enough to reach the border with either Russia or China, and then it is only an imaginary line drawn through the empty landscape.

Late in the afternoon of our thirteenth day on the Ider, we arrived at its confluence with the Moron River. Having flowed generally from the northwest, the Moron (which is actually pronounced Mu'run) heads south over its final few kilometres and collides with the Ider more or less head on. The resultant fusion of these two water flows is squeezed out in an easterly direction and henceforth is known as the Selenga [Selenge] River.

The sense of milestone, however, was almost completely drowned out by the dramatic nature of the merger. The Moron was in major flood, spewing out a thunderous torrent of milky-brown water. As a consequence, the banks of the Selenga were struggling to contain their inheritance.

In the wink of an eye, the river channel width doubled to over 100 metres. Our speed tripled. We went from serenely gliding along to bouncing along on a succession of standing waves up to one metre in height. The water seemed like a caged beast, determined to break free of its chains and swipe a claw. Whole trees, ripped from the earth somewhere upstream, surged beside us at a frightening pace. By the shore, vegetation debris had accumulated to form lethal snags.

Ben Kozel, Five Months in a Leaky Boat, *2003*

During the anti-Buddhist purges of the 1930s, many of Amarbayasgalant's temples were ransacked of their relics and several buildings destroyed. The Communist troops also removed the remains of the two Buddhist leaders from their vaults and burned them in a huge bonfire.

But the main temple complex was not destroyed and finally reopened as a fully functioning monastery in 1993. The pilgrims have returned and the monastery is again the site of important Buddhist gatherings. Every morning, young novices stand on the first-floor balcony above the main temple and blow conch shells to mark the start of services. Guided by young monks, tourists can visit the main temple, smaller temples and the two tombs. But, as a functioning monastery, visitors are not allowed into the innermost temple. A couple of kilometres west of the complex is the newly built **Dorje Shugden Temple** with its eight stupas honouring Mongolia's eight bogd gegeens, the last of whom died in 1924.

Top: The Onon River Valley is reputed to be Chinggis Khaan's birthplace (Carl Robinson).
Above: Traditional dress remains popular, revealing Mongolians' strong cultural roots (Leo Murray).

THE HENTII: CHINGGIS KHAAN'S HOMELAND

The **Hentii Mountain Range** rises out of the Terelj National Park (see page 200) northeast of Ulaanbaatar and runs some 200 kilometres (125 miles) across the Russian border, where it is the traditional homeland of the Siberian Buriats and long-time allies of the Mongolians. The Hentii is an ancient and heavily eroded range formed by different geological forces than Mongolia's other two major mountains chains, the Hangai and the Altai in the western half of the country. Unlike those two even grander ranges, which run in a southeast direction, the Hentii sprawls northeasterly. With an average elevation of 2,000 metres (6,562 feet), and dominated by the mighty bulk of sacred **Burkhan Khaldun** and its rugged surrounding gorges and valleys, the mighty Hentii gives rise to three of Mongolia's most famous rivers. Being also the birthplace of Chinggis Khaan, or Temujin, this region is – quite literally – the Heartland of Mongolia.

The Hentii Mountains from 2,067-metre Ikh Gazriyn, just east of Burkhan Khaldun (Don Croner).

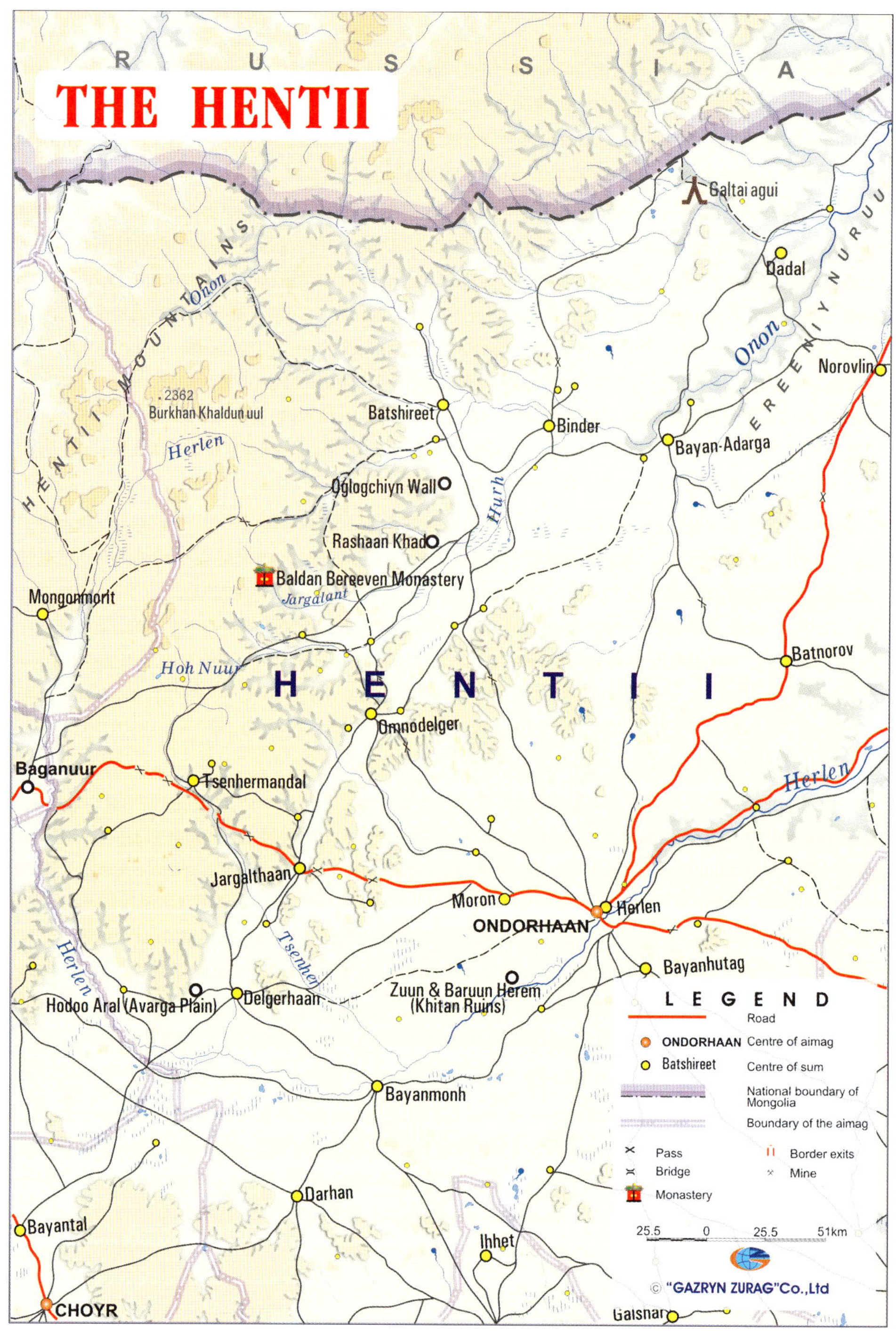
THE HENTII
RUSSIA
HENTII
HENTII MOUNTAINS
EREENIYN NURUU
Galtai agui
Dadal
Onon
Norovlin
Batshireet
Binder
Bayan-Adarga
2362
Burkhan Khaldun uul
Herlen
Oglogchiyn Wall
Rashaan Khad
Hurh
Baldan Bereeven Monastery
Jargalant
Mongonmorit
Hoh Nuur
Batnorov
Omnodelger
Baganuur
Tsenhermandal
Jargalthaan
Moron
ONDORHAAN
Herlen
Tsenher
Bayanhutag
Hodoo Aral (Avarga Plain)
Delgerhaan
Zuun & Baruun Herem
(Khitan Ruins)
Bayanmonh
Darhan
Bayantal
Ihhet
CHOYR
Galshar
LEGEND
Road
ONDORHAAN Centre of aimag
Batshireet Centre of sum
National boundary of Mongolia
Boundary of the aimag
Pass
Bridge
Monastery
Border exits
Mine
25.5 0 25.5 51km
© "GAZRYN ZURAG"Co.,Ltd

lakes offering a cosy and welcoming feeling of enclosure. But as elsewhere, there are very few people, lots of domesticated animals and fascinating wildlife, especially the comical-looking marmots and speedy ground squirrels. Away from the hustle and bustle of the capital, the entrancing tranquillity of the Hentii – even as the tourism infrastructure still develops – is only a few hours away.

For visitors, the Hentii makes a great first "extended trip" out of Ulaanbaatar (apparently the fishing's not bad either). Those not all that knowledgeable of Mongolian history will find a visit stimulating and provide mental images for further reading; for those already "read-up" on the origins of the Mongol Empire and today's Mongolia, seeing the reality of this region is absolutely fascinating – and so much more than you've pictured. To enrich your visit, do obtain a knowledgeable guide and make a point of reading John Man's seminal *Genghis Khan – Life, Death and Resurrection* which brings this whole region to life, even if you don't end up, like him, searching for the Great Khaan's grave atop Burkhan Khaldun. (Don Croner's blog at www.doncroner.net marvellously details the history through his own horse treks around this lovely region.)

The Millennium Road heads through the southern foothills of the Hentii Mountains (Carl Robinson).

From Ulaanbaatar, the paved **Millennium Road** heads east past the turnoff to Terelj with the Hentii range on the left and grassy steppe undulating off to the right. About an hour or 54 kilometres (34 miles) from the capital, you'll come over a crest and suddenly spot one of the strangest sights in today's Mongolia – a huge stainless-steel statue of Chinggis Khaan on a horse standing on a round concrete columned pedestal. The famous leader looks east and holds a golden crop in his right hand. Opened only in 2008, the **Chinggis Khaan Statue Complex** on the banks of the Tuul River was the creation of a local tourism company, the Genco Travel Bureau, which also owns UB's Bayangol Hotel (a smaller version of the statue sits outside its main entrance).

The massive, shiny statue certainly comes as a surprise and will no doubt become a popular tourist attraction, especially with the locals. The top of the statue stands 50 metres (164 feet) above the ground and from the restaurant, souvenir shop and amusement area below, visitors can ascend for a view of the surrounding countryside through the horse's head. Costing over US$50 million and planned to include a large tourist ger camp, the project clearly reflects the national pride, ambition and dreams of Mongolia's modern – and often still-young – entrepreneurs. (Genco also runs **13th Century National Park,** a replica medieval encampment with overnight accommodation some 40 kilometres (25 miles) to the southeast, and plans a spa and golf resort.)

Whatever your own reaction to the statue, you are now definitely in Chinggis Khaan Country. Not much further along, an unsealed road heads 100 kilometres (62 miles) north to the *sum* or district centre of **Mongonmorit**, the kick-off point for travel up to the sacred mountain of Burkhan Khaldun. Depending on road conditions, travel is up the **Herlen River Valley** by 4WD to the base of the mountain and then a 653-metre (2,144-foot) climb on foot, but it is preferable to make the entire journey by horse from the town. (The area can also be reached via the coal-mining town of **Baganuur** farther down the main road.) As the mountain is inside the **Khan Hentii Strictly Protected Area,** a permit is required and the journey takes a full day but also makes a pleasant overnight camping trip. By a tradition still widely respected, women are not allowed to climb to the summit and wait below at **Elegtseg Lake,** also the site of a present-day campground. (Non-Mongolian women and local female guides are exempt from this ban.)

With an elevation of 2,362 metres (7,750 feet), **Burkhan Khaldun** is where, according to legend, Chinggis Khaan prayed before going into battle and also where he is reputedly buried – although no grave has ever been found (see History, page 70.) Long a place of pilgrimage, a Buddhist temple once stood at the base of the mountain, but was destroyed in internecine fighting before the Manchu period; a second but smaller one was further

Right: A gigantic stainless-steel statue of Chinggis Khaan on a horse marks the entrance to the homeland of Mongolia's founding father (Carl Robinson). Top right: Up close, the statue is an impressive sight, showing Chinggis holding a golden crop (Chinneeb, licensed under Creative Commons ShareAlike 3.0).

up the mountain – this one was demolished by the Communists in the 1930s. With a growing number of pilgrims visiting the mountain since 1990, huge rock and pine *ovoo* bedecked in blue *hadag* or prayer scarves and piled high with gifts of tea, alcohol, dairy products and money now mark these two locations, as well as on the so-called **Black Crown** on the summit itself. (There is also a bronze plaque with a likeness of Chinggis Khaan, as on the cover of Jon Man's book.) Covered in snow for most of the year, in summer the saddle-shaped summit is a sprawl of black rocks, some seemingly in man-made patterns. But if the Great Conqueror is actually buried

A herdsman from Tov aimag rests at the ovoo *on the summit of Burkhan Khaldun (Don Croner).*

here, Mongolians prefer the simple mystery of an unmarked grave. For those not keen for a climb, a heady "glimpse" of this famous mountain's bald top is possible from the **Herlen Valley** below.

What could be called the Chinggis Khaan Heritage Trail leads for about 200 kilometres (125 miles) along a string of valleys at the base of the Hentii from the Herlen River below Mongonmorit to Dadal near the Russian border in the northeast. The day-long drive – all on dirt tracks – takes in not just sites associated with Chinggis Khaan's early life but those from the pre-Mongol period too. Interestingly, little physically remains from the Great Conqueror's days, only locations where important events took place. So, as one travels slowly along, it is intriguing to recall that the same older relics – and the untouched countryside – to be found in the region were all there when young Temujin was growing up, consolidating his power and becoming a tribal leader on the road to global domination.

The locations and stories quickly draw you in, such as **Burgi Ergi** on the Herlen River where Temujin hid after the dreaded Merkits kidnapped his young bride, Borte. (His father

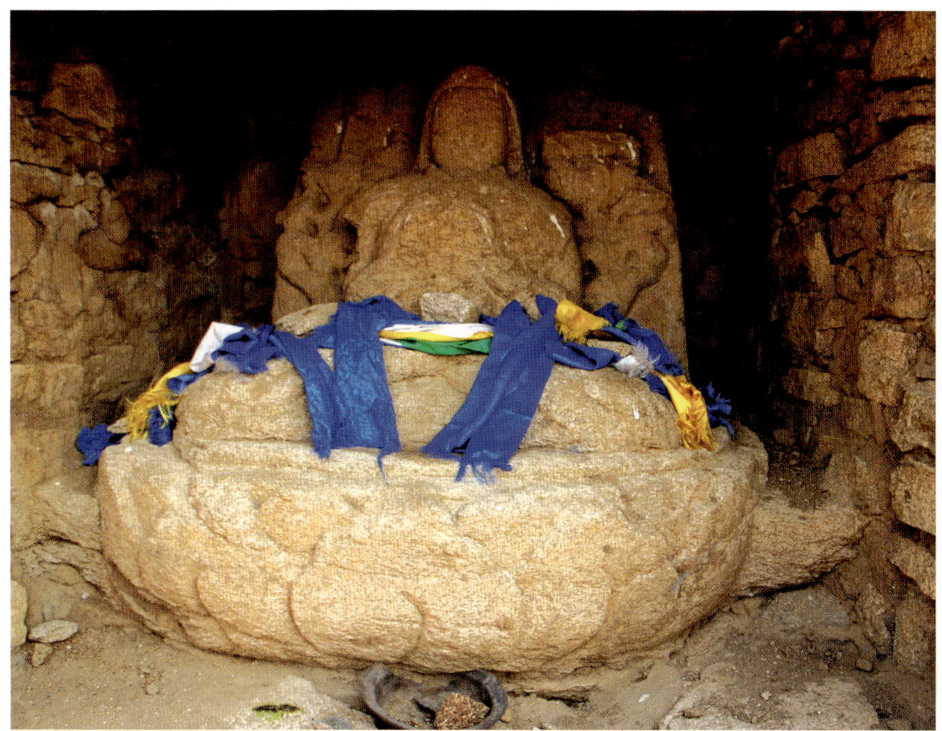

Badly damaged in the Stalinist purges, the Buddha of the Future is worshipped again at Baldan Bereeven Monastery (Carl Robinson).

Yesugei had kidnapped his own wife, Temujin's mother, from the same tribe so vengeance was doubtless a factor.) Further east up a shallow valley is **Hoh Nuur** (also Khokh Nuur), or the **Blue Lake of Black Heart Mountain**, where Temujin also hid, lost his horses to rustlers, settled down with Borte and – most importantly – was later proclaimed khan, or leader, of the Hamag Tribe. It is widely believed that he was also proclaimed leader of the Mongols here in 1206. Surrounded by low hills, the circular-shaped lake is a lovely spot but has lost its pristine tranquillity to tourism, and even private development, in recent years. Not all stories come from *The Secret History of the Mongols*, of course, and as Don Croner notes, local legends have created many "Chinggis Slept Here" spots along the route – such as a flat rock formation called **Chinggis Khaan's Table** and a Turkic-era grave where Temujin set up his ger and perched his pots. There are also modern stories to tell.

Streams flow down small valleys from the gentle larch-covered foothills, forming more small lakes – some with ger camps – such as **Hangal Nuur** where a Communist-era Young Pioneer Camp lies in total ruins, no doubt waiting for an ambitious entrepreneur to revive it. (With children dressed in red scarves, white shirts and blue shorts, the compulsory camps were one of life's summertime rituals in the old days and, like the old collective farms, many now lie derelict.) Not much further along, over a low ridge are the more poignant ruins of what was once the largest Buddhist monastery in eastern Mongolia. If this is your first experience of the devastation of the anti-Buddhist purges of the 1930s, you will probably be shocked by the destruction in such a beautiful natural setting.

First established in 1784, the **Baldan Bereeven Monastery** once boasted 8,000 monks with buildings made of local stone and wood, the most prominent a large, two-storey, thick-walled Tibetan-style temple, which now lies in ruins, totally destroyed

Left: Defiantly surviving the anti-Buddhist purges of the 1930s which obliterated the adjoining Baldan Bereeven Monastery is Mongolia's national symbol, the Soyombo, now repainted. Right: Chinggis Khaan would have seen this deer stone as a child growing up in nearby Jargalant Valley (Carl Robinson x2).

during the purges. Round stone platforms mark where the gers of the monks once stood. A simple wooden temple with its prayer wheels made from discarded fuel drums marks the monastery's post-1990 revival. Attempts at rebuilding the main temple are under way. Further up the hill are two smaller, more or less intact temples dating from before the monastery's creation. Thankfully not everything was destroyed: a majestic old pine, planted when the monastery was opened and known as the **Wish Granting Tree,** stands draped in hadag. The grounds are dotted with defaced statuary and in a grotto above one set of ruins is a faceless and one-armed figure of Maitreya, the Buddha of the Future.

But defiantly above this stands the symbol of Mongolia's endurance over recent centuries, a bullet-scarred *soyombo* engraved by a monk in the late 18th century but which the Communists could not destroy and is now vividly repainted. Another surviving feature is the **Mother Cave**, a shallow cave that believers crawl through and emerge cleansed of their sins.

Temples are always auspiciously located, of course, and nearby the lovely **Jargalant River** emerges out of the hills and flows down a widening valley to **Ayl Hargana,** an ancient pre-Mongol site where deer stelae date from the Bronze Age and stone graves from the Turkic period. Temujin played here as a youngster and later mustered his forces, and those from the Kereits further west, to attack the Merkits and rescue his wife. Protected by the surrounding hills, it's also easy to picture how Temujin and his followers settled here after dramatically splitting from his childhood friend and blood brother Jamuha. (The region is also full of locations where the two engaged in fierce battles for early control of the Mongols.) Farther downstream, the Jargalant meets the wider **Hurh River** in a lush but swampy valley which flows northeast to the Onon River. This entire region is the heartland of the Mongols.

On a prominent ridgeline to the west overlooking the valley – blasted by chilling spring winds and smoky haze from Siberian forest fires during my visit – is one of Mongolia's most ancient sites of human presence, and all the more important for its historic continuity: **Rashaan Khad.** Next to a huge ovoo is what appears at first as a mere jumble of eroded rocks. But this was actually an important sacred site for tribes over a period of thousands of years, with remains from the Upper Palaeolithic period (40,000–10,000 years ago) through medieval times.

Carvings and paintings etched into the sandy-coloured rock depict animals and humans, several hundred ancient tribal seals and a score of scripts in Turkic, Khitan, Arab-Persian, Chinese, Tibetan and Mongolian languages. *The Secret History of the Mongols* records

Left: With a continuous history stretching back to Palaeolithic times, Rashaan Khad is one of Mongolia's most important sacred sites with carvings, paintings and ancient scripts such as this in ancient Tibetan (Carl Robinson).

Temujin passing this way when he was on the run from the Taychuuds who'd kidnapped him earlier. Archaeological excavations over the years have discovered over 5,000 stone tools around the site. A natural spring once flowed from the rocks into a wading pool-sized depression, but less so in recent times. Further evidence of human habitation are Stone Age carvings and tools on a nearby hill, and a deer stele and grave complex on the valley floor below, some of the many you'll find in this region.

Not far to the west, up a valley with its slopes covered in pine forests, are the remains of a rather unusual structure called the **Oglogchiyn Wall**, also known as the **Almsgiver's Wall.** Built halfway up a hillside and made of stacked rocks three metres (10 feet) high and 2.5 metres (eight feet) wide, the wall is three kilometres (1.8 miles) long and has doors on its northern and southern sides. No evidence of buildings has been found inside the wall and most experts believe this was a fort during the Khitan period (947–1125). Its presence was certainly known in Temujin's day, when he hid here after escaping from his kidnappers. As John Man explains, both a Japanese team in the early 1990s and an American team in 2001 tried – in vain – to link Chinggis Khaan's grave to the site. Both expeditions were extremely controversial and aroused much public anger. A team financed by American entrepreneur Maury Kravitz found nothing conclusive and left behind a suitably cryptic sign at the site reading, "Place of the Great Ones". Their former camp, mostly wooden cabins, now provides tourist accommodation.

Further up the main valley, the Hurh joins the wide waters of the **Onon River** just southeast of the typically nondescript sum centre of **Binder.** Originating on the northern side of Burkhan Khaldun, the river – *Onon Gol* – is believed to be the origin of the word "Mongol" and is certainly surrounded by many legends, particularly as the birthplace of Chinggis Khaan. Coming out of the Hentii mountains, the river squeezes past an area famous for its hot and medicinal springs – plus anthropomorphic "man stones" (*balbal*) and Turkic graves from pre-Mongol times – and then broadens across meadows into several channels across a wide valley, narrowing again near Binder. But just where the famous World Conqueror was born remains in some dispute. Based on the words of *The Secret History of the Mongols* that Temujin was born at Terguun Onon, or a section of the river just above the Huhr, the edge certainly goes to today's Binder, and a memorial to this claim stands just south of the town. (Dadal, further northeast, also claims the title.)

With a length of 818 kilometres (508 miles), the Onon River passes into Russia, joining the Amur River and eventually reaching the Pacific Ocean. Swollen by the Hurh and other tributaries below Binder, the Onon carves sharp cliff faces across more level countryside as it flows northeast toward the border, narrowing briefly to cut its way majestically through the rugged **Ereeniy Range** just south of Dadal. For those interested in fishing, four salmonids inhabit its waters – lenok, grayling, taimen and the endemic Onon trout – plus the Amur pike. Kayaking and canoeing tours are also available.

Just getting across the Onon River at Binder can be an adventure as there's no bridge, requiring a very careful ford instead. Another alternative, used by motorcycles and smaller vehicles, is to "piggy-back" across on the back of a Russian-made 4WD truck. Then comes the final run – usually late in the day – to a real touch of Siberia around Dadal in the far northeast corner of Hentii aimag. Heading away from the river and with few physical features other than steadily rising grass-covered hills, the perfectly straight power poles alongside the road – electricity from Russia – are mesmerising as they lead you there.

Finally, you pass over a crest into an enchanted forest of Siberian pine and white-barked birch – and into the Lumberjack Capital of Mongolia. Just give them a sharp axe and they'll do the rest, it's said around here. All the buildings are made of timber with barely a ger in sight. Brand-new log cabins, including a disco bar with an outhouse in front, give the town a real air of prosperity. Log cabins in the tourist camps are warmed by huge wood-fired stoves, while lace curtains provide a Russian touch and hearty Mongolian meals really hit the spot.

The sum centre of **Dadal** is one of the most attractive in Mongolia and also makes a strong claim on the Chinggis Khaan heritage. While the town may be way up near today's Russian border, do recall that Mongol territory traditionally stretched all the way over to Lake Baikal. (Their close cousins, the Buriats, live right next door in Siberia and dominate the Mongolian side too.) Most dramatically from more recent times, Dadal is where a gutsy Communist Party Central Committee member named Tomor Ochir built a 10-metre (33-foot) monument to mark the 800th anniversary of Chinggis Khaan's birth in 1962. He'd wanted to counter Chinese attempts to co-opt nationalist sentiment at the time with the building of a "mausoleum" in Inner Mongolia. But with the Sino-Soviet dispute under way, Moscow hardly took kindly to such unideological behaviour in praise of this "reactionary" who'd certainly caused a bit of havoc in the Russian heartland in his day. Forced out of the Party, Ochir was exiled to an aimag museum and mysteriously murdered in 1985. But for whatever reason, the whitewashed concrete monument was never demolished and survived into the post-Communist period.

Built in the shape of a mountain peak, the **Monument to Chinggis Khaan** shows his portrait with his horsehair banner behind him. An inscription pointedly in Old Mongolian, not Cyrillic, reads: "I have exhausted myself to unite my people. If my body should suffer, so be it! But do not let my people fall into confusion." (Very cleverly chosen words by the "subversive" Tomor Ochir.) Located on the grounds of the tourist camp at **Gurvan Nuur** just east of town, the monument overlooks what's called **Spleen Lake** in reference to Temujin's mother preparing soup from the spleen of a white horse just before giving birth. Not far away is a small spring, **Khajuu Bulag,** from which Temujin supposedly drank and a hilltop called **Deluun Boldog** where locals believe he was born. A stone monument marks the 750th anniversary of the writing of *The Secret History of the Mongols*. (The more accepted site at Binder has the same name.)

With pine forests and grasslands covering the surrounding hills and gentle streams flowing down into the valley, plus all those log cabins around, the setting is definitely a more attractive birthplace than Binder. But there's no sign of the legendary Onon River although a major tributary, the Balj River, passes nearby. Dadal's stronger link to Chinggis Khaan comes from a nearby site where Temujin's wife Borte was kidnapped by the Merkits and a battlefield along the Balj where the future World Conqueror was soundly defeated by

Erected to much controversy during the Communist era, the Monument to Chinggis Khaan stands tall in Dadal (Carl Robinson).

A log cabin disco bar in Dadal, Mongolia's Lumberjack Capital on the Siberian border (Carl Robinson).

his erstwhile *anda*, or blood brother, Jamuha and took years to recover his momentum – and ultimate victory. But these little details need not distract you from what is a fascinating and lovely little corner of Mongolia.

The region is renowned for its mineral hot springs. For those interested in caves, **Galtai Agui** is located in a large national park about 70 kilometres (43 miles) northwest of Dadal and, at 80 metres (262 feet), is Mongolia's deepest. The park protects one of the few untouched examples of the transition zone between Siberian taiga and steppe. Due to its proximity to the Russian border, however, special permission is required for a visit. Nearby, **Agatsyn Gol-Altan** is a border-crossing point with Russia which, like most along Mongolia's northern border, cannot be used by foreigners.

From Dadal, another road – this one in better condition than the "Heritage Trail" above – heads southwards and crosses over the Onon River at a lovely spot where it narrows through the rugged **Ereeniy Nuruu** range. (The large modern concrete bridge is a real surprise and makes a great stop.) Further along, the land flattens out and the sum centre of **Norovlin** marks the turnoff northeast to the beginning of the vast **Ulz River Valley** (see The Great Eastern Steppe, page 250).

Following spread: Mongol hordes once mustered across the vast Avarga Plain before setting forth on campaigns of conquest (Carl Robinson).

Just to the south are the remains of what's known as **The Wall of Chinggis Khaan.** Not always easy to spot, these fortifications stretch for 600 kilometres (373 miles) through northern Hentii and Dornod aimags all the way into neighbouring China where the Manchu tribes once lived. But how old they are and what purpose they served is not clear – the nomadic Mongols and their marauding predecessors were never known for building walls and fortifications. In fact, as we know, the Chinese famously built walls to keep them out!

Passing through rolling steppe country, the road finally reaches the Hentii provincial capital, or aimag centre, of **Ondorhaan,** a pleasant enough settlement on the banks of the **Herlen River** some 330 kilometres (205 miles) east of Ulaanbaatar (the Herlen runs south from the Burkhan Khaldun area then makes a massive southwesterly loop – where Avarga, is located – before flowing roughly east-northeast.) The landscape here is flat and the river relatively wide. The neatly laid out town of 15,000 people has the usual mix of hotels, restaurants, shops, schools, hospitals and other government buildings – plus a few now-derelict Communist-era factories. There is a rebuilt Buddhist monastery and also both provincial and ethnological museums, the latter in a Qing-era palace.

A long park full of Soviet military hardware memorialises those killed in the **Battle of Halhgol** against the Japanese in early 1939. (For those unable to visit the actual battle site in far eastern Mongolia, a stop is well worthwhile.) Near the now unused airport, and certainly a bit unusual, is a large anthropomorphic balbal, or "man stone", dating from the Turkic period. After "roughing it" up in the Hentii for a couple days, the town makes a useful overnight stop – and the opportunity for a hot shower – before a full day's look at what comes next.

The paved **Millennium Road** provides a speedy trip west back to UB, but there are several points of interest along the way that get you back on the dirt. About 25 kilometres (16 miles) west of Ondorhaan south of the sum centre of **Moron** on the Herlen River's northern bank are the fascinating remnants of two fortified towns from the Khitan Period, in the same time frame as the Oglogchiyn Walls (see above).

Known as the **Zuun Herem**, or Eastern Walls, and **Baruun Herem**, or Western Walls, they are both roughly square with rammed-earth walls 7–12 metres (23–40 feet) thick and between 1.5 and three metres (5–10 feet) high, complete with gates. Excavations show pottery making, metalwork, construction and agriculture with evidence of grain and vegetable production. The reason for the two separate settlements, according to historical records, is that the second one was built to control and house upriver Mongols who'd rebelled in the early 11th century. In any case, this is the northernmost settlement established by the sedentary Khitans in the Mongolian heartland.

After the more confined spaces along the southern edge of the Hentii mountains, the valley of the Herlen River and its two main tributaries, the Tsenher and Avarga, is amazingly broad with foothills on the far horizon. The flat steppe is broken by solitary and heavily eroded ranges and even the odd swamp and lake. Here, squawking, floating and flying around a tiny lake over 1,000 kilometres (620 miles) from the nearest ocean are scores of seagulls. Conditioned over millions of years, the seagulls return every spring to an inland sea that is no longer there. (They're the biggest, fittest seagulls I've ever seen, too.) But there are only a few nomads tending their flocks and herds; the countryside is surprisingly empty as you cross the **Tsenher River**, which originates far to the north around Hoh Nuur.

The land remains flat but is slightly more elevated around **Delgerhaan,** a surprisingly neat sum centre on the banks of the **Avarga River** with its historic links back to the days of Chinggis Khaan. While the Onon River was his homeland, the **Hodoo Aral**, or **Avarga Plain**, which spreads 20 by 30 kilometres (12 by 18 miles) along the banks of the Herlen River, is where he consolidated his power. The plain is believed to be the first capital of the

A hadag-*swathed* ovoo *stands guard over the healing waters of the lake at Avarga Toson (Carl Robinson).*

Mongols and its first major population centre. (When they moved to Karakorum, today's Harhorin, this area became one of the four "hordes", or where a collection of several *tumen*, or military units of 10,000 men, was headquartered.) Backing this up are ruins found in 1969 at the archaeological site of **Avrgiin Balgas**, 12 kilometres (7.5 miles) south of the town, where remnants of what are believed to be the **Palace of Aurug** are located. Further work in the early 1990s by the Japanese team looking for Chinggis Khaan's grave found remnants of an elevated palace, columns and a Chinese-style temple which may have been built after his death. Evidence also shows craftsmen quarters, crop fields and other buildings on the site.

Also near the site is one of the first post-1990 monuments to Chinggis Khaan, a large granite block topped with his horsehair standard and the words, "My body will disappear, but our people will live on eternally". Funded by UNESCO, the **Monument to Chingghis Khaan** was erected on the 750th anniversary of *The Secret History of the Mongols* and a ceremony and Naadam was attended by over 2,000 people. (The complex also includes several royal gers with statues and portraits.) Another important connection to the Mongol Empire is at nearby **Herlen Tonoo Mountain** where in 1240 a Great Assembly, or *kuriltai* of tribal chiefs, chose Chinggis Khaan's son Ogedei as his successor.

Deer stones allowed religious and artistic expression among Mongolia's early societies (N. Bat-Erdene).

Just west of the town – and the main reason for its many tourist ger camps – are several spas with mud baths and mineral springs. Most notable is **Avarga Toson** where a huge ovoo, draped in blue hadag, overlooks the almost perfectly round lake. Swimmers indulge in its healing waters, and at the height of summer the place is absolutely packed. Similar lakes dot the surrounding plain. Without much effort, it is very easy to imagine those old days when the Mongol Horde was spread out across this lush and grassy plain with its gers, families and animals – just hanging out and taking in the waters until the next military campaign.

CULTURAL TABOOS

By *Ivana Grollova*

From its nomadic past, superstition, rigid customs and habits still dominate the lives of many Mongolians. However, a foreign visitor to today's Mongolia need not be afraid of being "dragged under the wall of a *ger* and beheaded", as allegedly happened when one violated the code of conduct during the Mongol Empire. Nowadays, it's enough for a stranger to show natural respect and interest; he or she can then turn down titbits and delicacies that are simply beyond his/her sensitivities.

Today, a foreigner's faux pas will generally be acknowledged with amused smiles – but nothing worse is likely to happen. Raw ram eyes as an appetizer or a wife offered for a night to please the guest belong more to some favourite myths about the "barbarian Mongols" spread by early Europeans. (In actual fact, even such legendary habits as wife-sharing might stem from very pragmatic reasoning, such as isolated families in remote areas instinctively fearing the dangers of degeneration. By offering their women for amusement, they may well have wanted the foreigner to enrich their own gene pool.)

In sparsely populated Mongolia, social competition was never as fierce, for instance, as in more urbanised Chinese, Japanese and Anglo-American societies. Mongolians therefore had no need to create such self-defensive clichés as permanently polite smiles, bows or superlatives, greetings and apologies. Even when foreigners are aware of this difference, however, they may be irritated when Mongolians are not ostentatious enough in their thanks and enquiries, or fail to knock on the door before entering a friend's room. The ger door was traditionally just a curtain and even nowadays stays permanently open for most of the year – so where to learn to knock on it? Similarly, Mongolians may be offended by Westerners' impertinence, albeit unintended.

Therefore, for the sake of a mutually pleasant atmosphere on your travels, it might be worth bearing in mind some basic rules so as to avoid the most flagrant cases of offensive behaviour:

Even in this land of hospitable nomads, a stranger should still not enter a ger completely unnoticed, as that would create suspicion about his intentions. Typically, the stranger attracts attention while still some distance away by yelling out, "Tie up your dogs!" (And they certainly have dogs – definitely not for cuddling!) If no one comes out to welcome him, the stranger must at least clear his throat at the front of the ger before peeping in. When crossing the threshold, even if a person is already known to the household, it is still polite to say "hello" or clear one's throat and not tiptoe inside silently. Once a visitor is called in, it is considered rude to leave for the toilet before actually entering. As a mark of respect, hats are left on but can be removed once the visitor is seated. Unrolling your sleeves down to the wrists is also polite.

Baskets, weapons and other tools, such as spades, must be left outside the ger, from an ancient tradition that only an enemy enters armed. Everyone else entrusts himself to the host's protection and goodwill, one of the most valued rules of nomadic society. Over the ages this habit has blended with a superstition that objects brought into the home for no particular reason, such as baskets or vessels, could take away wellbeing from the house or even cause death. When one returns borrowed kitchenware, for instance, one should therefore always place a small symbolic present inside, such as a few sweets, and place the item in a clearly visible spot in the kitchen or on the table.

A guest is expected to take his seat immediately where it is offered. It is not polite to walk around looking at family photos or relics on the family altar, or lean and touch the ger's two supporting posts. Neither is it polite to drink or eat other than when sitting. Guests must not interfere with the course of the meal, and passing along food or drinks from the housewife, however helpful, is considered impolite. If you pass anything to someone else, hold the object in your right hand supported with the left one below the wrist. When accepting a passed thing, both hands should be used, ideally below the giver's hands.

Once offered alcohol, it is polite to drink the entire glass or cup – or at least take a sip, especially for female guests. (One should also bear in mind that the glass will automatically be refilled three times in a row – most probably a Soviet era innovation!) A guest must never refuse offered refreshment and never make a visit too brief, at least not without some polite conversation. The traditional symbol to accompany a chat between men, the snuffbox, is received in the right palm. After taking a sniff, one returns it back only half-shut.

With food, the host himself offers morsels of cooked meat from the bowl or bids his guests to cut off bits with their knives when their turn comes. It is not appropriate to gnaw meat right off the bone; one should keep working small pieces with the knife all the time as long as the bone is not clean of meat or gristle. Fire must not be touched with a knife, nor liquids or rubbish placed on it or wood cut to pieces nearby. Leftover bones, usually shoulder blades, should be broken or chopped to break their magic power. They are used as a "magic mirror" in shamanism and it is therefore wiser not to give any otherworldly spirits the opportunity to use them against us unnoticed.

"Medals and tea are awarded, not just given," says an old Mongolian expression, illustrating the wisdom given this "common" drink. Enriched with pieces of meat or dumplings, tea may for some be the only meal during the day. When a housewife brings a bowl of tea, do not let her simply place it on the table. You should interrupt whatever you are doing, roll down your sleeves and take the bowl with both hands. Some believe their tea to be so tied to their household that they never even allow anyone to bring the teapot outside for serving.

Sacred places and sacrificial mounds, or *ovoo*, are circled in the direction of the sun, or clockwise. If your company dines outdoors, participants should pass the food or drinks in the same direction. By tradition, it is good if one slurps and smacks when eating, enjoying the meal with all your senses and as a compliment to the housewife's cooking.

It is considered impolite to lie down on a bed unless invited to do so. This might sound an odd warning, but after hours on the road and all the drinking and eating in a quite inconvenient and unusual position on the floor or in a tiny chair, one may soon feel tempted to stretch one's bones on comfortable-looking beds as the only other pieces of furniture around. When one *is* allowed to rest and take a nap, the feet should always point to the south and not the honoured northern side of the ger.

Tuesday is considered an unlucky day, and it is better not to force Mongolians to set out on a journey, start important work or even kill and disembowel a sheep on that day. Mongolians would most probably avoid doing any of these tasks if asked, or they will take them up only with the greatest unease.

Regardless of how deeply people feel their grief, Mongolians do not openly cry at a funeral. When leaving the cemetery after the ceremony, they will "purify" themselves with smoke, water, alcohol, milk or water by sipping or seemingly washing their hands, hats or scarves in them. This is a symbolic as well as practical hygienic custom going back many generations. A stranger is not expected to hypocritically persuade mourners of his or her compassion; the piety is rather expressed by silence and by avoiding uttering the late person's name out loud. For 49 days after death, nobody must visit the grave or publicly recall or celebrate the late person. According to Buddhist tradition, the deceased soul is wandering towards another reincarnation during this period and calling it back could confuse it, break its path through purification and plunge it into endless hell.

At a happier occasion, when seeing a newborn baby one should definitely not compliment the baby, as this might intrigue and attract evil spirits to call the baby's soul into the inferno. Instead, it is more appropriate to give the baby – who is called funny bad names – a small present or at least some symbolic amount of money, so that the mother does not feel offended and "the milk in her breasts does not harden". According to tradition, new mothers are considered "oversensitive" for 45 days after childbirth.

Even when meeting strangers, anyone is free to ask subtle details about children, livestock or weather. Mongolians are usually quite happy to answer and to ask their own questions in return. They are not just lonely herders grateful for news, but being still closely linked to a hunting culture, even in cities they show outstanding observational talents and peripheral vision, taking in a broad range of minute details. A "Yellow Man", or *shar khuun*, as the Mongolians call the light-haired foreigners who visit their country – regardless of how light our hair is in reality – is always a source of fascination and is warmly welcomed.

THE GREAT EASTERN STEPPE & DARIGANGA
RUSSIA
CHINA
CHINA (Inner Mongolia)
DORNOD
SUHBAATAR
CHOIBALSAN
BARUUN-URT
Onon
Baruun Tari
Zuun Tari
Soloviesk
Ereentsav
Chuluunhoroot
Hohnuur
Ulz
Deed Ulihan
Ulihan
Dashbalbar
Bayandun
Bayan-Uul
Marday
Wall of Chinggis Khaan
Norovlin
Havirga
Ar Hashaat
Dalay
Herlen
Ovdog
Bayanhoshuu
Buir nuur
Ikh Burkhant
Halhgol
Halh
Kherlen Bar Hot(Khitan Ruins)
Menengiyn tal
(Menen Steppe)
NOMROG NP
Great Hingan Range
Sangiyn Dalay
Matad
Erdenetsagaan
Bichigt
Zuun Hatavch
Hatavchiyn Havtsal
Lhachinvandad uul
1233
Shiliyn Bogd uul
1778
Dariganga
Ganga nuur
Moltsog els
Naran
Zamyn-Uud
Ereen
LEGEND
Road
Realway
BARUUN-URT Centre of aimag
Naran Centre of sum
National boundary of Mongolia
Boundary of the aimag
Pass
Bridge
Monastery
Border exits
Mine
60 0 60 120km
© "GAZRYN ZURAG"Co.,Ltd

THE GREAT EASTERN STEPPE

The word "steppe" – or *tal* – does seem a bit overused in Mongolia. Steppe refers to any area covered in grass – and that's most of the country! You'll find steppe in tight little valleys between towering mountain ranges and through undulating hill country. You'll even hear the almost contradictory "forested steppe" which actually refers to those mountains, especially in the northern regions, where trees only grow on the sunny northern slopes while their southern sides are all covered in grass. And how about "desert steppe"? But to finally drive on to the "classic steppe" of popular imagination is one of the great thrills of travelling around Mongolia. You're finally stepping out!

Stretching dead flat and wide to an unseen horizon, Mongolia's **Great Eastern Steppe** immediately conjures up images of massive human migrations and military invasions over the centuries – a mighty grassland stretching thousands of kilometres westwards to Eastern Europe. And back again, too, with Napoleon and Hitler's mighty invasions racing east across this same kind of steppe into the Russian heartland. Indeed, in a massive but little-known tank and air battle just before World War II, Japanese troops out of neighbouring Manchuria tried breaking onto the eastern end of this very steppe. The Soviets and Mongolians stopped them cold – and the Japanese were forced to shift their attention elsewhere, which led to their fateful confrontation with the Americans. Known as Mongolia's Serengeti, the steppe today is home to thousands of migrating white-tailed gazelles – while around its edges scores of rigs pump out oil for China.

Few tourists visit this fascinating part of Mongolia, which basically encompasses the province, or *aimag*, of Dornod, which means "east". Shaped like a giant capital "L" and bordering Russia to the north and China to the east, Dornod takes in the eastern part of the Hentii and its associated ranges, flattens out into undulating, grass-covered hills and then becomes vast, classic steppe. Shaped like the head of a camel, the easternmost tip of Mongolia pokes into the heavily forested **Great Hingan Range** of China's Inner Mongolia and Manchuria. The region is also renowned for its rivers, lakes, mineral hot springs, wild animals and birds, and national parks. Tourism infrastructure is still largely undeveloped, making this a more adventurous destination.

With its capital, **Choibalsan**, still named after the country's Stalinist dictator (see History, page 100) and Mongolia's fourth largest city (population 45,000), Dornod aimag is also the country's economic powerhouse – or potentially anyway – with rich deposits of coal, oil, gold, iron ore, feldspar, salt and uranium. During Mongolia's Communist period, the Soviets mined uranium at Marday in the northern part of the province, a secret operation not made public until after 1990. (A joint Canadian-Mongolian project is examining reopening the abandoned, and flooded, mine.) A Soviet-built railway, originally to defend Mongolia from a Japanese invasion in 1939, links Dornod with Russia's Trans-Siberian Railway – and China's Great Eastern, or Manchurian, Railway. Another – more modern – legacy comes from Mongolia's front-line position during the Sino-Soviet split of the 1960s and 70s when some 120,000 Russian troops squared off against the Chinese along the border. With their multistorey buildings visible far across the vast steppe, remnants of former Soviet bases lie looted and abandoned, today's Mongolians happier with the comforts of their traditional gers or wooden cabins. Perhaps these concrete relics will reopen one day as housing for mining companies – or even as five-star hotels for tourists.

Travelling directly from Ulaanbaatar, Choibalsan is 655 kilometres (407 miles) east of the capital on the **Millennium Road**, about a 12-hour drive, or 1.5 hours by scheduled flight into its civilian airport, a former Soviet airbase surrounded by sinister-looking former ammunition bunkers. Located on the **Herlen River**, the town was an important centuries-old caravan trading centre known as **Bayantumen** before it was renamed after the communist-era dictator, who was a native of the province. (Not content with that, the dreaded dictator named a *sum*, or district, centre just to the north after himself too.) Heavily industrialised, with a skyline dominated by a huge power station, the town is drab and unattractive but does offer hotel accommodation and restaurants, many full of Chinese businessmen and workers on various mining projects.

But for anyone travelling onwards along the sensitive Chinese border, a stop here is essential to obtain special permits at the imposing **Border Guard Headquarters** where new recruits, actually one-year draftees into compulsory military service, practise goose-steps in front of a statue of the Stalinist dictator. (The permits are also available in UB.) There is an above-average **Aimag Museum and Gallery** that includes material on Choibalsan and a nearby **Natural History Museum.** For those interested in military history, the **G.K. Zhukov Museum** honours the victor of the 1939 Battle of Halhgol against the Japanese (see below), who went on to become overall commander of all Soviet troops in World War II and oversee the ultimate conquest of Berlin, the Soviet Union's most famous general, or marshal.

By this point in its long journey from the Hentii range to **Dalay Nuur** (Dalay Lake) across the nearby Chinese border, the Herlen River is meandering widely across flat steppe. On its northern bank some 90 kilometres (56 miles) west of Choibalsan, best visited enroute rather than making a special trip, are the ruins of **Kherlen Bar Hot** dating from the Khitan Period (947–1125) and built at roughly the same time as the Zunn and Baruum Herem,

Top: A nomad's camel pulls a water cart home in the vast Ulz River Valley in northeast Mongolia. Above: Buriat Mongolians dominate this border region – here, two take a break along a riverbank (Carl Robinson x2).

Top: Vast herds of white-tailed gazelles can still be seen on the Great Eastern Steppe, though they can be harder to track down than in days gone by (R. Enkhbat). Above: Prosperity reflected in a new shop and truck in dusty Bayan-Uul near the Siberian border (Carl Robinson).

The rare white-naped crane finds safe haven on the Menen Steppe (Arpingstone).

Although relatively small (95 square kilometres, or 37 square miles), on an approach over hills from the west, the lake's waters are a stunning turquoise-blue and literally jump out of the surrounding flat, but still dun-coloured (in spring) landscape. Almost anywhere else in the world you would find resorts along its shores and inlets, but there isn't a ger in sight, just a few workers' cottages around the railway stop. The only signs of life are more birds and, strangely enough, herds of horses drinking the salty water. Skirting around the lake, you can spot white-tailed gazelles that often graze quite contentedly alongside the horses – but leap away at the first sign of a moving vehicle.

From here, the borders of Mongolia, Russia and China meet barely 70 kilometres (43 miles) to the northeast across the steppe. The railroad crossing into Russia at **Chuluunhoroot** is 45 kilometres (28 miles) north and China is now due east. (Mongolia's leaders hope to turn this rather remote region into a major transport hub linking northern Asia, including the Korean Peninsula, with Europe.) And you're also likely to spot at this point, high overhead, the contrails of airliners flying between Southeast Asia and North America (and checking into air traffic controllers at Choibalsan). (Another air route flies straight over UB from North Asia to Europe.) Operating only since the fall of the Communist regime in 1990, the overflights are a nice little earner for the Mongolian government.

Travelling south alongside the railway, another landmark appears across the now-rolling steppe – a grim collection of concrete buildings once part of a vast Soviet military base supporting Moscow's secret uranium mine at Marday to the west. Looking totally out of place, the three-storey buildings stand looted and abandoned – my guide advised against wandering inside as their rooms are now only used as public toilets. The few Mongolians around work for the railroad and live in neat wooden cabins along the tracks. A huge concrete bunker – protection against possible Chinese attack – and old maintenance sheds are used for storage, and horses shelter in buildings from the constant winds.

Right: Heading home after a three-day forage with his herd of horses, a nomad's long pole and rope provide a lasso for strays, or the next mount, as horses are rotated every two or three days (Carl Robinson).

Wandering around this relic of the Cold War and Sino-Soviet split feels eerie and tense – you half-expect a jeepload of armed troops to suddenly roar up and place you under arrest. And this nameless base is just one of many along this once tense border – all now in the same condition. Today, mining projects are scattered across the rolling steppe dotted with the odd salt lake, and commerce thrives across the **Havirga Port**, or crossing, into China's Inner Mongolia where the Dalay Nuur receives the waters of the Herlen River.

Special permission is required from the Mongolian Border Guard to travel across the steppe to easternmost Mongolia, along the sensitive Chinese border. As noted earlier, the region receives few foreign tourists but as that changes, procedures will surely simplify. But I don't see everyone sitting down for tea, candies and chitchat inside their high-security headquarters as we did! As my companions chatted and paperwork was completed, my eyes wandered over the large-scale military map behind the neatly uniformed, seated Border Guard sergeant that clearly showed sector-by-sector patrol zones all along the sensitive border, the Cyrillic words and abbreviations adding a sinister Soviet-era touch to proceedings. A thick UN handbook on refugee asylum was the only English-language book in the office. This was deadly serious. We were firmly warned to stay on marked roads and not stray too close to the border. In case of a breakdown or grass fire, stay with the vehicle. The manned towers – and patrols – all along the border would make sure of that. Sobering stuff, but hardly intimidating and most professional.

HUNTING "ANTELOPE" ON THE GREAT STEPPE

Regarded as the model for action-hero Indiana Jones and famed for his massive dinosaur discoveries at the Gobi's Flaming Cliffs in the early 1920s (see The Gobi, page 302), naturalist and explorer Roy Chapman Andrews already knew Mongolia from previous visits. Rumours that he was also an American spy always surrounded him, and his first visit by car to the then-capital of Urga in 1918, just as neighbouring Russia was collapsing after the Bolshevik Revolution, has some most intriguing overtones. Gathering scientific specimens aside, Andrews was also a keen hunter, as he relates in his book *Across Mongolian Plains*. (The animals he calls antelopes are Mongolian or white-tailed gazelles, now a protected species. Visitors fortunate enough to see them in their thousands on the Great Eastern Steppe will certainly vouch for the same crazy "cross your bows" behaviour noted by Andrews.)

Thus far the trail had not been bad, as roads go in the Gobi, but I was assured that the next 100 miles [160 kilometres] would be a different story, for we were about to enter the most arid part of the desert between Kalgan [Zhangjiakou in China] and Urga [Ulaanbaatar]. We were prepared for the real work of the trip, however, by a taste of the exciting shooting which Coltman had promised me.

I had been told that we should see antelope in thousands, but all day I had vainly searched the plains for a sign of game. Ten miles from Panj-kiang we were rolling comfortably along on a stretch of good road when Mrs Coltman, whose eyes are as keen as those of a hawk, excitedly pointed to a knoll on the right, not a hundred yards from the trail. At first I saw nothing but yellow grass; then the whole hillside seemed to be in motion. A moment later I began to distinguish heads and legs and realized that I was looking at an enormous herd of antelope, closely packed together, restlessly watching us.

Our rifles were out in an instant and Coltman opened the throttle. The antelope were five or six hundred yards away [450–550 metres], and as the car leaped forward they ranged themselves in single file and strung out across the plain. We left the road at once and headed diagonally toward them. For some strange reason, when a horse or car runs parallel with a herd of antelope, the animals will swing in a complete semicircle and cross in front of the pursuer. This is also true of some African species. Whether they think they are being cut off from more desirable means of escape I cannot say, but the fact remains that with the open plain on every side they always try to "cross your bows."

I shall never forget the sight of these magnificent animals streaming across the desert! There were at least a thousand of them, and their yellow bodies seemed fairly to skim the earth. I was shouting in excitement but Colman said:

"They're not running yet. Wait till we begin to shoot."

I could hardly believe my eyes when I saw the speedometer trembling at 35 miles [per hour, or 56kph], for we were making a poor showing with the antelope. But then the fatal attraction began to assert itself and the long column bent gradually in our direction. Coltman widened the arc of the circle and held the throttle up as far as it would go. Our speed increased to 40 miles [64kph] and the car began to gain because the antelope were running almost across our course.

They were about 200 yards away when Coltman shut off the gas and jammed both brakes, but before the car had stopped they had gained another hundred. I leaped over a pile of bedding and came into action with the .250 Savage high-power as soon as my feet were on the ground. Coltman's .30 Mauser was already spitting fire from the front seat across the windshield, and at his second shot an antelope dropped like lead. My first two bullets struck the dirt far behind the rearmost animal, but the third caught a full-grown female in the side and she plunged forward in the grass.

I realized then what Coltman meant when he said that the antelope had not begun to run. At the first shot every animal in the herd seemed to flatten itself and settle to its work. They did not run – they simply flew across the ground, their legs showing only as a blur. The one I killed was 400 yards away, and I held four feet ahead when I pulled the trigger. They could not have been travelling less than 55 or 60 miles an hour [88–96kph], for they were running in a semicircle about the car while we were moving at 40 miles in a straight line.

Those are the facts of the case. I can see my readers raise their brows incredulously, for that is exactly what I would have done before this demonstration. Well, there is one way to prove it and that is to come and try it for yourselves. Moreover, I can see some sportsmen smile for another reason. I mentioned the antelope I killed was 400 yards away. I know how far it was, for I paced it off. I may say, in passing, that I had never killed a running animal at that range. Ninety per cent of my shooting had been well within 150 yards, but in Mongolia conditions are most extraordinary.

In the brilliant atmosphere an antelope at 400 yards appears as large as it would at 100 yards in most other parts of the world; and on the flat plains, where there is not a bush or a shrub to obscure the view, a tiny stone stands out like a golf ball on the putting green.

Roy Chapman Andrews, Across Mongolian Plains, *1921*

Heavy spring rains belted down and flooded the streets of Choibalsan as we finally headed east over the swollen Herlen River – and straight through another abandoned Soviet military base. This one was full of rusty trucks and other equipment, broken-down barracks and storage sheds with a large complex of six-storey buildings off in the near distance. We were finally moving out onto the Great Eastern Steppe. The soil was heavily sandy and flatter than anything we'd seen before but rolled along gently – literally, like wide steps across the landscape – with watercourses collecting at the bottom of shallow inclines. The Russian Jeep was setting new speed records, hitting a full-blown 70kph (43mph) on the flats, but then slowing to a crawl to bounce and slide across muddy creeks and lakebeds. The sky cleared to reveal a low and heavily eroded ridgeline off to the south.

No, this steppe still wasn't flat enough in my book. We pulled into a roadside guest camp, a couple of gers where we spread out a lunch of black bread, pickles, sausage and cheese – one Russian legacy that thankfully hasn't gone the way of the old military bases. With typical Mongolian hospitality, the owners fired up the cow dung fire, served milk tea, kept us company and spoke of the dangers ahead. "Don't get lost out there," the old lady warned. "The Border Guards will first shoot out all your tyres!"

We'd travelled barely five minutes when we were pulled up at a Border Guard outpost to have our papers checked. A tiny checkpoint and raggedy chain blocked the road beside a collection of low masonry buildings without a trace of vegetation. A tall and sinister-looking steel tower with an enclosed observation platform stood on a nearby ridge, no doubt with a view straight over into China in the other direction. A uniformed female sergeant cranked away on an old-fashioned military phone to Choibalsan to double-check our permits. We were definitely on the edge of Mongolia now – and such stops every couple of hours became a routine of our entire journey. (Most stops are pleasant enough but, given these isolated outposts' paranoia, are more time-consuming than anything and allow plenty of time to stretch your legs. But definitely don't take pictures.)

I'd dozed off – which can indeed happen on Mongolia's rough roads – when we finally reached the classic steppe that I was so anxious to see. Startled awake, the landscape was totally flat, covered in yellow grass just starting to turn green. This was the legendary **Menengiyn Tal**, or **Menen Steppe** for short, a half-million-square-kilometre (193,000-square-mile) plateau that is the largest undisturbed steppe in the world. Declared a Strictly Protected Area in 1992 to safeguard the endangered **Mongolian white-tailed gazelle** (*Procarpa gutturosa*), the Menen is regarded as Asia's Serengeti Plain, where herds of 40,000 migrate at a time and up to one million permanently live. (The park also protects rare birds such as the white-naped crane, common pheasant, rough-legged harrier, steppe eagle and great bustard, plus many rare plants.)

From our single dirt track, the landscape was flat as far as the eye could see, bringing on that sweeping image of migrations and wars over the centuries. Another Border Guard checkpoint was right in the middle of this. We were entranced for hours as we kept our eyes peeled for migrating gazelles. But the only other sign of life through the long afternoon were a couple of looming oil-drilling rigs visible – like the masts of ships at sea – far across the steppe. Just how close the drilling was to the "protected area", or even inside it, we couldn't tell in this wide-open country. But everyone we spoke to over the next couple of days reckoned that oil exploration and drilling, a joint venture between Mongolia and resource-hungry China, had driven the gazelles away. Where, no one knew.

At the northeast edge of the vast Menen Steppe, we descended to what I'd call Mongolia's "East Coast", **Buir Nuur** (Lake), a traditional gathering place for Mongol tribes over the centuries. (The Halh River Valley, see below, was where today's majority of Mongolians originated and its waters, which start in the Hingan Mountains, flow into the northern end of the lake.) Stretching along the Chinese border for 40 kilometres (25 miles), this freshwater lake is the largest in eastern Mongolia, occupying 615 square kilometres (237 square miles) and varying in depth from 10 to 50 metres (32–164 feet). Rich in fish such as taimen, carp, lenok and pike, plus an endemic crayfish, overfishing disputes frequently arise with Chinese living on its northern shore, especially as Mongolians engage in relatively little fishing themselves. Unlike most other lakes in the country, Buyr Nuur is surrounded by bush. The few nomadic families living along its shoreline appear to live quite a hardscrabble existence in the sandy and windblown soil.

At the northern end of the lake, a Communist-era fish research station lies abandoned next to the only accommodation, the **Buir Travel Tourist Camp**, apparently a popular place in summer. But we hardly saw the "resort" at its best. The night before, a freezing spring storm blew down all its tourist gers, and its main building wasn't in much better shape, its hallways full of wet sand and no power. (With the restaurant closed, we settled into the overstuffed blue-and-white vinyl-covered furniture of the Presidential Suite, cooked a meal of mutton and vegetables on our gas stove, and warmed up with a cow dung fire in the ornate brick fireplace – certainly a memorable stop.) With lower-than-average rainfall, the lake's shoreline looked more like a vast tidal flat from its 20-metre-high (66-foot) sandy cliffs. A Border Guard tower was visible further to the north. On a pleasant midsummer day, the scene would clearly be a lot more inviting – and I certainly sympathised with the resort's owner who had a lot of rebuilding to do.

Following spread: The large reclining Lady Buddha at Ikh Burkhant is an important pilgrimage site but is rarely visited (Carl Robinson).

Travelling northeast from Buyr Nuur, we followed the **Halh Gol,** or river, here flowing widely and lined with shrubs and trees, including a plantation of birch trees outside a muddy and dilapidated former collective farm, or *bag*. There was no electricity, only tiny windmills and solar panels for power, but the kids all looked neat walking off to school. We roused the attendant from his tattered wooden cabin, and he grumpily hand-pumped more petrol into our jeep. (In some tiny settlements, if you can find the attendants in the first place, they sometimes refuse to sell their precious fuel if you've got UB licence plates.)

Cutting cross-country out of town, we stumbled onto a fascinating find – an old Soviet armoured car or BA-10M on a cement plinth, its wavy Art-Deco fenders straight out of the 1930s, and our first taste of the sites, relics, and memorials ahead from the battle against the Japanese in 1939. Clearly, this battered relic stood at the northernmost end of this vast battlefield. (Air battles also took place over Buyr Nuur.) Not much further, we came upon the towering "border gate" and bridge over the Halh River at **Bayanhoshuu-Ovdog,** a busy crossing point for Chinese trucks bringing in oil drilling and other equipment. (Although the Japanese occupying neighbouring Manchuria back in 1939 argued the river should be the boundary, the actual border between Mongolia and China from here follows the ridgeline on the eastern side of the Halh River Valley in a southeast direction all the way to Mongolia's easternmost point in the Hingan Mountains, where the river originates.)

Heading upriver, the Halh River Valley narrows to about 10 kilometres (six miles) across with gently rolling slopes below the surrounding steppe. Popping out of the valley, we soon spotted the remains of military positions, even bomb craters, from the battle. We expected to see more but the heart of this battlefield's massive 80-kilometre (50-mile) front was still hours away. Instead, coming back down off the steppe just past another guard tower, we stumbled onto one of the country's most important Buddhist pilgrimage sites, **Ikh Burkhant**, a large reclining image of the female Bodhisattva Avalokitesvara, known as Janraisig in Mongolia and Guanyin in China. Set on a slope beside the river and facing east, the 26.5-metre (87-foot) statue was built by a Halh noble named To Van between 1859 and 1864, during the Manchu period. (Conveniently, a Border Guard checkpoint is located right at its base, allowing plenty of time for a good walk around the two-hectare site while papers are checked.) Originally made of carved stone, the statue – topped by a line of Buddhist statuary – was damaged during the purges of the 1930s but restored in recent years, including Sanskrit characters down the slope on both sides of the statue.

Back up on the steppe, heavily weathered – even somewhat neglected – monuments to the battle between May and August 1939 start to appear. In many ways the first and simplest is the most poignant, three large steel x's – "**XXX**" – halfway up the valley's southern slope which mark the furthest Japanese advance into Mongolia on **Bayantsaagan Hill.** The broad vista stretches far across the valley into China's Inner Mongolia, providing a graphic sense of the battle's epic scale. On the flat grassy steppe beyond, and visible from miles away by their surroundings of tall poplar trees, are more elaborate monuments and a cemetery. Roads through the battlefield eventually lead south to the sum centre of Halhgol, site of a bridge crossing where more critical battles took place.

In brief, the little-known **Battle of Halhgol** of 1939 (also called the Battle of Khalkhin Gol, or the Nomonhan Incident to the Japanese after a village on its side) was the largest modern-style battle before World War II and saw the first massed use of infantry, artillery, armour and air power. (In fact, some historians claim the battle featured the largest aerial battle in history, with hundreds of aircraft on both sides taking part.) At the time, the Japanese occupied Manchuria and Inner Mongolia and had their eye on resource-rich eastern Siberia. Believing the Soviet military to be weakened by the Stalinist purges – and Mongolia too going through a similar upheaval – the Japanese were, at the least, testing Moscow's response when they claimed the Halh River as the western boundary of their puppet state of Manchukuo. (The region is actually part of Inner Mongolia.) Meanwhile, anticipating the threat ahead, a friendship pact in 1936 had already brought in thousands of Soviet troops and equipment, including the construction of the railroad down to Choibalsan.

The battle began simply enough on 11 May 1939 when Mongolian cavalry crossed over to the eastern side of the Halh River. Chased away by local Manchukuo troops, the Mongolians soon returned in greater force and reoccupied their land. Japanese troops then intervened but were badly beaten and retaliated with a damaging air strike against a Soviet airbase farther west on the Great Eastern Steppe. Then-Lieutenant-General **Georgy Zhukov** arrived in early June to beef up the Soviet-Mongolian forces as skirmishes continued. Using an estimated 30,000 infantry backed by tanks, artillery and aircraft, the Japanese launched a massive two-pronged offensive at the end of June. The northern taskforce broke across the river and occupied Bayantsaagan Hill. They were turning south to link up with the second force crossing the river when Zhukov sprang his trap. Using 450 fast-moving tanks and armoured cars but no infantry units, the Soviets virtually encircled the Japanese, forcing their withdrawal back across the river. The second crossing across Kawatama Bridge also failed and when the Japanese massed their troops and artillery for another attempt at the end of July, they were again defeated with heavy casualties.

Although the Japanese had suffered some 5,000 casualties, they'd reinforced themselves up to 75,000 troops backed by armoured vehicles and hundreds of aircraft, and planned a third offensive. Despite the appearance of a battlefield stalemate, Zhukov was busy building up a massive 50,000-man force of tanks, mechanised infantry, artillery and aircraft that included running scores of truck convoys from the Choibalsan railhead 400 kilometres (250 miles) away. On 28 August 1939, in a brilliant tactic that would become his trademark in World War II, Zhukov pinned down the centre of the Japanese line and then flanked them on both sides with the massive use of armoured units and totally encircled them. When the Japanese refused to surrender, Zhukov ordered massive air and artillery strikes. The battle ended on 31 August 1939, the day before Hitler invaded Poland, touching off World War II. The Soviets and Japanese signed a ceasefire two weeks later.

The cemetery for the 80 Mongolians killed during the Battle of Halhgol in 1939 (Carl Robinson).

Casualties were heavy on both sides. The official figures from the Japanese were 8,440 killed and 8,766 wounded, while the Soviets claimed a much higher 60,000 Japanese killed and wounded, and 3,000 taken prisoner. Archival work in post-Communist Russia puts Soviet casualties at 7,974 and 15,251 wounded. Reflecting their minor role in the battle, some 80 Mongolian soldiers also died, mostly from friendly fire, say present-day sources. In strategic terms, the Battle of Halhgol spelled an end to any Japanese thoughts of pushing west and joining up with Hitler. Instead, they now turned their eyes to the resources of Southeast Asia and began planning their surprise attack on the

Left: A marble Soviet-era statue of a Mongolian "war goddess" within the Yalalt (Victory) Museum in Halhgol. Right: A Soviet tank stands outside the museum's entrance (Carl Robinson x2).

Part of the huge Yalalt Monument (Carl Robinson).

Americans at Pearl Harbor in 1941. For the brilliant Zhukov, he was soon far to the west grabbing the Soviet Union's share of their deal with Hitler for the invasion of Poland. And when that strange alliance soured, starting with the Battle for Moscow, he'd already mastered all the right tactics to take on Germany – far across the steppe in easternmost Mongolia.

Travelling across this former battlefield is quite a moving experience, as it has also been for returning and now elderly Soviet veterans over the decades. Marked by a large white tomb-like slab and a Soviet-made Yakovlev tank on a sloping plinth pointing across the valley, one of the 450 that routed the Japanese from their furthest advance, a large monument on strategic Bayantsaagan Hill memorialises the battle with a brief inscription in Russian and Mongolian. A bit further along, and surrounded by a simple iron fence, is a cemetery for the 80 Mongolian soldiers killed, each grave marked with a red star. At its centre, a deteriorating concrete obelisk is surrounded with curved panels extolling the bravery of the troops and, of course, Soviet-Mongolian friendship. Surrounded by poplar trees, the nearby Soviet cemetery is dominated by a marble-covered obelisk with the names of various units and individuals. On the grounds are 90 graves of Soviet officers and men and other memorials, some topped with old tank turrets and other military objects.

But the most impressive of all these memorials, as one descends through a wide gully to the river below is the soaring **Yalalt Monument,** or Victory Monument. Built in the shape of a bayonet with a Soviet Star at the top, the 54-metre (177-foot) monument was dedicated at the battle's 45th anniversary in 1984 and constructed of copper plates attached to a steel frame. In the best Socialist Realism tradition, probably its very epitome, the bayonet's huge stylized 33-metre-wide (108-foot) handle is a surge of martial action – men, fists, flags, horses, tanks and aircraft lunging heroically across the valley and hills beyond. (Today, birds nest behind the warplane wings.) A Soviet and a Mongolian soldier stand proudly shoulder-to-shoulder. Behind them on the other side, a long-braided Mongolian "goddess of war" gazes back towards the home front. The monument has become a modern symbol for the battle and the focus of anniversaries. Below the monument are the sum centre of **Halhgol** and its so-called **Kawatama Bridge**, which the Japanese failed twice to cross.

While its tree-lined riverside setting is pleasant enough, especially viewed from the monument, the town is typically drab with Soviet-era apartment blocks, concrete-block streets and broken footpaths, an abandoned power station and factory or two, a tractor on a plinth, and a faded mural of Lenin on the sum administration offices. The highlight of any visit, though, is the three-storey **Yalalt Museum** (Victory Museum), which takes patience in first finding a caretaker and then dealing with power outages. (Coinciding with lunch, the delay allowed me to sample Mongolia's equivalent of the Aussie meat pie for the first time, deep-fried dumplings or *khuushuur*, dunked in tomato and soy sauce at the town's only eatery inside an old Russian-style four-wheeled trailer in the main park.)

A turquoise-coloured tank sits to one side of the museum, and in an open area where the Japanese have erected a **Peace Monument** are other pieces of military hardware, including the frame of a shot-down Japanese fighter. A large bas-relief over the museum's entrance extols Soviet-Mongolian solidarity. Using flashlights, we explored the museum's fascinating exhibits not just from the battle but a totally bygone era. On the museum's first floor, sunlight streams into a brightly lit inner sanctum dominated by a white marble statue of the "goddess" with wreaths at her feet and along the walls, clearly a place of reflection and quiet ceremony.

On the southern edge of town, we cleared another Border Guard checkpoint and crossed the broad river flat, dotted here with numerous metal markers where downed Japanese aircraft crashed, and then over looming **Khamar Davaa** (Khamar Pass), another battlefield landmark. Above was rolling grass-covered steppe with pockets of pine trees and a solitary track leading us to the easternmost tip of Mongolia. We finally spotted a few good-sized herds of white-tailed gazelles, which quickly vanished. Next to a lovely breast-shaped peak, we crossed the Halh Gol – here only a couple of metres across – and moved higher into a rugged range.

Finally reaching a crest, we looked far down to a grass-covered valley floor now drenched in the golden glow of the setting sun with a solitary military fort – like a scene from a romance novel. As we pulled up at this particular Border Guard outpost at dusk, no one wanted our papers this time. Instead, two smartly uniformed young privates rushed out and in double-time brought all our gear into the clean and pleasant guest quarters. The commander, a young lieutenant on his first posting, formally welcomed us. An excellent meal of rice, smoked mutton and potatoes prepared by the officer's wife was on the table even before we sipped our pre-dinner drinks. (In fact, this was just a "pre-meal" – a huge pot of mutton soup and spaghetti arrived an hour or so later!)

The neatly kept outpost is actually inside the boundary of the **Nomrog Strictly Protected Area**, a 310,000-hectare (76,000-acre) national park which stretches east from here up into the foothills of the **Great Hingan Range**, surrounded on three sides by China. On the far side of the lovely round valley is the **Nomrog River**, an easterly tributary of the Halh which, at one point, runs right along the Chinese border. With a shortage of rangers, the Border Guards patrol through and keep an eye on the park's rich collection of moose, deer, bears and other wildlife, including numerous bird species such as the rare Chinese parrotbill. (With their own patrols and those by the Chinese, plus a low population across the border, the commander claimed poaching is not a serious problem.) Because of the time and difficulty reaching this remote area, however, few tourists visit. But those who do are rewarded with lovely meadows, tree-lined streams and freshwater lakes and wildlife in what is a unique transition zone from the eastern steppe to mountain landscape across the border.

After a pleasant overnight stop, we headed back up to the mountaintop where we'd first viewed this entrancing spot and turned down the other side onto a little-used track along the border, supposedly a strategic road built by the Soviets back in the late 1930s. These are the western foothills of the Great Hingan Range, now visible off to the east, which were covered in the golden grass of spring with tinges of summer green. A few gazelles suddenly appeared – and then more and more of them in waves across the landscape, cresting the hills and disappearing. Scores, hundreds and soon thousands of these graceful animals were running alongside and would keep us company for the rest of the day. For any visitor, this will count as one of the most thrilling sights of their Mongolian sojourn.

We hadn't spotted a single gazelle across the famous Menen Steppe, but here they were, hard on the Chinese border. Perhaps everyone was right about the oil drilling chasing them away. Over here, where both countries physically fence their borders, they are probably running around in huge circles. At the next Border Guard outpost with an

EXTRA
+30G

Clockwise from top left: Salt workers at Sangiyn Dalay Lake; a boy wears a border guard's cap at a camp near the Chinese border; a stained-glass window in Yalalt Museum glorifies the defeat of Japan's 1939 invasion; the oilfields of southern Dornod feed the hungry Chinese market next door (Carl Robinson x4).

observation tower on the ridge behind, we thought something was wrong when we were asked inside. Instead, we were served huge bowls of noodle soup with beef and potatoes while the commander, another young lieutenant, waxed on almost poetically about the area's medicinal bushes – just lie down on them and you'll feel better – and the lovely flowers of summer when the grass nearly hides a patrolling horseman. And also how the gazelles are becoming a real "problem", so tame they come right up to the camp, eat the grass right down to the roots and raise fears of desertification. He also worried about the gazelles hurting themselves up against the border fence only 12 kilometres (7.5 miles) away. The openness and hospitality were amazing.

Travelling along Mongolia's unpopulated border region with only the rampaging gazelles and occasional Border Guard outpost for company was a fascinating experience. We stumbled onto a man-made ditch, possibly a wall, of indeterminable age extending across the flat steppe. Of more modern vintage was the "buffer zone" along the actual border, starting with a cleared and ploughed dirt strip to detect intruders and a broken-down barbed-wire fence. A more solid fence and guard towers stood a couple of kilometres away. (China has a similar fence on its side.)

From our more elevated position surrounded by rolling hills, we were literally on the edge of Mongolia and could see far down into heavily populated Inner Mongolia, including Chinese cities and power stations. After another checkpoint, a Border Guard patrol on horses flagged us down. Accompanied by several large dogs, including a couple of German Shepherds, the five-man patrol was heading out on a 10-day patrol and needed help hauling their gear and supplies to their outpost up the track. Mongolian hospitality means never saying no, not even when the higher-ranked guards squeezed into the back and left the two privates to bring up the rear.

Another day in Mongolia – and another surprise. Who'd ever believe we'd be giving Mongolia's elite Border Guards a lift along the Chinese border? They chattered away. One was a cadet from the Border Guard Academy in UB on summer work – and his first long-range patrol. Oh, yes, the gazelles are everywhere. But they couldn't prevent their dogs from attacking and eating this protected species. The Shepherds are specially trained to track down people, they said. But does anyone come across the border? Yes. Helped by sympathisers across 1,000 kilometres (620 miles) of Chinese territory, North Korean refugees come across in droves every late spring and summer. They walk openly so they'll be caught and detained by the Border Guard patrols. They immediately appeal for political asylum and are then flown from UB to South Korea. Now I understood that UN guide on refugees I'd spotted in the Border Guard Headquarters in Choibalsan.

Dropping steeply off the hills along the border, the endless flow of gazelles kicked up clouds of dust and followed us inland. The steppe levelled into long and steadily descending waves. Cresting over a rise, we saw a shimmering blue lake far ahead. But as we approached, we discovered this was just the sky's reflection off a large deposit of salt in a large dry lakebed, **Sangiyn Dalay.** The settlement of wooden shacks and gers was once a commune and its residents now work the mine as private individuals. The lake has a long history of trade with China, and the method of extracting the valuable salt has doubtless barely changed over the centuries. The locals work every day from 4am to 7pm using long-handled shovels and rakes to break up and stack the salt, which is then transported to shore on primitive steel-wheeled carts pulled by camels, and stacked up again for drying. Between 150 and 300 tons is shipped out every year. With recent price rises, the miners explained, they were doing well despite the long days of backbreaking work.

The flat steppe declined in long and gradual steps as we headed further south and came upon another surprise. Far ahead, we could make out the distinctive shape of oil-drilling rigs across the vast horizon, which increased in numbers as we approached. Forget those two exploratory wells up on the Menen Steppe to the north, this was serious drilling. Soon, we found ourselves in the middle of Mongolia's largest oil field, surrounded by blue-coloured pumps sucking the valuable liquid to the surface and into large shiny elevated holding tanks. After days virtually alone in an unchanged landscape, we were suddenly in the middle of a busy modern-day industrial site with wide dirt roads, tanker trucks and heavy machinery. We pulled up at a large housing compound for the operation's hundreds of Chinese and Mongolian workers hoping for a bunk and meal for the night, normally a possibility, only to be turned away because a high-powered government delegation was expected the next day.

Run as a joint venture, this field in southern Dornod aimag produces some 500,000 barrels of oil a year, all headed – one small tanker-truck at a time – across the border to China. Considering that nation's appetite for oil, that's like emptying the contents of a thimble into a 55-gallon barrel (but at least Mongolia is right next door). We drove a short distance and pitched our tent on the flat and windy steppe. A horizon of lights and the rumble of oilrigs and wells, plus the occasional passing China-bound tanker, kept us company through the night.

THE VOLCANOES OF DARIGANGA

Volcanoes are not an image generally associated with Mongolia. After all, most of the Earth's volcanic activity is found in coastal regions and islands, such as the renowned Pacific Ring of Fire stretching from Russia's Kamchatka Peninsula down through the Indonesian archipelago and out into the South Pacific. But to stumble onto more than 200 young volcanoes so far inland in southeast Mongolia, a good 1,000 kilometres from the Pacific Ocean, is yet another surprise in this fascinating country with its tortured geological history. (More solitary volcanoes occur in other parts of Mongolia.) Formed only 10,000 years ago, the **Dariganga Plateau** is a volcanic region covering 10,000 square kilometres (3,860 square miles) along the border of China's Inner Mongolia and located in a transition zone from steppe to desert, or *gobi.* With its mixture of dormant volcanoes – exactly 222 of them – canyons, caves, spring-fed lakes, steppe and sand dunes, but not much vegetation, Dariganga is one of the most fascinating – and charming – parts of Mongolia. This is a destination in its own right.

Early man – no doubt present as these volcanoes were formed – also found the Dariganga a fascinating place of settlement and worship. The area has Mongolia's richest collection of anthropomorphic *balbal*, or "man stones", as well as other statuary, some still venerated today. Its highest volcanic peaks are sacred and the site of long-established "men only" pilgrimages to revive one's spirits and prepare for war. Dominated by the minority Dariganga tribe, famous for their silver jewellery and blacksmithing, the region's lush grassland is where the Qing emperor grazed his vast herds of horses – and not without local resistance, either. This is the home of Mongolia's very own Robin Hood, who stole the imperial horses, gave them away to his own countrymen and, so the legend goes, was never apprehended. A new statue honouring him pointedly faces China. Comfortable in their unique surroundings, the Dariganga people are renowned for their friendliness and hospitality.

Dariganga is located in the southern part of **Suhbaatar *aimag*,** named after the famous revolutionary hero – as in Ulaanbaatar's main square – who brought the Communists to power in 1921 and whose father came from here. (Dornod lies to the north and Hentii to the west.) Most of the aimag is flat steppe and lower mountain ranges with no major rivers. Located in the centre of the aimag some 840 kilometres (522 miles) southeast of UB, its capital of **Baruun-Urt** is important for its mining of coal, wolfram and zinc. Although its

Previous spread: The ethereal moonscape of Dariganga Plateau (Elbegzaya Lhagvasuren).
Right: According to legend, Chinggis Khaan's mother Borte told her squabbling sons: "Together, a bundle of arrows cannot be broken". In this modern statue in the aimag centre of Baruun-Urt, the future World Conqueror, known then as Temujin, holds up the arrows in a traditional appeal to national unity (Carl Robinson).

THE 800 TH
ANNIVERSARY OF
GREAT MONGOLIAN STATE

Russian-built motorcycle sidecars provide taxi – and sightseeing – services in Baruun-Urt (Carl Robinson).

huge Soviet-era metallurgical plant now lies in ruins, the town is not unattractive compared to other centres and has good restaurants and hotels. The recently renovated museum has several balbal, including an actual grave, other pre-Mongol artefacts, the exquisite silver jewellery from Dariganga and lovely paintings of its traditionally dressed and bejewelled women. The busy town makes a pleasant lunch or overnight stop.

Employment in the mines provides good income and civic pride runs high, best seen at a pleasant and modern hilltop shrine with a seated statue of Chinggis Khaan's wife, Borte. With the young Temujin standing between her legs, she holds a bundle of arrows which, as the well-known legend tells, cannot be broken and are a salutary lesson on the need for unity. (We toured the town by Russian motorcycle sidecar while our driver repaired a flat tyre.) The local airport no longer receives flights – but hopefully will be reopened for travellers to Dariganga, another 150 kilometres (93 miles) away. Reaching the region directly today is a two-day drive from the capital. (Again, border permits are required.)

Continuing my own roundabout approach through Mongolia's eastern aimags, however, we entered Suhbaatar through its northeast corner after stumbling onto the country's main oil drilling operations on the southern steppe of Dornod (see page 269). Leaving behind

Left: Tapping into Mongolia's incessant winds, this German-donated wind turbine provides one-third of district capital Erdenetsagaan's power needs – the rest coming from coal-powered power stations across the nearby border in China's Inner Mongolia (Carl Robinson).

the gravelled main road and its convoys of China-bound oil tankers, we cut cross-country across the flat steppe and right into my first – but hardly last – Mongolian dust storm. Fierce winds blew light-brown clouds of gritty dirt and sand across the landscape obscuring the hills ahead, turning the valleys and canyons into wind tunnels. With the windows closed and no air-conditioning, temperatures inside the jeep rose uncomfortably.

The winds slowed as we rose high onto a range of hills cut by dramatic canyons and staggered into the sum centre of **Erdenetsagaan.** The town's major Buddhist monastery, **Eguzer Hutagt,** was destroyed in the 1930s and its remains used for other buildings, including large Soviet-era stone warehouses, and only a few Manchu-style buildings remain. (A new monastery is now open.) Towering over the town, and totally appropriate after what we'd just come through, was a huge wind turbine for power generation, an aid project from Germany and the only one in Mongolia. Able to generate one-third of the town's needs, its proud Mongolian manager wanted a couple more. But with electricity from a coal-fired power station across the border in China arriving soon, the prospects for his environmentally friendly alternative were hardly encouraging.

The border at nearby **Bichigt**, where the oil tankers cross into China and trade goods enter Mongolia, gives the town a busy air of prosperity. With stylish overhead streetlights, its paved main street zigzags past an attractive row of shops, restaurants and discos, each with a horse rail outside. The hilltop town was as dusty as a Wild West town but almost everyone was impeccably dressed in traditional silk *deels* as if they were heading off to a wedding, the men in cowboy hats. Right on the border is towering 1,233-metre-high (4,045-foot) **Lhachinvandad Uul,** a granite mountain that is part of a 1,000-square-kilometre (386 square-mile) nature reserve habitat for deer, gazelles, wolves, smaller predators and many rodents that was first declared back in 1965. (Most of Mongolia's national parks and reserves have only been created since 1990.)

The dust storm kicked up even worse as we travelled south into more hill and canyon country. For the first and only time, our driver became totally disorientated. (He drove up the nearest hilltop, spotted a ger family camp through the murk far below and drove straight down the other side to ask for directions. Even here, everyone was in immaculate deels.) The hills loomed higher and more rugged. Then, after passing a brilliantly white salt lake where horses drank and grazed on its green grass, the topography dramatically changed into a vast volcanic zone. We'd finally arrived in Dariganga.

The distinctive shape of volcanoes spread across the flat southern horizon all along the Chinese border. The rugged range we'd exited formed a backdrop to the north. We were looking for what is reputedly Mongolia's largest cave, expecting something above

Climbing the northern rim of Shiliyn Bogd volcano at sunrise is a rite of manhood (Elbegzaya Lhagvasuren).

ground, and instead found the entrance to **Taliin Agui**, or Steppe Cave, in a large hole in the ground. (The cave was fenced off after one too many vehicles accidentally drove into it.) Actually a lava tube, the cave's entrance is extremely narrow. But for those with flashlights who don't suffer from claustrophobia, the cave has seven chambers to explore, some filled with permanent ice. (With its main building's blue-coloured tin roof visible for miles, a tourist ger camp stands on the site and is particularly popular with those visiting the next attraction.)

Every Mongolian – but especially men – knows about **Shiliyn Bogd Uul**, the legendary and sacred mountain that is the highest peak in Suhbaatar aimag at 1,778 metres (5,833 feet). Located only 12 kilometres (7.5 miles) south of Taliin Agui, the mountain is actually an extinct volcano with a two-square-kilometre (0.7-square-mile) crater mostly open to the north, with its high southern rim overlooking the Chinese border.

Legends dating back to pre-Mongol days tell of warrior gatherings on the flat crater floor below and their climbing to the top of the rim to "revive their spirits", as Mongolians are fond of saying (a huge gathering of gers is certainly easy to imagine). The tradition lives on today in an annual "men only" pilgrimage to catch the first sunrise of the Lunar New Year, **Tsagaan Sar**, when the entire region is covered in snow and ice. One Mongolian I met follows up his annual visits with a round of wolf hunting. The new year climb is especially auspicious but virtually every Mongolian male aspires to climb Shiliyn Bogd at any time of year as a sign of manhood, especially at sunrise. It's a Mongolian macho thing.

The path to the summit is marked by numerous *ovoo*, many tied with blue *badag*, with the largest one at the summit. Despite the still-blistering and chilly winds, my two Mongolian companions barely hesitated before dashing up the steep 300-metre (984-foot) climb to the summit, where they sprinkled libations of vodka and returned with their now-blessed bottles (the vodka remained untouched for the rest of our journey, saved for sharing with friends back in UB). The view from the top of Shiliyn Bogd – especially on a clear day – is absolutely spectacular. The surrounding landscape is dotted with scores of volcanic craters and vistas stretch far across the steppe into Inner Mongolia. Unfortunately, less macho visitors have taken a much easier trip to the summit by driving their 4WDs straight up its northern grass-covered slope – in the process leaving behind a terrible scar on this most sacred site. (The problem here, as elsewhere in Mongolia, is the woeful lack of manpower to monitor its natural treasures.)

The sum centre of Dariganga lies 70 kilometres (43 miles) to the west across this wide volcanic region. One track leads to **Khurgiin Khundii**, a lovely valley 40 kilometres (25 miles) west where a dozen or so pre-Mongol statues lie on the ground, one legend telling that they represent women, forced to marry men they didn't love, who committed suicide off a nearby mountain. Another tells of a local lord who drove hundreds of gazelles over a cliff to their deaths and was then punished by Tengri, the Sky God. In any case, the area is now taboo and no domestic animals graze here. Pretty **Bichigt Shahaa** canyon is located nearby.

Another track closer to the border leads to a hillside with the statue of **Tooroi Bandi,** the "Robin Hood" who gave the Manchu such grief stealing and redistributing their horses while hiding out around Shiliyn Bogd. Erected only in 1999, the lifelike statue shows the handsome bandit in a traditional deel seated before an ovoo, an offering bowl in front of him and glaring towards China. Nearby is a huge brass cauldron once used for cooking.

The setting on the valley floor below requires a few moments to understand. In the middle distance are sand dunes that mark the eastern extremity of Mongolia's vast Gobi region (see next chapter), the **Moltsog Els** (*Els* is Mongolian for dunes). Running

Right: A statue of Tooroi Bandi, Mongolia's Robin Hood.
Above: A huge bronze cauldron once used for enormous feasts (Carl Robinson x2).

80 kilometres (50 miles) east to west and only a few kilometres wide, the dunes are not very high and are covered in vegetation. But combined with numerous natural springs, this sandy barrier has created a string of six lovely freshwater lakes along its northern side, protected as the 28,000-hectare (70,000-acre) **Ganga Nuur Nature Reserve.** The best-known and closest lake to the town is **Ganga Nuur**, where thousands of migrating swans congregate in late summer and autumn. This is a pleasant spot for a swim; its surrounds are like a lawn, a perfect spot for a golf course, where domestic animals – and once the Manchu horses – graze. A fenced-off spring feeds the lake and its water is most refreshing, especially at the end of a long day's drive. (Interestingly, there is no tourist ger camp around here.)

Dominated by the wide, dormant volcano **Altan Ovoo** (Golden Ovoo), the town of **Dariganga** is small and neat – so neat the locals even stack their cow dung in head-high rectangular piles. (Finding its legendary silversmiths, however, was a challenge. They'd all moved to UB!) Shops, restaurants and a hotel line the short main street and the town is dotted with fairly substantial buildings. Located atop the volcano is the **Bat Tsagaan Stupa**, now rebuilt after its destruction in the 1930s, and another "men only" pilgrimage site. The view from the top over the town with the lakes, sand dunes and mountains beyond, is quite stunning.

Like hundreds of other places around Mongolia, Dariganga's one-time Buddhist monastery, **Ovoon Khiid**, lies in ruins southeast of town. Dozens of pre-Mongol balbal are also located around the town with the three called **King, Queen and Prince** most easily accessible. Fenced off, they are still devoutly worshipped, their faces almost obscured by the large number of hadag and other colourful offerings that drape them. An ancient rock inscription named **Sudutiin Tsagaan** and more stone figures are located south of the sand dunes in remote **Naran** sum close to the Chinese border, a pleasant day trip for those able to spend some time in this wonderful region.

Another natural place of interest in the aimag west of the main road from Dariganga to Baruun-Urt is **Hatavchiyn Havtsal**, also known as Halzan, a narrow 20-metre-deep (66-foot) three-kilometre-long (1.8-mile) canyon formed by a dramatic fold in the Earth's surface during the Cenozoic Era (20 million years ago), which exposed Devonian sandstone from 400 million years before.

The Dariganga is also renowned for its ancient balbal, *or "man stones", that are still actively worshipped. Heavily draped in blue* hadag *and other scarves, this is one of three dominating the plain below a wide dormant volcano known as the Goldon Ovoo, another "men only" pilgrimage site (Carl Robinson).*

THE GOBI

The **Gobi Desert** is the most common mental image that outsiders have of Mongolia – a vast and inhospitable region that ranks as the Asian equivalent of Africa's lifeless and sandy Sahara (many think the entire country is like that). That view was certainly entrenched by tales of the hardship endured by early European explorers and reinforced by the famous American explorer **Roy Chapman Andrews** in the 1920s, who stumbled onto the world's mightiest dinosaur find in the harsh landscape of the South Gobi. The Gobi was a place of unbearable heat and sand dunes where man ventured at his own risk. Desert and Dinosaurs.

But the reality is surprisingly different. Certainly, there are bone-dry and stony plains, rocky outcrops, badlands, salt lakes and sandy wastes, but sand dunes only make up three percent of the region. The Gobi is also a land of semi-desert with a diversity of rugged treeless and even snow-topped mountain peaks, heavily eroded hills, springs and streams, rivers ending nowhere, a lush mixture of valleys and meadows, forests and scrubland, and classic and desert steppe. Even in the driest spots you can find the loveliest oases you'll ever stumble across.

The Gobi's rich animal and plant life includes some of the rarest on Earth. Although not as densely populated as the rest of Mongolia, a surprising number of people live in the Gobi, where they traditionally use the two-humped Bactrian camel. With the world price of cashmere wool – Mongolia produces the world's best – skyrocketing in recent years, goats are prolific now, but also bring growing concerns that their root-eating habits will increase desertification.

The word "*gobi*" is actually a misnomer – in more ways than one. First, the Mongolian term is actually *gov*, which means simply a desert, a place that receives little or no precipitation but is still prone to dramatic storms and flash floods. If you take a close look at a detailed map, Mongolia has some 33 gov. (In fact, you can see a gov on a quick day or overnight trip out of UB.) Most visitors do indeed visit just the **South Gobi**, but in our wide-ranging journey around Mongolia, the gov narrative will be much more extensive, allowing us to introduce some particularly beautiful places seen by few tourists, such as the **Bayanhongor Gobi**.

The entire Gobi region stretches nearly 2,000 kilometres (1,240 miles) across the bottom third of Mongolia, and in its wider definition extends in an arc from the **Great Hingan**

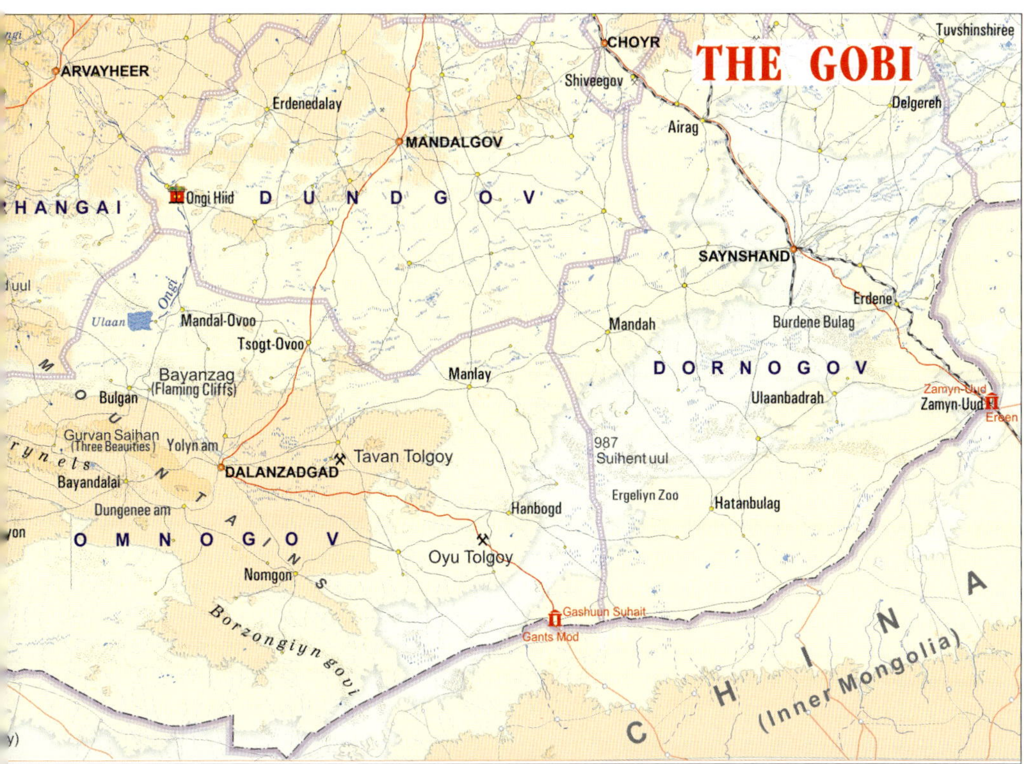

The Gobi's endless variety surprises in an outcrop of stark white limestone along the Road to China, an ancient caravan trail in western Bayanhongor aimag (Carl Robinson).

Range on the Manchurian border in the east, through Inner Mongolia and west to the **Tarim Basin** of China's Xinjiang Uygur Autonomous Region and then southwards to the edge of the **Tibetan Plateau.** In Mongolia, the Gobi runs from **Dariganga** in the east (see previous chapter), west through the aimags of **Dornogov (East Gobi), Dundgov (Middle Gobi), Omnogov (South Gobi)**, and the southern parts of **Bayanhongor, Gobi-Altai** and **Hovd** aimags.

The **Bogd Fault**, a massive and still active fault line extending down from the one forming the mighty Altai Mountains in the far northwest – cuts in a southeast direction and its fractures are clearly visible in several areas, most dramatically at the base of **Ikh Bogd** in Bayanhongor and also in the eastern Gobi. The Gobi's massive mountains, known as the **Gobi Altai**, are a lower extension of the range with peaks between 2,000 and 4,000 metres (6,500–13,000 feet) and lie along the fault's southern edge. They began forming only 20 million years ago when the Indian subcontinent crashed into Asia, pushing and rippling everything northwards against immovable bedrock in Siberia. The process continues today at a rate of 15 centimetres (six inches) a year.

The Gobi has a fascinating natural and human history. When volcanic activity was still present some 80 million years ago, the region was a vast sedimentary basin covered in savannah, a time when dinosaurs ruled the Earth. There were also forests, lakes, rivers and marshes. Periodically, huge sand and dust storms that dwarf those of today, as well as the sudden collapse of dunes, buried these creatures, leaving behind the world's richest collection of dinosaurs. The subsequent dry climate preserved them neatly for the "dragon

The Geology of Mongolia

Visitors to Mongolia can't help but be impressed by the dazzling variety of its physical features. In fact, the contrast between regions is so dramatic that as one moves between them, one often feels on totally different continents. And, in geological terms, this is precisely what's happened here. Mongolia is a landscape that's been glued together from everywhere, as professional geologist **Darrell Turcotte** explains:

Mongolia is a "tectonic collage" of six major terranes – blocks or fragments of the Earth's crust – which collided up against the primordial bedrock of the Asian continent, the Siberian Craton, some 120 million years ago. A collisional orogen, or a tectonic boundary marked here by the Sayan Moutains, indicates where present-day Mongolia abuts against this huge craton to the north. What is known as the Altaid Tectonic Collage consists of a series of orogenic belts made up of much more ancient tectonic units dating from the late Proterozic to early Mesozoic, or one billion to 540 million years ago (see Figure I).

Typically bounded by a series of large-scale or regional fault zones, the units making up the collage are fragments of accretionary wedge, or seabed sediments, and island arc, or volcanic, material created when a portion or a plate of the Earth's oceanic crust has subducted, or gone below a continental

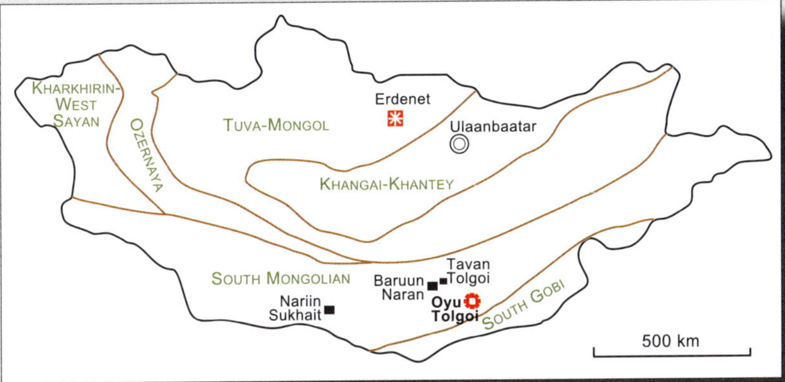

Figure I.

plate. (During obduction, the opposite happens with entire landscapes lifted over another.) Constantly affected by more distant geological forces and their own density, these terranes were also moved and squeezed in relation to one another (see Figure II).

At one time, a large body of water known as the Mongol-Orkhotsk Ocean characterised the region and was later squeezed shut as the terranes first amalgamated and then, over a period of millions of years and accompanied by significant mountain building activity, crashed into the Siberian Craton in the Late Jurassic to Early Cretaceous Period about 120 million years ago. Interestingly, Mongolia's famous dinosaurs – who lived here between 145 and 65 million years ago – were along for some of the ride.

Mongolia's six dominant geological terranes coincide remarkably closely with its geographical regions (see Geography, page 37). Its vast landscape of mountain ranges, valleys and steppe are, quite simply, the eroded surface of what geological forces had created. These are:

Tuva-Mongol and South Gobi Terranes: Located closest to the Siberian Craton, the Tuva-Mongol Terrane takes in the Hovsgol and Hangai regions of today's

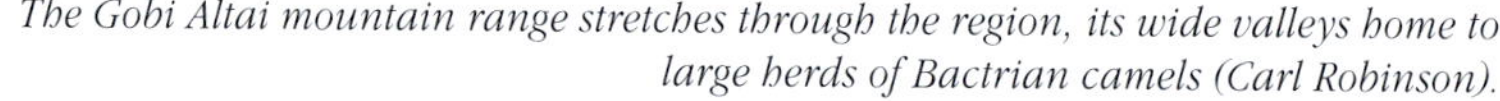

The Gobi Altai mountain range stretches through the region, its wide valleys home to large herds of Bactrian camels (Carl Robinson).

Mongolia. The rocks here date from the intermittent Vendian (650–540 million years ago) to Permian (299–251 million years ago) periods. As in the Hangai range, the landscape is dominated by granites, or arc igneous (magmatic) activity, and sedimentation, best seen in uplifted limestone southwest of Lake Hovsgol. These are in contact with the Precambrian (4,500 million to 540 million years ago) basement. While originally from the same period, the South Gobi Terrane was split or wedged over time by intervening terranes.

South Mongolian Terrane: Encompassing the vast Gobi region across today's southern Mongolia, this terrane is an accretionary wedge with superimposed magmatic arcs, or volcanic activity, with distinct mountain and basin characteristics and material dating from the Ordovician (488–443 million years ago) to Carboniferous (359–299 million years ago) periods. Most dramatically during the intervening Devonian period (416–359 million years ago), the terrane shifted from relative quiet to a period of major volcanic-tectonic activity and the development of a complex arc system. (In geological terms, these included continental, island-arc and back-arc basin settings.) The present-day relief shows sharp orogenic belts of igneous and sedimentary rocks with intervening valleys containing wide basins of piedmont-style deposited quaternary, or recent, sediments.

Today, this belt is host to some of Mongolia's major coal and mineral deposits. During the Permian period that followed 300 million years ago, volcanic activity quieted but tectonism, or instability in the Earth's crust, continued with dramatic folding, faulting and tilting. Volcanism also continued.

What geologists call "alteration" by these and other processes created the mineralogy seen today, including the landscape's distinctive features and colours. One is the widespread presence of distinctive green-schist (metamorphosed chlorite, actinolite and albite) across a wide swathe of southern Mongolia. Oxidised iron-bearing minerals provide the region's rusty reds, yellows and burgundy. Substantial mineralization, including rare earth metals, is associated with igneous activity along ancient fault lines, or orogenic belts, with a mixture of fascinating outcrops and colours, such as whites, blacks and more greens.

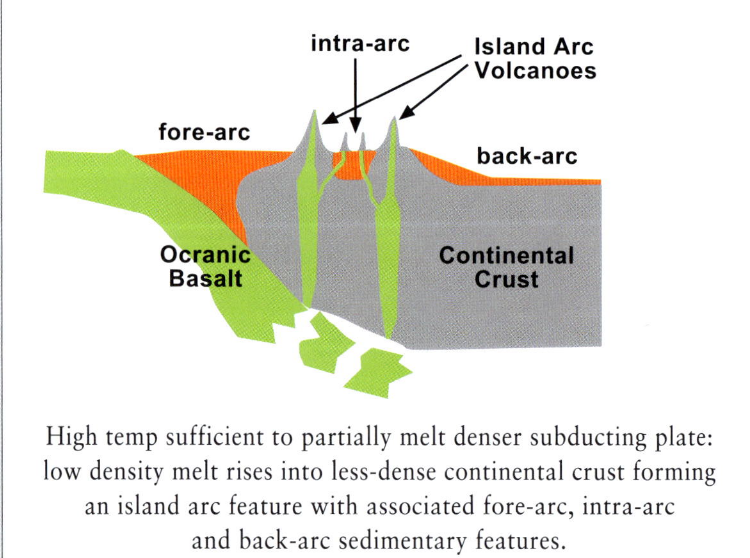

High temp sufficient to partially melt denser subducting plate: low density melt rises into less-dense continental crust forming an island arc feature with associated fore-arc, intra-arc and back-arc sedimentary features.

Figure II.

By the dinosaur era in the Jurassic and Cretaceous periods between 145 and 65 million years ago, this region was in all likelihood a tropical or subtropical environment. Continental drift later uplifted the region to its present-day elevation of 1,200 to 1,500 metres.

Ozernaya Terrane: Located in the northwest of Mongolia, this terrane is the result of the Tuva-Mongol arc migrating onto an accretionary wedge and is noted for the occurrence of an unusual late Neoproterozoic (circa 572 million years ago) ophiolite, or ocean crust. The ophiolitic complex contains intermediate to acidic lavas and sheeted dykes, and an igneous layered mafic complex typical of proto-arc subduction zone type ophiolites. Molybdenum-tungsten skarn type deposits occur in this terrane in northeastern Mongolia.

Kharkhirin Western Sayan Terrane: Coinciding with the main part of the Altai range in western Mongolia, this region is made up of basal turbidites, or sediments formed by currents, overlaid with volcanic and sedimentary rocks deposited in an intra-arc setting, or basin-like valleys between island-arc volcanoes, caused by the progressive western migration of the Tuva-Mongol terrane. Tectonic activity along the faulted edge of this and the South Mongolian Terrane after the Indian subcontinent crashed into Asia some 35 million years ago created today's Altai range which stretches down into the South Gobi.

Khangai-Khantey Terrane: Mongolia's Hentii range running northeast from the capital dates from the Vendian to Carboniferous periods (650–300 million years ago) and is characterised by ophiolithic, or oceanic crust, complexes, turbidites and iron and magnesium-rich and darker volcanics. Later intrusions in the later Permian to Jurassic periods (199–145 million years ago) brought in granites and other lighter-coloured igneous rocks, such as those in the Terelj National Park.

A geology graduate of Ontario's Carleton University, Canadian-born Darrell Turcotte specialises in reconnaissance mineral and coal exploration and has lived in Mongolia for the past 15 years, working mostly for Quincunx Gold Exploration, or QGX Ltd.

hunters" of the early 20th century, starting with the legendary Roy Chapman Andrews, and whose ranks tourists can join today, often totally unexpectedly. These remains are not only from the dinosaur period, but subsequent creatures heralding the modern Age of Mammals.

Despite its bleak appearance, the Gobi supports an incredibly diverse mixture of animals and plant life. Over 200 bird species and 50 mammals live here, but are not always easy to find. Like Central Asia farther west, the Gobi is home to argali sheep, ibex, Eurasian lynx, grey wolves, red foxes, hedgehogs, Asian wild ass, wild camels and gazelles – both the white-tailed and more endangered black-tailed species. The highly endangered saiga antelope lives in its western parts. Most illusive is the Gobi bear, of whom only 25 are thought to exist, living in the desert oases west of the Gobi Altai. Rodents are the most numerous, however, and include hamsters, jerboas, gerbils, voles, mice and pikas. Reptiles include lizards, iguanas and snakes.

Birds are perhaps the easiest to spot, starting with huge vultures and griffons that make the eagles and bustards look tiny in comparison. Falcons and other raptors abound, especially easy to spot when caring for their young in spring. Surprisingly, the dainty demoiselle crane, spotted throughout Mongolia, also lives in the Gobi. Smaller birds such as finches, larks and pipers are everywhere, often playing out alongside your passing vehicle. The Gobi bursts with life.

The type of plant life depends on moisture, of course, and varies dramatically with the heart of the South Gobi certainly the richest where remnant species from wetter times, such as birch, willow and dwarf juniper survive on north-facing slopes of the high ranges. Berry-bearing shrubs, wild roses and succulents are spotted. You'll also see an amazing amount of lush grasses, even alpine meadows, and a plethora of wildflowers. Some 28 of Mongolia's 128 endangered plants are found in the Gobi.

The Gobi is also renowned for its extremes of climate, with temperatures of -42°C (-44°F) in winter to over 40°C (104°F) in summer. Little rain falls, only 50–150mm (2–4 inches) a year, and there is no humidity. The Gobi's wind and dust storms are legendary, especially on the open plains and in spring. Occasionally, particularly severe winter conditions, which the Mongolians call *zud*, can devastate livestock; the region is still recovering from the last series back in the early 2000s.

For early man, the Gobi was a kinder place. A crystal-walled cave in Bayanhongor has revealed Mongolia's oldest Palaeolithic remains. Especially in what's called the **Borzongiyn Govi** southeast of **Dalanzadgad**, petroglyphs, walled settlements and carved stelae point to times when the entire region was more wet and liveable. There is even evidence of an ancient and still mysterious wall in the southern Gobi. Evidence of ancient canals and crops are seen in shallow valleys north of the South Gobi's majestic massif. (Indeed, regions right next to the range still grow fruit and vegetables, especially melons and tomatoes.) Just over the border in Inner Mongolia are the sand-covered ruins of legendary **Khara Koto** (Hara Hot), or **Black City,** near a now-dry desert lake. This was the thriving trade centre visited by Marco Polo and others, and only rediscovered by a Russian explorer in the late 19th century.

Over the centuries, great camel caravans to and from China sauntered along now-forgotten trails across the southern Gobi to Turkestan, now western China's Xinjiang Uygur Autonomous Region, and into Central Asia, the northernmost extension of the legendary **Silk Road.** The **Great Mongolian Road** and its more southern **Small Mongolian Road** passed on the northern and southern sides of the Gobi Altai range. (Another major extension of these two led to Qing Dynasty military strongholds in **Hovd** and **Uliastai** in always troublesome western Mongolia. North-south trails also ran from Mongolia all the way down to Tibet, intersecting with the main Silk Road. (Let us not forget, too, that at the height of the Mongol Empire, other caravan trails headed north to the capital of Karakorum, or today's Harhorin.)

Just across the border from southwest Hovd aimag in China's Gansu Province, was **The House of the False Lama,** the Legendary Dambijantsan, a man of total excess and dodgy title, who made the remote southwest Gobi his turf, preying on caravans in the early 1920s. Actually a Kalmyk from Russia, he drove the Manchus out of western Mongolia with his 1912 attack on Hovd. He later proclaimed himself the reincarnation of Amarsana, the last Oirad leader to succumb to the Qing in the 18th century. Not quite the unifying leader they were looking for, the Communists executed him in 1923.

American explorer Owen Lattimore mentions the incredible tale in his classic *The Desert Road to Turkestan* as he travelled on the **Winding Road** farther to the south in Inner Mongolia and Gansu in 1927 (upheavals in Soviet-run Mongolia had closed this ancient trade route). Today, modern caravans in 4WDs busily search for the Gobi's vast mineral wealth, principally gold, copper and coal. (The largest, and most controversial, is the massive copper-gold mine at **Oyu Tolgoy** southeast of Dalanzadgad, potentially one of the largest in the world. The South Gobi also has rich deposits of anthracite, or thermal, coal with four open-pit mines operating in 2009.)

The Gobi is clearly a "must-see" destination. Although mostly dry and flat, its eastern end – which visitors see on the Trans-Mongolian Train (see page 166) from Beijing – provides a taste. Windblown **Saynshand**, the capital of **Dornogov** aimag, is a stop on the railway and offers several nearby sights, such as **Khamaryn Khiid**, the rebuilt monastery of 19th century Buddhist monk, playwright and poet Danzan Ravjaa. Halfway to the border crossing point at **Zamyn-Uud, Burdene Bulag** are some of the Gobi's largest and most extensive sand dunes, including a lovely oasis with mineral springs.

The aimag centre of Saynshand is also a good starting point for a longer cross-country push to the South Gobi retracing the steps of Andrews' Central Asiatic Expeditions in the early 1920s. Few visitors come through this remote region and the trip includes the 6,000-square-kilometre (2,300-square-mile) **Ergeliyn Zoo Natural Reserve**, the nearby Jurassic-era **Siuhent Petrified Forest** and a smaller one at nearby **Tsagaan Tsav,** also home to the black-tailed gazelle. A granite fracture from the Bogd Fault which extends across this vast desert region is visible near the western border with **Omnogov**, or **South Gobi** aimag.

But the simple fact is most tourists head straight for the South Gobi, either individually or in groups, roughly 600 kilometres (375 miles) south-southwest of Ulaanbaatar. This is Mongolia's most developed – and popular – tourist destination. Typically, Omnogov – Mongolia's largest aimag – is the first stop on the so-called **Golden Circuit** that also travels overland to Harhorin, the ancient Mongol capital, in the centre and to Lake Hovsgol in the north-northwest. Others simply fly straight into the modern aimag centre of **Dalanzadgad.** Large tourist ger camps are everywhere, including what many regard as the most luxurious in Mongolia, the Gobi Three-Camel Lodge.

At the height of the summer tourist season, hundreds of tourists visit daily, crowding its three main scenic sites. But somewhat surprisingly for such a popular destination, the road infrastructure remains poor, even awful in places, and distances between sites are incredibly long. (This would be a great place for helicopters.) Remarkably, its famous ice-covered gorge (see below) is the only place in Mongolia sporting informative signage, including speed-limit signs on the winding dirt road down into the site. Personally, I'd been too spoiled by the remoteness and solitude of an earlier visit to Bayanhongor's version of the South Gobi (see below).

Still, the South Gobi belongs on your "to do" list. It's all a matter of when and how you make the journey, plus giving yourself extra time to relax and actually enjoy and explore the surroundings. The "context" of the place is also important and, while I understand time-pressed tourists flying in for a couple days, a road trip down through what is in between – the **Middle Gobi** – is certainly recommended.

On the main road, as the dark line of the Gobi Altai mountains, here the **Gurvan Saihan** or **Three Beauties**, finally appears on the southern horizon across an immensely wide valley – with still another two or three hours to go – there is a feeling you've reached the edge of the world. And a real sense of accomplishment, too, as this direct road from

UB is one of the busiest – but also probably most boring – in all of Mongolia. At some points, up to 15 old and new tracks form a scar across the landscape wider than an expressway. The straight-through high-speed run on **Route AO201**, popular with budget travellers, takes at least 12 hours.

A much more pleasant alternative is the unnamed southwest-running road past UB's international airport, involving a couple of nights spent in southern **Tov** and **Dundgov** (Middle Gobi) aimags along the way, staying in ger camps, camping out or, in my case, an incredible overnight stay with a ger family (see Special Topic, page 294.) The thrill here is a ground-level approach to the South Gobi's famous **Flaming Cliffs**, where Roy Chapman Andrews stumbled onto his massive dinosaur find in 1922 and, with newsreels rolling and cameras clicking, brought his heavily laden camel caravan to a picturesque halt the following year. (Most tourists only see the cliffs from an observation platform at the top.)

Not only did my hosts from Tseren Tours depart UB on a rainy and inauspicious Tuesday but the entire journey, returning on the main road, was done anticlockwise, another Mongolian no-no. (The only thing that went wrong? See below.) Ever in a rush, as travel writers are, we knocked off their seven-day Jeep Tour in a record five days.

I was assigned Tseren's best driver – crewcut, green-eyed Zorgo – and a pimple-faced guide named Zolbo who loves old rock 'n roll. Our vehicle was a second-hand Hyundai Galloper 4WD with, for some reason, Aussie-style "roo-bars" on the front. Zorgo's nickname is Eagle Eye, and those unusually coloured eyes spotted animals, especially bird life, miles away and provided an amazing undercurrent to the entire journey. We'd barely left UB when he was already off-road over trackless grass-covered hills looking for birds, settling for a few white-tailed gazelles instead. We spotted a dozen steppe eagles soaring over one immense valley. The first part of the journey through southern Tov aimag with stops at the **Ar Burdiin Els**, the closest sand dunes to UB, and **Zorgol Khayrkhan Uul,** a spectacular black-and-white wind-scarred mountain, were noted in an earlier chapter (Around UB, page 203) as pleasant day-trip or overnight destinations from the capital.

Entering **Dundgov** aimag, or **Middle Gobi**, the mountains disappeared behind us and the landscape opened up onto the steppe, here undulating with wide valleys. Zorgo suddenly turned cross-country and we pulled up right alongside a nest of three buzzard fledglings literally in the middle of the valley floor, their huge nest of twigs filled with detritus from modern Mongolia such as plastic bags, paper and plastic sandals. We then drove up onto a long plateau, the easternmost extension of Mongolia's massive Hangai Mountains to the northwest. Lakes, some quite large and others only patches of green, dotted the landscape with nomads herding sheep and goats along with the odd camel.

STAYING WITH A GER FAMILY

We were well into the first day of our overland trip to the South Gobi when my young guide Zolbo advised we'd be spending the night with a *ger* family. They are a feature of many tours around Mongolia, especially for budget travellers. And I was, after all, on an entry-level "camp and home stay" and not a more luxurious "tourist ger camp" tour.

By this stage of my travels around Mongolia, I'd already stayed in plenty of tour camps, rustic *aimag* and *sum* centre hotels and camped out a couple of times. I'd also visited many nomads in their gers, sharing milk tea, dried yogurt and boiled sheep. I'd even helped erect a ger or two in the middle of nowhere.

But I was a bit reluctant at the idea of actually staying overnight with a nomad family. Mostly, I just didn't want to impose. I also worried what we'd talk about, feeling out of place, or committing a gross discourtesy. Where would we all sleep? I certainly wasn't concerned about food. As things turned out, the stopover was one of my most pleasant and memorable experiences in Mongolia.

Separated from their kids and tied head to head in a line, cashmere goats await their evening milking (Carl Robinson).

We'd just passed through an incredible dust, rain, thunder and lightning storm in Dundgov (Middle Gobi) aimag, and out the other side the late afternoon sun was blazing on our now mud-drenched 4WD. Our driver Zorgo, or "Eagle Eye" for his bird-spotting skills, beamed as he spotted a couple of gers on a rise far to our left. Cutting cross-country, we were warmly welcomed by his long-time friends – "*Sain baina uu!*" (Hello!) – with lots of friendly nods and welcoming smiles.

But surely, we'd caught them at a bad time, I thought. With one long rope and in separate rows, the cashmere goats and fat-tailed sheep were tied head-to-head and ready for milking. Everyone was busy. Stools and buckets moved down the line, a few quick squirts from each animal. Grandma ripped clusters of wool off the sheep into another bucket to make felt. Her two-year-old granddaughter wandered around in only one shoe. A cat on heat meowed constantly, making everyone laugh. The big four-eyed Mongolian dog lay flat out and leery of any approaches.

It'd been a long day from UB and was now past 8pm with the sun slowly setting. Time to relax. Ducking low, I stepped over the low threshold of the open door into the ger, past the iron stove and its chimney and sat on a bed to the left, or male side. In a slight reversal of roles, our host Byambaa sat opposite on the floor of the woman's side. A low wooden table sat parallel to the stove, further inside the ger. He served milk tea and dried yogurt. He flattened a round ball of wheat flour and began slicing homemade noodles with a knife. He and Zorgo were catching up. Daughter Odnoo wandered in, chatting away and desperate to help, the smartest and most talkative two-year-old girl I've ever met.

But mealtime was still some time off. The milking was finished and mother goats and sheep turned loose outside the family's two gers, the smaller one a kitchen. We wandered outside to witness one of the loveliest – and most touching – scenes you'll see in Mongolia. Accompanied by Zorgo, Byambaa and his 13-year-old son, Tunjin, just home for summer from school in a nearby sum centre, walked far up the rise and out of sight. Minutes passed.

Finally, and to a rising crescendo of bleats from their mothers, scores of noisy young lambs and kids rushed down the slope at full speed for a massive reunion. This was more fun than a child day-care centre at the end of the day! Of course, the youngsters always find the right mother, nuzzling hard into her teats for a quick top-up. But I'd also spotted a lamb suckling a goat. Byambaa's wife Tsetsegee later explained they'd both suffered a loss and were now together.

Staying overnight with a ger family, instead of just a quick visit, the routines of nomadic life become totally absorbing. Unlike milk of other animals, for example, that of goats and sheep is mixed together. Soon, the freshly drawn milk arrived in a delicious newly brewed thermos of milk tea. Inside the kitchen ger, other portions went into making more dairy and a new batch of vodka, or *nermel.* Before dinner, Byambaa offered a welcome toast of the pleasant-smelling alcoholic beverage with the strength of beer. Our meal was homemade noodles with dried goat, cabbage, potatoes and carrots. Filling and delicious.

And then more vodka toasts and conversation. A parliamentary election campaign was on and Byambaa complained he couldn't get his work done for all the visiting politicians desperate for his vote. (Of course, he couldn't just grab a brochure and send them on their way – Mongolian hospitality requires tea and other homemade goodies.) I was touched when the couple pulled a present for Zorgo out of a cupboard, a Chinese-made multipurpose flashlight and mini-tool kit they'd bought months before not knowing when their friend would visit again. They'd only arrived here 20 days ago and might move soon because the grass was running out.

Occasionally, groups of cute kids and lambs bounded up to the door begging noisily to come inside, but were chased away with a "*choo*". (The only animal allowed inside was the desperately lonely cat.) The family were curious about me and asked about my family and life back in Australia. They flattered me how I didn't look my age, but from their lined and weathered faces I was surprised how much younger they really were, still in their 30s. The atmosphere was welcoming and convivial. I felt totally at home.

Typically, the ger had a satellite dish like I'd seen all over Mongolia. Elsewhere, I'd caught glimpses of NBA finals, wrestling and quiz shows, even interrupted a young man's favourite South Korean soap opera up in the Hentii. But I'd never figured out the technology. Using a solar panel, vehicle-sized batteries are charged up and then power a simple black-and-white television and its satellite-tracking device. After our meal, Byambaa's younger brother Epdenee was desperate to watch his favourite late-night soap. While one brother watched the TV and gave instructions, the other one outside manoeuvred the dish until the picture zeroed in, all a bit fuzzy but definitely watchable. (They have four channels.) Considering how often nomads move, usually with the satellite dish on top of everything, the technology was amazingly rugged.

The ger – pronounced "gair" – is a fascinatingly simple structure and ideally adapted to the nomadic lifestyle. (Some families have more substantial buildings, including corals, at their winter camps.) For nomads, the ger – known as a yurt elsewhere in Central Asia – is the ideal mobile home. Ger walls are made of foldable wooden lattice, the number of pieces dependent on how large they want their home to be, with a wooden door that always faces south away from the prevailing winds.

The main support for the ger comes from two solid wooden poles that hook into a large round ring overhead (never lean or hold onto them – it's bad manners). Numerous longer and thinner poles are then stretched from holes in the ring to the upright lattice and tied with string made from dried cow or camel hide. The wooden structure is then covered in huge sheets of homemade felt for insulation and then weatherproofed in canvas secured by long ropes made from horsehair. The iron stove sits directly below the hole or *toono*, which provides the main light into the ger and is also the exit point for the chimney. (The hole also acts as a clock during the day.)

In bad weather, the ger's hole is covered by a separate piece of canvas pulled over by a rope. In particularly windy conditions, more ropes are draped directly over the entire structure and weighed down by heavy rocks or discarded machinery. (In style, the gers of the minority Kazakhs of western Mongolia have steeper roofs and are generally more colourful inside.) Putting up a ger takes barely an hour.

The feeling inside the ger is cosy but hardly claustrophobic. Everything has its place and the family altar, usually just to the left of the far wall, is always the first of the furniture put into position when the ger is assembled. Typically, the altar has a Buddha and other religious objects, often a photo of the current Dalai Lama and those of family members, both living and deceased, and is where incense is burned daily. (Do make a point of clasping your hands together and bowing here.) The altar and other wooden cupboards dominate the far side of the ger with the beds on either side separated by a table. More furniture sits near the entrance with the front right, or female side, acting as a pantry. TVs are on the left, the male preserve, along with the "*airag* bag" to make fermented beverages.

The family was relatively prosperous, running a couple of hundred sheep and goats. They had a few camels but sadly now only a handful of horses after most of the herd was stolen by rustlers. The family also had a motorcycle, tractor and water trailer. The nearest settlements were 30 kilometres (18 miles) away. Their main income came from selling cashmere wool.

The floor of this ger was covered in linoleum. The table was moved away, our three sleeping bags laid out in a row. The lower walls were lifted to provide a draft and we were soon asleep. Grandma Nadmid, still amazingly active for her 82 years, slept on one bed while the brother watched late-night TV on the other. (The couple and the children slept on the floor of the kitchen ger.) The only sound during the night was the occasional barking of the patrolling dog – both far and

near – keeping the marauding wolves away from the goats and sheep that huddled together outside.

Up with the sun at 5am, I finally met Mongolians who shared my early-morning habits. Grandma was lying in bed making yarn out of camel hair with a spinning top. Using binoculars, Byambaa was sussing out where he'd send the herds out to graze for the day while Tsetsegee was working the milk products in the kitchen. She kindly boiled water for my instant coffee, a beverage Mongolians generally don't drink, and I set up a portable table and chair for my daily diary. The view was superb. A low range stood to the east and the valley spread out far in front. A couple of lumbering double-trailer trucks with goods from China kicked up dust as they headed north towards UB.

The kids and lambs were a constant nuisance, trying to break into the kitchen ger or lick at a muslin bag of curd weighed down by a rock. I helped "choo" them away with a long stick with a piece of cow hide dangling at its end. I was soon rewarded with a bowl of warm yogurt – and only wished I'd brought along my muesli from back home. It was delicious!

A couple of hours later, my Mongolian travelling companions finally awoke. Breakfast was yogurt and fried bread. I dug out a few gifts for the family with pencils for the boy and a cuddly toy for the girl. We chatted about the day ahead. I asked Tsetsegee how she'd met her husband and heard a charming love story. She also made a point of showing me how she makes her vodka. Soon, Byambaa or the brother would follow out the herds and shepherd them from harm, all part of their daily routine. We were back on the road.

Home from school for the summer, young Tunjin helps with the milking of the family's flock of fat-tailed sheep. Their wool is used for felt (Carl Robinson).

A new stupa on a solitary hilltop overlooked ramshackle **Rashaant,** a *bag* or former collective farm, and the more substantial sum centre of **Erdenedalay** offered a small and well-preserved 200-year-old Buddhist monastery that somehow missed the dreaded purges of the 1930s. Just before reaching the town, Zorgo went off-road again. On the crossbar above the town's now-unused entry gate, five falcon chicks were nesting. Mom was off catching rodents and other small creatures for their crying, hungry mouths. (You can easily see how bird poaching is a serious problem in Mongolia.) The long plateau was ending and the vista stretched far out below us with few landmarks, only distant ranges. This was all very nice but I was wondering if the Middle Gobi wouldn't be a bit of a "hard sell" for tourists.

Then, coming down into heart of the wide valley, dark grey storm clouds loomed off to the right and strong winds kicked up, sending sand and debris across the road. Ploughing ahead at full-speed – another one of Zorgo's many skills – we were suddenly in the middle of a blinding dust *and* rainstorm. Strong winds blasted the 4WD from the right and the light turned an eerie green. Lightning struck and rolling thunder overwhelmed the howling winds. Muddy rain pelted down. We slipped off the trail and ground to a halt in bushes. In minutes, the storm passed, the wind subsided and sun returned. We headed up the other side of the valley to find Zorgo's friends, a nomad family, at their traditional spring encampment. The 4WD was covered in mud. They welcomed us to spend the night, one of my most pleasant in Mongolia (see Special Topic, page 294).

Dundgov can't always promise you an epic dust storm like that one, although we did run into another – a simpler all-day blow – at its eastern end returning on the main road. In a remote desert plain northwest of the pleasant-looking aimag centre of **Mandalgovi** is **Baga Gazriyn Chuluu,** a lovely rock-strewn range full of canyons, caves, a couple of old monasteries and a solitary lake. Tov aimag's **Mother Rock** is located to its northeast. (These destinations are detailed in the Around UB Chapter as day or overnight trips.)

In hilly country cut by gorges in the southwest corner of Dundgov aimag are the ruins of **Ongi Hiid**, a once-large Buddhist monastery destroyed in the 1930s, which spread across a small and lovely river valley after which it is named. Now functioning again, including a souvenir shop and musical performances, the monastery is a good opportunity for visitors who haven't already to witness this sad legacy from nearly 70 years of Communist rule in Mongolia. (Nearby tourist ger camps set in sandy, tree-lined gorges are an overnight stop for travellers cutting cross-country from the South Gobi to Harhorin.)

Shortly afterwards, we crossed into **Omnogov** aimag, or **South Gobi** province, and entered an amazingly flat steppe that brought back fond memories of the Menengiyn Tal far to the east (see Great Eastern Steppe, page 256). Known as the **Otogon Hoovoriyn Tal**, this is "classic steppe" – totally flat with dead-straight power lines paralleling the road. The shimmering heat warped isolated gers and herds of camels and sent mirages of shimmering lakes up into the air. Off to the right, the steppe abruptly ended with the sharp banks of the **Ongi Gol** (River), flowing below us in a wide valley. A range of hills – foothills of the Hangai – rose on the far horizon above the opposite bank. Zorgo was making an incredibly speedy run – until we came off the steppe and loudly blew out the left rear main spring. We staggered on, passing through the sum centre of **Mandal-Ovoo** where canals once fed lush farms in its still-green and lush tree-lined river valley. Just to the west, its waters join those of the Ongi River to fill **Ulaan Nuur**, a square-shaped lake that ends in desert sands.

The variety of landscapes at this northern end of Omnogov was incredible. Quite suddenly, we passed over a low ridge and were in a barren heavily volcanic landscape, mostly flat but surrounded by heavily fractured and eroded ranges and rugged ravines. The ground was covered in black, wind-eroded pebbles, a characteristic of the so-called Black Gobi. We were inside a large rift zone created north of the fault line that formed the Altai range farther to the south and west some 20 million years ago. This quickly gave way to flats that looked like an ancient seabed and then, from a low roller-coaster ridgeline, we spotted the distinctively red colour of the **Flaming Cliffs** across the wide valley, still far ahead and below a flat-topped plateau. The dark-coloured Gobi Altai stood far on the horizon beyond. Closer to our side of the valley, forests of saxaul trees covered low sandy hills. In the clear air, this was a unique and amazing landscape on an absolutely massive scale.

We dropped down into flatter sandy country, stopping at a dry river crossing where a large camel herd crowded around a well with the trough dry. Its waters were impossible for them to reach. Still springtime but already blazing hot, these two-humped Bactrian camels looked decidedly uncomfortable and half-naked as they shed ragged, thick coats of winter hair. In a real act of kindness, Zorgo and Zolbo jumped out and took turns filling the trough as the camels pushed and shoved and bellowed for a drink. (I was intrigued by the empty grey plastic oil container around each camel's neck, sometimes two, but couldn't imagine them carrying their own water! More likely, this was a novel way for the owner to identify his herd.) We should've lingered more back along the ridge for soon we'd left the trees behind, forded a wide stream and were surrounded by tourist ger camps – back in civilisation. We forged on and pulled up for lunch in the shade of the Flaming Cliffs. It was an incredible way to arrive in the South Gobi.

With snow already dusting the peaks of the Gobi Altai back in August 1922, American explorer Roy Chapman Andrews was anxiously wrapping up his first Central Asiatic Expedition to return to his winter quarters in Peiping, now Beijing. But a bit lost, the team was looking for the main trail back when, as one still does, they spotted a ger camp and drove up to ask for directions. While waiting for the other cars to catch up, expedition photographer J.B. Shackelford spotted an unusual outcrop and literally plucked out a white fossil bone sitting atop a small pinnacle of rock. The team's palaeontologists recognised a reptilian but had never seen anything like it. The ground was littered with bones and others were eroding out of the walls. Someone else picked up fragments of a fossilised eggshell. This was the fossil gold mine they'd been searching for all summer.

The expedition pitched camp right next to where we were having lunch. Borrowing from Charles Gallenkamp's *Dragon Hunter* (a great companion to have on your trip), this is how Andrews described the spot: "[It] is one of the most picturesque spots that I have ever seen. From out tents, we looked down into a vast basin, studded with giant buttes like strange beasts, carved from sandstone... There appear to be medieval castles with spires and turrets, brick-red in the evening light, colossal gateways, walls and ramparts. Caverns run deep into the rock and a labyrinth of ravines and gorges studded with fossil bones make it a paradise for palaeontologists." They named this the **Flaming Cliffs**.

The expedition returned the next year in 1923 and then in 1925, firmly establishing the Flaming Cliffs as the world's most significant fossil find from the Cretaceous Period, 145 million to 65 million years ago. Most were of the relatively small, or 2–3 metre-long (6–8 foot), parrot-beaked and heavily plated *Protoceratops* at every stage of its life cycle. Most sensationally, the team discovered dozens of fossilised dinosaur eggs and pieces of eggs, even embryos.

Other early dinosaur remains were the bird-like *Oviraptorid* and the deadly and swift *Velociraptor*, a model for the movie *Jurassic Park* although this was really the Cretaceous Period. Also found were those of the *Turbosaurus*, an ancestor of the famous *Tyrannosaurus Rex*, and even a species of crocodile named *Shamosuchus*. The discovery took the scientific world by storm and stirred wide public interest, turning Andrews into a folk hero upon whom, many say, the Indiana Jones character was later based. The later 1925 expedition found links to the "Age of Mammals" and early sign of mankind.

The expeditions funded by the American Museum of Natural History (AMNH) could easily have continued for years. But the increasingly suspicious Soviet-dominated regime in Ulaanbaatar banned any further exploration. During the Communist period Polish, Russian and Mongolian expeditions visited the Flaming Cliffs and went on to discover even more significant sites on the southern side of the Altai massif in the huge **Nemegt Basin**, an area over the range visible from the Singing Dunes (see below). After 1990, the AMNH and other Western and Asian expeditions joined the hunt. Discoveries are still coming to light – even by tourists in more remote spots.

The Mongolians know the Flaming Cliffs as **Bayanzag**, or "many saxauls", such as those we'd just driven through. In earlier times they were prolific here, but as their wood – which roars like a jet engine when lit – is widely used for fires by nomads, as well as tourist ger camps, they are far fewer today. Bayanzag today is one of the South Gobi's top three tourist destinations. Interestingly, the landscape above is almost totally flat desert steppe with water and wind erosion exposing the red sedimentary layers below and forming the brightly coloured cliffs on its edge.

Most visitors arrive at the Flaming Cliffs from their nearby accommodation on the flats to an observation platform overlooking the incredible formations below. Locals sell warm soft drinks and souvenirs, including supposed fossils, and one particularly enterprising young lady has a payphone to call your friends! Unfortunately, there is no signage or brochures explaining the location's importance.

Left: Shabby from losing their thick winter coats, Bactrian camels mill around an isolated well in a dry riverbed in the South Gobi (Carl Robinson).

A Bone to Pick

By *Mark Norell*

There are a few great places in the world to look for dinosaur fossils, but one of the best is Mongolia. Here I am in the aimag of Omnogov in southern Mongolia, leading the 12th instalment of American Museum of Natural History (AMNH) expeditions that began in 1990. Working closely with colleagues from the Mongolian Academy of Sciences we have collected an impressive array of fossil bones – dinosaurs, mammals, turtles and lizards. These specimens are now part of the collection of the Mongolian Academy of Sciences and are part of the pantheon of great discoveries made in Mongolia by successive groups of palaeontologists.

If anyone ever thought the life of an international dinosaur collector was a romantic, thrilling endeavour they should be right here, right now. It is hot (well into the 40s Celsius), I haven't bathed in weeks, and I am filthy. Empty beer cans (a great source of liquid and carbohydrates – especially when heated to ambient temperature) and broken glass obstruct every elevation of my vehicle's clutch; every gear change is a surprise. I am exhausted and hungry as I muscle a heavy Unimog (a truck-size 4WD all-terrain vehicle) full of gasoline barrels that last few kilometres towards our base camp – our little city filled with my stinking companions – and the place on the desert floor I call my bed.

The history of dinosaur discovery in Mongolia has to be old. People have been out in the Gobi for a long time. In places, we come across Neolithic stone tools, Bronze Age remnants, Turkic burial platforms, Chinggis Khaan era pottery and coins, and the latest in discarded Chinese plastic kitchenware. In some areas dinosaur bones are so obvious that you cannot miss them. Eighty-million-year-old fossils can be so well preserved, so white, so pristine that they look like any other bones – like the smashed sheep, camel, horse and yak carcasses that litter the desert floor. The locals must have seen this stuff for millennia. Adriene Mayer, in her book *The First Fossil Hunters: Palaeontology in Greek and Roman Times*, has even speculated that dinosaur bones from the Gobi Desert may have been the root cause for mythological monsters. Perhaps, as the caravans moved across the Gobi, their stories about unusual animal bones with beaks, bumps and big teeth metamorphosed into stories of dragons and gryphons. It is also almost certain that some of these fossils ended up in powder form as "*longgu*" (a traditional Chinese sedative and tranquilliser also used for the treatment of palpitations, insomnia and bad dreams), in the dimly lit pharmacies to the south.

The modern era of dinosaur palaeontology began in the 1920s when the American Museum of Natural History conducted a series of expeditions to Mongolia and other parts of Asia. Termed the Central Asiatic Expeditions, their goal was to find the ancestry of humankind. In this aspect they were unsuccessful – but along the way they collected spectacular remains of dinosaurs and other fossil animals and demonstrated that Mongolia was a treasure trove of fossils.

Roy Chapman Andrews led the expeditions. Andrews was by most accounts a brilliant expedition leader and a vigorous self-promoter. The excellent biography by Charles Gallenkamp (*Dragonhunter*, 2001) portrays him as a complex person, confident in the Gobi Desert as well as New York

A team of paleontologists drive across the Gobi's apparent desolation (Mick Ellison).

Roy Chapman Andrews' desert camp (American Museum of Natural History).

social circles. These desert expeditions were some of the largest and most expensive ever developed. From the field quarters in an old Ming Dynasty palace near Tiananmen Square in Beijing, the expeditions were meticulously planned. Camel caravans were sent out in advance carrying supplies and fuel, and the armed party (chaperoned out of China by military guard) traversed the Gobi Desert in open touring cars.

Andrews was able to convince some of the wealthiest men of his time to shell out huge sums of money to finance his ventures. Although he was not much of a scientist (yet, he did hold a PhD from Columbia University), the success of these expeditions was due to Andrews' leadership and planning. After retiring from the Museum, he was able to turn the exaggerated accounts of his exploits into a money stream that supported him for the rest of his long life.

Fossils were found early on in the first Central Asiatic Expedition, but the most famous locality was discovered in 1922, on the last day of the field season. Andrews' notes record that they were lost on an old caravan road on their way back to Beijing. While Andrews went to get directions at a small garrison, Walter Granger, second in charge and the chief palaeontologist, accompanied by the expedition photographer J.B. Shackelford, went in the other direction to look at a few small hills of red rock. When they approached, a vast bright-red cliff – invisible to the north – lay exposed before them. Immediately fossils were found. Because of the late date, they only collected a few specimens, and the caravan continued towards Beijing. This locality became popularly known as the Flaming Cliffs, because of the bright orange colour of the rocks and "the way they burned deeply in the sun in the afternoon". The Mongolian name for the area is Bayanzag, which in characteristic Mongolian fashion is a simple descriptor meaning "many zag trees". The fossils that were found included a small skull of a dinosaur and the remains of a single egg – thought at the time to be that of a bird.

The next year, in 1923, the expedition headed straight for Bayanzag. It was here that they found the first unequivocal dinosaur nests. During the 1923 season alone they collected three of the most important theropod (the meat-eating dinosaurs that are closely related to modern birds) dinosaur specimens ever discovered – *Oviraptor*, *Velociraptor* and *Saurornithoides*. These were reported on in a seminal paper simply titled "Three new Theropoda, *Protoceratops* zone, central Mongolia". In addition to describing these animals, this paper spun an account of how the Oviraptor died while raiding the nest of a plant-eating dinosaur called *Protoceratops*. The Oviraptor specimen had been found lying on top of a dinosaur nest, at the time thought to be the nest of the small herbivore Protoceratops. It was not until our own expeditions, 70 years later, that conclusive proof was found that these were not the eggs of a Protoceratops being devoured by a marauding Oviraptor. Instead it is the nest of the Oviraptor itself, which died while sitting atop it, probably brooding its yet to be hatched eggs – just as modern birds do.

Today tourists often visit Bayanzag with the idea of following in Andrews' footsteps. It is close to several tourist camps and the airport at Dalanzadgad. In the late 1990s an entrepreneurial nomad even opened a camel riding concession where tourists could be led around on a camel and have their picture taken with the cliffs as a backdrop (and I am sure pick the fleas off themselves on the bus back to the tourist camp). Yet, important specimens

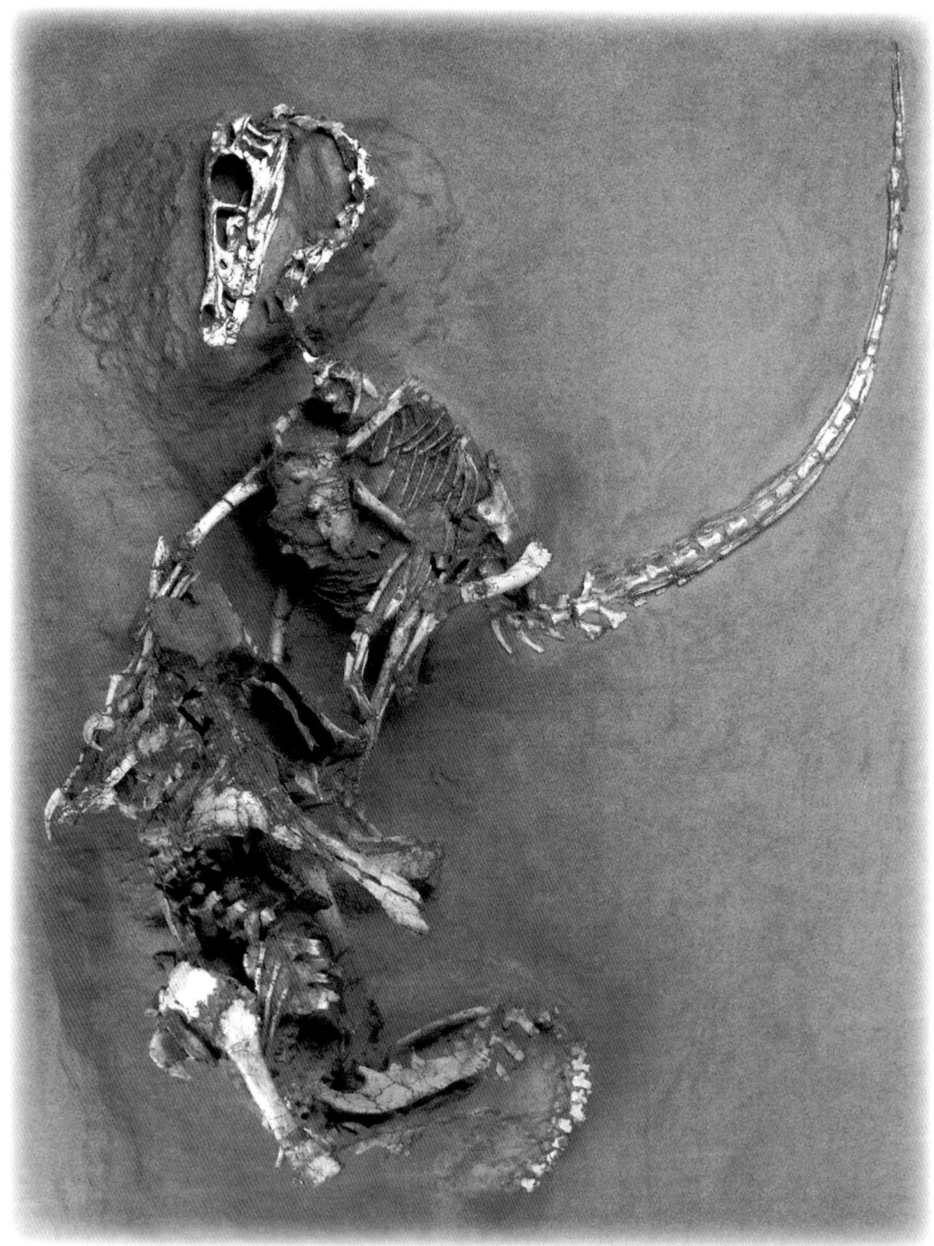

The famous "Fighting dinosaurs" specimen (Mick Ellison).

An Oviraptor nest (Mick Ellison).

are still to be found there, and our expeditions have collected several. Although the area looks much the same as Andrews described it, it has suffered from the depredations of modern tourism. Trash litters the valley, roads are cut on every cliff rim and traverse the valley floor, and human excrement lies mixed with that of ibex, goat and sheep in every area protected by the red cliff face.

By the end of the 1920s a changing political climate caused the cessation of AMNH activities in Mongolia until our involvement began anew in 1990. The storm of political purges of the 1930s ensured that no outsiders, particularly US scientists, would be allowed to explore and map Mongolia. It was not until

An AMNH-funded expedition excavates at Ukhaa Tolgod (Mick Ellison).

after WWII that large-scale palaeontology expeditions were reinitiated in Mongolia. This time it was the Soviets, using a variety of military equipment, who were able to extend operations far outside of the relatively specific areas explored by Andrews. In one of these areas, within the Nemegt Basin, they found some of the greatest dinosaur localities ever discovered. Places with names like Altan Ulaa, Kheerman Tsav and Tomb of the Dragons produced spectacular dinosaurs like the *Tyrannosaurus* relative *Tarbosaurus*, the armoured *Talarurus*, and the duck-billed *Saurolophus*.

Following the Russians were the Poles, who conducted a series of expeditions throughout the 1960s and 70s called the "Polish-Mongolian expeditions". Under the leadership of Zofia Kielan Jaworska, these expeditions collected many new kinds of dinosaurs and their mammalian and lizard contemporaries. They also discovered significant new localities. Research on these materials is still ongoing – led by many of the scientists who took part in the expeditions.

Undoubtedly their most famous discovery was the "Fighting Dinosaurs" found in the white sands of Tugrugeen Shireeh, near Bayanzag, in 1971. This

Roy Chapman Andrews and his team pack fossils into crates, ready for the long journey to New York (American Museum of Natural History).

specimen represents an adult Protoceratops locked in a death struggle with a Velociraptor. The Protoceratops is crouching, while the Velociraptor is lying on its right side. The talons of the Velociraptor's right hind limb are embedded in the neck of its prey, while its hands rake across the skull, the right arm caught between the powerful jaws of the Protoceratops. Caught in a sudden dune collapse, this fossil is a snapshot of a battle that raged between these two animals about 80 million years ago. This treasure of dinosaur palaeontology is on display in the Natural History Museum in Ulaanbaatar along with other fossils collected by Soviet, Mongolian and Polish palaeontologists.

For nearly two decades my colleagues and I have been patrolling much of the same terrain in search of dinosaurs and other fossil animals. Much of our effort is concentrated at Ukhaa Tolgod, which we discovered in 1993. One would like to think that careful planning and perseverance were needed to make such discoveries, but Ukhaa, like the Flaming Cliffs, was discovered as much by happenstance as it was by skill. In fact we had driven by the place on a number of occasions, when one day in 1993, with our caravan mired in the sand, we decided to take a short look. After only a few minutes we knew it was the best place we had ever seen. Ukhaa Tolgod has become one of the best localities for dinosaur remains in Mongolia, itself one of the greatest areas to find dinosaurs on the planet. So far we have found remains of hundreds of dinosaurs and, just as importantly, thousands of specimens of mammals and lizards that lived with them.

At Ukhaa Tolgod we have discovered the remains of an animal we named Citipati – a close relative to Oviraptor (Citipati is the Tibetan protector of the funeral pyre). In addition to beautiful Citipati specimens, we have found animals sitting atop nests brooding them, and even embryos. What does this tell us? A few things, one of which is that because the animals were sitting atop their nests in the same fashion as birds, we can determine that the behaviour of nesting that we see in today's birds has a history that extends well into the dinosaurian ancestors of our fluffy friends.

What accounts for this great preservation? Usually when an animal dies or has been killed, the carcass is scavenged and the skeletons disarticulated. It is a rare occurrence for such fossils to be buried quickly – usually in a stream or river – and preserved. At some Mongolian sites something else happened that suggests that the animals were buried alive. Geological evidence tells us that at Ukhaa Tolgod, the Flaming Cliffs and perhaps Tugrugeen Shireeh, the landscape of 80 million years ago was one of large, sparsely vegetated sand dunes occasionally dissected by ephemeral ponds and rivers. The sand that made up these dunes had a peculiar quality so that it soaked up water, and the sediment that the dunes lay on was not porous. Thus, if enough rain fell the dunes became saturated, and just like sand castles built too close to the water, the dunes catastrophically liquefied, running out as large debris flows. These flows captured all in their wake, burying animals on their nests, fighting, in their burrows and perhaps even in social groups.

A shovelful of Gobi sand goes flying as the dinosaur hunters inspect a fossil site (Mick Ellison).

The history of scientific dinosaur excavation in Mongolia is not even a century old. Compared to most other continental areas, only a handful of expeditions have been active. The locality of Ukhaa Tolgod was a great discovery, yet we are still out here looking for the next astonishing place. Each year we follow a familiar route – out from Ulaanbaatar, across the steppe and into the desert. The regions in which to look are expansive, and palaeontologists have so far barely scratched the surface. There is much to do. Undoubtedly the next hundred years will completely change our contemporary view.

Mark Norell is chairperson of the Division of Palaeontology at the American Museum of Natural History in New York.

Right: The Hongoryn Els – Mongolia's longest stretch of sand dunes (Elbegzaya Lhagvasuren).

From the platform, visitors are welcome to explore, although the cliffs are rather precipitous. It's better to drive down a rough track below and follow the footsteps of those first dinosaur explorers into an incredible maze. In the searing heat of summer, however, when temperatures soar above 40°C (100°F), such wandering is best done early or especially late in the day when the cliffs earn their colourful name.

For those without the time to visit the Singing Dunes, the **Moltzog Els** are 25 kilometres (15 miles) northeast of Bayanzag. Surrounded by saxaul trees, they are smaller but beautifully formed and provide a pleasant alternative. Another interesting site in this area is **Togrogyn Shiree** where the Fighting Dinosaurs, now on display at the Museum of Natural History in UB, were discovered.

Bayanzag is actually outside the boundaries of the **Gobi Gurvan Saihan National Park**, the largest in Mongolia and occupying some 27,000 square kilometres (10,400 square miles) stretching 400 kilometres (250 miles) east to west and 80 kilometres (50 miles) north to south. (Its western tip stretches into southern Bayanhongor aimag, see below.) The **Three Beauties**, as the name translates, is named after three ranges at the park's eastern end, **Zunn Saihan** (East Beauty), **Dund Saihan** (Middle) and **Baruun** (West), but also includes a series of ranges stretching farther south and across its entire length, including the **Zoolon, Sevrei** and **Nemegt**.

This massif is the easternmost extension of the Altai Mountains starting in Mongolia's far northwest. Its interior offers a dramatic and rugged variety of scenery and landscapes.

But from its northern side, which most visitors first see, Gurvan Saihan is surprisingly deceptive. With the valley floor around Dalanzadgad already at an elevation of 1,000 metres (3,280 feet), the range – fronted by a wide and gentle slope of desert steppe – rises only another 1,000 or so metres. But for those with time, the northern face hides remnants of plants and trees from cooler and wetter times. The beauty definitely lies within.

From Bayanzag, the main entrance into Gurvan Saihan looked close but was still a couple hours away. But that would wait for a more roundabout – anticlockwise – approach. First, we headed to the nearby sum centre of **Bulgan** – famous for its cold and drinkable springs – for much-needed repairs on our own vehicle's springs. That done, we spent the late afternoon speeding west – and listening appropriately to Boney M's "Rasputin" at full volume – across a wide and surprisingly grassy plain. The Three Beauties disappeared behind and in the far distance I could even make out Bayanhongor's glacier-peaked Ikh Bogd which had so enthralled me only weeks before (see below.) We finally turned south up a canyon cutting through another range, **Bayan Bor Nuruu,** and found a camping spot. The narrow valley was lushly green and covered in white-headed grasses, multiple coloured flowers and a lovely-smelling sage. Argali, or wild sheep, roamed the sharply rising rocky cliffs above. We even had a full moon.

Running for 180 kilometres (112 miles) on the southern side of this last range, the **Hongoryn Els**, also known as the **Hongor Els**, is Mongolia's longest stretch of sand dunes – and the second of the South Gobi's three most popular tourist destinations. Unfortunately, the dynamics which created these majestic dunes – lots of wind – can also ruin your visit. The previous day was perfect, but as we descended onto the flat valley floor and its tourist ger camps, we could barely see them. But up close, the dunes are indeed spectacular, rising sharply at their highest point over 200 metres (650 feet) with bushes and grasses growing near their base. Many visitors climb the dunes or do camel treks. Their name, **Singing Dunes**, comes from the roaring sound of moving sand, either from strong winds or hikers setting off mini-avalanches down their steep faces.

Averaging about 12 kilometres (7.5 miles) across, the dunes do not stand alone, as I'd pictured, but are squeezed onto the southern side of a valley and up against another massive range that runs parallel to the Three Beauties. Narrow at its western end, the valley acts as a massive funnel of wind and sand from open flatlands to the west. Widening out, the valley is remarkably lush and green. A small spring-fed creek, the west-flowing **Hongoryn Gol,** runs along the dunes' northern face forming the occasional oasis and lake, home to an unusual assortment of amphibians, birds and other animals. (A day trip northwest from the dunes leads to one of Mongolia's few remaining saxaul forests, with trees several metres high at **Balar Tsong**.)

This lush valley also has a surprisingly large population of people and goats – certainly the healthiest such animals I saw in Mongolia – who've made the South Gobi the country's richest producer of cashmere wool (though the goats' eating habits also raise fears of increased desertification). From their encampments along the valley floor, the nomads also run camel treks for tourists.

We'd come around the long way to the Hongor Els, but most tourists use more direct routes from Dalanzadgad and ger camps on the northern side. Still, even on the best roads travelling through passes between the Three Beauties, visiting the dunes is an all-day trip. (A better alternative is to spend a second night at a ger camp near the dunes.) Slightly longer but most interesting is the road running through **Gegeetyn Am**, a narrow gorge through **Baruun Saihan** (Western Beauty) known for its Lammergeier vultures. From the dunes' highest point, we travelled east along the main tourist road.

Off to our right, or south, against the backdrop of the rugged **Sevrei Range** and its 2,631-metre (8,632-foot) summit, the dunes constantly changed in shape and character but turned gradually lower. A turnoff cuts through the dunes and over the Sevrei and then west along the **Nemegt Mountains**, with the park's highest peak of 2,788 metres (9,147 feet), to the red hills of **Ukhaa Tolgod** and **Nemegt Canyon**, both significant for dinosaur finds, and to remotest **Hermen Tsav** and **Zulganay Oasis** – a trip for the adventurous (see below).

But with a steady string of alluvial fans full of round rocks and boulders off the rugged and steep-sided northern ranges, the main road east was incredibly and bone-jarringly rough, even getting on Zorgo's nerves, broken only occasionally by a smooth and grassy high-speed ridge. At one point off to our right, the line of dunes abruptly stopped and turned into separate but still large, solitary piles of white sand, "baby dunes" which will perhaps grow up one day into more solid dunes in the neverending process of nature. Smaller lines of dunes then continued on the southern side of the now-much wider valley, which was dotted with the occasional lake. We finally reached the sum centre of **Bayandalai**, the largest settlement in the valley and actually outside the park boundary, with the main turnoff to its northern side. The Middle and East Beauties were still far ahead – and the trip had taken so long that I thought we'd already passed them!

On its southern side, the Gurvan Saihan range is a dramatic contrast to its more benign northern side. Rising sharply from the valley floor, there was absolutely no sign of vegetation, just jumbled rock to challenge even the best mountaineer, and no distinctive summits. Pulling off the main road, we were travelling across level ground when it suddenly opened up into a small U-shaped valley. At the bottom down a sharply descending track lay the ruins of a small Buddhist monastery, **Hushuu Huralyn Tuuri**, a lovely spot beside a creek leading out of a narrow gorge at the very foot of Zuun Saihan, or the East Beauty.

The vehicle barely squeezed through the watery entrance of **Dungenee Am** (gorge), and wound past groups of university students celebrating graduation by camping out in large tents. (A bit of romance going, too, as couples cuddled in tiny caves along the gorge's sheer wall.) They yelled greetings – and warnings too. The gorge ahead was full of ice and we'd never get through. By now the wind had turned to rain and we stopped at a barrier of thick ice to explore the gorge ahead on foot. With the warmer weather, a steady stream flowed beneath and I seriously wondered if the ice would carry our heavy 4WD. But not Zorgo; leaving us to walk, he drove up onto the ice and forged ahead. Soon, the gorge widened into a lovely grass-covered valley through thc heart of the range. The rain stopped. We'd entered another world. Wild goats scampered in the hills and falcon lairs dotted the surrounding cliffs. On a wide ledge just above the valley floor, we found a spot to camp. The sunset was spectacular and my Mongolian companions played chess.

The lammergeier can be seen soaring over the Gobi on massive wings (Richard Bartz, reproduced under the Creative Commons Attribution ShareAlike 2.5 licence).

Yolyn Am's "glacier" is a popular attraction among Mongolians as well as foreigners (Elbegzaya Lhagvasuren).

The valley widened and was covered in grass as we drove high up into the heart of the **Zunn Saihan** (East) range early the next morning. Side valleys opened up, and we spotted a fledgling steppe eagle learning to fly. Nobody lives up here and we were surprised to see a huge black-and-white *hainak*, a breed of half-yak and half-cow from Mongolia's higher and cooler regions, wandering over the hills, obviously very lost. The valley narrowed again and we crested the range onto a totally unexpected alpine meadow, bright green and covered in spring flowers. A narrow canyon with its walls soaring high above appeared. Precariously, the track headed straight down to the canyon floor into an even lusher and deeper valley. Soon, we turned onto a well-maintained road and arrived at the entrance to **Yolyn Am.** Also known as **Eagle Valley**, or more correctly Vulture Canyon, for the endangered Lammergeier vultures who live here, this is the third of the South Gobi's most popular tourist spots and receives thousands of visitors every summer.

First established as a park back in 1965, Yolyn Am is well managed, restricts speeds on the incoming road, limits vehicular access to the site and even includes informative signage on the local wildlife such as ibex and argali sheep. These are difficult to spot, along with the vultures, but not the small, hamster-like pika, a round-eared member of the rabbit family, who must be paid to entertain visitors, popping in and out of their burrows and scampering through the grass. The main attraction of Yolyn Am is a year-round "glacier" – actually layers of accumulated snow and ice – which is sheltered by the soaring canyon walls and survives through the South Gobi's hottest summer days. The tiny valley is the best example of the park's biological diversity.

Left: A good game of chess at the end of a hard day's driving can become a nightly ritual (Carl Robinson).

From the entry gate, the walk to the "glacier" is three kilometres (1.8 miles) but local nomads hire out horses and camels in the summer months. The trail follows a gurgling stream along a lush valley floor covered in flowers – and scampering pikas – and becomes increasingly narrow and winding as the canyon walls, made of the same twisted sedimentary rock throughout the Altai range, rise steeply above, placing its floor in deep shadow. Old-timers say the ice has shrunk considerably in recent years, but on my 2008 visit it still stretched in chunks over 500 metres (1,640 feet) before becoming totally solid at its narrow exit, where it is only metres wide. Annual layers can clearly be seen in the three-metre-thick (10-foot) blue-tinged ice, but its surface is hardly smooth or pristine and is covered in Gobi dust.

Judging from the graffiti left behind, Soviet soldiers on duty in Mongolia were once tourists here too. On a hot summer's day, the canyon certainly provides a pleasant tonic to the searing, dry heat outside. At the park's exit on its northern side is an information centre and souvenir shop – with great views back across the wide valley. But for those heading into the range, there is little hint of the incredible sights inside this mountain wall.

As noted earlier, by cutting through a dip in the Hongor Els and crossing over the Sevrei range and then west on its southern side, visitors can travel to more remote parts of the South Gobi, including fossil-rich hills and canyons. Eventually, this route ends at the massif's westernmost point where even more dramatic scenes await in southern Bayanhongor aimag, the latest and furthest extension of the vast Gurvan Saihan National Park. A more direct track – obviously used by the teams of fossil-hunting palaeontologists spending their summers here – passes through the sum centre of Bayandalai, skirting around the eastern end of the Sevrei. (Other trails west lead past the Hongor Els or on the northern side of the range.)

This run across the western end of the **Gobi Altai** massif is tough country and shouldn't be done without two or more vehicles, and these should be totally self-sufficient. From the rugged southwestern edge of the huge Gobi Altai massif, flat desert plains stretch down to the nearby Chinese border, actually Inner Mongolia. This region is certainly remote but there is a border crossing at **Shivee Huren-Sehe**, not open to foreigners, and the Chinese are building a link from their main east-west rail network to exploit a huge anthracite coal deposit at **Naraan Sukhait** at the foot of the massif.

With its remoteness and sparsely developed tourist infrastructure, Mongolia's **Bayanhongor Gobi** makes quite a contrast to the popular South Gobi which most tourists visit. But this fascinating region is – without too much arm-twisting and aware of the country's incredible variety – my most recommended destination in Mongolia. (This was my second extensive expedition out of UB after the Great Eastern Steppe, and before my high-speed reconaissance as detailed previously.) Some travellers continue the journey from the South Gobi.

The most direct approach is to travel west from Ulaanbaatar on the paved **Millennium Road** towards the ancient Mongol capital of Harhorin, another popular destination, and after crossing the **Tuul River** head southwest through **Ovorhangai aimag** and its capital **Arvayheer,** at the southeast foot of the **Hangai Mountains** (see page 390). Getting into position at a comfortable tourist ger camp at this end of the Gobi is a comfortable two-day trip with an overnight stop en route, usually around **Rashaant** and the **Mongol Els** sand dunes (see Around UB, page 208). (Seemingly oblivious to blown tyres and busted springs, our high-speed companion 4WD took 16 hours straight through.)

Arvayheer is a large and beautifully positioned aimag centre where, in spring, the Hangai Mountains behind are still covered in snow and provide the headwaters for the **Ongi Gol** (River) which heads across a wide valley and into the southwest corner of **Dundgov** (Middle Gobi) and northwest **Omnogov** (South Gobi) to empty into **Ulaan Nuur** (above). (The valley is also a wheat-growing region.) From here, the Millennium Road turns to dirt and skirts across a high plateau into Ovorhangai's southwest where the trails to the Bayanhongor Gobi begin. (The Millennium Road winds its way on to Mongolia's far western aimags.)

Travel is down into the same rift valley observed in northern Omnogov but which here is squeezed much more narrowly – and dramatically – between the Hangai and Altai ranges with a string of landlocked and salty lakes. Starting from a higher elevation, the journey is an hours-long but high-speed descent through a stark and barren landscape cut by the occasional watershed and dotted with the odd volcanic range, coal and gold mine.

Finally, the **Valley of the Lakes** appears with the sharply rising **Ikh Bogd Uul** (3,957 metres or 12,982 feet) rising sharply behind, Mongolia's fifth highest peak. Another massive range, **Baga Bogd Uul** (3,590 metres or 11,778 feet) rises 80 kilometres (50 miles) farther east-southeast. Higher and more solitary masses than the South Gobi's Gurvan Saihan, they are also part of the Gobi Altai**.** Both peaks are capped in snow year-round, a dramatic and welcoming sight in this brownish desert setting of saltpans, lakes and small sand dunes under a cloudless blue sky. The rift valley is about 40 kilometres (25 miles) wide and dominated here by **Orog Nuur**, a salty lake that varies in size over the years depending on precipitation.

Adding to the drama of this location is actual evidence of a massive earthquake that struck on 4 December 1957, and is still remembered by older nomads. The 8.1 magnitude quake along the 250-kilometre-long (155-mile) **Bogd Fault** left a long and visible crack up to six metres high (20 feet) at the base of the mountain, and even divided a lake in two. Ikh Bogd's summit is mostly flat, an uplifted plain with a shorter fault line on its southern side. From the lakeside of the mountain, a road winds precariously to the top where a small community live and raise yaks surrounded by the forest. (From here, the rift valley rises in a northwest-trending arc, eventually widening out into Mongolia's Great Lakes Region, see page 376.)

The **Bayanhongor Gobi** lies on the far southern side of these two massive ranges. A road leads up a long river valley and reaches a grass-covered watershed sloping down and across a wide valley to mountain ranges on the far horizon. With the ground rising sharply off to our right up the side of Ikh Bogd, and more gently to ranges on the southern side, the view was absolutely breathtaking, a sense of space and distance that goes on forever. Just how much so was the long run still to come before finally reaching the flat valley below and the tiny sum centre of **Bayangovi** on the mountain's southern side. The morning light from our nearby tourist ger camp, The Gobi Camel, revealed an absolutely stunning setting across a grass-covered valley and straight up the heavily eroded southern side of Ikh Bogd to its wide and snow-capped summit. (The hike straight up takes 12 hours.) A white stupa stood on a low ridge just to the south, once part of a Buddhist monastery. I felt wonderfully cut off from the rest of the world.

For the next few days, just as for those endless camel caravans that once crossed this same valley, this entrancing mountain, which dominates the northern horizon, became our beacon in the desert. Double-teaming with two fully equipped Japanese 4WDs, including a highly skilled local guide, we clocked up over 2,000 kilometres (1,200 miles) exploring this remote part of the Gobi and ventured far south nearly to the Chinese border. Few tourists visit here, and while the more popular South Gobi offers its own unique and relatively close-together destinations, the strongest attraction here is its very isolation and

Right: The Ikh Bogd massif in Bayanhongor aimag (Don Croner). Above: A stupa looks out over the lush valley on the southern side of mighty Ikh Bogd, or Buddha's Mountain (Carl Robinson).

constant new discoveries, sights you'll stumble across and be unable to find on a map. Forced to choose between the two destinations, I'd strongly recommend Bayanhongor's more mysterious, often totally unpredictable, version of the vast Gobi.

Like other parts of the Gobi, few nomads live here and those that do traditionally raise camels, although many are now switching over to more lucrative cashmere goats. Up near the southern side of Ikh Bogd, we turned east up into hills and visited briefly with a family whose large herd of goats has just produced a bumper crop of kids, a sign of real prosperity to come for this nomad family. The undulating hills were lushly covered in green grass and the northern-facing slopes of the mountain range behind had distinctive bands of colour – dark brown, tans and a military-like green I'd never seen in nature. (Determined by underlying sedimentary layers, the unusual combination of colours is constantly repeated in a huge band way up into northwest Mongolia.) In the other direction, one-time volcanic vents appeared and then a rugged wall-like ridge, also volcanic, with a sharply dipping valley and vistas beyond to snow-capped **Baga Bogd** on the horizon.

Home for the summer, nomad girls help tend their family's cashmere goats (Carl Robinson).

We cleared the end of the range and the landscape changed completely – one of those constant surprises of Mongolia. We looked south far across a vast slope, an alluvial fan of water-borne rocks, to the flat plain below. Mirages waffled up in the shimmering heat. The southern side of the same range was totally different – a wind-blasted surface of pale-coloured rock. Walking up a gorge, we found a large cave entrance. Behind an overhanging sill, the floor slanted sharply upwards forcing us onto hands and knees to enter the main chamber.

Inside, the cave's ceiling towered 50 metres (160 feet) to a small opening to the sky. The cave's dusty walls were covered in pink crystals as revealed here and there by the chippings of previous visitors. We were inside **Tsagaan Aguy**, or **White Cave**, the oldest Palaeolithic or Early Stone Age site in Mongolia (roughly 750,000 years ago) and where researchers recently found more than 800 stone artefacts. Back then, the climate was considerably wetter and the plains below teeming with wildlife. (A similar site is located farther west at **Chikhen Agui**.) The excitement is palpable.

Down on the plain below, an extension from our camp, a solitary volcano stood tantalisingly off on the eastern horizon as we crossed the river flats where camels grazed. Following a riverbed up the plain's southern side, we crested onto a plateau marked by unusual rocky outcrops and down into a new watershed marked by black shiny mountains that looked like huge dumps of coal, but were clearly volcanic in origin. We were in the **Ikh Bayan Nuruu**, or range, and soon entered the mysterious **Bichigt Had**, or **Valley of the Writings**.

On its northern side, the rock walls of this narrow valley – actually more like jumbled stacks of black rocks – are literally covered in amazingly well-preserved petroglyphs from the Bronze Age some 5,000 years ago. Scratched into the rocks' oxidised black surfaces are sun symbols, depictions of men and women, hunters, deer, wolves, gazelles, ibex, scorpions and even wheeled carts. Wandering up the valley along a small creek that dead ended at a herder's ger, I spotted more modern graffiti, thankfully well away from these precious relics. With only one way in, the valley clearly had an important ceremonial function. (Actually inside the Gurvan Saihan National Park, travellers to the South Gobi can visit Bichigt but it's a very long return journey and best as part of an ongoing itinerary. Besides, this is hardly Mongolia's only well-preserved collection of petroglyphs, which are even more numerous in the far west.)

Out of the range and speeding home across a plain covered in tussock grass, its fluffy white tops oddly visible from only one direction, snow-capped Ikh Bogd loomed far ahead in the late afternoon sun. On the plain's southern edge is **Tsagaan Bulag**, or **White Spring**, an unusual lump of shiny white marble at the base of a hill where water trickles down to a pool and into a green-bordered creek beyond. (When the spring is not running, as on our visit, local nomad kids use its surface as a slide.) Interestingly, the rock's flat surface is marked with several chiselled handprints and dozens of small round holes, perhaps an ancient work area for fashioning tools, arrowheads or even starting a fire – nobody seemed to know. But after hearing that ancient caravans once passed this way, the springs would've made an ideal stop.

Above: The entrance to the White Cave, Mongolia's oldest Stone Age site dating back 750,000 years. Following spread: The refreshingly lush Zulganay Oasis leaps out of Bayangovi's dun-coloured landscape (Carl Robinson x2).

If you are not already fascinated by geology, Mongolia certainly changes that. The first thing professionals say is that Mongolia's geology is "complicated", but there is also an amazing simplicity that will enrich your travels – and help pass the time (keep in mind the flows of water and wind). On the long run from **Bayangovi** to the southern Gobi, the trail first clears a low range and the massive landscape spreads out into a wide valley a couple of hundred kilometres across through clear desert air and bright blue sky to the distant South Gobi Altai.

Simply, what is a long and sloping alluvial plain of eroded rocks and debris runs south, crosses an ancient watercourse and then rises again up through a similar feature to the massif beyond. First laid down when the surrounding mountains and precipitation were dramatically higher, these thick deposits – often full of coarser material, including rounded rocks – are further eroded by more recent water action. Mighty winds might have smoothed the scrub-covered landscape deceptively flat. But quite suddenly, you'll almost stumble into a sheer-walled gully or valley cutting through the original deposits, even the odd oasis. (Just make sure the driver has good brakes!)

We were heading around the western end of the Gobi Altai's southeasternmost range and the latest extension of the **Gurvan Saihan National Park** (see above). After bouncing across the wide valley's main watercourse, here hosting thick brush and poplar trees from the underground water, we headed up into the range on some sort of "short cut" only to get totally lost inside a Chinese-run gold mine full of workers, ger camps, heavy equipment and fuel depots. They'd bulldozed so many new tracks that our normally unflappable guide was totally confused. He frantically ran up tiny hillocks looking for a way out. We escaped this totally incongruous scene back down to the flats below, and followed another wide valley down to where cliffs formed along its northern banks.

Just below the 20-metre-high (66-foot) cliff face lay the bright greens and golden yellows of the **Zulganay Oasis**, an amazing contrast to the surrounding landscape of dark browns and whitish sands, including low dunes and scrub. A shallow sandy creek ran past to form a lake further downstream, a desert home to courting ducks and other birds. There are plenty of oases in the area, and they make a great late lunch stop, but be warned, the stinging flies and bees can spoil the mood – especially in summer.

Crossing this wide sand and scrub-covered valley and then a stony plain, we reached the base of a spectacular and heavily eroded line of red-coloured cliffs with coal black and grey swirls of pebbles blown by the fierce Gobi winds. We were at the westernmost end of the range and turned around the corner to enter a red sandstone world of monumental proportions, the South Gobi's hidden gem. On the left, cliff faces like modern balconied

The Gobi's oases are rich with succulent grasses, streams, lakes and wildlife (Carl Robinson).

apartment blocks rose sharply above us along with solitary buttes. We drove further inside a valley of more buttes, dry creek beds, red sand dunes and saxaul bush. Its southern wall a couple of kilometres away was a wind and water-eroded string of isolated cliffs and buttes. Wide-sloping fans spread down from the plateau above.

Often compared to the South Gobi's more famous **Flaming Cliffs** (page 302), **Hermen Tsav** is even more dramatic, especially after the long drive to get there. We camped out of the wind and explored more the next morning. Once a lakebed, the Gobi's red sandstone is a common indicator of dinosaur remains, and Hermen Tsav has also yielded important fossils over the years. I'd have loved a couple more days here just hiking in the shady little canyons and relaxing. Hermen Tsav is truly one of the most charming highlights of the entire Gobi.

The view from our elevated position looked far out across an open plain, a vast continuation of that ever widening watercourse we'd crossed coming down from Bayangovi. Out here are more scattered oases such as the one we'd seen. The largest, **Ehiyn Gol,** was an experimental horticulture commune during the Communist period growing vegetables and fruit, especially melons and tomatoes. Still continuing on a smaller scale and now

Following spread: Dawn over the South Gobi's hidden jewel, Hermen Tsav, and (inset) its gigantic red sandstone cliff faces (Carl Robinson x2).

privately run, the markets are indeed far away. These oases are where the illusive Gobi bear still lives, though only an estimated 25 are left. (The False Lama, Dambijantsan, raided caravans from here in the 1920s and an ovoo is named after him.) Way down here 100 kilometres from the border, China feels very close and the radio is full of Chinese programmes. Out there is even a "Road to China" – actually an ancient north-south caravan trail – we travelled on the next day. But with a very low western horizon and a huge sky overhead, the sunsets and starlit night to follow were magnificent; as were the sunrises too – a classic desert scene.

From here, the route back to Ikh Bogd was in a huge northwest-running trajectory. Back across the watercourse, we barrelled up to full speed across bare, coarse, undulating hills ever westward, eating the escort vehicle's dust as he screeched to a sudden halt so the guide's "Mongolian GPS" (see page 164) could kick in. Finally, we were up on a limestone plateau. From red and tan, the landscape was all white – a mysterious feeling.

We hit the high-speed gravel road dubbed the **Road to China** – identifiable by the green Chinese beer bottles tossed out by passing drivers. Following an ancient caravan route, the road is an important transport link for this part of Mongolia, especially to the aimag centre of Bayanhongor to the north. The wind was blasting gritty sand across the gravelly plateau and only leafless scrub grew by the road. The two 4WDs suddenly stopped and everyone beat out against the wind to "souvenir" what were actually saxaul bushes less than a metre high (they bring good luck and soon the top of our 4WD looked like a giant tree; you'll certainly get envious looks driving back into UB).

Left: Dawn reflects off isolated buttes and a lone saxaul bush at Hermen Tsav. Above: Searching for fossils across the white limestone plains of Bugiin Tsav in Bayanhongor Gobi (Carl Robinson x2).

Bypassing a couple of lovely tree-filled valleys set in rounded white hills, we ploughed out into a sloping white and grey desert landscape capped in picturesque buttes called **Bugiin Tsav**. The guide rushed out ahead in the burning heat, others scampering after him. In five minutes, he'd unearthed a treasure trove of fossil bones, including lots of turtles, teeth and leg bones. A few large-boned animals too, judging by the heavy knuckle we found; these were the remains of early mammals rather than dinosaurs found in the red sandstone further east.

We headed cross-country – as one does in Mongolia – and quite soon, just in time for lunch, we dropped out of a rocky range of hills and down onto the edge of this same vast white region. Lush desert trees known as *tooroi* lined an unseen sandy creek. There was even a solitary ger. **Zunn Mod** is another Gobi oasis, but very different. Up a sandy and tree-lined canyon, we stopped just below a monolithic rock face where a creek dribbled down. After lunch in the shade, we scrambled up the sharp rock face to a natural courtyard where a large pool of water had formed on one end, fed by a string of even higher and tinier ponds up into the rock's vast catchment area.

At the other end of this unusual round platform, a waterfall dropped 20 metres (66 feet) to another rock pool where a solitary tree grew tall, even a bit of grass around its feet. Lizards abounded. The waterfalls ended in a grassy pond feeding the creek where a horse-operated waterwheel and trough drew water up from a well. At "full operation" – such as after a massive Gobi thunderstorm – this would be a mighty waterfall indeed, like a giant natural water fountain. This would be a great place for an overnight stop.

Now looping back across this southern part of Bayanhongor aimag, we headed across a touch of the Black Gobi, a flat landscape of volcanic pebbles cut by the odd perpendicular gully where waters have rushed through. At some points, this was like driving on a good gravel road. We sped across at full speed only to screech to a halt at the gullies (where

Above: Fossil bones gathered in minutes at Bugiin Tsav. Right: Heavily eroded by water and wind, the monolithic cliffs of Zunn Mod oasis are full of ponds – and spooky character (Carl Robinson x2).

THE HOUSE OF THE FALSE LAMA

US-born Owen Lattimore remains one of the most highly respected Mongolists of the 20th century, whose lifelong interest in the Mongolian people dated from a 1926 camel caravan from Beijing to western Xinjiang province, formerly Turkestan. By then, the Soviet-dominated regime in Mongolia had shut down its traditional east-west caravan routes, forcing traders onto a more southerly route through Inner Mongolia and Gansu province. Quaintly descriptive of people and place, *The Desert Road to Turkestan* tells the story of the Mongolian renegade who raised the so-called Winding Road to its brief moment of glory. The location is northern Gansu along the southern border of Mongolia's Hovd aimag.

Already the legend of the False Lama has been elaborated beside the tent fires into many versions, but from the choice of details it is possible to throw together a picture with life in it, of an adventurer who, during those years when Mongolia echoed again for a while with the drums and trampling of its mediaeval turbulence, proved himself a valiant heir in his day to all the Asiatic soldiers of fortune from Jenghis Khan to Yaku Beg of Kashgar.

I have heard men say that the False Lama was a Russian. Certainly the thing they remember most vividly about him, next to his harem, is the habit he had of changing his clothes every day or so, dressing at different times like a Russian, a Chinese or a Mongol. Others maintain that he was a true Mongol, so it may have been that he was Buriat, a Russianized Siberian Mongol. The most substantial story of all is that he was a Chinese from Manchuria who had served in Mongolia as a herder of ponies for the princely firm of Ta Shen K'uei. In this employment he learned the language and customs of the Mongols. [In fact, he was a Kalmyk Mongol from Russia's Volga region.] *They say that he rose suddenly to power and notoriety during the violent period about 1920-21 when first the White and then the Red Russian "partisans" overran Mongolia. He began by claiming himself a Lama, and a lama of high rank, a Bogdo or Great or Holy One, taking a title that belongs only to the several degrees of Living Buddha.*

While winning his early successes he got himself the repute of being immune from fire and invulnerable to bullets. It is declared positively that he was captured by the White Russians at Kobdo [Hovd] who burned him for three days, but to no purpose. Escaping from them, he led the Mongols back to the sack of Kobdo, the massacre of the Chinese, and the eviction of the Whites. The caravan men never seem to have counted it against the False Lama that he gave over their countrymen at Kobdo to a Mongol massacre...

When the Urga Khutukhtu [Eighth Bogd Gegeen] *was acclaimed ruler of all Mongolia, with the title of Bogdo Khan, he gave the False Lama – or so it is said – large territories in Western Mongolia for a fief, including Kobdo, the Altai country, the hoshun* [province] *of Mingan, and the temple trading centres of Yunbeize and Dabeize. The False Lama, however, afraid either of intrigues against him or of the recoil of his own intrigues against others, fled westward and stopped for a while near Ku Ch'eng-tae, representing himself in a friendly way to the Governor of Hsin-chiang* [Xinjiang]. *Later, probably in an understanding with the Governor, he moved again to these oases in what for many years had been a No Man's Land...*

[The False Lama's] *followers were a mixed lot, lifted from all over Western Mongolia, some of them his own fighting retainers, the rest whole families he had swept up on his way in order to establish a population about him. This was in the end the weakness of his position, for not only had a large number of his subjects not come willingly, but they did not like his high-handed way of keeping all the men at call for service under arms and seizing all women at his will for the harem that was his especial princely recreation.*

For a year at least he ruled boldly and successfully at Kung-p'o Ch'uan [Gongpoquan]. *He must have been a man of vision and energy, for the caravan men say that it was he more than anyone else who pieced together the Winding Road, linking little-used Mongol routes to the byways of the opium runners... These were the days of his pride, remembered by the caravan masters who used to be invited to sit with him in his high room overlooking his stronghold, to smoke decorously and talk of roads and travel and the growth of trade... Also being full-blooded men, they dwell more on the memory of his harem than on the help he gave them...*

At the height of his power he had more than two hundred yurts [gers] on permanent foundations of stamped clay under the shadow of his walls, while other families herded his thousand head of camels, his hundreds of ponies, and his many thousands of sheep, dispersed through the central chain of oases and over the slopes of the Ma-tsung Shan [to the south]. His road, however, was not more than well founded and his fortress well built about him when the wrath of Urga [Ulaanbaatar] *sought him out; in the year 1923 or 1924, as I understand it. Ten men rode out of the desert to his north saying they were lamas of the Bogd Khan, sent to invite him to council at Urga on matters of high policy. Three of them, as chiefs of the mission, were admitted to his chamber in the central keep, from which he could overlook almost all the frontiers of the kingdom he had brought into being as if out of a vision. When they were brought before his face, in the same moment that they saluted him they shot him with automatics, thus ending a legend with murder and the vulgar proof that his invulnerability was not equal to his incombustibility.*

Other ways of telling the story are that the emissaries from Urga came in one or two motor cars; that the False Lama was taken out and shot before his people; that he was taken to Urga and shot; that his head was cut off and his body bound down with chains to make sure of him; and that he was never captured at all, but another man in his stead, and that he is yet alive, an outlaw in hiding...

[Lattimore visits the ruined fortress next day, accompanied by a travelling companion "because it was a bad country, no place for a man alone".]

...In the fortress itself there is a cramped and sinister feeling. I did not feel happy. Withered in the light of the noonday sun almost to the dingy color of the utter emptiness of marsh and hill, brief patches of living land and long stretches of desolation, the rifled ruins seemed to be oppressed by something uncanny. I did not wonder that the few frequenters of the wilderness should avoid them and whatever ghost they harbor.

Owen Lattimore, The Desert Road to Turkestan, *1929*

someone could easily put in a few culverts and make this a real Mongolian speedway). Far ahead was another mountain range with a string of red cliffs at one end, just like Hermen Tsav. Anxiously, I thought we'd done a full circle around this incredible mix of landscapes and were back to where we'd started. But no, I was told later after we'd travelled up into a steep-walled Afghan-style canyon at the middle of the range. (There is a nameless mini-version of Hermen Tsav out there just waiting for a visitor.)

Mongolia's valleys are always fascinating to travel – and you usually come out alright at the other end. Although this island-like range, called **Tsaramyn Nuruu,** is just another eroded extension of the Altai, its valleys exhibited the same brown igneous material seen throughout this wide region (similar to Dungenee and Yolyn Am). Typically, the floors of the valleys rise with the elevation and peak on to wide, lush meadows, here even with trees. Several ger families tended their animals, the first people we'd seen all day.

After this brief and refreshing temperate zone in the middle of the Gobi, a new watershed stretched far down into our now familiar valley. The 20-kilometre-long (12.5-mile) sheet of ice atop blue-tinged Ikh Bogd was clearly visible. With the other vehicle far in the lead, kicking up only a tiny cloud of dust, and the sprawling vista out ahead, this was a journey you wish would last forever – and almost does. Two hours later and right on sunset, we finally pulled into camp. The feeling of distance covered was immense.

We bade our farewells the next morning, first stop filling our bottles at a mineral spring right outside the camp. Then, Sunday morning was spent in neat little **Bayangovi.** Everyone was in their finest for Mothers & Children Day, when gifts are lavished on children and single women. No one survives financially in Mongolia on just the tourist season; our camp's owner and tour operator, who also comes from here, had joyously supplemented his annual income with a huge buy of cashmere off the locals, now bundled higher and higher onto an old Russian-made trailer for the long run up to UB – and a happy payoff. In formal Mongolian tradition, we all drove to the edge of town, pulled off onto a low hill overlooking the vast plain and parked, us going that way and him returning home. Speeches were made, with best wishes for a safe journey.

Driving back out of this memorable valley left a certain melancholy. We tracked upward through steppe and then back down the riverbed to the **Valley of the Lakes.** On the other side of the lake, both vehicles stopped next to an ovoo on flat land. It was our companion vehicle's turn to say goodbye and now attempt to smash the record dash back to UB. We were heading north into the **Hangai** portion of **Bayanhongor aimag.** In his yellow T-shirt and baseball cap, Elbegee – some of whose work illustrates this book – jumped out with a bottle of Chinggis Khaan vodka. We gathered round and he poured a single plastic glass to pass around (it was only 10am). Across the wide dry lake and a small string of dunes, soaring straight up from its very own fault line, was the sharp face of Ikh Bogd, our companion on the southern side. Buddha Mountain, its name means. Elbegee pointed to the treacherous trail up to its snow-covered flat summit. As we chatted away, a white baby camel – good luck, Mongolians say – walked past. More rounds. It'd been an incredible run. And finally a formal farewell.

From southern Bayanhongor, the **Western Gobi** stretches in a narrowing band for another 700 kilometres (435 miles) in a northwest direction along the border of China's Xinjiang Uygur Autonomous Region to the legendary **Dzungarian (Junggar) Gobi**. (This fascinating border region was the scene of the last determined resistance by the Oirads to Qing occupation in the 18th century with its empire stretching west into today's eastern Kazakhstan.) Located in the southern lee of the now much higher Altai range, the region consists of vast plains, valleys, oases and isolated mountain ranges. Most notable in southern **Gobi-Altai aimag** is the soaring **Ajbogdyn Nuruu** massif with the highest of its three peaks, **Huren Tovon Uul** standing at 3,802 metres (12,474 feet).

Clearly, this region is Mongolia at its most remote, and much is now protected as natural reserve, with very few tourists visiting. For those that do, from the aimag centre of **Altai** on the northern edge of the same rift valley a circular itinerary takes in the fascinating vegetable-growing **Biger Valley**, in the actual depression, and then up to **Burhan Buudai Uul** (3,765 metres or 12,352 feet) and solitary **Eej Hayrhan Uul** (2,275 metres or 7,464 feet), both sacred mountains of the Western Gobi. Travelling on west through desert provides an opportunity to meet Mongolia's reintroduced wild horses, or *takhi*, before reaching the pleasant sum centre of Bulgan, and then over the range on a historic caravan route to the aimag centre of **Hovd** (or Khovd, see page 343).

In addition to its famous vegetables and fruit, the southern Bayanhongor oasis of **Ehiyn Gol** is the ranger headquarters of one of the largest and most remote natural reserves in the world, the **Great Gobi Protected Area.** Covering over 5.3 million hectares (13 million acres) of largely undisturbed desert, it provides a vast refuge for the endangered fauna of Central Asia, including nearly 50 mammals, 15 reptiles and amphibians, and over 150 bird species. Protected flora includes over 410 plant species. Visitors require special permission to visit this area.

Divided into two parts, the **Southern Altai Gobi** (Gobi A) covers the southern parts of Bayanhongor and Gobi-Altai aimags while the **Dzungarian Gobi** (Gobi B) is separated by 300 kilometres (186 miles), including the above massif, and located in southern Gobi-Altai and Hovd aimags. The Southern Altai is the traditional home of the extremely rare Gobi bear, *Ursus arctos*, mentioned earlier. Wild Bactrian camels also live here. (On a map, Gobi A takes in the south-southwest tip of Mongolia and the Dzungarian Gobi is closer to its southwest corner. See The Altai & Great Lakes map, page 344.)

Located closer to the Altai range, the Dzungarian Gobi is more lush than its eastern section and is home to the last remaining herds of *khulan,* or wild ass, and the increasingly rare black-tailed gazelle and saiga antelope. This region was also the last refuge of the world's only real wild horse, the takhi or Przewalski's horse, which is now being reintroduced to Mongolia from Western zoos. Much more isolated than the Hustain Nuruu Reserve outside UB, few tourists visit the second Mongolian Wild Horse release site just on the northern side of the **Tahiin Shar Nuruu**, on the Chinese border in southwest Gobi-Altai aimag. (There is a research station where visitors can drop by and perhaps meet these unique horses before their release into the wild.)

At the southern edge of the main range, the **Mongol Altai**, the lovely sum centre of **Bulgan** sits on the banks of a swift-flowing river of the same name which flows into Xinjiang's Dzungarian Gobi. Because of its clear desert air, the town was a popular destination for the full eclipse of the sun in 2008. Two major border posts cross into China in this region, but unfortunately they are closed to foreigners.

Also from Bulgan, an ancient caravan trail from Tibet and Xinjiang travels eastwards past an incredible ovoo, a canyon of stone carvings and collection of deer stelae and then over the famous **Ih Ulaan Davaa** (Pass) into the heart of what was once the Dzungarian Empire around the modern-day city of Hovd. Renowned throughout Mongolia, historic **Kharuul Ovoo** (Guardian) is made of solid rock and looks more like a tower, standing 25 metres (80 feet) above an isolated peak and 50 metres (160 feet) across.

Near the tiny settlement of **Uyench** further east, in a steep-walled canyon where caravans once passed, is one of Mongolia's most fascinating archaeological sites, **Yamaan Us Gorge** (Goat Water), which boasts several hundred rock drawings. Believed to date back to the Xiongnu (Hunnu) period (third century BCE to first century CE), the well-preserved drawings show humans shooting at ibex, deer, antelope and wolves – and one poor fellow about to get axed in the back. Most famous are the widely reproduced ones of wheeled carriages discovered here. South of the pass near the tiny village of **Bayanzurkh** is one of Mongolia's largest – and most southern – collection of deer stelae. (More typically, however, visitors will be entering this region from the north, or via Hovd.)

THE ALTAI

Located at the western end of Mongolia, the Altai is the highest – and most spectacular – of the country's three main mountain ranges. Many of its summits are capped with perennial snow and surrounded by glaciers. Known as the **Mongol Altai**, these majestic mountains form one branch of the **Altai-Sayan**, which stands as a massive barrier – and unique ecosystem – between the steppes and deserts of Central Asia to the south and the great taiga forests of Siberia in the north.

From a central area in the northwest tip of Mongolia, this mountain system branches off in three directions: the main Altai range runs due west through a northern sliver of China's Xinjiang Uygur Autonomous Region and then along the border of northeast Kazakhstan and Russia's south-central Siberia. An eastern spur of the Altai, the **Sayan** runs along Mongolia's northern border with Russia and over the top of Lake Hovsgol. The **Mongol Altai** stretches southeast, reaching far down into the heart of the Gobi Desert.

Overall, the western Altai is actually higher with the highest peak being the UNESCO World Heritage-listed and twin-peaked Belukha (4,506 metres, or 14,783 feet), situated along the Russian-Kazakh border not far west of the point where Russia, China and Mongolia meet. Rising just east of this junction is the Altai's second highest – and Mongolia's highest – mountain at 4,374 metres (14,300 feet), **Khuiten Uul**. Flanked by

four other peaks and the source of a massive glacier, they are more commonly known as **Tavan Bogd**, or Five Saints.

Fronted on its eastern side by a massive fault line, the Mongol Altai is more mountainous and rugged than its western counterpart with hundreds of summits ranging over 3,000 metres (9,843 feet) and stretching in diminishing elevations for nearly 1,000 kilometres (620 miles) southeast into Mongolia's Gobi region, the so-called **Gobi Altai** (see page 318). Four peaks over the 4,000-metre mark (13,123 feet) are widely scattered through the bulk of the range, which runs roughly 500 kilometres long and 100 kilometres wide (310 by 62 miles). Even as the range stretches out into more isolated massifs towards the Gobi, some peaks are still at the high 3,000-metre mark, such as Ikh Bogd in Bayanhongor *aimag* (see The Gobi, page 319).

Geologically, the Altai Mountains are a result of the collision of the Indian subcontinent with Asia some 20 million years ago, a process that continues today at 15 centimetres (six inches) a year. Although the point of this collision was more than 2,000 kilometres (1,243 miles) away, the landscape in between has been effectively pushed up against the solid primordial rock of the so-called Siberian Craton north of Lake Baikal. This region is one of the most seismically active in the world.

Tsambagarav Uul – at 4,195 metres high this mountain and its surrounding massif is a major landmark for those heading to the Tavan Bogd region from Hovd (Elbegzaya Lhagvasuren).

The Altai is a rocky range with glaciers along many of its high ridges and punctuated by deep valleys, clear lakes, springs and hundreds of streams. Three of Mongolia's largest rivers originate here – the Hovd, Buyant and Bulgan – even though their waters never reach the sea. Because of its position and isolation, and because its biodiversity is immense, the Altai is considered one of the world's most important– and perhaps last – refuges for many plants and animal life. The range is home to Argali sheep, ibex, *maral* (large Siberian deer like elk), brown bear, marmot, fox and wolf, as well as the endangered snow leopard and lynx. Birds include saker falcons, Altai snowcocks and golden eagles. Often located in tight little pockets, its plant life crosses through a wide range of habitats from alpine tundra down through pine forest to grassy steppe and semi-desert.

With its wild and diverse terrain, and still rustic infrastructure and rough roads, the Altai is a favourite destination for adventure tourism, especially horse trekking, mountain climbing and hiking (there are also some great whitewater activities). The Altai is totally different from any other part of Mongolia and definitely belongs on your itinerary, even if it means camping out for a couple of nights.

The entire Altai-Sayan region also has a long human history dating back to Palaeolithic times, and is the traditional home of the Turkic people, where the Altaic family of languages originated (see People & Culture, page 116). Although now part of Russia, proto-Turks also ranged up into the headwaters of the Yenisey River, today's Tula, with proto-Mongols, now the Buriats, living east of Lake Baikal.

The Altai is rich in archaeological sites dating back to the Palaeolithic Era. A cave complex at the southeast edge of the Mongol Altai shows evidence of human habitation between 40,000 and 12,000 years ago during and after the last Ice Age. Elaborate graves of Scythian warriors and princesses have also been discovered. Visitors today can easily find Bronze Age petroglyphs and deer stelae, along with burial mounds or *kurgan*, ceremonial stacks of rocks and anthropomorphic "man stones" called *balbal* from the later Turkic period. The gold, copper and iron of the Altai – which translates in both Mongolian and Turkic languages as the "Mountains of Gold" – have been mined since prehistoric times. Today, traditional nomadic-style herding continues, even in the heart of the **Tavan Bogd National Park**.

Even today, the Altai is the most ethnically diverse region of Mongolia. Although its Kazakh minority is the best known and most obvious, they are relatively recent newcomers, migrating out of the turmoil of western China and Central Asia only in the 19th and early 20th centuries. Other Mongolian-speaking tribal groups are Oirad groupings: the Dorvod, Uriankhai, Zakhchin, Mayangad, Torgut, Oold, Khoton and Tuva. Administratively, the

Mongol Altai occupies most of the westernmost aimag of **Bayan-Olgii**, and the western and southern parts of **Hovd** and central **Gobi-Altai** aimags. Another more isolated spur of the Altai occupies western **Uvs aimag.**

The main gateway to the region is the town of **Hovd** (also spelt Khovd), capital of the aimag bearing the same name and located some 1,425 kilometres (885 miles) or three hours by air west of Ulaanbaatar. (The western aimags are also on a different time zone, one hour behind the capital.) Located in a shallow valley of the wide **Buyant Gol** (River), flowing from the Altai to the west, Hovd is a large settlement of 35,000 dating back to the bloody conquest of western Mongolia by the Manchu Qing Dynasty in the 1700s (see History, page 83). Known as the Front Camp, Hovd was the furthest extension of Qing military power into Mongolia. (Its main military headquarters, or Rear Camp, was farther east at Uliastai in the western foothills of the Hangai Mountains, see page 416.)

In summer, the town's surrounding sharp-edged, reddish-brown, rocky hills provide a dramatic contrast to its poplar-lined streets and the lush green of its riverside pastures dotted with dozens of circular white gers. Beyond these close-in hills, the snow-capped peaks of the blue-tinged Altai line the western horizon. To the east, vast lakes mark the southern end of Mongolia's Great Lakes Depression and the lower ranges and sand dunes beyond.

Established as a Qing military outpost and trading centre in 1731, the poplar trees along the town's paved streets were planted by its conquerors in the 1800s. (Now an environmental pest, poplars are always a sign of a previous Chinese presence, in nearby Uliastai and UB also, and in spring their fluffy white seeds blow everywhere, sprouting like weeds.) At the town's northern end are the mud walls of a fortress, the **Sangiin Herem**, built by the Manchus in 1762. Once surrounded by a moat and including a barracks, administrative buildings, homes, temples and a cemetery for the Chinese, the fort was destroyed in a bloody siege and battle in 1912 when the local Manchu governor refused to surrender, despite the fall of the Qing Dynasty the year before.

At the terminus of the **Great Mongolian Road**, the main northwesterly running caravan trail from China across the vast Gobi Desert, Hovd had a large Chinese population engaged in trade, and created market gardens on its river flats, even growing rice. Another even more historic trail led south across the Altai's **Ih Ulaan Davaa** (Pass) with its huge, renowned *ovoo*, into Xinjiang and farther south into Tibet. (The Oirads sent troops there to keep the Dalai Lama in power in the 1700s.)

THE ALTAI & GREAT LAKES
RUSSIA
Handgayt
Borshoo
Uureg
Uvs
Tashanta
Tsagaannuur
Bayramyn davaa
ULAANGOM
Turgen Uul Range
3965
4082
Nairamdal uul
4374
Khuiten uul
Achit
Tsagaan
Tsengel
Ulaanhus
Hovd
UVS
Booroog Deliyn els
GREAT LAKES REGION
Hoton
OLGII
BAYAN-OLGII
Hyargas
Hurgan
Dayan
Tolbo
Altai
Sambagarav uul
Airag
Hunshanzi
Dayani
Buraatyn davaa
Hungiy
Urgamal
Bor Hyaryn els
Buyant
HOVD
Deluun
HUH SERH
Har Us
Har
Zavhan
Zavhanmandal
Chandmani
Dorgon
Dorvoljin
Gurvan Tsenher
4204
Monkh Harkhan uul
Ih Ulaan davaa
4090
Sutay uul
Takashiken
Bulgan
HOVD
Uyench
Shargyn Tsagaan
Sharga
CHINA
(Xinjiang)
Laoemyao
Burgastay
LEGEND
Paved and cravel road
Earth road
HOVD Centre of aimag
Bulgan Centre of sum
National boundary of Mongolia
Boundary of the aimag
Pass
Bridge
Border exits
Mine
15.6 0 15.6 31 km
© "GAZRYN ZURAG"Co.,Ltd

When the Russian Civil War spilled over into Mongolia in the early 1920s, the region was the scene of the last decisive battles between the Reds and Whites. Later in 1944, Soviet separatist intrigues in neighbouring Xinjiang led to a bold Nationalist Chinese invasion in pursuit of a troublesome Kazakh insurgent named **Ospan Batyr** (Osman Batur). With Soviet-backed cavalry, they were soundly defeated on the eastern bank of the Hovd River north of the town, their grave mounds still visible today.

Despite its tranquil setting, history weighs heavily over Hovd, homeland of the western Oirads who formed the short-lived **Dzungarian Empire** extending through Xinjiang and into Central Asia in the late 17th century. Regional pride still runs high. The town centre is dotted with new statuary and now overwhelms the one of Ayush, the politically correct *ard*, or "proletarian herdsman", of the early Communist era. (He rebelled against a corrupt local noble, reinforcing the Marxist view of the Mongolian aristocracy's "collaboration" with the Qing Manchus.)

The most recent addition to the downtown square is a bold statue of **Galdan Khan**, or Galdan Boshigt, who attacked eastern Mongolia in 1688, sacking Erdene Zuu at Harhorin (Karakorum) and other monasteries near today's Ulaanbaatar, and forcing its theocratic leader Zanabazar to flee to Inner Mongolia, where he succumbed to Qing vassalage three years later. The statue of the horse-borne warrior in a park off the main square is the legendary **Amarsanaa**, whose Oirads held out against Qing forces until 1757, when he fled into Russia and later died (see History, page 83). Portraits of him and others related to this defiant period are displayed in the local museum.

Still publicly unrecognised, however, is the colourful **Dambijantsan**, a Volga or Kalmyk Mongol who was one of the leaders of the 1912 siege of the Hovd Fortress. Claiming descent from the legendary Amarsanaa, he returned years later as the **False Lama**, who lived a life of banditry and debauchery at the southern end of the aimag before his execution at the hands of the Communists in the mid-1920s (see Literary Excerpt, page 334).

Today, dominated by a mobile phone tower atop a dry and rocky outcrop on its northern outskirts called **Yamart Ulaan Uul** (Red Goat Mountain), Hovd is the largest settlement in western Mongolia. It is a neat and busy provincial city with many stone administrative and office buildings, multistorey hotels, restaurants, shops and a university, as well as a few derelict old factories. The main poplar-lined street leading to the fortress was once Hovd's Chinatown, but no buildings from that era remain. An "imperial" monastery funded by the Qing Emperor, **Shar Sum** or **Yellow Temple**, was destroyed in the anti-Buddhist purges of the 1930s and has recently reopened in this street.

A large market occupying the southern part of the town sells, among other things, vegetables and fruit still grown in the region (Hovd is famous for its watermelons). Typical of Mongolian towns, Hovd also has several ger districts of wide, unpaved streets with each property surrounded by wooden palisades, here with each "suburb" occupied by a different ethnic group.

The **Hovd Museum**, with its replica of the famous cave paintings at Gurvan Senkher, interesting historical exhibits such as a scale model of the old Qing fortress, and others relating to the region's ethnic diversity and wildlife, makes a worthwhile stop before continuing your journey – or while your driver is refuelling or repairing his vehicle. Another interesting spot near the fortress ruins is the **Ahmet Ali Mejit**, a mosque built in 2000 to cater to the local Kazakh community. (Like the Buddhists, Mongolia's Muslims suffered during the Stalinist purges of the 1930s.) For those with time, Hovd makes a pleasant and comfortable base to explore the surrounding region, perhaps even engage in an early morning hike to the top of Red Goat Mountain.

For those anxious for an early taste of the Altai, only 40 kilometres (25 miles) due west of Hovd where the Buyant River emerges from the range is the **Huh Serh Protected Area** (Blue Ibex), also called Khokh Serkhii, a 65,900-hectare (16,280-acre) habitat for the rare Argali sheep, ibex, snow leopard, Altai snowcock and stone marten. Its highest peak, snow-covered **Takhilt Uul**, stands at 3,776 metres (12,388 feet). The park can also be accessed through Deluun, famous for its Kazakh eagle hunters, in neighbouring Bayan-Olgii aimag on the other side of the range south of Tolbo Nuur (see below).

Ninety-two kilometres (57 miles) south of Hovd across the grasslands of the **Mankhanii Tal** (steppe) in the foothills of the Altai is **Gurvan Tsenher**, also known as **Tsenkheriin Agui**, two remarkable caves about 20 metres (66 feet) deep which were inhabited by humans between 40,000 and 12,000 years ago during the Palaeolithic Era. The walls of the entrance cave are covered in numerous Stone Age rock paintings, drawn in deep ochre or brown paint against the yellow and white walls. In addition to paintings of animals still prevalent today – such as cattle, ibex, argali, camels and gazelles – are now extinct mammoths, buffalo and ostrich (one that looks suspiciously like a kangaroo is actually a camel). Others depict birds, snakes and trees.

The caves – which rise 25 metres (85 feet) to their ceilings in places – were only discovered by Soviet and Mongolian archaeologists in 1967. Although the setting on the slope of a small mountain along the banks of a small river is quite picturesque, many of the cave paintings have been defaced by vandals in recent years.

Another couple of hours further south from the caves is Mongolia's second-highest mountain, **Monkh-Harkhan** (Munkh-Hairkhan), with its snow-covered peak rising to 4,204 metres (13,793 feet). Regarded as one of the country's most beautiful mountains, the climb up its northern face is relatively easy, although basic mountain-climbing equipment is required to deal with the snow and ice. The mountain's deep canyons offer a lovely mixture of streams, lakes and colourful flower-covered slopes. Down a valley on its western side is the lovely but extremely remote **Bulgan River**, which flows southwards through the top of the Dzungarian Gobi into China's Xinjiang Uygur Autonomous Region.

This southern region is more easily accessed over the ancient caravan trail which crosses over the southern end of the Gobi Altai at **Ih Ulaan Davaa** (Red Pass) which offers spectacular views down the range to solitary **Sutay Uul** (4,090 metres or 13,419 feet), one of Mongolia's highest peaks, at the southern end of the Mongol Altai (from this point, the Gobi Altai begins).

Because of more frequent air connections, many visitors fly into Hovd and then travel 220 kilometres (137 miles) northwest by road to **Olgii**, the aimag centre of Bayan-Olgii that is the closest town to the crown jewel of the Mongol Altai, the **Tavan Bogd National Park**. Although the dirt road has improved in recent years, the six-hour plus trip can be quite tiring, especially for those straight off a flight from UB, and the rush to Olgii an irritating distraction from enjoying the stunning countryside.

Travelling north up the grass-covered Altai foothills with the lushly green Hovd River Valley off to the east, the road turns west up the rugged **Namarjin Valley** and past the mud-brick remains of a small settlement damaged by flash floods several years ago, which opened up a small collection of Turkic graves, or kurgan. Turning right, the road follows the starkly bare and rocky valley up a straight and surprisingly long incline – and finally out onto a lovely alpine meadow crisscrossed by streams and covered in grass and flowers. (This picturesque place is perfect for a coffee break.)

Looming off to the northeast above a shallow valley is the soaring massif of **Tsambagarav Uul**, Mongolia's third highest mountain (4,195 metres or 13,763 feet), with its wide triple-peaked summit covered in eternal snow and glaciers. Jutting east out of the Altai range, this magnificent mountain is a stunning landmark visible for huge distances all across the Great Lakes region beyond. Even brushed by low-hanging clouds, as during my stop, the broad mountain evokes an air of majesty – even mystery – as its halo-like cover of snow and ice flashes fleetingly in the sun. I was hardly surprised to hear later that Tsambagarav is famous for its sightings of the legendary *Almas*, Mongolia's yeti (see Literary Excerpt, page 400). Protected as a national park, climbing the mountain is relatively easy, again with proper gear, and accessible from several directions.

Off to the left of the vast meadow rise the double peaks of 3,984-metre (13,070-foot) **Buraalyn Davaa**, also known as Sayryn Uul, a travelling companion for the next stage of the journey. The road gently rises out of the meadow around the northern side of this snow-capped mountain, through a dramatic pass and down into a high and wide glacial valley containing the clear blue waters of **Tolbo Nuur**, or Frog Lake. Located at an altitude of 2,080 metres (6,824 feet), the lake covers 185 square kilometres (71.4 square miles) but even in summer its waters are extremely cold. When the Russian Civil War spilled into Mongolia, the lake was the scene of the decisive 42-day battle in 1921 where White troops were finally defeated by the Bolsheviks, or Reds, with help from a local general named Khasbaatar. The event is memorialised by a couple of lakeside plaques at the southern end of the lake.

From the *sum* centre of **Tolbo**, at the foot of the pass back up the valley, a rough road leads over the Altai range and down the remote Bulgan River

Clockwise from above: A cave drawing in Tsenkheriin Agui (Elbegzaya Lhagvasuren); a young eagle awaits training (Carl Robinson); a Turkic balbal *shows distinctive physical features such as hands and facial detail (Gotsbayar Rentsendorj); beautiful Kazakh weaving (Leo Murray).*

OVOO OFFERINGS BOTH OLD AND NEW

Given Mongolia's constant surprises, running into someone from the former Belgian Congo (now the Democratic Republic of the Congo) where I grew up seemed totally natural. A trained anthropologist, Gaby Bamana came to Mongolia in 1995 with the Catholic Church and is now a university lecturer and researcher. Fluent in Mongolian, he is no doubt the world's only African Mongolist. In his self-published book, *On the Tea Road, A Journey into Mongolian Life and Culture*, he uses the historic Tea Road – and the overriding importance of tea itself – as a metaphoric journey through contemporary Mongolian life and culture. Available in UB, this 200-page book is a great companion for your travels around Mongolia. The following excerpt looks at the ovoo's place in the modern Mongolian world:

This particular ovoo *[in the Gobi Altai] we came to was a small one as there were few stones in the sandy, deserted place to pile up a much nicer and bigger heap. As far as we were concerned, this was a good happening because at least we had something to do and break away from the monotony [of the journey]. We stopped to greet the ovoo and perform the prescribed ritual of going around the heap clockwise three times. We managed to add a few stones to the heap and our driver was able to offer a cigarette and a prayer. Since we were going into a foreign land, we needed the permission of the local genies and spirits of that particular land and waters for us to travel safely, to eat of the food, and to drink of the water of this region without any harm. Yet I was not expecting the surprise awaiting me on this little ovoo. Among the many items offered on the ovoo, there was a tea brick. Definitely, we were on the road of tea. Why would people offer a tea brick to the ovoo?*

My enquiry about this brought long and sometimes contradictory explanations. Some people just said that you do not offer any tea brick or any tea at all to the ovoo, while some others said you should. These were just two different traditions, and I never found out the reason behind the difference. However, tea, being the prime of the entire foodstuff, was a normal offering to the genies and spirits of the land and waters. Originally, the ovoo was a shrine for the exchange between humans and the sacred. Our driver explained that the ovoo is the place where one gives back to nature what nature has previously given in form of sustenance. In fact, people say the more the ovoo has the more it is able to constantly provide for human beings. In this case, people offer in gratitude and thanksgiving for nature's clemency.

However, our driver insisted that nature is more than what one sees. Nature is alive and that is how it cares about humans. It is important to understand that Mongols do not worship nature as such; otherwise, there would be shrines everywhere. The spots for erecting shrines are carefully chosen, and one of the criteria behind those choices is that these places are mirrors to something beyond human reach. It is not nature as such that people worship; rather people worship what nature tells us about the sacred. Nature is transparent and expresses a reality that overwhelms the human mind. People feel that they are and should be connected to this reality, and they create spaces for communication and connection with the sacred. I was really wondering what concepts such as naturalism and animism have ever meant. Nature is like a large painting; people admire it and worship the painter. Any aesthetic mind would admire nature's charms, and the Mongolian landscape has some charms indeed.

It is amazing what one finds on the ovoo as offerings. It often includes tea bricks, milk, candies, cigarettes, a watch and a can of beer. People on a journey offer drops of vodka before they drink themselves. Most of the items offered are foodstuffs or the remains of foodstuffs or of game such as bones, horns, hoofs. They are intended to be food for the spirits of the ovoo but, more significantly, they are offered in gratitude for the abundance of food that sustains people's lives. Besides, there is a consistent presence of scratches and broken bowls on most of the ovoo. Here, one understands the role of the ovoo as a place for some kind of recycling. People believe that what they possess is nature-granted and, if it happens that they could not use it any longer it is given back to nature via the ovoo. It is not good to throw things out anywhere, for that is dirtying nature; such dirt makes nature impure and this may bring about disharmony and misfortune. In the same order, people have thought of placing empty vodka bottles on the ovoo instead of throwing them just anywhere in nature. Yet the trouble with empty bottles is that nature cannot absorb them and there are so many nowadays. Thus, many ovoo have become deposits for vodka bottles which makes the spirits very angry. Goods that are placed on the ovoo are supposed to be absorbed with time and thus nature is nurtured and recycled. In the same line and since money has become the medium of exchange in the global economy, money bills are offered so that the spirits can purchase whatever food they prefer. Thus, even for the living spirits of the ovoo, the bells of globalization have rung.

Gaby Bamana, On the Tea Road,
A Journey into Mongolian Life and Culture, *2008*

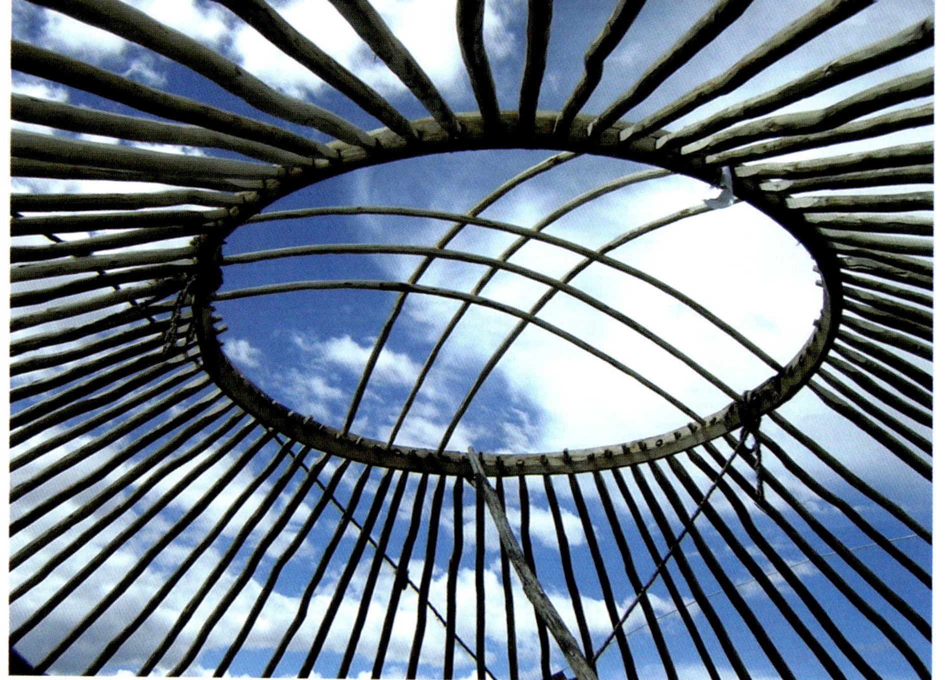

A Kazakh yurt's roof opening, or shangyrak, *is its symbolic – and physical – apex (Leo Murray).*

to the southern end of Hovd aimag. The region around **Deluun** and its lovely mountain lake, **Doroo Nuur,** is famous for its Kazakh eagle hunters (see Special Topic, page 356). The settlement is also a departure point for popular horse treks up into the solitary Buraalyn Davaa massif. Another point of interest is a large collection of Bronze and Iron Age petroglyphs along the **Boregtiin Gol** (River) at the foot of **Buyan Nuruu** (Mountain), about 25 kilometres (16 miles) southwest of Tolbo Lake. Only discovered in 2002, these are not nearly as numerous as those at Tsagaan Salaa (see below). From Tolbo Lake, Olgii is another 50 kilometres (31 miles) down the valley.

Created out of western Hovd province in 1940 as part of Soviet intrigues to control neighbouring Xinjiang, **Bayan-Olgii aimag** became a refuge for Muslim Kazakhs fleeing vicious separatist fighting in that Chinese province. (Already in control of Kazakhstan and other Central Asian states to the southwest, the Soviets wanted to create a puppet state in Xinjiang using a Kazakh-dominated Mongolian aimag as a rear base. Of course, the movement of different tribal groups through the region had gone on unhindered for centuries before Russia and China imposed modern-day borders over former Dzungaria starting in the 18th century.

Mongolia's western region had first provided refuge for Kazakhs – the second largest tribal group in Xinjiang after the Uighurs – in the late 19th century. The movement of Kazakh refugees grew after Mongolia's independence from China in 1921 and jumped dramatically as rebellions and civil war swelled through the province in the 1930s and 40s. (Refugees continued to enter into the 1950s as Beijing brought the last of the rebellions under control.)

Today, the Turkic Kazakhs make up over 90 percent of the aimag's 90,000 population, and its capital of **Olgii** (30,000) has a distinct Central Asian feel. (Kazakhs, who are Mongolia's largest ethnic minority at roughly five percent, also have a strong presence in neighbouring Hovd. Renowned for their mining skills, they are also heavily represented in coal and other extractive industries, as well as in the long-distance transport sector.) In physical appearance, Kazakhs have a slight Caucasian look rather than being overtly Asian. Typically, the men wear moustaches and skullcaps and women wear long dresses and cover their heads in colourful scarves. (And, yes, despite religious strictures, the men don't mind a drink either!) Most are bilingual but speak Mongolian with a distinct accent.

Compared to other Mongolian settlements, Olgii has a unique appearance and atmosphere. Located along the southern bank of the swift-flowing and tan-coloured **Hovd River**, the modern town has a distinct layout with solid buildings and shops and signage in both Cyrillic and Arabic. Homes in residential areas are made of mud and twigs with flat roofs. More outside the town, Kazakhs also live in yurts (the Turkic equivalent of the ger) which are easily distinguishable by their high, curved roofs. Instead of a market, Olgii has a bazaar, plus a mosque and *madrasah,* or Islamic school. The cuisine, too, is different with the smell of flat oven-baked bread and *shashlyk,* or kebabs, heavy in the air. Stores are stocked with local goods and those imported from Kazakhstan, located to the west but separated from Mongolia by two small wedges of Russia and China. A border crossing south of Olgii at **Dayan-Hunshansi** connects with northern Xinjiang but is forbidden to foreigners. The northern crossing into Russia, which is open, is at **Tsagaannuur,** 130 kilometres (80 miles) north of the town. (Weekly flights connect with Almaty in Kazakhstan.)

By air, Olgii – pronounced with a "U" sound – is some 1,636 kilometres (1,017 miles) from Ulaanbaatar, usually four hours with a stopover en route. (Driving day and night, trucks take about three days.) The town receives fewer flights than Hovd, but for those flying directly into the airport just north of town, the view out over the highest part of the Mongol Altai is absolutely magnificent. There is a very remote – and different – feeling to this westernmost part of Mongolia.

A visit here is not only an opportunity to see Mongolia's most magnificent mountain scenery but to absorb the Kazakh lifestyle which, in many ways, is more traditional than in their "native" country. (After the break-up of the Soviet Union in the early 1990s, the

Following spread: The hospitality guests receive inside a Kazakh yurt seems boundless (Colin Monteath).

THE EAGLE HUNTING FESTIVAL

By *Peter Oetzmann*

The most spectacular event in Mongolia during the autumn takes place in the far west, in Bayan Olgiy. The people in this area are mainly Muslim Kazakhs and they still practise one of Asia's oldest arts, the use of eagles for hunting. The festival takes place at the beginning of October on a date that – like many things in Mongolia – is subject to change.

Participants come from miles around, riding for days and travelling along a route that has been passed down through generations (a few entrants even make the journey from Kazakhstan through Russia into Mongolia to compete). The opening ceremony takes place with the smell of food and alcohol in the air, and the many *yurts* (the Kazakh equivalent of the Mongol *ger*) offer their usual hospitality and warmth.

In this land of eternal blue sky the autumn sun provides a photographer's dream, with the Kazakh hunters sporting their finest embroidered jackets, fur overcoats and colourful fur-lined hats. The hustle and bustle of what for many is an opportunity to catch up with long-parted friends and family, and for the younger generation to make new acquaintances, creates a heady atmosphere of celebration. The sound of musical instruments, song and dance illustrates the Kazakh love for music and poetry – two art forms that are intrinsic to nomadic culture. Kazakh minstrels and singers, known as *akyns*, compete in joyful public contests called *aytis*, verbally and musically sparring with each other to show the greatest wit and improvisational skill. And all around the food and drink flows; as a visitor, be sure to try everything offered at least once – this festival is a fantastic chance to try many traditional Kazakh dishes.

At the main event, the hunting eagles are not fed prior to hunting and ride on the arms of the hunters, supported by a piece of wood jutting from each rider's saddle. The hood is removed often at a gallop and the eagle soars up into the sky, scanning the terrain below for its prey. The silent sweeping curves of these magnificent birds as they cut through the sky is an awe-inspiring sight; as the target animal is spotted they descend in a crescendo of speed to hit their prey with shocking force, engulfing and holding it until the hunter arrives and issues a reward to his eagle. (The power of an eagle's strike, talons outstretched, will often kill an animal outright, even prey as large as an adult wolf.)

As well as the hunting of live prey with eagles, usually in the form of a released wolf cub, the Eagle Hunting Festival includes many other varied events, enabling the Kazakhs to show off their prowess not only in hunting but also in horsemanship, strength and bravery. These tests include the sport of *kokpar* (known in southern Central Asia as *buzkashi*), a sort of horseback rugby where two teams of horsemen compete to grab and win possession of a headless sheep or goat carcass then carry and throw it over the opposition's goal line; *auderyspak*, or wrestling on horseback to try and unseat your opponent; and the traditional game of skill and daring called *kumis alu* or "pick up the coin", whereby a rider must, while galloping at full speed, bend low over his mount's back to grab a coin from the ground. These days a handkerchief or other everyday object is usually substituted, but the courage and remarkable technique required prove a rider's ability beyond doubt. None of these events is for the faint-hearted, whether as a spectator or competitor. Of course horse racing also takes place, which can often involve a few private financial transactions.

Eagle hunting is thought to have originated in Mongolia among Turkic-speaking tribes such as the Kyrgyz, Uighurs and Kazakhs, later spreading west and south as these tribes migrated, then into Europe along the trading routes of the Mongol Empire. This is an event that captures much of what makes nomadic life in Mongolia fascinating – the epic landscapes lit by a cloudless sky; the realities of hunting for food; the friendships which exist between people who for prolonged periods live an isolated and relentlessly demanding way of life. Kazakhs are fiercely competitive individuals, a trait that is born through the struggle for survival in this harsh, open and unforgiving landscape. For the visitor, attending the Eagle Hunting Festival is an opportunity of a lifetime to be awed and inspired by a centuries-old culture that lives close to and in harmony with the natural world within an epic landscape.

Also a freelance journalist and photographer, British-born Peter Oetzmann is a tour director for Tseren Tours (www.tserentours.com).

government of now-independent Kazakhstan subsidised the migration of thousands of Mongolian Kazakhs to the west. Many returned disillusioned.) Kazakhs are celebrated for their artistic skills, in particular poetry, singing and music (played on their own unique instruments, such as the *dombra*, a double-stringed mandolin-like instrument with a rich timbre), as well as colourful felt carpets, wall hangings, embroidery and leatherwork (these are immediately obvious on entry to a Kazakh yurt). They also engage in some agriculture, as visitors can see just outside the town.

Most Kazakhs here continue their centuries-old nomadic lifestyle herding domestic animals: sheep, goats, horses, camels and cattle, especially yaks and crossbred *hainaks*. As elsewhere in Mongolia, they move at least four times a year, returning to solid winter quarters on southern-facing slopes, and their hospitality is equally legendary.

But what makes the Kazakhs unique is their use of trained eagles for hunting, especially in late autumn and winter. (Interestingly, the eagles are not held for life but released back into the wild after only three years.) Bayan-Olgii's Eagle Hunting Festival every October draws participants from Kazakhstan and attracts hundreds of domestic and foreign tourists (see Special Topic, page 356).

The main destination for visitors is the **Altai Tavan Bogd National Park** right up against the Chinese and Russian borders. Established only in 1996 and occupying 6,361 square kilometres (2,456 square miles), the park takes in the Mongol Altai's highest peaks and is a breathtaking collection of rugged, snow-capped peaks, huge glaciers, glacial valleys, lakes, streams and rivers. With its many valleys and wide variation in altitude, the park hosts a range of habitats from rock and ice through luxuriant tundra and thick forests and on to grassy steppe – with wildlife to match. At the same time, nomads are permitted to continue using the park; their growing herds are now beginning to present environmental challenges.

Although the park's two entrances are only 150 kilometres (93 miles) west of Olgii, just getting there over rough roads takes at least half a day, while the park itself requires a minimum of several days to explore properly. The park is ideal for hiking and backpacking, but most visitors find horse treks a much better option, even for brief journeys. Tour companies and locals are well set up to assist in all these options.

The main part of the national park runs southeast from the Tavan Bogd peaks, parallel to the Chinese border (the wildest parts of the park are actually along this difficult-to-reach border region). The main road leads past the village of **Ulaanhus** on the banks of the Hovd River and then through the picturesque town of **Tsengel** farther upstream. This

Previous spread: Camels and horses lead a mountaineering group through the lush meadows of Tavan Bogd, with Potanin Glacier behind (Colin Monteath).

COLDEST MOUNTAIN: THE FIRST WINTER ASCENT OF MT KHUITEN

By *Graham Taylor*

Why attempt to climb a mountain in winter with ambient temperatures of -40°C? Insanity springs to mind, but so does the challenge of going where nobody else has gone before. "Khuiten" means cold in Mongolian, and by the late 20th century it remained one of few if any significant peaks in the world without a winter ascent... perhaps with good reason!

It all started back in 1999 with a quest to find somewhere unique and memorable to celebrate the passing of the millennium: on top of Mongolia's highest peak, I thought, how remote is that! It didn't seem too daunting a task at the time; after all, I had already made two summer ascents and had started operations of summer tours in the region. Sylvia Haye, another long-term resident of Ulaanbaatar, shared my enthusiasm for this adventure, so it wasn't long before we were making plans. It all seemed fairly straightforward really – take lots of warm clothes, fly to Bayan-Olgii, drive to Tavan Bogd National Park, ski up the glacier, climb the mountain and come back. We had little idea how much snow there would be, or the conditions, as people (even locals) didn't venture so deep into the mountains at this time. Even Atai, a dear friend and National Parks Director at the time, bought into the project – so we were to be a party of three.

Slyvia and I flew to Bayan-Olgii on 27 December 1999, kitted out for an expedition, but with many extra layers of clothing. We met Atai in Olgii and made the day's drive to the Tavan Bogd National Park... my feet were cold just sitting in the jeep. On arrival at the National Park, Atai introduced us to a herder friend "Kadelmaa", who would be providing the packhorse – "packhorse", what packhorse? This was a mountaineering trip! In any event we proceeded through snowy conditions and arrived at Camp 1, close to the location of our summer base camp, at dusk on 30 December. Our three-person tent was cramped to say the least, and after a cold and uncomfortable night we awoke to a blizzard and the realisation that the summit was a long way away. That evening it was with great entertainment – though not from any summit – that we celebrated the new millennium with toasts of vodka.

Roll on year 2000 and the start of a mission: with good planning, preparation and equipment, a winter ascent of Mt Khuiten would be achievable. Sylvia and Atai politely declined a second attempt, so it was up to Andy Smith to pick up the baton. This time we decided to "do it properly", with a sponsorship programme, media coverage, equipment deals, and a lean, mean, lightweight party of two. Following a near identical itinerary to the 1999 expedition, we reached a high camp beneath Mt Malchin, a typical launch point for summit attempts in summer. Faced with clear skies, an ambient temperature of -25°C but high winds, we decided to make a summit attempt... until disaster struck when our tent blew away as we were breaking camp. As we watched the tent bounce down the Potanin Glacier like a giant beach ball, our summit dreams faded – tentless, our only option was to retreat.

Having shelved any plans for a third attempt, it was only the enthusiasm of Greg Leonard, an American geologist and Mongolia old-hand, that rekindled any ideas of going again ("Greg, do you have any idea how cold it is up there?"). With Greg's persistent encouragement a plan started to evolve. Now armed with the experience of two failed attempts, this would be the third and final one – no holds barred. We would be light, fast and fully kitted out: Everest-class climbing boots; down suits, mitts – the works. By this stage I had 12 summer ascents under my belt and could almost walk the glacier in my sleep!

The winter solstice seemed the only logical time to do a "real" winter ascent, so retracing the steps of previous years we arrived at Tavan Bogd on 20 December 2006. The plan was to make the ascent Alpine style, almost non-stop, to avoid the debilitating effects of condensation and ice build-up in clothing and tent. Given that the days offered only five hours of sunlight at this time of year, we were mentally prepared to travel mostly by night. Leaving the jeeps late morning on the 21st, we set out in good conditions, clear skies, -15°C and a light wind. With dusk falling at 4pm, we proceeded under torchlight and reached base camp at 8pm – camp being a frozen creek bed. We dug a platform for our tiny two-person tent into the side of a deep snowdrift and, after a quick brew, turned in for a short night's sleep.

At 1am, with light snow and light wind, there was no reason not to make a summit attempt. We made good progress up the Potanin Glacier under torchlight with light snow falling, our "Yowie" snowshoes working a treat (made in Australia of all places!). Dawn broke at around 8am with thick cloud building and an orange hue – generally not a good sign in the mountains! As we negotiated the upper reaches of the glacier visibility dropped to a few metres and the wind began to howl, but we pressed on up the summit ridge. Beaten by driving snow at -25°C and buffeted by wind gusts up to 100kph, we reached the summit at 2pm on the shortest day of the year. With no view to speak of, and a feeling of being a very long way from anywhere warm, we retraced our steps off the summit and back down the glacier in the worsening blizzard, arriving at the security of our tent at 9pm. Although dehydrated and somewhat delirious, we were warmed by the comforting knowledge that we had conquered Mongolia's highest peak in winter!

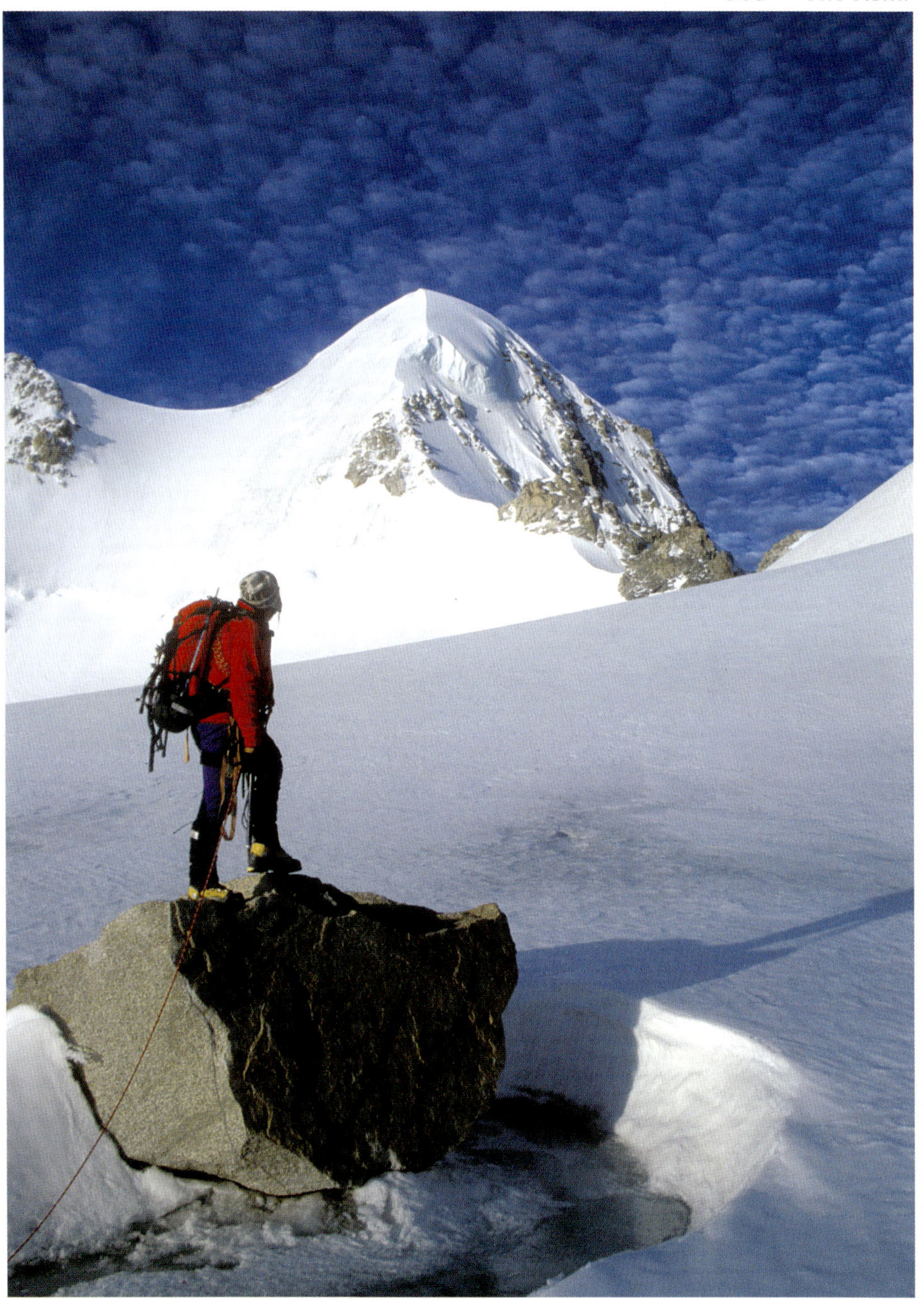

A mountaineer stands surrounded by beauty within the upper regions of Tavan Bogd, on his way to the summit of Khuiten Uul (Colin Monteath).

A Feeling for Felt

Born in Berlin but growing up in Britain, Louisa Waugh travelled to Mongolia in the mid-1990s where she worked for two years as a journalist and foreign correspondent. In 1998, she moved to a village in the remote Altai Mountains of westernmost Mongolia to spend a year teaching and living with the local people, mostly minority Tuvans and Kazakhs. Her unique and unsentimental account of an incredible year, *Hearing Birds Fly*, is one of the best reads on modern Mongolia.

Gansukh and I were on the endless search for dung when the sky above us rumbled and bruising clouds began to roll. The rains, which had started months ago in spring but released nothing more than a few days' downpour, finally seemed imminent. The air began to feel hot and thick. Deri-Huu and Manike called me to help them gather the nets of sheep's wool that were still lying on the riverside hassocks, and were now dry and stiff. Some of it we bundled into sacks, the rest we spread evenly across a large mat woven from reeds, and then we all knelt around the run and beat the wool soft with sticks.

This was harder than it sounds. Deri-Huu gave me two sticks and showed me how to cross one on top of the other, so the wood didn't splinter on impact. It was one of the few times we all worked together, and we sang out loud as we whacked the wool. Webs of fluff floated above and around us, until we were enveloped in a hairy cloud. It was several hours before the lanolin had been beaten soft and the wool was fluffy. We rested inside the cool ger *and drank tea for a while.*

But Deri-Huu was soon back on her feet. "Come on, Elizaa – I'm going to show you how to make esgii *with this fresh fleece before it rains."*

Making esgii, *or felt, in Mongolia is like harvesting a diverse crop, and it is work that only women do. Felt provides walls for the gers, it's used as mattresses and blankets for the narrow beds, is dyed and stitched into elegant rugs, or moulded into huge stiff, knee-high winter boots for the men. Felt boots are perfect for wading through the snow – your feet don't get wet at all.*

Deri-Huu and Manike spread the fleece evenly across the tightly woven reed mat. Then Gansukh appeared with two large pails of warm water.

"Now watch..." Deri-Huu poured a thin stream of water into her dark palm, her fingers splayed open. Drops trickled on to the dry fleece. "We have to soak the fleece before we can roll it into esgii*," she said. "If the wood isn't wet, it won't bind."*

When the whole fleece was damp, the four of us rolled the mat and fleece slowly and tightly into a long, thick sausage. Deri-Huu swaddled it with lengths of grey rope, binding it fast. When she'd finished, we knelt down again on the dry grass and rolled it backwards and forwards, backwards and forwards, until our singing was parched and even Deri-Huu admitted she was weary. We had a rest, drank tea and then started rolling all over again. We worked until Shilgee herded the flock back to camp for the evening and we had to milk the goats and the yaks. Gansukh and I were shattered, and spent the late evening comparing our throbbing arms and backache.

The next morning we slowly unfurled the rigid mat. "If the fleece hasn't bound properly, we'll have to roll it again this afternoon," said Manike casually, as she released the ropes. I couldn't even bear to think about that prospect.

The emerging fleece was pale as a newborn, the wool fibres meshed and inseparable. Gansukh nudged me and grinned. "It's OK," she said in English. "It is good esgii*. Look."*

Together we'd rolled a stiff white wall of felt.

Louisa Waugh, Hearing Birds Fly, *2003*

is the mixed Kazakh and Tuva community where Louisa Waugh spent her memorable year described in *Hearing Birds Fly* (see Literary Excerpt, page 364). A winding road then leads up the V-shaped Hovd River valley for another 45 kilometres (28 miles) and crosses a rugged wooden bridge at the park's eastern entrance. Dominating the southern horizon, but outside the park boundaries, is snow-capped **Tsengel Khairkhan Uul** (3,943 metres or 12,936 feet) which can also be seen from Olgii.

Shaped by glacial forces during the last Ice Age, the heart of the park is the distinctly U-shaped **Hoton Nuur Valley** (also Khoton) where constant streams feed into the park's longest lake, **Hoton Nuur**, and **Hurgan Nuur** (also Khurgan) just to the south, both formed in troughs left behind by receding glaciers. The valley's western side rises sharply up to the range's main ridgeline, while its eastern side consists mostly of gravelly moraines and the distinct levels of previous glaciers.

Coming into Hoton Nuur from the north is the **Tsagaan Us Gol,** or White Water River, one of its three tributaries, which flows down a narrow valley of the same name from the Tavan Bogd glaciers high above. Its waters are distinctly white from the suspended powdered rock ground by the glaciers, called glacial milk, which contrasts dramatically with the grassy meadows along its banks. A road leads partially up this valley with a hiking – and horse trekking – trail then running far up the spectacular valley and into high country to the peaks 60 kilometres (37 miles) away.

At the southern end of this section of the park is another large lake, **Dayan Nuur** and its smaller southern neighbour **Har Nuur**, where the Hovd River originates, its waters flowing north to join an outflow from these other two lakes. (To give readers an idea of the distances involved in this rough and wild landscape, the sum centre of **Dayan** at the southeast corner of the lake is a full eight hours by road from Olgii.) As one of the major rivers of western Mongolia, the 516-kilometre-long (320-mile) Hovd River eventually exits the Altai and then flows down its eastern foothills into the Khar Us Lake and the Great Lakes Region east of Hovd (see next chapter).

Evidence of a continuous human presence and migration routes through the Altai-Sayan region goes back several hundred thousand years to Palaeolithic times. Relics of this fascinating history are scattered throughout the park, with one just outside its northern end. These include petroglyphs, large rock mounds, slab-edged graves and anthropomorphic balbals. Encircled by boulders, one large stone mound sits above the Hovd River near Hoton Nuur.

Previous spread: The rare snow lotus, or vansemberuu, *is found in crevices and cracks high up in the Altai. A perennial herb, it is used in Chinese medicine – a major reason for its increasing rarity (Elbegzaya Lhagvasuren).*

Just past the park entrance, another road leads north through the smaller **Mogoit Valley** where there are several Turkic-era balbals dating from the 6th–8th centuries, their heads thankfully not lopped off by the succeeding rulers. (More such statues are also found on the flats above the Hovd River to the south.) Offering several smaller alpine lakes with a lovely backdrop of snow-capped peaks, this road leads to the northern end of the park.

Closer to Olgii, a second less-scenic road to this end of the park leads past Ulaanhus, up another valley and then over a pass where one branch heads due west to a ranger station. The other heads south into the upper reaches of the **Tsagaan Gol**, or White River, its glacial milk an even richer white than its southern counterpart. (The Mogoit Valley road joins the river at this point and travels along its southern bank.) During the summer months, the valley provides summer pasture for nomadic Kazakhs and Tuvans whose yurts and gers dot the surrounding landscape. On the glaciated slopes of **Sheveed Uul** (3,350 metres or 10,990 feet), home to a large herd of ibex, is a small collection of Bronze Age petroglyphs carved into the blackened granite.

Farther up the Tsagaan Gol Valley, the road ends and a trail leads for another 10 kilometres (six miles) higher to the **Tavan Bogd Base Camp** located in lush alpine tundra and glacial moraine at the foot of the mountain's main glacier. The base camp is the kick-off point for the climactic journey to the top of the Mongol Altai.

Against the backdrop of the Tavan Bogd's five sharp-edged peaks, the wide **Potanin Glacier** occupies some 23 square kilometres (8.8 square miles) and slopes gently eastwards. This is, quite literally, the top of Mongolia. Marked by crevasses and full of eroded rocks and dam-like grey moraines on its flanks, the glacier breaks off into a small lake where the waters melt and flow milky white into the Tsagaan Gol. In the summer melting period, the river can rise quickly during the day, making fording hazardous. Mongolia's highest peak, **Khuiten Uul** (4,374 metres or 14,350 feet) is the most southern of the five overlooking China, while the top of 4,082-metre-high (13,392-foot) **Nairamdal Uul,** or Friendship Peak, straddles the border of Mongolia, China and Russia. Ever practical in their nomenclature, Khuiten simply means Cold while the others are Malchin (Herder), Ulgii (Cradle) and Burgd (Eagle).

Requiring an experienced guide and full mountaineering equipment, climbing Mongolia's Five Saints is developing a reputation as one of the world's great mountain climbs, if for no other reason than its remote location. Australian expat Graham Taylor, who runs Karakorum Tours and the Xanadu Wine Shop in UB, has climbed the Tavan Bogd on several occasions, including in midwinter; he advises that Khuiten Peak is an "advanced trekking peak, more technical than Mera or Island Peak in Nepal". The most difficult part is traversing the eight kilometres (five miles) of the heavily crevassed Potanin Glacier, with some crevasses up to two metres (six feet) wide. "Rope climbing teams regularly find members slipping waist-deep into crevasses," he warns, "and on occasion complete falls." As an experienced climber, Taylor emphasises the glacier is serious stuff and anyone who shows up at the base camp thinking they can solo-climb the mountain is "irresponsible and highly dangerous". With a scree of rocks to scramble over to the snowy summit, Nairamdal Uul also requires caution. For those who prepare well and travel in groups, one reward is spotting the ever-elusive snow leopard across Tavan Bogd's vast snowfields – or at least its delicate tracks.

For those with time, Mongolia's largest collection of petroglyphs – over 100,000 images going back 10,000 years – lies just outside the northern end of the park at **Tsagaan Salaa** up near the Russian border. (The find is also referred to as **Baga Oigor**.) Extending over 20 kilometres (12.5 miles) along the rocky slopes of two rivers, the complex is regarded as one of the oldest and largest open-air rock art sites in North Asia. The images show a wide range of wild and domesticated animals, human activities and even diagrams of chariots. A smaller and more recent complex is located along the **Upper Tsagaan** but shows exquisitely preserved images from the Bronze and early Iron Age (2nd–1st millennia BCE) and the Turkic Period (7th–9th centuries CE). The complex also includes ancient altars, stone images and even ancient cemeteries.

From the aimag centre of Olgii, the tree-lined Hovd River – its waters swollen to near bursting point in late spring – flows northwest, first meandering through a wide plain with the hulking Tsambagarav Uul massif on the southern horizon and then squeezing through a spectacular canyon as it hurriedly exits the Altai range. (The road heads up a pass and hugs the foothills before joining the roaring river through this narrow canyon.) Quite abruptly, the mountains end – rising sharply from an unseen fault line – and the land slopes gently down into a wide valley dominated by a lovely lake with another snow-capped range in the far distance. Off to the right, the river valley spreads out into a lovely expanse of green – covered in grass and lined with willow and poplar trees, its many gers an obvious sign of rich pastures.

Straddling the border of **Uvs aimag**, **Achit Nuur** is the region's largest freshwater lake and with distant snow-capped mountains in almost every direction and calm reflective waters makes quite a spectacular sight, especially at sunrise and sunset. The lake's waters exit through a natural embankment at its southern end where its lush grass provides a summer home for dozens of nomad families, the distinctly Kazakh-style yurts set apart from the others. (While the roads are all-dirt, a solidly built concrete bridge straddles the fast-flowing river.) The rest of the shoreline is dotted with patches of grass and sandy beaches between the odd heavily eroded rocky outcrop. Fed by streams flowing down from the range across the northern Russian border, the lake is home to geese, ducks and the increasingly rare Dalmatian pelican.

The calm surface of Achit Nuur reflects the shifting clouds. This freshwater lake is home to a host of water birds (Carl Robinson).

To the west and stretching north is the snow-topped frontal range and lower foothills of the Altai while due south looms the mighty bulk of Tsambagarav Uul, a lovely backdrop to the entire scene. On the eastern side is a string of bare and rugged hills – their composition remarkably similar to those far to the east and north of the Gobi. Our driver Byambaa was born right near the bridge and took us on a pleasant drive downstream from the lake past a mini-oasis, sand dunes and odd ancient stone monument, and then through rugged hills and down a narrow defile to where the amazingly wide and lush valley of the Hovd River suddenly opened up before us with the snow-capped mountains behind (the constant contrasts of Mongolia never cease to surprise).

Along the slopes of the narrow gully leading now sharply to the valley below were at least a dozen large rocky mounds. These are the graves of Nationalist Chinese troops killed in that little-known battle in 1944 with the Kazakh insurgent Ospan Batyr. Almost on cue, a lone Mongolian horseman clattered down the same steep hillside where Soviet cavalry swarmed down to trap those invaders from far across the distant Altai Mountains all those years ago. Byambaa knew the story, now part of local folklore.

We travelled to the nearby riverside sum centre of **Hovd** (not to be confused with the larger aimag town of Hovd in the aimag of the same name to the south) for lunch with his family and a much-needed rest. Later, as we prepared to leave this obscure spot, a group of mostly French-speaking Europeans bounced into town on their mountain bikes, part of an adventure tour. All they wanted was a shower. I suggested the Hovd River – but just don't get swept away! We'd tried, but no 4WD truck was prepared to ferry our Russian Jeep across to the other side and we backtracked past Lake Achit.

The last part of Mongolia's Altai region lies between Achit Nuur and the country's largest lake, salty **Uvs Nuur** at the northern end of the Great Lakes Region (see next chapter). Some might argue with this definition, but the stunning – and almost solitary – **Turgen Uul** range is a clearly a spur off the larger Altai-Sayan system which juts southeast into Mongolia. From the Uvs aimag centre of **Ulaangom** to the east or approaching from out of the rest of the Altai, this is an absolutely stunning pocket of Mongolia renowned for its beautiful scenery and particularly famous for the rarely seen high-altitude snow lotus flower. Known in Mongolian as the *vansemberuu* and bearing the scientific name *Saussurea involucrata*, the flower, an alpine saw-wort, only grows between 2,600 and 3,000 metres and has become increasingly rare.

Just one part of the surprisingly diverse Great Lakes Basin and protected as one of only 10 UNESCO World Biosphere Reserves in the world, the **Turgen Uul Nature Reserve** is dominated by the twin peaks of **Hanhiraa** (4,037 metres or 13,245 feet) and **Turgen** (3,965 metres or 13,008 feet) and accessed from the massif's southeast side. (On the plane in, I met a group of Canadians who planned to spend two months just hiking around the reserve.) But from whatever approach, the first full view of this snow-covered massif definitely takes your breath away. Flanked by lower but still-spectacular mountains on either side, a stunning 60-kilometre-long (37-mile) valley dominated by ancient tombs and a large lake connects the Turgen with the main range just across the Russian border.

On the western side of this entire range, the foothills east of Achit rise higher but remain dry and rugged with only a sharp valley and its rock-strewn watercourse hinting at the massive snowy range inside. With a superb view back toward the lake and the main Altai range beyond, we stopped at some large mounds made of round rocks – not a single such rock visible in the immediate area and obviously brought from some distance – and heard a story of an untamed area beyond the Qing's reach. Of a different style and later than others in Mongolia, these were the tombs of highly revered local leaders.

Past a small Kazakh-run coalmine, the road heads up a long grass-covered incline strewn with granite boulders where yaks, hainaks, goats and sheep graze. But the permafrost has made the road surface irritatingly rough and slow, making walking a better option. In fact, the worst roads in Mongolia are through precisely such terrain, where granite boulders are heaved up and down by changing seasonal temperatures, posing a serious challenge to modern road builders. On the positive side, the constant jostling is like an exercise machine at an expensive gym – and great for weight loss. The Russian Jeep Weight-Loss Programme!

At a crest in the range, **Bayramyn Davaa** (Pass) makes a welcome break. Several years ago, its huge ovoo was shifted to one side for an international team of archaeologists to explore a burial chamber beneath; they found jewellery, clothing, sheep knucklebones and other relics of an obviously important personage. (Not all ovoo have graves, of course, and this is most unusual.) Next to the now covered chamber, the new ovoo rises draped in blue hadag and even the odd yak skull.

Grassy alpine meadows dotted with flowers stretch eastwards and overlook the above-mentioned valley with the glistening waters of **Uureg Nuur** and the 3,500-metre-high snow-capped **Tsagaan Shuvuut Uul** beyond (this range is also part of the Biosphere Reserve). Off to the north and just across the Russian border only a short distance away rises solitary **Mongon Uul** (3,970 metres or 13,024 feet) and its glistening snow and glacier-covered peak. It is quite a majestic sight and only gets better further down.

Descending into the valley, the northern side of the range – as elsewhere in Mongolia – is covered in larch forests and then opens up into lush pastures dotted with the herds and summer gers of nomad families. Clearly, humans have lived here for centuries. In a choice position with the lake and range beyond is one of the largest circular gravesites in Mongolia – carefully laid stones more than 50 metres (165 feet) across with a large mound at its centre and a dozen smaller ones around it. Farther down the valley is a large man-made pyramid of rocks.

With no outlet, **Uureg Nuur** is mildly salty and heavily mineralised and its shoreline is dotted with numerous sandy beaches and rocky inlets. A small island is home to thousands of migrating ducks, which feed off the lake's huge stock of fish. Just off the main road from Olgii to Ulaangom, the lake makes a wonderful camping spot with lovely views at sunrise as the sun reflects off Mongon Uul and the eastern range. (Still undeveloped, it's only a matter of time before someone builds a tourist ger camp along its lovely shores. I can already see water skiers scooting around this lake!)

Coming out the eastern side of the valley at the pass of **Ulaan Davaa**, the snow-capped bulk of the **Turgen Uul** is now clearly visible off to the south. Our driver was looking forward to taking his family up into the range for the summer – and tracking down its legendary snow lotus flower once again (his family album had pictures of his entire clan posing beside one they'd found). Between its two main peaks, the park boasts a beautiful mixture of forest, meadows, lakes and creeks. From the pass, too, the vast waters of **Uvs Nuur,** the most northerly of Mongolia's Great Lakes, can be seen far off in the distance. Unlike this mountain region's western side, however, the drop down is quite precipitous.

Following spread: A large, circular gravesite, marked out by carefully placed stones, overlooks Uureg Nuur and the Tsagaan Shuvuut range beyond in Mongolia's remote northwest (Carl Robinson).

THE GREAT LAKES

Mongolia's **Great Lakes Depression** – or Basin – is located between the **Altai** and **Hangai** mountain ranges and is a vast semi-arid region containing hundreds of fresh and saltwater lakes in a unique landscape that includes some of the last remaining reed beds in Central Asia. Technically, the Great Lakes is not a depression, or below sea level, but as part of the Central Asia Internal Drainage Basin none of its waters exit into any other river system. (In geological terms, the depression is an "intermontane basin".) The region's elevation averages between 750 and 2,000 metres (2,460–6,562 feet) and covers roughly 100,000 square kilometres (38,610 square miles) of western Mongolia.

From the **Tannu-Ola Range** along the Russian border, an extension of the **Altai-Sayan** mountain system, the depression runs south and southeast for some 650 kilometres (404 miles). In width, it varies from 250 kilometres (155 miles) in the north to only 100 kilometres (62 miles) in the far south. The Great Lakes Depression contains over 300 lakes of various sizes but derives its name from its half-dozen larger fresh and saline lakes, which start in the arid north with the country's largest lake, salty **Uvs Nuur**, and continue – in roughly four separate sub-regions – down to smaller and more isolated **Shargyn Tsagaan Nuur** in the southeast, now a protected area for the highly endangered saiga antelope. (*Nuur* means lake in Mongolian.)

The Great Lakes region covers parts of the *aimags*, or provinces, of **Uvs, Zavhan, Hovd** and **Gobi Altai.** Geologically speaking, the depression continues eastwards as a rift valley north of the Gobi Altai Mountains dotted with many other isolated lakes, such as **Orog Nuur** just north of Ikh Bogd in Bayanhongor aimag (see The Gobi, page 319) and **Ulaan Nuur** in the northern part of Omnogov (South Gobi) aimag.

With an extremely cold climate and little rainfall, this semi-arid region offers quite a variety of landscapes, from arid steppe in the north to semi-desert and desert in the south. Wide, dry valleys on the lower parts of surrounding mountains slope down to rivers and lakes. The actual floor of the depression is a mixture of saltpans, marshes, lakes and hills, including many jagged rocky outcrops, with sparse desert and semi-desert vegetation. Many lakes and salty marshes are covered by some of the last reed beds in Central Asia. These wetlands provide a summer haven for thousands of migratory birds, including the endangered Dalmatian pelican, Eurasian spoonbill, black stork, osprey and a rare sub-species of the saker falcon, making this region a birdwatcher's paradise. Seagulls fly thousands of kilometres into the depression from the south coast of China. The region's drier areas are also a haven for the threatened saiga antelope. The eastern parts of the region are covered in large sand dunes. Those east of Uvs Nuur are the most northerly dunes in the world, while farther south are some of the largest dunes – by area – in all of Mongolia. As a unique ecoregion, much is protected as national park, but it faces threats from overgrazing, population growth, poaching and even a hydroelectric dam.

With its distant and often snow-crowned mountain ranges, the dazzling contrasts of the Great Lakes Depression provide an evocative remoteness and extreme solitude. The dark blue waters of its vast lakes and yellowish green reed beds stand out starkly against the surrounding brownish landscape of rugged hills and bright blue sky. Fringed only by shadings of grass, the rivers flowing through this vast desert region from faraway mountains have an almost unreal quality. Equally surprising are the lush and marshy deltas where their waters enter the lakes. This is most dramatic where the fast-flowing Hovd River ends its mighty journey out of the highest part of the Altai at **Har Us Nuur** at the southern end of the Depression.

Few venture into the heart of the Great Lakes Depression – and only the most avid ornithologists make this a regular destination. Rather than simply a passing glance, such as a quick half-day trip out of Hovd, an itinerary that cuts through this amazing region and provides plenty of vistas is definitely recommended. (But one early word of warning: bring plenty of insect repellent, as summertime mosquitoes are a real nuisance.) This region is indeed quite fascinating – and is another surprise in a country of constant surprises.

My own cross-country journey through the Great Lakes between the Altai and the Hangai Mountains was certainly one of my most memorable – if slightly spooky – travel experiences. Across a flat desert landscape of saltpans and dry scrub at high noon, the only other sign of life through the shimmering heat was the odd frighteningly emaciated camel. With no real landmarks, I felt totally disorientated. We stopped an oncoming Russian Jeep to double-check we were on the right track through this incredible wasteland. A dead wolf was draped across its spare tyre. We finally reached a wide river crossed by a totally incongruous concrete bridge. The two gers on the riverbank below looked like the loneliest in Mongolia. Travelling east, vultures fed atop rocky outcrops, flying away only lazily at our approach. There's definitely an otherworldly feel to this part of Mongolia.

The town of **Hovd** is the main gateway to Mongolia's western region, including the southern part of the Great Lakes Depression. (With its good hotels and restaurants, Hovd makes a pleasant base to explore the immediate region.) Due east of Hovd and occupying a large part of the aimag's northeast, the vast 3,200-square-kilometre (1,240-square-mile) **Har Us Nuur National Park** includes three of this region's largest lakes and was created to protect its wetlands and rich bird life, including wild ducks, geese, wood grouse, partridges and seagulls, including the rare relict gull and herring gull.

Following spread: Intense colours and contrast mark the meeting of Har Nuur's brilliant-blue water with the mighty sand dunes on its banks ((Elbegzaya Lhagvasuren).

Overwhelming feelings of remoteness characterise the Great Lakes region (Carl Robinson).

of the main Altai range to the west, and which hems in a large area of marshland and reed beds at the lake's southern end. The contrast of the bright yellowish-green of the reeds with the blue lake and dark, rocky mountains behind makes a pleasant impression.

We were on the trail to where Mongolia's famous *hoomii,* or throat-singing (see People & Culture, page 137), originated – the small settlement of **Chandmani** on the other side of the massif west of **Dorgon Nuur.** But just getting across this southern end of the main part of the Great Lakes region was a challenge – and in more ways than one. Our driver

Above: A satellite image shows the Great Lakes region, the lakes' differing colours and the watercourses that feed them (Courtesy of Jacques Descloitres, MODIS Land Rapid Response Team, NASA/GSFC).
Below: Scores of small lakes contain some of Central Asia's last marshlands, and are a favourite habitat for migrating birds (Carl Robinson).

Byambaa was great around his birthplace beside the Altai's lovely Achiit Nuur, but became increasingly lost the further we travelled, a situation hardly helped by growing problems with his old Russian Jeep. The odometer, crucial for his per-kilometre livelihood, broke coming out of Hovd and brake failure was next on the agenda.

Making our way across the lush wetlands, we asked for travel advice from a nomad family who'd just arrived at their summer encampment, their knocked-down ger and belongings still in a heap but taking time for milk tea and a quick meal, which they gladly shared. Daylight was fading and the legendary throat-singers too far away, so as Byambaa showed off his own skills, we pressed on for another couple of hours through a sandstorm and on a barely visible and rough track around the massif's northern tip to a lakeside camping spot, where mosquitoes swarmed but were easily controlled with repellent.

At dawn, a nomad on a white horse fortuitously wandered up and provided new travel instructions for the journey ahead. Travelling northeast from Har Us Nuur through the centre of the park, we made good time across a flat landscape dotted with conical hills, small lakes and marshes. Close up, the shores of the lake are soft and easy to sink into with stands of gold and green reeds that extend out into the water, a haven for a constant flow of noisy ducks and gulls. Under the bright blue sky and with the snow-capped Altai Mountains on the far horizon, the scene was wonderfully relaxing. A bit further on, a huge expanse of marshland running for several kilometres was covered in reeds. At the northern end of the lake, these wetlands stretched far into the distance.

In this vast expanse, there was no sign of any inhabitants, only a few straggling Bactrian camels, which only accentuated the feeling of remoteness. We climbed a low rocky range with a distant view backwards, bidding farewell to our constant companion from the Altai – snow- and glacier-covered Tsambagarav Uul to the north of Hovd. We descended down into a wide valley where the outlet from the Har Us Nuur flows eastwards. About 20 metres (66 feet) across, the river was flowing surprisingly swiftly on its way to nearby Har Nuur with its grass-covered banks supporting a couple of nomad families and their herds. Beside a rustic wooden bridge, looking like a small fort with its mud-brick walls and dropping flag, was a neat ger *guanz*, or canteen, serving meals.

Even by Mongolian standards, the family and handful of customers were unusually quiet, even sullen. The hot sun blazed down, wiping out any shadows. Straight off his Russian motorcycle, a moustachioed nomad in snazzy *deel*, big belt and broad-brimmed hat looked like a character from a cowboy movie, hardly uttering a word. Byambaa had another go at fixing his odometer. My guide Daddo tried fishing but with no luck. The dog outside had a huge gear axle dangling from his collar – presumably to stop him chasing passing vehicles or biting arriving customers. This place felt on the edge of the world.

Located about 75 kilometres (47 miles) north of the Har Us Nur National Park, and now inside Uvs aimag, is the next of the Great Lakes, **Airag Nuur**, a small freshwater lake where the **Zavhan Gol** ends its long journey from the Hangai. Fed by a couple of other desert rivers, the lake's waters then flow north into **Hyargas Nuur**, a salty lake over twice as large as Har Us Nur, or 2,688 square kilometres (1,038 square miles). Protected as part of the 3,330-square-kilometre (1,285-square-mile) **Hyargas Nuur National Park**, the two lakes provide another refuge for water birds and also boast abundant fish life. Airag Nuur also protects about a dozen breeding pairs of Dalmatian pelicans, whose population of several hundred in the early 1960s has dwindled drastically due to poaching for their beaks, which are used for cleaning horses. There are also some hot springs at **Har Termes** on the northwestern side of the lake.

Finally, a further 80 kilometres (50 miles) north past the east-west running and relatively low (2,200–3,000 metres, or 7,218–9,843 feet) **Han Hohiyn Range**, is huge **Uvs Nuur**, the northernmost of the Great Lakes and the closest Mongolia has to an inland sea – in fact, five times saltier than the ocean. Although relatively shallow at 12 metres (40 feet), the lake's surface covers some 3,423 square kilometres (1,322 square miles) and at 759 metres (2,490 feet) above sea level is the lowest point in western Mongolia. Fed by rivers inside Mongolia and from neighbouring Russia but with no outlet, the lake's waters are highly saline. With an extremely marshy shoreline, access is difficult although there is a small beach and camping area on its southwestern shore closest to the aimag capital of **Ulaangom**, 10 kilometres (6.2 miles) away.

With over 200 species recorded, the lake's bird life is quite prolific and includes cranes, spoonbills, geese and seagulls. The best spotting apparently is around its northeastern side, where the **Tesiyn Gol** (River) forms a delta after its long journey from the Hovsgol region through Russia to the lake.

Because of a permanent anticyclone in winter, Uvs Nuur is one of the coldest places in Asia and renowned for its low winter temperatures, a record -58°C (-72.4°F). At the same time, its summer temperatures sizzle above 40°C. For this reason, the Uvs Nuur and three adjoining areas are one of only 10 UNESCO World Biosphere Reserves to study the effects of climate change. Together, these form part of the huge 71,250-square-kilometre, or 27,510-square-mile, **Uvs Lake Basin Strictly Protected Area**. In addition to two mountain ranges – the Turgen and Tsagaan Shuvuut – the biosphere includes the **Altan Els,** the world's northernmost sand dunes. Also known as the **Boorog Deliyn Els,** these remarkable dunes stretch east for some 150 kilometres (93 miles) from the eastern side of Uvs Nuur.

Following spread: Nomads lasso their next batch of riding horses in the shadow of the spectacular Bor Hyaryn Els in the east of the Great Lakes region (Carl Robinson).

THE ROADS OF MONGOLIA

Mongolia's roads have a notorious reputation. But quite perversely, they are also one of its attractions – that rare ability to just head straight across an unfenced countryside stretching to the far horizon. Mongolia has an astounding 49,000 kilometres (30,450 miles) of roads but barely 1,000 kilometres (620 miles) are actually paved. Most are gravel and dirt, and when one track wears out, drivers simply start another one alongside.

On really busy roads, such as the main road from Ulaanbaatar to the South Gobi provincial capital of Dalanzadgad, up to 15 old and new tracks sprawl across the vast steppe, narrowing only to cross the odd modern concrete bridge. The environmental impact of these multiple tracks is plainly obvious; rain and melting snow erodes the old tracks into ugly gullies. Often, the tracks expose soft sand below and blasting winds further aggravate the erosion.

Road travel can be achingly slow – three hours to travel 100 kilometres is typical. The roads are worst in the permafrost regions of northern Mongolia where the road surface is heaved up and down with the seasons, exposing the unyielding granite below. Travellers are jostled about like clothes in a washing machine. Elsewhere, just as the vehicle picks up speed and you start to relax, the driver brakes hard to stagger slowly through another watercourse. The best runs are across the vast steppe, such as the Great Eastern Steppe, but even here channels, even the odd lake, interrupt the flatness. Be patient and don't get too irritated.

Fortunately, things are finally changing. In 2001, Mongolia's State Great Hural, or parliament, authorised construction of the Millennium Road, a paved 2,600-kilometre (1,600-mile) east-west network across Mongolia. The road's construction was seen as essential infrastructure for Mongolia's economic development. (Interestingly, the country's tourism department is part of the Ministry of Transport.) With financial, engineering and construction assistance from a range of international aid agencies and both local and foreign companies, Mongolia has seen some remarkable progress, even as many grumble about corruption allegations and endless delays. With such a brief construction season, basically over the brief summer, the Millennium Road and other road constructions were never going to happen overnight. On the positive side, the works have provided hundreds of new and often highly skilled jobs to the local population.

In mid-2008, an important "missing gap" on the Millennium Road just west of Ulaanbaatar was finally finished and now allows all-asphalt travel to the ancient capital of Harhorin (Karakorum), 365 kilometres (227 miles) away. (From there, another paved road leads 45 kilometres, or 28 miles, north to the ancient Turkic capital of Khooshoo-Tsaidam, a donation from the Turkish government.) The main highway is paved for another 120 kilometres (75 miles) southwest to the aimag centre of Arvayheer – and then quickly reverts to a dirt track all the way to Mongolia's far west. Back closer to the capital, paved roads run 200 kilometres (124 miles) north to the Russian border and west to the mining town of Erdenet. The old Tea Road to China – alongside the Trans-Mongolian Railway – is paved only to the industrial town of Choyr, 194 kilometres (120 miles) southeast of the capital. The border remains an unpaved 226 kilometres (140 miles) away.

East of the capital, the Millennium Road is paved for 338 kilometres (210 miles) to the Hentii aimag capital of Ondorhaan and in patches eastward towards Choibalsan in Dornod aimag where the road will cross into China's Inner Mongolia. Other engineering and construction work is taking place around the country, often in the most surprising places, such as over a rugged pass from Hovd to Olgii in the west or coming through the northern Hangai Mountains. In early 2008, Mongolia was granted funding for a main road linking China's western Xinjiang Uygur Autonomous Region up through the eastern Altai to Russia, part of the vast Asian Highway, an ambitious 141,000-kilometre (88,000-mile) network that will link Asia to Europe through 32 countries.

While these roads have certainly improved travel around Mongolia, they've also come at a price. The number of highway deaths and injuries has spiralled dramatically, either from collisions or flipping off high embankments. (Burnt-out engines in vehicles not used to high speeds are another problem.) In other places, ugly quarries for material to build the new roads are a new scar on the landscape. But where the new roads run, it is heartening to see the old dirt tracks slowly fading away – even if more could be done to physically rejuvenate the landscape.

THE HANGAI

Located in the western half of Mongolia starting some 400 kilometres (249 miles) west-southwest of Ulaanbaatar, the **Hangai** are the country's largest mountain range. Also referred to as the Khangai, or **Hangayn Nuruu** in Mongolian, this southeast-running range is 800 kilometres (500 kilometres) long and roughly 200 kilometres (124 miles) wide. The Hangai is Mongolia's third major mountain range after the Hentii northeast of the capital and the Altai along its far western border (running only 200 kilometres, or 124 miles, the Hentii is Mongolia's oldest range while the 1,000-kilometre-long, or 620-mile, Altai is the longest, youngest and highest).

Each of Mongolia's three main ranges has a very different appearance and character. The Hangai – literally "what satisfies a need" – is generally a broad and gentle range of domed summits covered in meadows. Considered a transition zone from the Siberian taiga to steppe, the Hangai's mountainous slopes are covered in thick forests, mostly deciduous larch, with a high diversity of other flora and fauna. Its main mammals are *maral* (elk), musk and red deer, brown bear, wild boar and wolf. The region's lush, grass-covered valleys are fed by a multitude of streams, rivers and lakes.

Fantastic views can be seen on flights from UB to western Mongolia (Leo Murray).

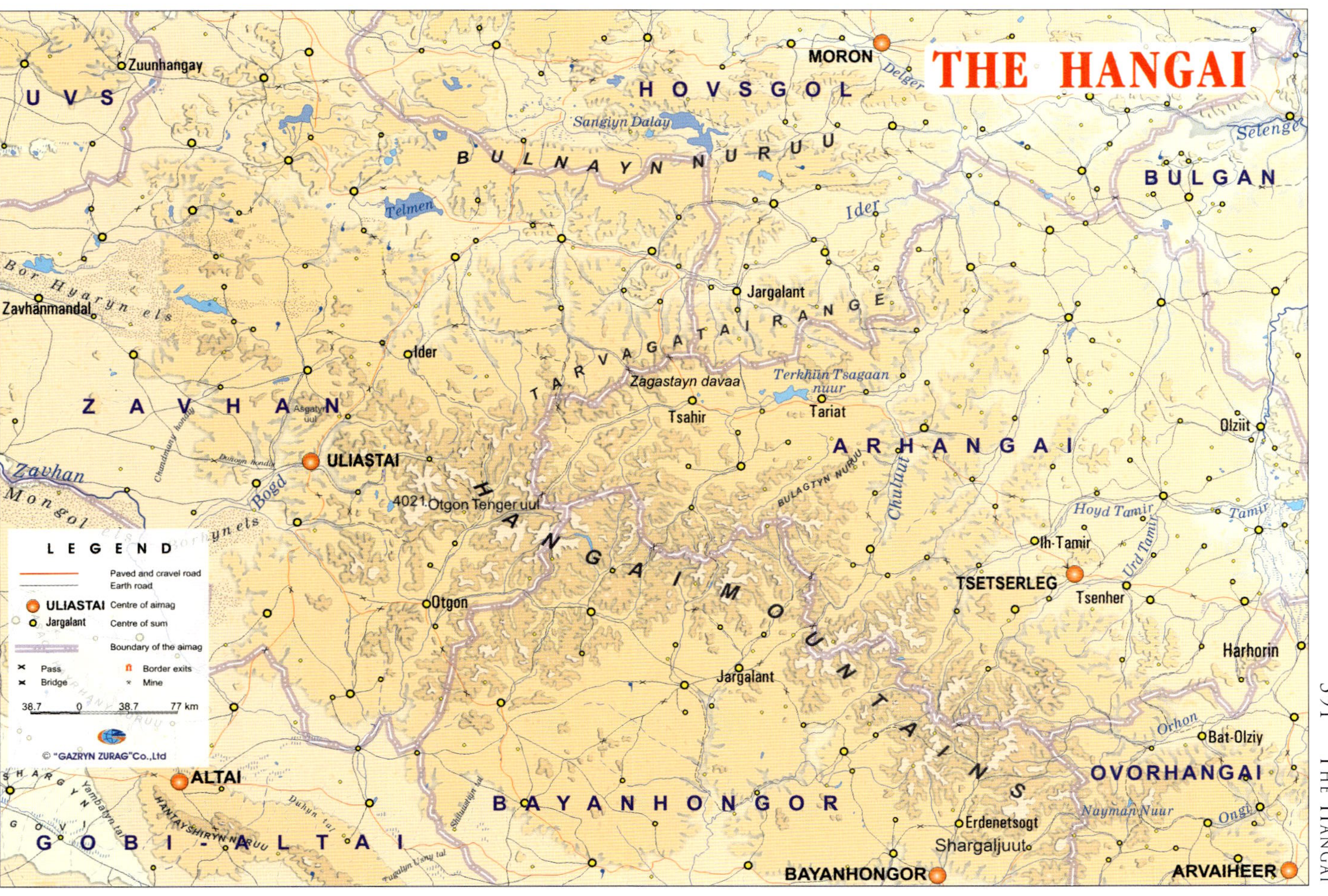
THE HANGAI
UVS
HOVSGOL
BULGAN
BULNAYN NURUU
ZAVHAN
TARVAGATAI RANGE
ARHANGAI
HANGAI MOUNTAINS
BAYANHONGOR
OVORHANGAI
GOBI-ALTAI
MORON
ULIASTAI
TSETSERLEG
ALTAI
BAYANHONGOR
ARVAIHEER
Zuunhangay
Zavhanmandal
Ider
Jargalant
Zagastayn davaa
Tsahir
Tariat
Terkhiin Tsagaan nuur
Olziit
Ih-Tamir
Tsenher
Harhorin
Bat-Olziy
Erdenetsogt
Shargaljuut
Otgon
4021 Otgon Tenger uul
Asgatyn uul
Bulagtyn nuruu
Hantayshiryn nuruu
Sangiyn Dalay
Telmen
Delger
Selenge
Ider
Chuluut
Hoyd Tamir
Urd Tamir
Tamir
Orhon
Ongi
Nayman Nuur
Bogd
Zavhan
Bor Hyaryn els
Mongol els
Duhyn tal
Yambatyn tal
LEGEND
Paved and cravel road
Earth road
ULIASTAI Centre of aimag
Jargalant Centre of sum
Boundary of the aimag
Pass
Bridge
Border exits
Mine
38.7 0 38.7 77 km
© "GAZRYN ZURAG" Co.,Ltd

The Hangai's average elevation is above 2,500 metres (8,200 feet) with many peaks permanently covered in snow. The range's highest peak is 4,021-metre (13,192-foot) **Otgon Tenger**, located near its western end just east of **Uliastai**, the Qing's old military capital, with a couple of peaks near its southeastern tip around 3,500 metres (11,483 feet). Dating from the Permian-Triassic Periods between 250 and 280 million years ago, the Hangai are heavily granite but also reflect extensive and more recent volcanic activity, some as recently as 5,000 years ago. The range is renowned for its hot springs.

At the main range's northern end, but still considered part of the Hangai, are two east-west trending branch ranges, the **Tarvagatai** (also **Tarvagatayn Nuruu**) and **Bulnayn Nuruu.** The northern boundary of the entire Hangai system is the **Bulgan Fault**, the world's longest active fault line, which stretches 340 kilometres (210 miles) west into Uvs aimag (province). Open fissures from the last major earthquake in 1905, in places 60 metres (197 feet) deep and over 10 metres (33 feet) wide, are still visible today.

The Hangai is also the source of two of Mongolia's most significant north-flowing rivers, the headwaters of the Arctic-bound **Yenisey River**, the **Ider**, and the legendary **Orhon** and its principal tributary the **Tamir**. These flow in a generally northeast direction and, after the Orhon is joined by the **Tuul** which runs through UB, eventually form the **Selenge River** just south of the Russian border which flows into Sibera's **Lake Baikal** (see Around UB, page 203). Rivers on the Hangai's southern side flow into what's called the **Central Asian Internal Drainage Basin** where they dead-end.

Given its huge size, the Hangai range covers parts of several Mongolian aimags. At its southeast corner, closest to Ulaanbaatar, the range occupies the western parts of **Ovorhangai** (South Hangai) and **Arhangai** (North Hangai) – the flat grassy steppe of its foothills home to successive empires over the centuries, including the Mongol Empire's Karakorum, or today's Harhorin (see Orhon Valley, page 428). The Hangai's northern and western parts are in southern **Hovsgol** and eastern **Zavhan** aimags. Across the Hangai's southwestern side is the northern part of **Bayanhongor**, an extremely varied aimag that extends far into the South Gobi (see The Gobi, page 282). Four aimag centres, or capitals, are located around its fringes.

Evidence of age-old settlement is literally everywhere throughout the Hangai and its immediate surrounds. Deer stones are particularly numerous in the western Hangai and burial sites from various historic periods are so frequent that visitors barely give them a second glance, unless they are especially large or unusual. By Mongolian standards, many of its lush valleys are literally crowded with the gers of nomadic families and their animals, with the funny-faced and shaggy-haired *hainak*, a cross between a cow and yak, clearly the most numerous. (The other main domestic animals are horses, sheep and goats but not many camels.) With its numerous forests, logging for timber – both legal and not – is a major industry and the region also has several mines, especially for gold.

Many visitors to Mongolia do see the Hangai Mountains, most frequently on the popular road run – the so-called **Golden Circuit** – taking in the South Gobi, the Orhon Valley and Lake Hovsgol. After a stopover at the ancient Mongol capital of Karakorum (Harhorin) and other sites in the Orhon Valley, travellers typically continue up the Hangai's eastern edge and then northwest to an absolutely beautiful mountain lake before experiencing the worst road in Mongolia north to Moron, the capital of Hovsgol aimag, and then on to its eponymous lake. (Some will argue, however, that the worst road is actually the one from Erdenet to Moron through Bulgan aimag.) The permafrost – which extends far down into the range – combines with all that granite to make building and maintaining roads through the Hangai and northern Mongolia an unceasing challenge.

There are, of course, many more destinations in the sprawling Hangai Mountains: stand-alone ones such as the snow-capped **Otgon Tenger**, now a popular horse-trekking and hiking destination, or just passing through on less-travelled tracks between other far-flung destinations. And there is always so much more to discover. Probably the least-visited region is along the Hangai's southern side in northernmost Bayanhongor aimag, the headwaters of the Baydragiyn which feeds south into Boon Tsagaan Lake in the Gobi Altai's rift valley.

Starting in Hangai's southeast, mention has already been made of the attractive Ovorhangai aimag centre of **Arvayheer** and its lovely mountain backdrop as the source of the **Ongi River**, which heads southeast across the flat steppe into Dundgov (Middle Gobi) and Ulaan Nuur in northern Omnogov (see The Gobi, page 319). Located 430 kilometres (267 miles) southwest of the capital on the paved Millennium Road**,** Arvayheer is a good starting point for horse trekking and nature trips up into the southern end of the range. Up in the mountains here, 116 kilometres (72 miles) west of town is **Nayman Nuur,** literally Eight Lakes, one of the most spectacular places in central Mongolia. A string of mostly round lakes is dominated by a large extinct volcano covered in forests and grass with even an ancient Bronze Age deer stone to round off the idyllic scene. From this cosy pocket-sized valley, the distant southern vista stretches far out onto the flat steppe. Closer in are steep-sided valleys and gorges where the Ongi and more famous Orhon rivers begin their respective journeys.

Another approach into this end of the Hangai is through neighbouring **Bayanhongor,** another 209 kilometres (130 miles) farther west, and capital of the aimag of the same name. Originating on the southern watershed of the Hangai, the **Tuyn River** flows south through the town, then across steppe country – and even a touch of older volcanic landscape – to

A herd of shaggy hainak, *a cross between cows and yaks, graze beside the spectacular Terkhiin Tsagaan, or White Lake (Carl Robinson).*

Orog Nuur at the base of snow-capped Ikh Bogd Uul (see The Gobi, page 319). There isn't much to this town, beyond an incredible number of noisy dogs, but up in the mountains about 60 kilometres (37 miles) to its northeast is the well-known health spa of **Shargaljuut**, which boasts over 300 hot and cold springs along the banks of a river flowing between two high mountain peaks. Water is delivered to indoor and outdoor pools, and even individual gers. The spa also has a Soviet-era sanatorium where many Mongolians come for treatment (the waters are believed to cure rheumatism and skin disorders).

Travelling north up the picturesque **Tuyn River Valley** for 29 kilometres (18 miles), the large Buddhist monastery at **Erdenetsogt** was destroyed in the purges of the 1930s. But one remarkable survivor, although only built in 1903, is the double-storey lama's residence on the grounds of a now reopened temple and well worth a quick look. From here, the main road continues high over the crest of the range to **Tsetserleg** on its northern side (see below). Another track leads up a string of grassy valleys typical of forest steppe, dotted with large granite outcrops and home to families and herds in their lush summer encampments, before finally clearing a high rocky pass into the wide expanse of **Nayman Nuur**.

(Continued on page 403)

A solitary and remarkably well-preserved deer stone stands firm through the centuries, evoking a distant age and culture (Graham Taylor).

Deer Stones and Khirigsuurs

By *William W. Fitzhugh*

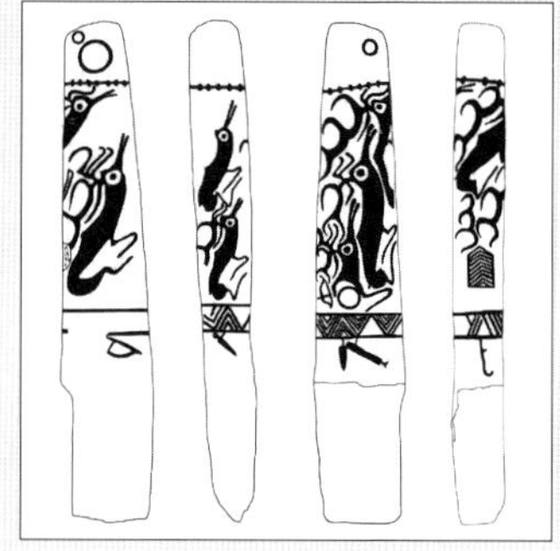

Standing among the rolling hills of northern and western Mongolia, stone monuments known as "deer stones" evoke a past that seems still very much alive today. Local herders sometimes refer to deer stones as "our old stone men", revering them almost like their living elders. In fact, these visitors from the Bronze Age have been standing alone or in clusters, facing the rising sun every day for the past 3,000 years. Their partners in this vigil are burial mounds made of piles of boulders known to Mongolians as "*khirigsuurs*". Together, deer stones and khirigsuurs (also "*khereksurs*") are the most widespread monumental features of Mongolia's ancient past. They are the earliest prehistoric monuments still visible today.

Deer stones vary in size from small, simple stones 50cm high to spectacular 2.5-metre-high examples that display some of the finest stone carving in the ancient world. More than 1,000 deer stones have been found in northern and western Mongolia, with a few also occurring in nearby regions of Russia, Kazakhstan and China. Many more have fallen and await discovery. Archaeologists and art historians have studied deer stones for decades, but only recently have their secrets begun to be revealed.

Deer stones are named from the beautifully carved deer whose iconic image wraps around the rectangular-sided stone like an envelope. However, the stelae actually represent stylizations of individual Bronze Age warriors. The tool belt is frequently shown as a cross-hatched band around a deer stone "waist". Attached to these belts one sees swords, daggers, battle-axes, whetstones, chariot rein hooks, quivers with arrows and compound bows, fire-starting kits, and other objects of male apparel. Different deer stones display different sizes, shapes and styles of implements, suggesting they were carved as portraits of real historical figures.

A unique personality is also suggested by deer images carved on the deer stone "torso". These are not regular deer; they are magical creatures, having the body and antlers of the Siberian red deer (*Cervus elaphus sibiricus*), known in Asia as *maral* and in North America as elk. However, the head is that of a bird with a round eye and elongated bill, parted at its bulbous end as though speaking or calling. These deer-bird images, always identical in form, must represent a codified central deity

Above: An accurate rendition of a deer stone at Khushuutin Gol site – the stone's actual size is 282cm x 54cm x 29cm (Jamsranjav Bayarsaikhan).

combining the power of Asia's largest stag and a shamanic bird, thus uniting master-spirits of land and sky.

The precise function of the deer-bird spirit is not known, but these images may have been tattooed on the bodies of warriors they represent to protect them from harm or help their spirits reach the sky-world after death. Like the weapons, these images differ from stone to stone, providing further evidence that they represent real images on the bodies of living persons. Also found in the torso area are pentagonal "sergeant stripe" motifs, perhaps representing shields, together with round discs that represent shamanic mirrors used for fortune-telling, as well as bows and arrows and other items.

At the top of the stone, separated from the torso by a looping beaded necklace of pits, is the warrior's head. In a few instances, as at the Ushgiin Uver site near Muren (Moron), a face is carved into the top of the stone. In this case its mouth is open, as though shamanizing. In most cases, however, the face is indicated by two or three diagonal slash marks. The faces and slashes always face east or southeast. On the north and south sides ring grooves represent earrings, sometimes with attached pendants. At Ushgiin Uver these rings are clearly attached to the warrior-shaman's earlobes.

In addition to representing warriors, deer stones encapsulate Bronze Age cosmology. As well as shamanic and animal spirit imagery, celestial themes are seen in juxtaposition of smaller ring grooves adjacent to the larger "earrings", and it is difficult not to see the deer-bird spirits as the flying steeds of shamans. Despite human and spiritual symbolism, deer stones are not human grave markers, although they may be found near khirigsuurs that do have human burials. Around the bases of deer stones, archaeologists have found carefully buried bundles, each containing the skull, neck bones and hooves of a horse, whose head faces east, just like the stone men.

These ancient monuments reveal Bronze Age Mongolia at a crossroads of history. Earlier shamanistic religion shared popularity with new ideas supporting a militaristic society whose leaders came to be immortalized in deer stones, surrounded by their finest horses.

As the sun swings around Mongolia's blue-heaven sky, the god-force known to early Mongols as *Tenggeri* (Tengrii), the stone heroes of ancient Mongolia come to life, etched in shadow and light, as they have every day for the past 3,000 years.

William W. Fitzhugh is head of the Arctic Studies Centre, Natural Museum of Natural History, Smithsonian Institution in Washington, DC, and the world's leading expert on deer stones. He travels annually to Mongolia working closely with the National Museum of Mongolian History in Ulaanbaatar.

Following spread: Horses graze along the headwaters of Mongolia's legendary Orhon River (Carl Robinson).

Legends from the Steppe: The Almas

For centuries Mongolian nomads have told legends of huge, wild creatures that bear a vague resemblance to man roaming the mountains of Central Asia. Since ancient times these animals have traditionally inhabited immense, snow-capped ranges such as the Himalayas, the Urals, the Tien Shan and the Altai.

The name *Almas* translates as "snow man", and this creature is bear-like, with thick, coarse, dark-brown hair covering its entire body. Many places in rural Mongolia have been named after this strange phenomenon. Researchers claim this confirms the Almas once existed in Mongolia.

Even today, with Mongolia becoming increasingly urbanised and sophisticated, herders still tell stories of sighting the Almas, or claim to have discovered huge, unidentified footprints or the outline of a large, heavy body laid to rest in deep snow or soft mud. Harsh, continuous wails have been heard echoing across the open steppe. The Almas supposedly still lives in remote corners of the Altai Mountains, and several have traditionally lived in isolated areas of the Gobi Desert, which covers much of southern Mongolia. The Almas is solitary, always living alone, but occasionally seeking a companion of the opposite sex. There are, of course, both male and female of the species and female Almases are said to be even more ferocious than males when roused to anger. The Almas usually lives in a well-concealed cave, emerging only under cover of darkness and eating a diet of raw meat, seeds, plant and tree roots.

Romantic, religious, at times gory and even comical, the truth of the Almas legends has become less important than their telling – they are an integral part of Mongolia's ancient oral tradition. Usually told in the candlelight of a *ger* during the long, dark winter evenings, this is the first translation of the Almas legends published in English. The following stories describe some of the most famous sightings of the Almas, and men and women who even spent time with this strange, almost silent creature.

A GOLDEN BURDEN

In 1837 a young mendicant lama was trekking across the southern Altai mountains, on his way from Mongolia to the Tibetan capital of Lhasa. The lama, Altan, always travelled alone and on foot, as this was the tradition of his monastery. As he journeyed he taught the Dharma to all those he met and was offered food and hospitality in return for his wise words.

Altan found the corpse of a dead Almas in the Tsenkher Nomin desert, part of Mongolia's vast Gobi region in the south of the country. He skinned the whole creature and carried it, with the stomach bile of the Almas, to Bogdyn Khuree, the former name of the Mongolian Capital, Ulaanbaatar. Almas bile was renowned as a cure for many serious diseases and Altan sold the bile to a doctor named Lu, who attended the Bogd Khan, Mongolia's religious leader. In return Altan was presented with a bar of gold the size of his index finger.

He had already given the heavy, coarse-haired Almas skin to Galbyn Ulaan monastery in the Gobi desert. The monastery craftsmen stuffed the skin and created a huge, lifelike model, which they placed in the midst of their temple. One of the lamas, Luvsandorj, frequently spoke about this strange Almas model, which dominated the temple while he was a young lama. He said it looked strangely human, although it was almost entirely covered in thick, rough, dark-brown hair. Measuring more than two metres in height, it had an immense, broad chest, narrow hips and very long, thick, hairy arms. Along its spine, the Almas had long hairs similar to a horse mane, but its face was hairless, except for eyebrows, incredibly long eyelashes and a thin growth on its chin. The large feet were thickly callused.

Tragically, when Choibalsan's government destroyed more than 700 monasteries and temples across Mongolia in the 1930s, Galbyn Ulaan monastery amongst them, the Almas figure was lost forever. It was only the testament of Luvsandorj that has kept the story of this discovery alive.

A BIZARRE KILLING

In the winter of 1922 a hunter named Mend from Bulgan village in Khovd province had a bizarre experience while hunting. He was riding horseback along deep, bushy ravine, when he heard loud noises as though one animal was in pursuit of another. From one side of the ravine a very strange man-like animal covered with hair appeared and ran toward the nearest tree where he broke off a long, jagged branch. After a short while three wolves appeared and lunged after the strange creature.

Mend was staring at the strange animal with his mouth wide open, when it started to howl as the three wolves drew close. The animal held the tree branch tightly in both its huge hands and fended off the lunging wolves. It hit and knocked down one wolf, which died instantly at the creature's feet.

But the creature's branch had snapped in half and the two other wolves attacked more savagely from either side. As it struggled to defend itself from the larger of the two wolves, the other charged and bit the animal, ripping into its leg. Stunned, the creature turned, as the biggest wolf bit and ripped open its belly. The creature screamed in agony and fell to the ground.

When the animal died the two wolves began howling to call others. As wolves roam the steppe in packs and share their prey, many others appeared to share the kill.

As Mend was an experienced hunter he knew he wouldn't be able to kill all these excited wolves, and that if he did fire his gun the entire pack might turn on him. He quietly urged his quivering horse in the opposite direction and moved up the steep ravine bank, fleeing the site of this strange killing.

Battulga Tumurdash (edited by Louisa Waugh),
The Sun Eater & Almas, 12 Amazing Snowman Legends *(2009)*

A lone horseman searches for errant steeds to round up (Leo Murray).

At the other end of this picturesque lake area, the road drops precipitously down into a narrow valley – pines growing on its northern slopes and grass on the other with a view far into the distance – where the famous **Orhon River** begins. Fed by more tributaries, the river quickly widens and continues its journey into Mongolia's historic heartland – a great back-door entry into this fascinating region. Detracting from an otherwise idyllic scene of rock-strewn, fast-flowing streams with herds of horses, hainaks and isolated gers against a backdrop of forested hills, however, are beetle infestations from Siberia, which in recent years have decimated huge portions of larch forest in the southern Hangai. (This environmental problem is also evident in the Hentii.)

Located 116 kilometres (72 miles) northwest of the former Mongol Empire capital of Karakorum, today's Harhorin, along the Hangai's northeast-facing slopes is **Tsetserleg,** capital of **Arhangai aimag**, regarded by many as the most attractive town in Mongolia. Dominated by a rugged and heavily eroded pyramid-shaped mountain of granite, the settlement of 18,000 is neatly laid out with its streets lined with trees, hotels and restaurants, and several immediate attractions. Rising over 300 metres (984 ft) above the town, **Bulgan Uul** (1,980 metres or 6,496 feet) is protected as a nature reserve and its larch and white birch forests are a habitat for roe and musk deer, wild boar and rare bird life. Its

(Continued on page 411)

TRADITIONAL MONGOLIAN MEDICINE

By *Ivana Grollova*

Medical methods born on the Mongolian steppe have been passed down by herdsmen from generation to generation for centuries. They differ not only from Western medicine but even those of neighbouring countries, such as China, in the same way that nomadic life differs from the settled life of peasants.

Evidence of the use of copper and silver needles in Mongolia goes back to the Hunnu or Xiongnu Period (third century BCE–first century CE). Singeing (moxibustion), massage and related chiropractics are originally herdsmen's treatment methods. Local tradition and close contact with India enabled the growth of famous "master healers" who were invited to eighth century Tibet to compile the first medical encyclopaedia.

The "Four Roots of Medicine", translated into many languages, was the key work and methodology for Indian, Chinese, Tibetan, Korean and Mongolian physicians for centuries. Mongolian experts, known as *maaramba*, also created their own reference books. Even when Mongolian medicine absorbed other cultural influences, particularly from Tibet, it still retained its own distinctive form.

Mongolian traditional medications used hundreds of medicines of vegetable or animal origin, dozens of salts and minerals, numerous healing herbs, trees and fruits. Some of them may inspire an indulgent smile: wolf's stomach, bleeding deer antlers, fish bile, the "meat" of spiders, musk from the Siberian musk deer, mercury, mother-of-pearl, coral, turquoise, an infusion of daisies which had been chewed and spat out by a rutting deer, and a mixture of a boar dung, gentian, a herb called *dzhugan* or the bark of a "yellow tree".

Healers, or *otoch*, combined five or six – but often 20 to 40 – vegetable, animal or mineral components into one medication. Their "pharmacies" had drugs for stomach cancer, plague, tuberculosis and inflammation. Prevention and diet were considered a necessary part of therapy.

A general knowledge of various natural remedies and their effects was an essential part of everyday life. Among Mongolians, there's no doubt that a woman who's just given birth, or an exhausted person, is best helped by the broth of boiled mutton leg. As part of their dowry, young Mongolian women often received a wreath of rare dried white mushrooms, its soup known to contract the uterus after childbirth. Certain meats must be eaten fresh, while others should be salted, dried or set aside in the cold for several days or weeks before consumption. Otherwise, these meats would have a poisonous effect on humans and cause the spread of diseases from wild game to domestic cattle sharing the same pastures or watering holes.

Conventional nomadic dietary practice is a font of wisdom. Mongolians do not drink water without boiling it first. From the age of two, children stop drinking milk and, like adults, only consume it mixed with tea. In winter, when the body needs energy to survive the bitter cold, herdsmen eat a lot of fat meat. In summer, their diet consists mostly of cheese, yogurt and *airag* (*kumys* in Turkic languages). According to the 13th century travellers Plano de Carpini and William of Rubruck, Mongolian warriors drank airag for months and did not need any other sustenance.

Even now, airag is a frequent beverage and a "meal-in-one" in summer. The chemistry of mare's milk does not, with the exception of its sugars, change during fermentation. On average, airag comprises 1.85 percent fat, 1.99 percent protein, 2.03 percent sugars, 0.44 percent minerals and 1.5–2.3 percent alcohol. It is easily digestible and stimulates metabolism. By drinking airag, the human body can be perfectly purified of the high doses of animal fat accumulated in winter.

In addition to this, dairy yeast and bacteria destroy foreign microbes. That is why airag is prescribed even for the treatment of scurvy, tuberculosis, anaemia, digestive disorders or exhaustion. But airag is not recommended for open wounds and fractures.

Other dairy products can also heal: warm milk vodka, or *shimin arkhi*, is used against cold, tiredness and spring vitamin deficiency, and in the form of a poultice against pneumonia; butter (*shar tos*) or cream crust (*öröm*) are massaged in for stomach ailments, and they heal infant hernia or chafe. They decrease high blood pressure, but are too strong for a sick heart. They also help against poisoning and ear inflammation. Hard curd and cheese (*aaruul*

Following spread: Few places rival the beauty of Mongolia's legendary Great White Lake (Carl Robinson).

and *byaslag*), served warmed with flour, can ease tiredness and maintain acidity. Served cold, they can counteract febrility. The milk of a white goat or the special airag made from it, heals liver and tuberculosis. Children have airag spread on their chest during the summer months, so that their lungs and bronchi are strong and immune to illness in winter.

Mongolia has one of the world's few deposits of a mysterious stone called mumio (*baragshin*, or "accumulating heat"). Mumio was already highly valued in medicine as far back as the Egyptian pharaohs, Aristotle and Avicenna. Some theories explain mumio as the tarred excrement of prehistoric rodents, consisting of acids, resin and at least 20 different minerals. In mumio, nature itself blended a medicine against inner maladies, neurological disorders and for the regeneration of bones and tissues.

In Mongolian traditional medicine, drugs and infusions are always supplemented with the "five remedies" (*tavan dzasal*). These methods require few materials, and this is one reason why the Institute of National Medicine trained field doctors and nurses in these long-forgotten methods when traditional medicine was revived after 1990 and the collapse of the Soviet Bloc.

Most remarkably in Mongolian medicine, large-scale massages and remedies (*barikh*, or "to grasp") can actually dissipate a blood clot from brain concussion, usually within a week. Herdsmen, who often suffer falls from horses, apply a "shock against shock" technique to deal with a situation for which European patients are prescribed weeks of bed-rest. Even more importantly, besides the speed of recovery, is that the blood clot is dissolved and massaged back to its original liquid state. (In Western treatment, the blood clot often remains, and pressure can result in further disorders.) In addition to the healer's own talents and perceptiveness, a perfect knowledge of the vascular system, cerebral cortex and glands (even in months-old babies) is an important prerequisite for successful treatment by this uniquely Mongolian method.

In a sense, small pulse massages, or *ilbekh*, are an elaboration of the principles of acupuncture. According to the nature of the problems suffered by the patient and the spot of the bloodstream which is activated, the physician massages the patient's veins and nerve receptors with several fingers (so-called "skating"), flat palm ("ironing") or with the back of his hand ("planing").

A method of "grooming" or sucking drops of blood out of the skin (*samnuur*) and bleeding veins off (*khanuur* or *khatgakh tüünekh*) may seem gory. Westerners know about the tradition of applying leeches or bleeding a vein. In Mongolia, ancient and highly professional drawings have survived showing the human body with a complete vascular system and dozens of points – and this has now been revived by traditional healers. These points are for the application of a retort as an exhauster or for small wounds to be cut with a scalpel or a needle to drain away superfluous blood. The blood's black colour and thickness is shown as proof of how much the body needed to be freed of its burden.

Wounds made by a scalpel are closed without risk of infection by being sprinkled with ash or daubed with garlic. The procedure aims to lower blood pressure in the afflicted area. In the Golden Age of Mongolian Traditional Medicine, experts could even carry out optical surgery using this method!

Nowadays, such bleeding, along with acupuncture (*dzüü tavikh*) and singeing (*toonuur*), are respected healing methods again and provide a valuable alternative to Western-style medicine in Mongolia. No doubt the theory of such methodology is close to that of Chinese medicine. There are, however, some unique features from Mongolia's nomadic environment.

Although not obvious at first, every non-pharmaceutical method must be based on excellent knowledge of anatomy and the vascular system. (A few books have been preserved which suggest Mongolian medical science considered "pulse diagnostics" an independent branch of medicine.) Mongolian practitioners identified more than 50 types of pulse (shallow, deep, slow, fibrillar, empty and so on) and of vein ramifying (divergence). The pulse can also change according to atmospheric influences, seasons, days, hours or even quarters of hours, and the momentary body condition. Not only blood, but also blood gas and the overall temperature of the organism are important factors for determining a diagnosis.

Mongolian medical science classified 404 kinds of illnesses, which in mutual combinations represented 1,616 various health problems. The first

(Continued on page 412)

Above: An altar honours Otgon Tenger, the Hangai's highest and one of the three holiest peaks in Mongolia (Leo Murray). Below: A rickety bridge across the Ider River at Jargalant (Carl Robinson).

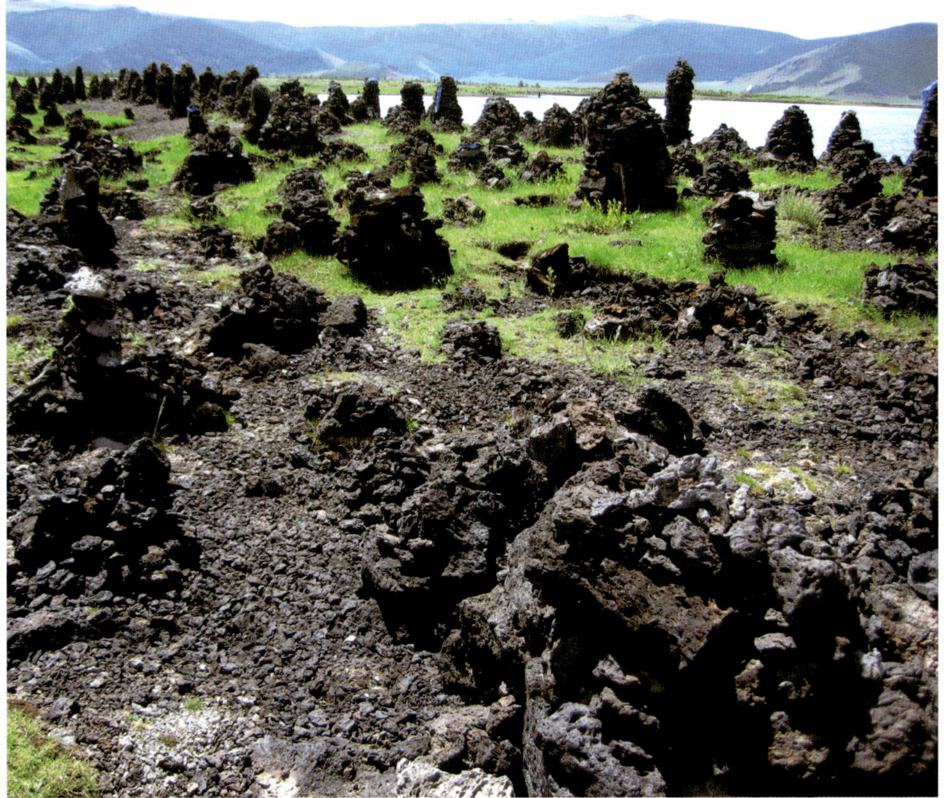

Ovoo *made of volcanic rock adorn the shoreline of Great White Lake (Carl Robinson).*

(Continued from page 403)

remarkably intact **Zaiyin Hiid Monastery** dates from 1586 and its six temples serve as the aimag museum. An abandoned temple on the hill above the town provides great views. Just outside of town near **Tsagaan Davaa** (Pass) are several Bronze Age deer stones. And for those looking for hot springs, the **Tsenher Jiguur Health Spa** 30 kilometres (19 miles) south of the town caters especially to tourists.

The two principal branches of the **Tamir River,** itself a major tributary of the Orhon, pass near Tsetserleg and out onto the flat steppe beyond. Located in grasslands along its northern branch 16 kilometres (10 miles) to the north is mysterious **Taihar Chuluu Rock,** a granite pinnacle that rises sharply 25 metres (82 feet) from the flat landscape. A regular stop for tourists heading north, the rock is highly revered and worshipped by locals who have placed an *ovoo* at the top.

Travelling further northwest, the main range drops away to the south and a fascinating volcanic region opens up separating it from an east-west running branch to the north, the **Tarvagatayn Nuruu**, also known as the **Tarvagatai Range.** As in Mongolia's Dariganga region (see page 272), finding volcanoes so far inland is extremely rare and still puzzles geologists, who have described this zone as part of the **Baikal Rift System** that runs

(Continued from page 409)

group (101 illnesses) pass without the need of any treatment. The second are illnesses cured by healthy diet and staying outdoors. The third represents the worst illnesses, which must be cured by medicines, while the fourth is the incurable illnesses, which can only be averted by prevention. Psychology plays an important role here, as in the shamanistic approach to healing. According to interpretation based on shamanistic teaching, some illnesses originate as a result of bewitching or due to the impact of evil powers. While the reasoning may be different, the healing methodology, such as interviews, magic formulas and hypnosis, used in the tradition of an official Mongolian medicine for centuries, was in fact almost identical with those from the shamanistic practice.

Even if all the theory of Mongolian medicine could be studied and assimilated from books and taught by an experienced teacher, a healer would only be considered a real professional after 30 years of practice. As part of its repression of the Buddhist religion during the 70-year Socialist Period, however, much was lost. Traditional medical treatises, prescriptions and tools were destroyed and many monastery doctors, like disciples of the Aquamarine Buddha (*Binderyaa Manal*), and countryside healers were declared fakes and persecuted or imprisoned by the regime.

Present-day Mongolia is attempting to link up the fragments of its traditional medicine with Western medical science, itself critically important for a society that has drifted away from its natural roots. Traditional healing procedures are closely connected to the traditional lifestyle, diet and full confidence in their effectiveness. Once removed from this context, they often do not hit home, because they can hardly keep up with how today's impatient, undisciplined and sceptical patients destroy their own health.

southeast of the Siberian Craton (see Special Topic, page 285). (Russia's Lake Baikal is only 500 kilometres, or 310 miles, to the northeast.)

But compared to the Dariganga of eastern Mongolia, the volcanic activity here is much more recent – Miocene to Holocene (25,000 years ago to present day) – and dominates the lower reaches of the **Chuluut Gol** (River) where its waters have created a wide and dramatic canyon through layers of black basalt. (The Chuluut joins the Ider north of the Tarvagatai and later the Selenge River into Russia.) With its mixture of larch and other pines, the gorge offers some beautiful scenery and great opportunities for fishing and bird watching. Interestingly, this volcanic activity would have taken place at the end of the last Ice Age – a fascinating period of floods and climate change.

But for sheer spectacle and even a touch of the exotic, few places in Mongolia can rival the beauty of **Terkhiin Tsagaan Nuur,** or **Great White Lake**, another 54 kilometres (34 miles) up the road from the gorge. Located at an elevation of 2,060 metres (6,760 feet) and up a major tributary of the Chuluut River, this magnificent lake was formed only over the past 10,000–20,000 years when a major volcanic eruption blocked the eastern end of the valley. A large body of water built up behind this natural dam and eventually forced a narrow gorge out of its southern side at the foot of a volcano that is the lake's most dramatic and dominant feature.

Believed to have last exploded only 5,000 years ago, the **Horgo Volcano** looks amazingly fresh. One of six cinder cones in the area, this classic-looking 200-metre-wide (656-foot) volcano towers about 50 metres (164 feet) above a blackened landscape of lava flows dotted with pine trees. A trail leads up to its summit where a lake has formed in its 100-metre-deep (328-foot) crater. The views from here and other high points around the lake are absolutely perfect. An unusual feature on the nearby lakeshore is a line of ovoos made from piles of volcanic rock

With its numerous headlands, beaches and crystal-clear waters, Terkhiin Tsagaan stretches for 300 square kilometres (116 square miles) over a wide valley with the hills sometimes coming right down to the water's edge. As usual in Mongolia, but here in such an exquisite setting, the lake's northern-facing slopes on the southern side are a thick forest of pine while the opposite slopes are covered in grassy steppe. Vast and lush expanses of grassland lead across to the northern range, perfect pasture for the valley's many nomadic families and their hainaks. The lake is renowned for its fish and bird life. Pike is in abundant supply and so is the great cormorant that feeds on them. Always in pairs, the ever-trusty ruddy sheldrake is also present.

ADVENTURE TRAVEL IN MONGOLIA

Just "showing up" is an adventure in Mongolia, and once you've headed out of Ulaanbaatar into the wide-open countryside, the adventure really begins – even if you're just travelling by road. But Mongolia is also developing quite a reputation as a destination for some truly adventurous travel. One tour company even runs a marathon – admittedly in the cooler autumn – through the Gobi Desert's famous Flaming Cliffs, where the runners might even stumble onto a dinosaur bone or two.

Like Mongolia's tourism industry itself, the range of outdoor adventure activities is still developing, but the list is already quite impressive. These include hiking, mountaineering, horse and camel trekking, yak cart journeys, bicycle and motorcycle tours, quad-bike expeditions, rafting, kayaking and paragliding. (Fly-fishing is another popular activity, see the Special Topic on page 446.) With its crystal-clear air, huge landscapes and vast horizons, Mongolia is an open invitation for physical

Horse trekking around the Great White Lake is a popular pastime (Carl Robinson).

activity. Even the most basic tours provide opportunities for hiking and brief horse, camel and yak cart rides. (Do remember to keep up your liquid intake though, as the dry climate can be quite dehydrating without one realising it.)

Hardly surprisingly in a land, culture and history so dominated by the horse, the most popular of these activities – and certainly the easiest way to venture off the beaten track – is on horseback. Well organised and supported by plenty of guides and staff, including cooks and their packhorses, horse treks typically travel between 15 and 30 kilometres (10 to 20 miles) a day in tours lasting between one and two weeks. Accommodation is mostly in tents. These tours are particularly popular in mountainous areas, the closest in the Hentii Mountains outside UB and further away in the Hangai and Altai ranges, and the Lake Hovsgol region in the north. Travellers drive or fly into kick-off points where horses and local guides await, and then begin a circuitous journey. This is Mongolian Nature at its best, through a landscape of magnificent, often snow-capped, mountains and wildlife. Also part of the experience are visits with isolated nomad families, even taking in the odd *aimag* or provincial-level Naadam Festival which, in many ways, are much more intimate than the national one held in the capital every July. Camel treks, using Bactrian camels, are more focused on Mongolia's South Gobi region.

Mountaineering (see Special Topic, page 361) and hiking are not nearly as popular and take even more organising. The Turgen Range, an eastern branch of the Altai in

Left: Horse trekking is probably the most popular adventure activity, allowing access to very remote areas – although beginners should perhaps consider riding helmets for safety's sake (Leo Murray).

western Mongolia, is a particular favourite. Although hiking can certainly be done on one's own, guides are recommended, especially as weather conditions can change literally in minutes, particularly around Lake Hovsgol. (It's best to bring all your own gear, including camping equipment.)

More focused on overland journeys covering longer distances, cycling – using mountain bikes – has grown rapidly in popularity. Travelling with support vehicles and guides, these trips range over the entire country. One tour from Active and Adventure Tours travels first by train to Erdenet northwest of UB, and then overland to Lake Hovsgol and back down through the eastern side of the Hangai Mountains. (They are not the only company offering cycling.) Again, the pace is reasonable, meals are provided and accommodation is camping in tents.

For those looking for a bit more speed, motorcycle tours are also available with one company (Off the Map Tours) using a fleet of tough and lightweight Yamaha WR250 Enduros for long-distance expeditions to the Gobi and Terhiyn Tsaagan, or White Lake, in the Hangai. (The company boasts a helicopter on standby in case of serious accident.) Quad-bike tours, while available, are usually limited to specific locations. Another option is to rent or purchase an old Russian motorcycle and, with a GPS and good maps, create your own tour. (Ever reliable, these bikes are easily repaired in even the most remote areas; the Chinese-built ones less so.)

While still a fairly limited activity, Serena Travel offers paragliding in a national park east of UB. More of a novelty, yak cart tours are becoming more popular but, without the luxury of springs or rubber tyres, short-duration trips are a better choice. Kayaking and whitewater rafting are other possibilities but with much potential. Right now, kayaking is mostly on Lake Hovsgol and rafting along western Mongolia's Bulgan River, but given the country's many other lakes and rivers, there is nothing holding back visitors from arranging other locations.

Safety is, of course, always of paramount concern in these more adventurous activities, all the more so given Mongolia's vast distances, scarcity of medical facilities and few helicopters. One friend leading a horse trek through remotest Mongolia thought the entire journey over when one of his clients badly cut her leg in a fall. Just then, a New Zealand couple – both veterinarians – appeared over the horizon, sewed up the wound and the journey continued. (Another saviour is there is less distance to fall off a Mongolian horse!) So, do travel well equipped with a GPS, satellite phone, good medical kit and a basic knowledge of first aid. The rule: have fun but don't take any unnecessary risks.

With a choice of swimming, fishing, horse trekking and hiking, the Terkhiin Tsagaan is a wonderful place to spend a few relaxing days. Quite frankly, I'd even recommend Terhiyn Tsagaan over highly praised Lake Hovsgol for the ease and access to extra activities and exploration. (Besides, where else in Mongolia can you find a beach... and a volcano?) Protected as a national park, its entrance is across a bridge just past a lovely *sum*, or district, centre named **Tariat.** The park offers several tourist ger camps for visitors.

Parting from such an idyllic scene is hardly easy – and the mind quickly returns there for comfort on the terribly rough journey north over the top of the Tarvagatai Range which, as noted earlier, is a top qualifier for the title of Mongolia's Worst Road (blame this on permafrost, which lifts up the underlying rocks in freezing winter and sinks the entire lot in blazing summer – the result is an amazingly bouncy ride). But patience and forbearance must win out, as your vehicle first crests out of the grass-covered slopes north of the lake at a magnificent ovoo. Then comes a slow and delicate descent through the thick forests of larch and pine and rushing streams of the range's northern side, the land gradually opening up into meadows and then grassy valleys.

Relief on this northward journey finally comes in the richly scented Siberian pine forests of **Jargalant** – Mongolian for "happy" – on the southern bank of the **Ider River**. Moron, gateway to Lake Hovsgol, is still seven or eight hours away across the lower, but still tough, **Bulnayn Nuruu,** another branch range of the Hangai to the north. (In what's a long 12-hour day on the road, not untypical in Mongolia, many operators push all the way through lake-to-lake. But after camping out for days, I settled for the hot springs and comfort of a tourist ger camp on the town's southern side. Most of my fellow guests were from Poland!)

To the north and west is a less well-known side of the Hangai Mountains. Out here the dominant feature is **Otgon Tenger Uul**, the range's highest peak at 4,021 metres (13,192 feet), 72 kilometres (45 miles) east of the **Zavhan** aimag capital of **Uliastai**. Located at the western end of the range, its massive bulk is the watershed for two important – if slightly obscure – Mongolian rivers.

The first is the **Ider River**, which originates on its northern slopes and is regarded as the actual headwaters of the mighty **Yenisey River**, which runs 5,540 kilometres (3,442 miles) north to the Arctic Ocean and is the world's fifth longest river, and second in Asia. (In his *Five Months in a Leaky Boat*, Australian adventurer Ben Kozel tells early on of his search up the mountain for the river's source. See page 213 for a Literary Excerpt from later in his journey.)

Following spread: A highlight of the Naadam Festival are lengthy horse races, the horses ridden by young boys and girls (Elbegzaya Lhagvasuren).

73

828

Below: Marksmen shoot at distant targets from behind a marked line at a rural Naadam event (Leo Murray). Right: Archery is a test of strength, concentration and skill – for women as well as men (Colin Monteath). Bottom: Wrestlers enter the "battlefield" (Leo Murray).

But given the reverence Mongolians have for their horses, it's hardly surprising that racing is the real highlight of any Naadam Festival and takes full advantage of Mongolia's wide open spaces. More of a cross-country event, the races cover distances of between 15 and 30 kilometres (10–20 miles) with their length determined by age class, with the older horses in the longer races. The races are also all about the skill and stamina of the horses – not the jockeys, who are children basically along for the ride of their lives. Colourfully dressed, the young jockeys are both male and female and range in age from five to 13 years old. The winning jockey, however, is given the honorary title of "leader of 10,000", or *tumny ekh*. But the real champions are the winning horses, some of whom receive the ultimate accolade of a statue in a town square somewhere around the country. The horse races are surrounded by much singing, feasting and celebrations, with medals profusely distributed. Even the very last two-year-old horse is serenaded with a song for better luck next time.

Above left: Young participants prepare for an upcoming horse race. Above right: A victorious wrestler performs the "eagle dance" at a provincial Naadam (Leo Murray x2).

The western Hangai's second major watercourse, the **Zavhan River**, runs west past massive dunes and through semi-desert for 800 kilometres (500 miles) into the heart of Mongolia's **Great Lakes Depression** (see page 376). From this region, powerful prevailing winds funnel down the Hangai's northwest fringe creating the massive sand dunes east of the lakes. One particularly fascinating string of dunes is the **Bor Hyaryn Els**, which runs from for nearly 200 kilometres (124 miles) to just outside Uliastai. Coloured an unusual reddish brown, the accumulating sands billow up around island-like remnants of the range. Closer to Uliastai, the Hangai rises higher to enclose the town which served as the Qing Dynasty's military headquarters during their 200-year occupation of Mongolia until 1911.

Located along the banks of the **Bogd Gol**, a tributary of the Zavhan River, **Uliastai** is an attractive town of 20,000 with a well laid out downtown area, its streets lined with poplar trees introduced by the Chinese (the Mongolian name for the tree comes from the town). The **History Museum** is particularly fascinating and its **Museum of Famous People** an interesting insight into the aimag's best-known personalities and the eras in which they lived. Rugged foothills rise immediately above the town to the west and, just a short walk up from the main roundabout, the small hilltop of **Javhlant Tolgoi** and its pavilion with nine stupas provides great views out over the valley.

Surrounded by higher hills and accessed up a narrow river valley, Uliastai's strategic importance is easy to understand. Established by the Qing in 1733, the town served as its Rear Camp to keep an eye on the still-unruly eastern Mongolians, or Halh, on the other side of the Hangai Mountains. But more crucially, the town was a secure base for repeated and massive military offensives against the rebellious Oriads around Hovd, or Front Camp, to the west, a campaign that took another 50 years to complete (see The Altai, page 343). As at Hovd, the town has remnants of an old Qing fortress just to its northeast, but it is now just a rubbish tip. Canals where Chinese market gardeners diverted water for crops are still plainly visible.

Instantly recognisable by its distinctive shape and a round and slightly skewered snow-covered summit, Otgon Tenger is Zavhan's proudest symbol and can be spotted everywhere around Uliastai, including in murals on restaurant walls. Located inside the 95,510-hectare (2.4 million-acre) **Otgon Tenger Uul Strictly Protected Area**, the mountain – which has a massive granite face on its southern side – is one of the three most sacred in Mongolia, after Burkhan Khaldun in the Hentii and Bogd Khan in Ulaanbaatar. Otgon Tenger is the Hangai's highest, and also the only peak in the range with a permanent glacier on its summit.

Because of its sacred nature, climbing the mountain is not actively encouraged. And as adventurer Ben Kozel (see above) discovered, the climb can in any case be quite a gruelling experience and easily turn into an overnight expedition. Established in 1992 to protect its fragile alpine ecosystem, the park includes rare plants, including juniper, and its forests provide a habitat for argali, red deer, ibex and musk deer with the endangered snow leopard at its higher elevations.

With lovely **Hoh Nuur** (Lake) at its base, a better option is to view the mountain from **Dayan Uul**, a couple of hours east of town, or south past the town of **Otgon** by road. Another increasingly popular activity is horse trekking out from Uliastai or smaller settlements around the mountain's base. Located in the valley of the **Rashaan River,** the **Otgon Tenger Hot Springs** are high in sulphate, bicarbonate and soda and are renowned for their curative qualities.

From Uliastai, the main highway from Altay in the south leads over the Hangai for another 390 kilometres (242 miles) northeast to Moron, the capital of Hovsgol aimag, over the spectacular **Zagastayn Davaa**, or **Fish Pass**, some 50 kilometres (31 miles) north of the town. Marked by a large ovoo, the pass offers some spectacular views – if somewhat distracted by a power line running straight up the valley. From the pass, the road drops down into a wide green valley featuring many ancient gravesites where the **Ider River** makes its descent from the northern slopes of Otgon Tenger.

For those coming from the Altai and Great Lakes to the west but intent on visiting Terkhiin Tsagaan (above), a roundabout loop is required that takes you northeast along the Ider River Valley between the Hangai's two northern branch ranges, and passes through **Tosontsengel,** Zavhan's second largest settlement and a major timber town. Past smaller Ih-Uul, the road then heads south over **Selongotyn Davaa** (Pass) to the river system feeding into the lake from the west. The long climb up the pass – actually a section of the **Millennium Road** and full of long-distance trucks – crosses through grassy steppe and then the Tarvagatai's heavily forested northern slopes. Like most summits through the round-domed Hangai, however, the pass is more of a wide and marshy meadow with the water from its melting snows flowing confusedly in several directions.

Normally, the journey from Uliastai would've been an easy enough run, but with a late start after fixing our Russian Jeep's failed brake system – definitely something we'd need up in the mountains – we settled instead for a roadside *guanz*, or restaurant, at the sum centre of **Tsahir**. In what was a new experience in my travels and for the cost of a simple meal, we were given space on a raised room-length platform covered in mattresses to spread our sleeping bags. A memorable night in a Mongolian Inn. The lake would wait… and just as well, as our morning approach from the west to Terhiyn Tsagaan was absolutely breathtaking. Even the hainaks were grinning!

Following spread: The Orhon Waterfall in full flow – part of a UNESCO World Heritage-recognised "Cultural Landscape" (Elbegzaya Lhagvasuren).

THE ORHON VALLEY: MONGOLIA'S HEARTLAND

Chinggis Khaan's choice of Karakorum as the capital of the Mongol Empire was no coincidence. The surrounding **Orhon Valley** was the centre of preceding nomadic empires for centuries and had enormous symbolic importance. Protected by the gentle bulk of the Hangai Mountains and blessed by easy-flowing rivers across wide, grass-covered steppe, the valley's microclimate had attracted humankind since Palaeolithic times some 750,000 years ago. By the Stone Age, or Neolithic period, some 7,000 years ago, a pattern of migration had developed where groups moved out of the northern forests – the Siberian taiga – and settled onto these steppes, where they adopted pastoralism and eventually moved south and west.

"Whether the movement was in response to pressure from other groups to the north or east (pushing) or new opportunities to the south and west (pulling) remains an important arena for research," explain US archaeologists David Purcell and Kimberly Spurr, who have worked one of the sites, "but the pattern was persistent for millennia." This pattern continued into the Iron and Bronze Ages, with evidence of settlement in the Orhon Valley from the Hunnu or Xiongnu period (third century BCE–first century CE) onwards which is only now coming to light.

While the physical setting may not necessarily dazzle, Mongolia's Orhon Valley is actually one of the world's most important cultural regions – and recognised as such by its listing as a "cultural landscape" of the **UNESCO World Heritage** in 2004. The 1,220 square kilometres (470 square miles) of the **Orhon Valley Cultural Landscape** encompass extensive pastureland on both sides of the Orhon River and ancient archaeological sites, including Karakorum. While recognising the valley's influence on world history, trade and culture, the listing quite simply – and importantly – recognises the strength and persistence of nomadic culture. "Underpinning all the development within the Orkhon valley for the past two millennia has been a strong culture of nomadic pastoralism," reads part of UNESCO's "justification for inscription". "This culture is still a revered and indeed central part of Mongolian society and is highly respected as a 'noble' way to live in harmony with the landscape."

Clearly, the Orhon is the source of much national pride, including post-1990 calls for Mongolia to move its capital there, now apparently shelved. Located 365 kilometres (227 miles) west-southwest of Ulaanbaatar, the Orhon Valley – more specifically **Karakorum**, or today's **Harhorin** – is a staple on travel itineraries for visitors to Mongolia. But do keep in mind the region's crucial cultural and historical importance as first impressions – if my Mongolian friends will forgive me – can be a bit disappointing.

However, this is a very symbolic place. With a high-speed paved road now all the way from UB, the last range of hills opens out onto a wide valley with the Hangai Mountains on the far horizon. Fed by the **Zegstiyn Gol** (River), this looks like a perfect spot for growing wheat, as indeed the expansive valley is, with farm buildings and machinery appearing across the landscape.

In front of a low range of hills that rises higher at its northern end is a large, drab-looking town, the *sum* or district centre of Harhorin dominated by a large flour mill and other industrial buildings. There is no sign of the Mongol Empire's legendary city. But on the flats just east of the town are the white stupa-topped walls of Harhorin's famous monastery, **Erdene Zuu**, dwarfed by the surrounding town and landscape (frankly, you may be expecting something much larger). Many tourists find themselves asking, "Is this all there is?"

The physical setting of the Mongol Empire's famous capital is remarkably ordinary – but absolutely perfect for nomadic societies. Plenty of summer grass for their herds and room to pitch literally hundreds of *gers*, even grow grain as the Mongols and their predecessors did as well. There's lots of room also to muster those hordes for world conquest. The protected valleys of the nearby Hangai provided winter shelter. Just past the northern tip of the hills behind the town, the **Orhon River** flows in from the west and joins the Zestyin and other streams to form an even wider valley roughly 100 kilometres (62 miles) long.

At the valley's northern end, the **Tamir River** arrives from the west. Rounding off the picture on its northeastern edge is tiny 25-square-kilometre (10-square-mile) **Ogiy Nuur** (Lake), famous for its bird life and fishing and a popular stopover. From here, the Orhon River – Mongolia's longest at 1,124 kilometres (698 miles) – narrows, is later joined by UB's Tuul River and then flows north into the Selenge and on to Russia's Lake Baikal (see Around UB, page 203).

Stretching from the river's headwaters in the Hangai in the southwest, this wide and lush expanse of rivers, marsh and grasslands comprises the historic Orhon Valley. Here, within 100 kilometres (62 miles) of Karakorum, where Chinggis Khaan established his capital in 1222, are the former capitals or settlements from the Xiongnu, the Rouran (5th–6th centuries CE), Turks (6th–8th centuries CE) and Uyghurs (8th–9th centuries CE.) The Kyrgyz in the mid-9th to mid-11th centuries were more intent on simple destruction and revenge, but there is also evidence of a Khitan presence from the early 10th to 12th centuries

Following spread: The outer wall of Erdene Zuu stretches 400 metres on each side, is topped by 108 white stupas and has a gate at each cardinal point (Graham Taylor).

not long before the ascendancy of the Mongols (see History, page 64). Relatively small, the region is actually split between two *aimags*, or provinces, taking in the northernmost tip of **Ovorhangai** and southeastern **Arhangai** (see The Hangai, page 390). Other important relics stretch across southern **Bulgan aimag** to the northeast.

Discussion will return later to the Orhon Valley's older sites, but in Chinggis Khaan's day in the late 12th and early 13th centuries, this region was the territory of the Kereit, his earliest tribal allies who lived immediately west of his native Hentii northeast of today's Ulaanbaatar. Once his control grew, the Great Khaan first used the valley as his western encampment, or horde, for his massive military campaigns to the west and south. (The Hentii's Avraga Plain was home of the eastern horde.) He then followed tradition by naming the Orhon Valley as the capital of his Mongol Empire. Located at the junction of long-established trade and nomadic routes crisscrossing Mongolia with southward links into China and along the famous Silk Road, his son and successor Ogedei turned Karakorum into the Empire's political, cultural and economic capital.

Much of our knowledge about Karakorum comes from two separate diplomatic and religious visits by Roman Catholic missionaries in the 13th century, Giovanni Di Plano Carpini and William of Rubruck, frequently referenced in books on the Mongol Empire, such as Tim Severin's *In Search of Genghis Khan* and Jack Weatherford's *Genghis Khan and the Making of the Modern World*. (Stanley Stewart's *In the Empire of Genghis Khan* actually retraces Rubruck's entire journey.) Despite its close call in 1241 (see History, page 72), Europe had long heard of the legendary Prester John and Nestorian Christians far to the east and was desperate for allies to retake Jerusalem, which fell to the Muslims in 1244.

But the renowned religious tolerance of the Mongols made these visitors more the object of curiosity, including a ludicrous theological debate where the audience got roaring drunk. In 1246 the Italian Franciscan Carpini was sent packing back to Rome by Kuyuk, Ogedei's successor, who demanded the Pope's submission and threatened Europe with renewed invasion. Rubruck did better under Mengkhe, the next Great Khaan, and stayed for nearly a year after his arrival in December 1253. Ironically, when Mengkhe's brother Hulegu had the Muslim World nearly on its knees in 1262, Rome refused to help the Mongols. And by then, another brother, the famous Kublai, had abandoned Karakorum for Dadu, today's Beijing and Marco Polo's Cambaluc.

The best description of Karakorum at the height of its four decades as the centre of the Mongol Empire comes from the Flemish Franciscan Rubruck. Located on flat ground east of today's Erdene Zuu Monastery, the city's earthen walls ran in a rough 1.5 x 2.5 kilometre (1 x 1.5 mile) rectangle and were designed more to control access rather than for defence. Its main street was paved in stone with all economic activities, merchant residences and religious buildings within its walls. The city had four gates, each with its own specialist market, such as horses at the northern and grains at the eastern gates. Illustrating the Mongols' religious tolerance, the city had a Nestorian Christian church, two mosques and 12 "idolatrous" temples, presumably Buddhist and Taoist. "Given what we know about the settlement and movement patterns of the Mongols," explains Daniel C. Waugh of the University of Washington, "it is clear that at the times when the Khan's court was present, the population of the town would have grown substantially by the temporary residents of Mongols in their gers in the adjoining territory." A model of Karakorum can be seen at the National Museum in UB.

With most Mongols living outside the city itself, its inhabitants were mainly foreigners, a fascinating and cosmopolitan collection of diplomats, princes, religious leaders, merchants, bureaucrats and scholars from Persia, Central Asia, India, China and Russia. Muslims were traders and the Chinese skilled craftsmen. The artists were mostly prisoners whose skills the Mongols needed, including a small group of French captured in Hungary. The most famous was a Parisian goldsmith named Guillaume Boucher, who created a large and ornate silver fountain outside the main palace shaped like a tree with a trumpeting archangel at its top. Through an elaborate hand-pumped system, fermented mare's milk and other intoxicating drinks poured out through the mouths of protective dragons. (Rubruck's description of this magic fountain inspired 18th century drawings which produced today's replica outside a tourist ger camp near Erdene Zuu, a model at the National Museum in UB, and the image on the reverse of the 5,000 tugrug bill.)

The **Palace of Ogedei** was located in the southwest corner of the city on the shores of an artificial lake. But the building was only used for ceremonies and receptions with even the Great Khaan living outside the walls in a traditional ger. Descriptions from the period describe a two-storey building with a red and green tiled roof, containing a vast central reception hall supported by 64 columns, decorated with paintings and with floors covered in green tiles. To date, no evidence has been found of its remains.

As things turned out, Karakorum was the Mongol capital for barely 40 years before Kublai moved to Dadu, today's Beijing, where he established the Yuan Dynasty. While that dynasty continued until 1368, Kublai's eastward shift also spelled the beginning of the empires' disintegration, with Karakorum now the focus of dissidents, followers of Ogedei's grandson Kaidu who'd opposed his controversial accession. After the dynasty's collapse, Ming troops launched a series of punishing raids into Mongolia, culminating in the total destruction of Karakorum in 1388 and the capture of 70,000 troops. Despite several attempts by the now-divided Mongolians to revive Karakorum, the old capital lay in ruins for nearly 200 years until its rubble was used to build today's Erdene Zuu Monastery, which occupies only a small portion of the old city.

Unfortunately, little remains from Karakorum's days of glory, although a Mongolian-German archaeological team working since 1999 has uncovered a wealth of new objects to supplement those first discovered in 1949. These show buildings made of sun-dried bricks, some still bearing the trademark of their manufacturer, and warmed by an underfloor heating system. From gold and other mines up in the mountains, Karakorum was a centre of metallurgy, illustrated by the cast-iron hubs of wheels remarkably similar to today's yak carts. From administrative, craft and trading quarters have come fragments of porcelain and glazed pottery, bits of Chinese silk, farming implements, craft tools, domestic utensils and ornaments in gold, silver and bronze. Coins discovered are mostly Mongol and Chinese. After discovering Buddhist frescoes on the site of what earlier archaeologists believed was the Palace, the latest thinking is either the building is somewhere else or was converted into a temple after Kublai Khan's move to Beijing.

Some of these important objects are on display at the small museum at Erdene Zuu with larger pieces, such as several large stone sculptures, on the grounds outside. (Other objects were taken away to Germany for further study and exhibition.) But the site where the archaeologists explored was simply covered over. Considering Karakorum's critical historical importance, and its huge number of visitors, a quality showcase museum – including an open-air facility – is desperately needed here.

The most important relics are two of the four large granite Chinese-style tortoises that once stood outside the city, and were topped with inscribed stelae. One is located on flat ground some 300 metres (984 feet) northeast of Erdene Zuu near what would have been Karakorum's north gate. The tortoise is still actively worshipped with libations. Offerings are also made at a nearby ovoo marking the site of the tomb of the wife of the monastery's founder, Avtai-Khan, the great-grandparent of Mongolia's First Bogd Gegeen, or theocratic leader, and noted artist Zanabazar. Sometimes a small souvenir market is set up nearby.

Old Karakorum's second tortoise is located atop what's appropriately named Tortoise Mountain, or **Melekhit Uul**, a hilltop a couple of kilometres southwest of the monastery, which provides a great orientating view over the immediate region. At the foot of this hill and pointing up a small cleft-shaped valley at the base of the hill is the remarkably evocative **Phallic Rock,** or **Booviin Chuluu**, lying at a slight angle, its tip wrapped in a blue hadag, with a large stone offering bowl to hold libations – and hopefully provide fertility. (No one quite knows from what period this unusual sculpture dates but, with its Indian-influenced lingam theme, it is more likely post-Mongol Empire.) The money and offerings in the bowl, and the rustic little fence protecting it, show the rock is still actively worshipped. (Another story says the rock symbolises a castrated monk who'd broken his vows of celibacy and serves as a warning to others.) On the hill above, this second tortoise has an inscribed stele draped in a hadag. At the far end of this small hill is a traditional ovoo with a line of horse skulls, an offering to the mountain spirit by their owners, and which provides a great panoramic view over the town and monastery.

Of course Harhorin is a popular tourist destination – the mid-point of the so-called **Golden Circuit** which travels first to the South Gobi and then diagonally cross-country to Lake Hovsgol in the far north. Other travellers come directly out from UB with an added stop around **Rashaant** for its sand dunes and old monastery (see Around UB, page 205), or Ugii Nuur. If you've arrived from the solitude of the Mongolian Outback, however, as I did, Harhorin can't help but come as something of a shock. From capital of the Mongol Empire to Tourist City today! Scattered around the town are more than a dozen tourist ger camps, some quite large and one boasting the biggest ger in Mongolia as its dining room. Traffic is busy and everyone ends up at Erdene Zuu.

Souvenir markets are everywhere – near the first turtle, the Phallic Rock and especially inside the monastery grounds. On tables or spread out on the ground, mostly women hawkers sell a fascinating mix of statuary, boxes, metalware, knives, jewellery and other stuff that's at least worth a browse – and you may wish later you'd actually bought. The sellers are slightly reserved, not pushy – and do not bargain. (The number of arrowheads is

A line of ovoo *overlook the plain where the Mongol capital of Karakorum once stood, now the site of the Erdene Zuu Monastery, seen in the near distance. The horse's skulls are offerings to the mountain spirit of favourites who have passed away (Carl Robinson).*

enough for a horde!) Of questionable provenance – most likely Chinese-run Inner Mongolia, I was told – be sceptical of assurances of 200-year-old objects made of yak bone. (Back home, my grime-covered, dusty and rusty-hinged foldout Buddha polished up like new!)

Some decorum is essential at Erdene Zuu – this is Mongolia's oldest surviving Buddhist monastery and is now primarily a museum, except for its Tibetan-style temple. One of my Mongolian companions was shocked to see a European couple drinking beer just inside the main gate. Other tourists, especially those in groups, were just plain loud. Personally, I was surprised to suddenly see so many other foreigners about and didn't know what to expect. Slow down – this is a sacred place to be savoured. Even if you have to wait an hour for an available guide, as we did, the reward makes Erdene Zuu an incomparable Mongolian destination. A woman in her 40s, my guide was well informed and as she opened old-fashioned locks into each temple, we imagined ourselves on a personalised journey back into the dusty past. (Another great source of information on Erdene Zuu is Don Croner's *Guidebook to Locales Connected with the Life of Zanabazar.*)

Right: Of the four large Chinese-style tortoises which once guarded Karakorum, only two survive, this one on Tortoise Hill southwest of today's Erdene Zuu Monastery and still actively worshipped (Carl Robinson).

Erdene Zuu – which translates as "precious master" – was Mongolia's first Buddhist monastery after the religion's revival in the early 16th century (see History, page 77 and People & Culture, page 128). In search of a unifying religion for the Mongolians, a descendant of Chinggis Khaan himself, Altan Khan from today's Inner Mongolia, had proclaimed the head of Tibetan Buddhism's then minority Yellow Hat sect the very first Dalai Lama in 1578. Shortly afterwards, he bestowed the honorary title of Tusheet Khan on Avtai Khan who controlled the Orhon Valley, one of the three domains of eastern Mongolia. Using the stone monuments, bricks and other building materials from the ruins of Karakorum, construction of the monastery began in 1586 and quickly became Mongolia's most important. In 1639, a portable monastery known as **Ih Huree**, or the Great Circle, departed from Erdene Zuu along the Orhon River and the other northern rivers, finally arriving at present-day Ulaanbaatar 60 years later in 1779. Only then was Erdene Zuu displaced in importance.

Surrounded by a brick wall 400 metres (1,312 feet) on each side, and topped with 108 white stupas and gates at its four cardinal points, Erdene Zuu occupies 160,000 square metres (1,722,226 square feet). Regarded as a holy number in Buddhism, each of the 108 stupas holds a sacred object such as the remains of a revered lama, scriptures or relics, and they are spaced roughly, but not consistently, 15 metres (50 feet) apart. Its four gates are solid and impressive with huge wooden doors, including a smaller one for entry,

and a Chinese-style pavilion above the turreted rampart. The heavily defensive look of this monastery wasn't just for show, as some very unholy wars against the majority Red Hats were still raging in its early days, and it was later subjected to attack by the western Mongolians in 1688.

At its height, Erdene Zuu had 62 temples, hundreds of other buildings and over 2,000 lamas, or monks. During the Communist purges of the 1930s, most of the temples were destroyed and lamas either executed or imprisoned. The monastery was simply locked up but allowed to reopen as a museum in 1965. Today only 14 temples remain. Worship began in the Tibetan-style temple on its northeastern side after 1990 but most of the complex remains a museum. All remains are on the northern side of the grounds and include temples, small buildings and a large Golden Stupa.

Located in the northwest quadrant of the grounds, the three Zuu temples are the monastery's most important structures and a guided visit provides an informative introduction to the Tibetan Buddhist hierarchy and its Mongolian variations. (Building up a sense of anticipation, the guide slowly opens old-fashioned brass locks and then swings open wooden doors into the darkened labyrinth within, each temple a new surprise.) Built from the ruins of a Buddhist temple inside old Karakorum, the **Central Zuu Temple** was built by Avtai Khan in 1586 with the Left and Right Temples constructed over the following decades. The buildings are built in a distinctly Chinese style, with a raised platform and a large courtyard across their entire frontage that includes a large incense burner. The two tombs to each side of the stairs leading up to the temples are those of Avtai, the monastery's founder (and Zanabazar's great-grandfather), on the left and Gombodorj, his father, on the right.

The main temple, also known as **Gol Zuu**, houses a statue of Shakyamuni, the historic Buddha, with Amithaba, the symbol of spiritual enlightenment on the right and Otoch Manal, the god of medicine, on his left. (Erdene Zuu was renowned for its doctors and astrologers.) This temple also has statues to the sun and moon gods, co-opted from Mongolia's original religion, Tengriism. Decorated with a ceiling of Taras, or female Buddhas, and *mandalas*, the **Left Zuu Temple** contains the more familiar statues of the past, present and future Buddhas while the **Right Zuu Temple** has one of the adolescent Buddha and also Tsongkhapa, founder of the Yellow Hat sect. Smaller buildings off the courtyard contain ancient mandalas and paintings of the perils of hell. Outside the front of this complex is the modest but attractive Dalai Lama Temple, commemorating his visit in 1673. Among the items of particular interest are *tangkas* depicting Sonam Gyatso, the first Dalai Lama. (Working retrospectively from his naming by the Altan Khan, he is regarded as the Third.)

To the left strolling toward the next temple is a long complex of stupas with the largest, the **Golden Prayer Stupa**, or **Bodhi Suburgan,** dating from 1799 and honouring Mongolia's Fourth Bogd Gegeen. Hidden away amongst them is the very first structure built on the site by Avtai, the small **Khoh Sum**, or Blue Temple. At the northeastern corner of the grounds, the white- and gold-fronted **Laviran Temple**, also called Labrang, is built in a very different Tibetan style and is the only active part of the Erdene Zuu monastery. Only the ground floor of the three-storey building is open but visitors are welcome to enter during services, which begin daily at 11am. (It's best to simply sit down, relax and even meditate, for a few moments absorbing the atmosphere and droning chants before taking a quiet clockwise stroll past its many altars, including colourful decorative cakes made of yak butter. Don't forget to clasp your hands and bow, too.) A shop in a large white ger just in front of the temple looks slightly out of place but is an important source of funds. What was once the heart of Karakorum lies in the flat fields outside the nearby **East Gate** – certainly worth a stroll for those with time.

Another point of interest inside the grounds is near the main entrance, just south of the pathway containing a fascinating collection of stone relics. Known as the **Bat-Olziit**, or the **Courtyard of Happiness and Prosperity**, this circular rock platform dates from Zanabazar's early days as Mongolia's theocratic leader in 1658 and is where a huge ger some 45 metres (150 feet) in diameter, 15 metres (50 feet) high and capable of holding up to 300 people was erected. (The ger was later moved to Ih Huree, where its presence was noted by a visiting Russian ethnographer in the late 19th century. No one knows what happened to it.) Just south are the remains of a large circular pond.

For many visitors, Erdene Zuu is the main stop before heading onwards, usually northwest to Lake Hovsgol. But for those with an interest in the wider sweep of Mongolian history, there is plenty more to see. A good first stop is the new **Great Imperial Map Monument** on a crest in the range just behind Harhorin. Built only in 2004, the monument's three sides show various empires based in this valley, including the Hunnu (Xiongnu) and Turkic periods.

Starting with the oldest relics in the Orhon Valley and located some 75 kilometres (47 miles) north-northwest of Harhorin along the banks of the Tamir River are the ruins of the Hunnu or Xiongnu settlement of **Tamiryn Ulaan Hoshuu.** Explored in detail by an American-Mongolian team only in 2005, this 5,000-year-old settlement yielded evidence not just of a mixed sedentary and pastoralist lifestyle but a wealthy society with extensive trade links with China. Among the nearly 300 graves at a site near the river's junction with the Orhon, the team – funded by the Silk Road Foundation – discovered old coins,

Erdene Zuu's Tibetan-style Laviran Temple holds regular Buddhist services (Carl Robinson).

lacquerware, silk, glass beads and gold jewellery. Earth-walled fortifications further west yielded evidence of a Xiongnu settlement but few artefacts. But the jury is still out on whether this was the Hunnu's capital (other important sites are found north of UB, in the Hentii and Dornod).

Relics from the Turkic era, specifically its second period or khanate beginning around 680 CE, are much more evident – and easier to reach on a brand-new Turkish-built highway direct from Harhorin. Located on the east bank of the Orhon River some 45 kilometres (28 miles) north of the old Mongol capital, **Khooshoo-Tsaidam** was the capital of the Eastern Turks between the sixth and eighth centuries; they left behind over 40 stelae, many with inscriptions known as the Orhon Script, with runic on one side and Chinese on the other. (These are the oldest example of Turkic writing, and account not just for the paved road to reach the site but the intense cultural interest from faraway Ankara.) Dating from between 732 and 735, the more famous of the two is the massive **Bilge Khan Stele** (3.3 x 1.3 metres, or 11 x 4 feet), recently restored by a team of Mongol and Turkish archaeologists who work from a large hangar nearby. (A replica is located in the excellent Turkish Gallery of UB's National Museum.)

The Turks were followed in 751 by another tribe from the Orhon and Selenge River valleys who set up their capital 20 kilometres (12 miles) to the southwest at **Har Balgas** or **Ordu Baliq**, 45 kilometres (28 miles) due north of Harhorin. Known as the **Black City** and also on the east bank of the Orhon, this walled fortress was the Uyghur capital for about 100 years into the mid-ninth century, when they were routed by the iconoclastic Kyrgyz from the Yenisey River to the northwest. The large, brick-walled, five-hectare (12-acre) fortress had two gates, one north and the other south, was surrounded by a moat and its layout is clearly visible. Canals brought water into the town and for irrigating crops. Inside the fortress is evidence of a Buddhist stupa and the ruler's palace. Archaeological evidence points to a sophisticated mixed society with handicrafts, printed books and trade relations with China. (Fleeing south into western Xinjiang and Central Asia, the Uyghurs would later provide the Mongol Empire with its own written script and many of its administrators.)

Top: Dating from 1586, a beautifully rendered historic Buddha, or Shakyamuni, takes central position in Erdene Zuu's Main Temple.
Above: The deity Gongor, or Sita Mahakala, stands protectively to one side of the altar (Carl Robinson x2).

East of Ogiy Nuur and inside the southernmost part of Bulgan aimag are the ruins of the **Har Buhiyn Balgas**, or Khitan Balgas, from the last pre-Mongol empire, the Khitan, who ruled from the early 10th to 12th centuries. Renowned as city builders, ruins from this era are also found in eastern Mongolia (see The Hentii, page 232 and The Great Eastern Steppe, page 247), but these are the westernmost ruins.

Back in the other direction from Harhorin and west up the Orhon Valley are several worthwhile attractions, in particular the much-photographed **Tovkhon Khiid,** or monastery, with its "easy chair" setting up a rugged cliff face west of the river. Another one of Zanabazar's creations, and apparently where he did much of his writing and bronze works, the monastery was magnificently restored in the early 2000s. The main temple complex is located on the "seat" of the chair and a trail leads up to its summit with spectacular views out over the Hangai Mountains. On the way to the summit is one of the monastery's most popular attractions, the so-called **Mother's Womb,** a narrow passageway from which pilgrims exit symbolically reborn and cleansed of their sins. (Access is from the Orhon Valley or past the long-time hot springs town of Hujirt.)

The monastery is located on the way to the **Orhon Waterfall,** also known as **Ulaan Tsutgalan,** some 82 kilometres (51 miles) southwest of Harhorin, and a popular tourist destination. But the volcanic activity and thick layers of basalt which created this attraction also make the road one of the worst in the country, all the more shocking as the waterfall is formally inside the valley's UNESCO World Heritage-protected area. (Entry fees should contribute to some serious road maintenance.) The trip can take up to three hours, and another turn-off is the presence, right next to the waterfall, of a rather tacky tourist ger camp and an amazing amount of rubbish. On our visit, arriving from the west and the headwaters of the Orhon River in early June, the 20-metre-high (66-foot) waterfall was totally dry. Locals assured us the waterfall would be running by the height of the tourist season in July; Mongolia doesn't have many waterfalls, but do make sure this one's running before undertaking the long drive.

Having said that, however, the drive up – or down – the rest of the Orhon Valley can be quite pleasant with some lovely views out to the distant hills and the picturesque river. At one particularly photogenic spot, legend says that a large battle once took place between the Red and Yellow Hats for control of Mongolian Buddhism, with the dead and injured falling down the precipitous cliff face. In our travels, we also stumbled upon Bronze Age petroglyphs in a volcanic stretch of the Orhon farther downriver, and a large collection of Turkic-era graves up a narrow valley.

THE HOVSGOL

As it does for many visitors, our long clockwise narrative journey around this wonderfully diverse country nears its end on the pine-covered and mountainous shores of pristine **Lake Hovsgol** in Mongolia's far north. The Mongolians call this **Dalai Ej**, or Mother Sea, while others know it as the **Dark Blue Pearl of Mongolia.** Many regard the Hovsgol region as the most beautiful in Mongolia. Personally, as my last stop after weeks of intense travel around the country, the beauty and tranquillity of Lake Hovsgol was just what was needed. I totally relaxed and for the first time in years even got up on a horse. The place is indeed magical.

Located north of the Hangai Mountains hard up against the Russian border, the mountainous Hovsgol region is dominated by Mongolia's mini-version of gigantic Lake Baikal, **Hovsgol Nuur**, or **Lake Hovsgol** (from the Turkic "Blue Water Lake", it is also spelled Khovsgol, Khuvsgul and even Khubsugul). In size this spectacular clear-watered lake is Mongolia's second largest after salty Uvs Nuur (see The Great Lakes, page 385), but its tremendous depth makes it Mongolia's largest by volume – and by fresh water, too. Part of the Baikal Rift System, Lake Hovsgol is younger, smaller and higher than its Russian counterpart located less than 300 kilometres (180 miles) to the east.

Formed by tectonic activity 2.5–3.5 million years ago (compared to 25 million years for Lake Baikal), Mongolia's north-south trending Lake Hovsgol is 136 kilometres (85 miles) long, 36.5 kilometres (23 miles) at its widest point, and covers 2,760 square kilometres (1,066 square miles), with a maximum depth of 262 metres (860 feet). (Comparable figures for Baikal are nearly 32,000 square kilometres [12,355 square miles], 636 kilometres long by 81 kilometres wide [395 miles by 50 miles], and a much deeper 1,642 metres [5,387 feet].) Lake Hovsgol contains 65 percent of all the fresh water in Mongolia (1–2 percent of the world's supply), and is amazingly clear and pure. The lake's surface is frozen from December to June and at the height of summer its water temperature is between 14°C and 20°C. At an altitude of 1,645 metres (5,397 feet), Lake Hovsgol is at the top of the watershed of the same name, and is fed by some 96 streams with water flowing only out of its southern end, from where it winds its way in a long, roundabout course to the Selenge River and then into Lake Baikal, which sits at an elevation of 454 metres (1,490 feet).

Located just south of the **Sayan Mountains**, the eastern spur of the Altai-Sayan mountain system that runs along the Russian border, Lake Hosvgol is part of the transition zone between the great Siberian taiga and the steppe and deserts of Central Asia. As in the heart of the Altai, the region has the same delicate ecosystem with its own unique flora and fauna. The highest peak in the region, **Monh-Saridag** or **Burenkhaan** (3,491 metres or 11,453 feet) sits spectacularly at the northern tip of the lake, its snow-capped, pyramid-shaped peak straddling the Russian border.

A steep north-south range of uplifted dolomite, or limestone, runs along its western shore, the **Horidol Saridag Range,** which has permanently snow-capped peaks over 3,000 metres (9,800 feet) high. (This western shore even includes an extinct volcano.) By contrast,

the eastern shore of the lake has a very different character of gentle forested hills, grassy steppe, bays and meandering rivers. The lake, its shoreline and the mountains are all a protected national park. Considered an "ancient lake", Hovsgol was present during the last Ice Age, which ended 20,000 years ago and left behind a legacy of glacial valleys, moraines and other debris.

(Continued on page 456)

A herd of stocky horses gallop through a stream in the Hovsgol region in autumn (Gotsbayar Rentsendorj).

CASTING FOR GIANTS: ANGLING IN MONGOLIA

By *Andy Parkinson*

Since opening up to Westerners in the early 1990s, Mongolia has rapidly earned a reputation as an outstanding angling destination both for the unique adventure of fishing its wild untamed rivers and for the chance to catch a legendary fish called the **taimen**. Of course, the fish have been there all along. It's only that traditionally Mongolians did not eat fish – leaving the rivers in a pristine state.

Taimen can be described as prehistoric mega-fish. They are renowned for feeding on small mammals and ducklings and willingly take a surface fly imitating a mouse. An ancient ancestor of the salmon, they exhibit many similarities. But unlike salmon, taimen do not run out to the oceans, instead spending their entire life cycle in the river where they were spawned. Left alone and growing slowly to great size, taimen can live over 50 years, reach 70 inches (180 centimetres) in length and over 200 pounds (100 kilograms) in weight. The largest sport-caught taimen range from 50 to 60 inches (127–152cm), but even these giants are rare; the average size is nearer to 30 inches (76cm) and 10–12 pounds (4.5–5.4kg).

Scientists estimate the maximum potential population density of this top predator in Mongolia's rivers is only around 20 taimen per kilometre, and that is in the most productive and pristine rivers. The implication is that taimen need to be protected. Every one caught should be carefully released to the river after taking a photo, and you shouldn't expect to catch great numbers.

FLY-FISHING FOR TAIMEN

The thrill of fly-fishing for these freshwater giants is experiencing the strike when the fish takes the fly. They will explode on the fly, sometimes coming completely out of the water, or even smashing the fly with their tail first. They clearly intend to swallow their prey whole or otherwise stun and drown it first. On witnessing this great commotion many anglers strike too soon and miss hooking up with their quarry; the trick is to keep stripping until you feel the weight of the fish, then lift the rod to set the hook. Once the fight is on, taimen will charge around the pool, often going airborne, or boring deep to the sanctuary of the depths, shaking their head like a dog with a bone. Just as you think it's ready to come into the bank, the taimen will turn, charging back to the middle of the river.

Once the taimen is tamed, bring it to the shallows; keeping the fish in the water, grasp the tail with one hand while using your pliers to flip out the barbless hook with your other hand. (Best to have a guide or buddy on hand also to help unhook and photograph your catch.) The best photos are with the taimen held just in or slightly above the water – never wrestle the fish out of the water or haul it up by the gills. (A big one will put your back out anyway!) Then gently revive the fish, holding it until it regains the strength to swim off; it'll soon be fully recovered to terrorize the grayling population and spawn again next spring.

LENOK, GRAYLING AND MORE . . .

It is easy to forget that there's much more to fishing Mongolia than chasing taimen. For starters there's abundant lenok trout and grayling. The **lenok**, another ancient member of the salmon and trout family, occupies a similar ecological niche to trout, feeding on prolific mayfly hatches and readily taking a dry fly.

There are several different species of grayling – new ones are just being classified – and trying to catch all species would take you on a fly-fishing odyssey all around Mongolia: from the Altai Mountains and the eagle hunters of the west for **Mongolian grayling**; north to the taiga home of the reindeer herders for the strikingly coloured gold-tailed **Arctic grayling**; to Lake Hovsgol for the endemic **black grayling**; and east to the birthplace of Chinggis Khan on the Onon River for **Amur grayling**.

Taimen are only found in the catchments draining to the Arctic and Pacific, while in the Great Lakes Basin other unique fish such as several species of **osman** can be found. The eastern rivers of the Amur catchment also have remarkable diversity of fish, including the leopard-spotted **Amur pike**, and a second species of lenok.

Remember there's a three-foot-long (one-metre) predator in the water so it's not uncommon for taimen to attack a hooked lenok, or to gulp down the grayling you just released.

Following spread: A fishing site at a secret location in the Hovsgol (Carl Robinson).

CONSERVATION

Unfortunately, it is no longer true that Mongolians don't fish; while still little subsistence fishing occurs, the pressure from irresponsible sport fishing and commercial fishing is increasing. Taking a trophy taimen for the table or to nail its head to the wall can rapidly decimate the population of large older fish; but more significant is the threat of commercial fishing, especially poaching with nets in the winter for export to China or Russia. Gold mining is also a threat: illegal artisanal miners, the so-called "Ninjas", can now be found panning for gold in some rivers.

Fortunately the threats remain localised and you can still find good fishing. Responsible fly-fishing outfitters have initiated conservation projects and are actively protecting certain rivers, sponsoring ranger patrols, and working with local communities to protect river resources for the benefit of all. In fact, conservation has become an integral part of business for the most responsible outfitters.

The Eg-Uur watershed project initiated by Sweetwater Travel and the Taimen Conservation Fund was the first of these projects; the science team working here has advanced our understanding of taimen ecology and collected important data for the future conservation of the species. Companies like Fish Mongolia and

Above and right: The handsome "fighting" taimen is Mongolia's most prized fish – but a catch-and-release system is strictly enforced (Courtesy of Dan Bailey/Fish Mongolia x2).

Mongolia River Outfitters are also partnering with communities and conservation organisations to protect important taimen rivers.

"Catch and Release" is now required by law. Both spinning and fly-fishing methods are permitted using only single barbless hooks when angling for taimen. Treble hooks are banned. The fishing season officially opens on 15 June to allow taimen to spawn undisturbed during May. Post-spawning, the taimen are hungry and aggressive so the early season is one of the best times to fish, while September is the other popular season when the larch trees turn golden and the onset of the short autumn brings stable, sunny weather, with clear and cool waters.

Who to Fish With?

Pioneers of taimen fly-fishing operations included the Vermillion brothers of Sweetwater Travel, who with their local partners, Hovsgol Travel, established the first fly-fishing only taimen camps on the Eg and Uur rivers in Hovsgol aimag. Sweetwater Travel conducts a professional, high-end operation and can be commended for initiating Mongolia's first major taimen conservation effort.

You'll find the best fishing furthest from the roads and it is better to be on the water in a boat to access the prime pools. Some camps use jet boats to distribute their guests efficiently along the river, although some herders along the rivers object to the disturbance caused by their motors. Other fly-fishing outfitters like Fish Mongolia and Mongolia River Outfitters now allow you to experience

the best that Mongolia's rivers have to offer in a more tranquil manner on float trips with inflatable rafts rowed by your guide. You can get even further off the beaten track on horse-packing expeditions into remote rivers.

Enter "Mongolia Fishing" into Google and you'll find that many tour companies now offer fishing tours, but it's worth checking their credentials, especially that they have the necessary licences and permits for the river where they intend to take you, and also that they know a thing or two about fishing. It would be laudable to support outfitters who are actively involved in community-based conservation efforts. Any photos of dead or mishandled taimen on a tour company's website should immediately alert you.

Going it alone on an unguided trip is not a viable option in Mongolia as it is almost impossible to obtain the necessary taimen permits without going through an outfitter. However, for a fee, some companies like Fish Mongolia may help you arrange permits and local services to provide access to fishing beats on certain rivers. Elsewhere, you can get a permit to fish for lenok and grayling from the National Park offices at Lake Hovsgol and Terkiin Tsagaan Nuur.

The Experience

Stop casting, take a seat on a riverside boulder and look around. Last night, you sat around the campfire while your local guides sang haunting Mongolian songs under the bright stars. This morning, you watched a group of herders ford the river on horseback, off to scythe hay along the riverbanks. There's a white *ger*, flocks of sheep and goats, a herd of shaggy yaks in the distance. The scenery is stunning, dramatic cliffs, golden larch trees, no fences. Quite possibly, you just had the craziest hour of casting dry flies to rising lenok trout, a take on almost every cast. Perhaps you fished a huge mouse fly through the half-mile-long (800-metre) pool from riffle to tail out without a bite. Or maybe you just caught the largest freshwater fish of your lifetime on a fly rod. Whichever way, fishing in Mongolia is a truly remarkable experience.

British-born Andy Parkinson has operated fishing tours in Mongolia since 2003 for Fish Mongolia, a joint venture with a local partner. Fluent in Mongolian, Parkinson emphasises community-based tourism, offers a wide range of other tours and plans individualised trips (www.fishmongolia.com).

Following spread: A group of Tsaatan, or Reindeer People, on the move – as well as serving as mounts, reindeer dairy products provide much of the Tsaatan's staple diet (Elbegzaya Lhagvasuren).

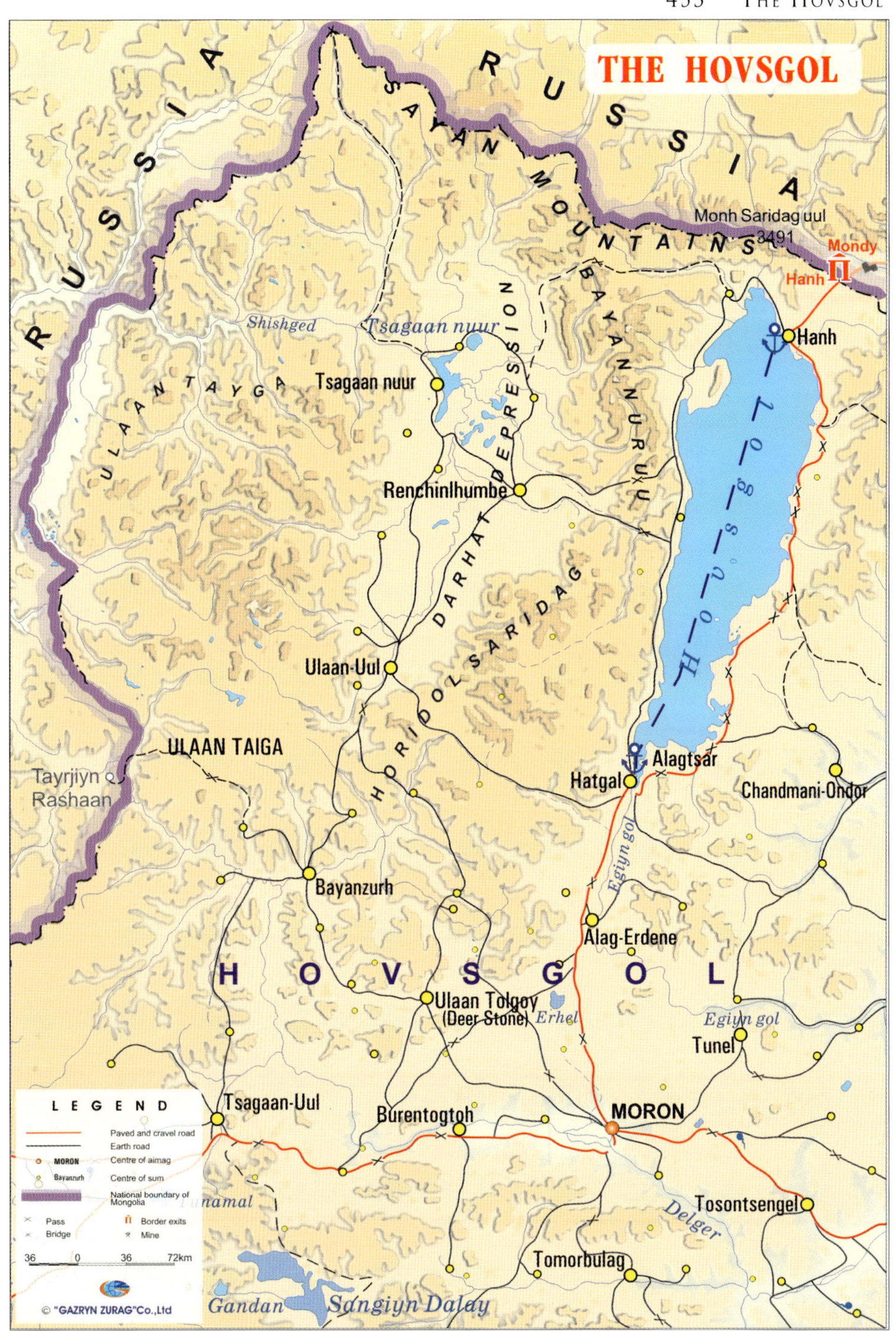
THE HOVSGOL
RUSSIA
RUSSIA
SAYAN MOUNTAINS
Monh Saridag uul
3491
Mondy
Hanh
Hanh
Shishged
Tsagaan nuur
Tsagaan nuur
ULAAN TAYGA
DARHAT DEPRESSION
BAYAN NURUU
Renchinlhumbe
Hovsgol
HORIDOL SARIDAG
Ulaan-Uul
ULAAN TAIGA
Tayrjiyn Rashaan
Alagtsar
Hatgal
Chandmani-Ondor
Egiyn gol
Bayanzurh
Alag-Erdene
HOVSGOL
Ulaan Tolgoy
(Deer Stone)
Erhel
Egiyn gol
Tunel
Tsagaan-Uul
Burentogtoh
MORON
Tosontsengel
Delger
Tomorbulag
Gandan
Sangiyn Dalay
LEGEND
Paved and gravel road
Earth road
MORON Centre of aimag
Bayanzurh Centre of sum
National boundary of Mongolia
Pass
Bridge
Border exits
Mine
36 0 36 72km
© "GAZRYN ZURAG"Co.,Ltd

On the western side of the range is the remote **Darkhatiin Hotgor Depression**, also known as the **Darhat Valley**, once occupied by a lake the size of Lake Hovsgol with the **Ulaan Tayga Uul** on its western side. Today, surrounded by forested hills and steppe, the heart of the depression is a collection of marshland, ponds and streams emptying into **Tsagaan Nuur** and other smaller lakes. The fast-flowing **Shishged River** is the lake's only outlet, flowing northwest into Russia's **Yenisey River**. The northern end of this depression and up into the Sayan Mountains is the homeland of Mongolia's fascinating **Tsaatan**, or **Reindeer People**, who now number less than 300 still living a nomadic lifestyle (see Special Topic, page 458).

The Hovsgol region is blessed with a rich natural ecosystem dominated by species suited to its colder climate. Bird life is prolific and plant life amazingly varied. Its 68 species of mammals – many more than around Lake Baikal – include ibex, argali, maral, reindeer, musk deer, brown bear, lynx, marten, wolf, beaver and moose. Although unspotted in recent years, the high peaks of the Horidol Saridag are a traditional home of the snow

Below: A group of anglers prepare for another legendary day of fishing along Hovsgol's remote wild rivers (Carl Robinson). Right: An aerial view of the Darhat Valley, close to the border with Russian Siberia, reveals its myriad marshes, lakes and streams (Elbegzaya Lhagvasuren).

THE REINDEER PEOPLE

By *Morgan Keay*

Amidst the colourful pictures of Mongolia that populate brochures, books and websites about the country, one expects to find the obligatory images of Mongolian *gers* (yurts), and the "Big Five" Mongolian livestock (horses, cows, camels, sheep and goats). One might be surprised, however, to come across unexpected images of teepees and reindeer, but indeed these are part of the cultural landscape of Mongolia as well.

Mongolia is home to the southernmost indigenous reindeer-herding people in the world, the *Tsaatan* (or ethnic *Dukha*), who originate from Tuva in Siberia. The Tsaatan's unique lifestyle, and the taiga environment in which they live, represent one of the most distinct cultural and ecological pockets of Mongolia. Residing in the rugged taiga ecosystem of Hovsgol's Sayan Mountains, the Tsaatan are Mongolia's smallest ethnic minority, and are a highly nomadic, reindeer-herding people who have moved throughout the Mongolian-Siberian border region for millennia. Unlike their steppe-dwelling counterparts, the Tsaatan live in teepees, which are better suited for their forest environment, and which are more portable than gers allowing the Tsaatan to move with their reindeer as often as 10 times per year.

At the centre of Tsaatan life are domesticated reindeer, on which the community depends primarily for milk and transport. Reindeer dairy products make up the bulk of the Tsaatan diet, and reindeer are used as pack and riding animals in their mountainous landscape. Contrary to popular belief, the Tsaatan do not typically slaughter reindeer for meat due to their perception as sacred animals by the community, instead relying on wild game as their main protein source. The community's shamanic religious tradition is credited as one of the most vibrant and intact of any in Mongolia, informing much of daily life and adding to the Tsaatan's popularity among anthropologists, filmmakers and tourists alike.

In recent decades, the Tsaatan have confronted a disproportionate number and diversity of challenges as compared to most Mongolian communities, such as restrictions on subsistence hunting and fishing, forced relocations out of the taiga, unstable reindeer populations, inability to engage in public sector activities, and limited access to healthcare and education. They are Mongolia's smallest ethnic minority – with less than 300 individuals living in the taiga, and only a couple of hundred more living in towns and cities – and rank among the country's poorest inhabitants.

Their vulnerability, remoteness and cultural uniqueness have recently contributed to the Tsaatan's growing visibility in the public forum, generating much-needed attention, but also a myriad of stereotypes and misunderstandings about the community. Among the most common myths about the Tsaatan are that they are uneducated, lazy and inbred. In reality, most Tsaatan children travel great distances to attend schools, and the literacy rate in the taiga parallels that of Mongolia as a whole. Hardly lazy, the Tsaatan lifestyle and taiga habitat demands that constant effort be made simply to survive. And thirdly, despite the fact that there are less than 300 Tsaatan individuals living in the taiga region, the community has staved off inbreeding through marriages with neighbouring ethnic groups, a practice that is growing in frequency in the community.

A young Tsaatan boy rides one of his charges (Bruce Smith, courtesy of The Itgel Foundation).

Today, the Tsaatan continue to work towards self-realisation and sustainability, integrating aspects of modernity with a proud commitment to maintaining their cultural heritage. Several nongovernmental organisations (NGOs) are working with the community to provide support in the form of educational scholarships, veterinary treatments and training, and natural resource management programmes, which have contributed to improvements in Tsaatan quality of life in recent years. Among the most successful of these programmes has been the establishment of the **Tsaatan Community & Visitors' Centre (TCVC)**, an initiative supported by an NGO called The Itgel Foundation that has taken advantage of the growing trend of tourism to the Tsaatan to bring vital economic, social and other benefits to the community.

A reindeer's mighty antlers mask its benign nature, making it a relatively easy animal to keep as livestock (Jessica Shutz, courtesy of The Itgel Foundation).

Teepees make more convenient homes for the Tsaatan, who live in a remote environment of mountain and taiga forest (Katrina Shum, courtesy of The Itgel Foundation).

Despite rapid increases in tourism to the Tsaatan and their taiga region from the late 1990s onward, little benefits were directed to the Tsaatan people themselves prior to the establishment of the TCVC. Tour operators and independent travellers spontaneously arrived in the taiga allowing for little or no opportunities for the Tsaatan to be involved, much less benefit economically. Tsaatan were essentially props in the tourism experience, and at best were given handouts of flour or candy to thank them for their time. Seeking to redefine this trend, the Tsaatan worked with The Itgel Foundation to establish the TCVC, a fully Tsaatan-owned and operated hub for trip coordination to the community. Through the TCVC, visitors can obtain goods and services provided by Tsaatan individuals, and learn how to visit the community in a culturally and environmentally sensitive manner. Hiring Tsaatan individuals to work as guides, cooks and horsemen brings vital economic opportunities to the remote Tsaatan, and ensures that trips are facilitated by knowledgeable community members, allowing for the most authentic and responsible experience possible.

The TCVC's unique profit-sharing model enables all Tsaatan to benefit from a shared community fund, and encourages cooperative planning as opposed to competition in the close-knit community. One hundred percent of revenue goes directly to the Tsaatan, who have independently owned and operated the TCVC since May 2008, after three years of start-up support from The Itgel Foundation. Since its establishment, the one-of-a-kind TCVC has enabled household income among impoverished Tsaatan families to increase by as much as 300 percent, and has created greatly improved access to health, education and information for the remote community. All tour operators, independent travellers, and even commercial and NGO entities headed for the taiga are encouraged by the Tsaatan to utilise the TCVC, thereby ensuring that all visits fairly involve the community. (For more information check out www.gotcvc.org.)

Though the Tsaatan do welcome visitors, travellers should be advised that the community lives in an incredibly remote corner of Mongolia, and reaching them involves long, costly and often uncomfortable travel. From Ulaanbaatar, it can take as many as five days just to reach the taiga via a combination of plane, Russian jeep and horse, and services are extremely limited along the way. Border permits are critical for visiting the area, and must be obtained from the Border Protection Authority in Ulaanbaatar or in Murun (Moron), Hovsgol. Logistics are complicated and should be coordinated with support from travel professionals. Weather conditions are extreme, and many routes are impassable at different times of year due to mud, ice and snow. A trip to the taiga should only be considered by those prepared to invest the time, money and effort needed to make the trip enjoyable, safe and sensitive to Tsaatan requests. That said, perhaps no other community in Mongolia evokes the imagination and offers the potential for unforgettable experiences as does the Tsaatan.

Morgan Keay is Executive Director of The Itgel Foundation, a non-profit Mongolian NGO which is dedicated to protecting Mongolia's cultural and environmental legacy through grassroots projects (email: itgelfoundation@yahoo.com, www.itgel.org).

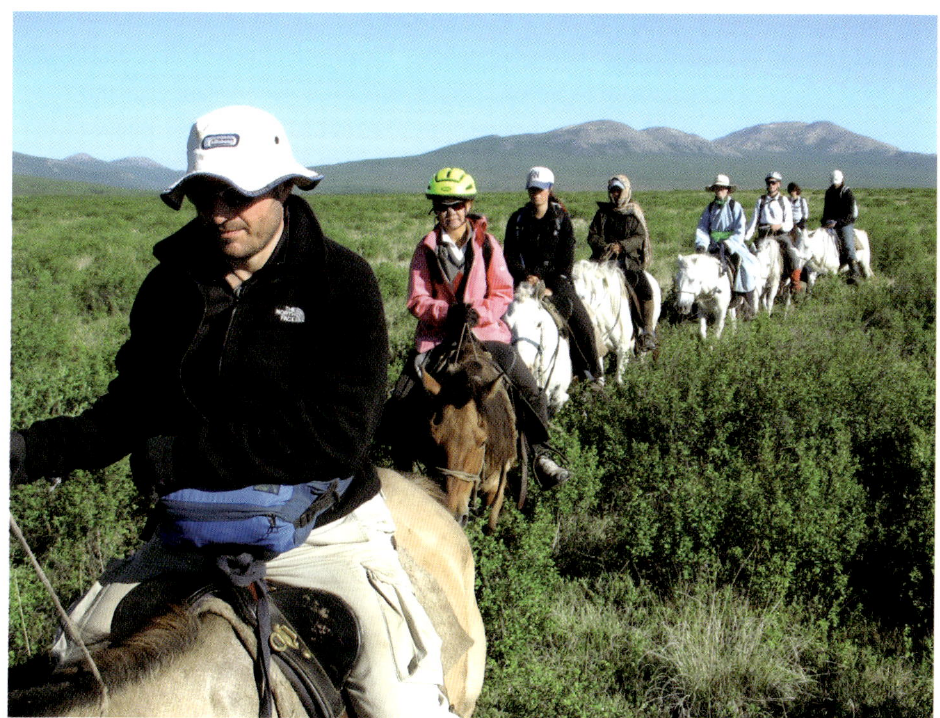

Horse trekking is the best option in regions where walkable trails are scarce or nonexistent (Leo Murray).

leopard. Lake Hovsgol is a habitat for nine different types of fish, including the Siberian grayling, Arctic cisco, freshwater cod and a Siberian catfish. Thankfully for them, the giant carnivorous taimen, a relative of the salmon, does not inhabit the lake. But these voracious predators are present downstream and in the region's other many rivers, and attract scores of keen anglers every year (see Special Topic, page 446).

With its colder climate, the Hovsgol's human history is not as old as other parts of Mongolia, perhaps only 7,000 years; this was an ancient "meeting point" between tribal groups, principally the Turks to the west and Mongols in the east. Consequently, the region boasts the single richest collection of deer stones and burial mounds, or *khirigsuur*, and is a primary focus of research by the Smithsonian Institute (see Special Topic, page 396).

In addition to the majority Halh Mongolians, the region's population includes a strong proportion of Buriats from around Lake Baikal and Darhats, a tribal group from the Darhat Valley who achieved special tax-exempt status as livestock breeders for the Buddhist Church around Mongolia in the late 17th century. Back home, though, they always maintained the hunting and fishing lifestyle and culture of the original Mongolians, and speak in a more archaic language with a strong emphasis on oral tradition, songs and rituals. Most importantly, the Darhat are regarded as the guardians of Mongolian Shamanism (see Special Topic, page 466). The region around Lake Hovsgol is notably less Buddhist than other parts of Mongolia – and shamanistic rituals are even a tourist attraction.

Lake Hovsgol is located about 900 kilometres (560 miles) northwest of Ulaanbaatar in Hovsgol aimag. Its capital of **Moron** (pronounced Mooroon) is 782 kilometres (486 miles) or 1.5 hours by air from the capital. The region is a popular destination for tourists and the last stop on the **Golden Circuit** by road first to the South Gobi and then diagonally across the country through old Karakorum in the Orhon Valley. (Whether coming this way past lovely Terhiyn Tsagaan Lake or from the east through Bulgan aimag, these two roads are regarded as the worst in Mongolia.)

Located in a broad valley on the banks of a river of the same name, Moron is a relatively large and well laid out town (population 35,000) with many shops, hotels and restaurants. Unlike other towns, homes in its residential area are made of timber, which is abundant in the region. Few visitors stay here, however, quickly heading north up the 110-kilometre (68-mile) improved dirt road to Lake Hovsgol, with perhaps a couple of sightseeing stops en route, including a large collection of deer stones. (The journey takes a good three hours.)

Moron is also a popular starting point for fishing expeditions in surrounding rivers where the taimen is particularly prized (but everything is strictly licensed and on a "catch-and-release" basis only, see Special Topic, page 446). This was my own introduction to the Hovsgol region as we travelled to a "top-secret location" along the **Tsagaan Bulan Gol** some three hours northwest of Moron. Again, the amazing geographical diversity of Mongolia struck as we drove through another type of "mountain-steppe", tighter valleys dotted with volcanic cones and melting permafrost drenching grassy hillsides, even in June.

Across wide undulating steppe, then quite precipitously down into a valley of uplifted limestone full of caves and recesses, and finally into a pocket-size, steep-sided, grass-covered valley with a wide, clear, rushing river. My host, Andy Parkinson of Fish Mongolia, was prepping a four-day rafting expedition with a small group of Canadian and American anglers and we'd just dropped in to say hello and stay overnight. (I've never seen such a happy bunch of fishermen!) It was a perfect hideout, too: "The Whites once took refuge in this valley," he explained, referring to the Russian Civil War of the early 1920s (see History, page 85). "They've found boots and equipment over there." He works closely with the local community who also benefit both financially and employment-wise from the operation.

After one last rubbish patrol, with the rafts under way and everyone already pulling in the taimen, we travelled back out of this marvellous valley – impossible without a 4WD – and headed cross-country to the main road north, visiting a nomad family along the way. About 40 kilometres (25 miles) north of Moron and due west of **Erhel Nuur**, a small salty lake, is one of the largest collections of deer stones in Mongolia, **Ulaan Tolgoy**. Just as Buddhist monasteries are never poorly sited, the setting for these Bronze Age stones was absolute perfection. Surrounded by the southern foothills of the Horidol Saridag, the wide valley sloped gently down to the lake and then far across to a distant range of hills. Definitely a place for contemplation.

Not far north, the main road crests a ridge to reveal the valley of the **Egiyn Gol**, the only outlet from Hovsgol Lake, which from here heads east on its long and wandering journey to the Selenge River. (The two rivers join not far north of the copper-mining city of Erdenet far to the southeast.

The fast-flowing Tsagaan Bulan flows past an outcrop of dolomite, or uplifted limestone, a geological feature that dominates much of the Hovsgol region (Carl Robinson).

SHAMANISM

Shamans are distinguished from other people in that they have a shaman spirit which selects and initiates them. This spirit is known by many names, including *utha*, and *onggor* among the Buryat (Buriat) and Dagur. It acts like an extra soul and is a source of power and controls the shaman's encounters with other spirits, some of which may also become helper spirits. While a shaman may show a proclivity for shamanizing from an early age, the utha will manifest itself suddenly, resulting in mental or physical illness. During the course of the illness the shaman-to-be will have a vision in which the utha will initiate him. Common elements in the vision include travel to the upper world and the dismemberment and reassembly of the shaman's body so that it will be new and empowered for his work. When the new shaman falls ill, the shaman who examines him will recognise at once that he has been selected by an utha spirit. At that point if he agrees to become a shaman he can be healed, otherwise he will usually die. The training and initiation which follow his recovery are only a confirmation of the initiation which he experienced in the spirit world.

The duties of a shaman include healing, blessing, protection, hunting magic, and occasionally weather magic. Healing is the most important of these because spirits are believed to be the cause of illness. Spirits can also be called to provide protection and improve luck. Hunting magic rituals put the shaman in touch with the animal and nature spirits who provide or withhold game. Weather magic usually involves rainmaking or sending lightning back to the sky, and requires direct contact with Tenger, or Tengri, Father Heaven. Some rituals such as the *oboo* ceremony and *ominan* ritual last for several days and are meant to promote the welfare of the entire community. Shamans' work may vary from simple fortune-telling to grand rituals lasting several days. Depending on the difficulty of the task, a shaman may invoke his spirits to help him or to actually enter his body when a lot of power is needed. Shamans usually sing, drum and dance during performances.

Shamans use several different tools in their work. Their costume and *ongons* (or spirit houses) are actual residences of their helper spirits. A one-sided, hand-held drum, usually 60cm or more in diameter, is used to drive the singing and dancing which are a part of most ceremonies. After the drum the most important tool of the shaman is the *toli*, a metallic circular mirror. A shaman will attach many toli to his costume if he can obtain them, but one toli over the chest is most important. A toli acts like armour, deflecting spirit attack; it can reflect light to blind spirits, and also absorbs energy from the universe to increase the shaman's power. Most shamans usually also have one or two staffs that represent horses which they ride on spirit journeys. Another tool found in many tribes is the *dalbuur*, a ritual fan used to drive out spirits from patients. Other musical instruments may be used by shamans, the jaw's harp (*aman huur* or jew's harp) being the most common. Shamans from some tribes use masks, but the most common one is the bear mask used for the ominan ritual.

Although shamans are noted for going into trances to do their work, not all rituals require it and the shaman performs many tasks in an ordinary state of consciousness. When an altered state of consciousness is required, however, there are many techniques which boost the shaman into the ecstatic state of mind that allows him to take on the qualities of a spirit and become clairvoyant and capable of spirit travel. Most rituals employ several of these techniques together in order to bring the shaman to ecstasy.

The setting of the ritual is crucial to the effectiveness of a ritual. Shamanizing at night is conducive to achieving the trance state; in fact many spirits are not as effective when called during the day. The people attending the ritual can help the shaman reach a trance state by echoing parts of his song, beating drums, or shouting along with the drumming. Circle dances can raise energy and propel the shaman into the upper world.

The beating of the shaman drum is the most powerful way to induce trance. Scientific studies have shown that repetitive rhythms at certain frequencies can induce a hypnotic state similar to the trance of shamans. Shaman drumming, however, does not have a metronome-like steadiness, but rather will slow down or speed up, get louder or softer depending on the state of the shaman's mind at a given moment. Mongolian and Siberian drums are generally large in diameter and have a deep, resonating sound that will vibrate through the shaman's body, and the drum is frequently held near the face or over the head so that the beat will resonate through the head and upper body with great force.

Intoxicants may be consumed before or during the ritual. Shamans frequently drink alcohol before shamanizing and pause at points during the ritual to smoke tobacco. Juniper, which is mildly hallucinogenic, is used in practically all rituals in Mongolia and in many parts of Siberia. The fumes of juniper will be waved in the face and inhaled, and the air of the ger will become thick with juniper smoke during the ritual. Sacred smoke is believed to raise the windhorse and is pleasing to the spirits. A more potent hallucinogen, the muscaria mushroom, has been connected with Siberian and Mongolian shamanism from ancient times. Mushrooms may not always be consumed during shamanist rituals, but shamans may also consume the dried mushrooms on order to achieve ecstasy during times between rituals.

Climbing the *toroo* tree is another path to ecstasy. In Mongolian the word to go out and to go up are the same word: *garah*. Researcher-writer Krystyna Chabros has suggested that the connection between those two meanings lies in shamanism. By symbolically ascending the representation of the World Tree the shaman is literally going out of this world into the world of spirits. The toroo tree has nine steps, and as the shaman climbs higher and higher, at the same time singing, the drumming and the encouragements of his audience will bring him to the ecstatic state. Some shamans will show their contact with the spirit world by singing *hoomei* (overtone or throat singing), which consists of a base note and a whistling overtone note. The overtones represent the contact with the spirit world while remaining physically on Earth (represented by the base tone).

A shaman trance entails travel on the spirit plane of existence, and the shaman usually experiences this as either flying or riding an animal which will carry him to the place in the three worlds where he is needed. These spirit journeys may take the shaman to places in this world, or may require him to travel to the upper or lower worlds. Lower world journeys are usually only required in cases of soul retrieval or bringing a dead person's soul to Erleg Khan (the lord of the lower world). Most other rituals will require the shaman to travel on Earth or ascend to the upper world. Lower world journeys are the most difficult, and only the strongest shamans can go there safely.

Spirit journeys usually start by moving upward, and even when going to the lower world the trip will start with flight, frequently out through the smoke hole of the ger. The shaman may take the form of a bird or ride a flying supernatural mount. During the course of the journey the shaman may change form several times, at one point being a bird, at the next in human form, and then taking on the form of a bear, depending on which spirits are guiding him or entering his body. The shaman may utter animal sounds as he goes through these transformations. He may appear to be unconscious during the journey, or may remain conscious but in a trancelike state and will be capable of moving around, dancing, or even telling his audience about what he sees. While in this state of mind the shaman is capable of acting completely out of character and can perform dangerous feats that he would be incapable of doing otherwise, such as stabbing himself or walking on fire. Most Altaic shamans speak of passing nine landmarks (*olobs*) during a journey regardless of which world they are travelling in.

The mount which a shaman rides during his travels is usually a flying horse or deer. These are physically represented by the one or two shaman staffs which he keeps handy during the ritual, or may be represented by his drum. Before a ritual starts the drum is warmed by the fire, this is called *amiluulah*, making the drum come alive. The drum not only drives the vision by its steady beat, but is literally the steed upon which the shaman rides to his destination.

Upon returning from his journey the shaman will cough or belch to expel the spirits that were riding with him inside his body. He then sings in praise of his spirit helpers before completing the ritual.

Excerpted from "A Course in Mongolian Shamanism – Introduction 101" at the Golomt Centre for Shamanistic Studies, Ulaanbaatar.

Tempting visitors for long and relaxing stays, Lake Hovsgol offers many of Mongolia's most luxurious tourist ger camps (Carl Robinson).

Clearly glaciated in the last Ice Age, the valley and river are full of round granite rocks with only small patches of grass for nomadic herds. The last part of the journey crosses over a rock-strewn tributary of the Egiyn Gol from the now-high range to the west. (Judging by the road's washed-out condition, the melting snows must pour mightily down this valley.)

Located at the southern end of Lake Hovsgol on the river, **Hatgal** is a rather run-down place, actually a port that has definitely seen much busier and more prosperous times. Its large wool-scouring plant is derelict, Communist-era concrete buildings lie unused and little remains of a large warehouse complex from the once busy trade with the old Soviet Union. In those days, truck convoys crossed the frozen lake in winter (40 fell through into the icy waters below, and now the practice is banned for ecological reasons). Hatgal's port, which even has a small museum, is full of rusty old freighters and barges not going anywhere. And there is no sign of the classic high-smokestack vessel, still seen in the odd travel brochure, that once plied the lake up to its northern port of **Hanh,** roughly 130 kilometres (80 miles) away, close to the Russian border. (It sank, apparently, but no one knows whether from rust or by accident.)

But there is a certain rustic charm to Hatgal, particularly around its small shopping area and the line of charming Russian-style wooden cabins on the road to the port. Already popular with backpackers for its plentiful budget accommodation, the town may well turn itself into quite a pleasant spot, Mongolia's only Port City! Certainly, everyone passes through the town. The **Lake Hovsgol Visitor Centre** is a most useful stop for its informative displays on the region's culture and natural attractions.

The Lake Hovsgol region is a wonderful place simply to relax but also offers plenty of activities such as hiking, kayaking and fishing – with horse trekking particularly popular. Most of the tourist ger camps are at the lower western end of the lake, sometimes literally cheek-by-jowl, with only a couple along its remote eastern shore. More camps are located around Tsagaan Nuur in the Darhat Valley.

But getting around the region by road is hardly an option. In fact, just travelling to the tourist ger camps closest to Hatgal is an incredibly bumpy affair over the rocky and permafrost-affected track, which stops after only 40 kilometres (25 miles). Although only 30 kilometres (19 miles) away on the east shore, the trip to our wonderful camp at a lakeside cove named **Alagtsar** – famous for its bird life – took a tortuous two hours. (No wonder visitors just want to relax after these in-bound trips.) Travelling farther up the same

Mountains reflect off Lake Hovsgol's crystal-clear waters from its more isolated eastern shore at Alagtsar (Carl Robinson).

One of Mongolia's largest collections of deer stones is easily visited at Ulaan Tolgoy between Moron and Lake Hovsgol (Carl Robinson).

road to the northern port of Hanh can take 12 hours – and with no regular ferry service, the same all the way back. (Wisely, some ger camps offer transfers by water but no one does lake cruises – at least not yet.) Travel to the sum centres of **Renchinlhumbe** and **Tsagaan Nuur** in the **Darhat Valley** takes two days or longer, depending on water levels at river crossings, on a northwestern route from Moron.

So, in true wilderness fashion, it's either the boot or the hoof if you want to see the sights – and I'd certainly recommend even just a few hours out exploring what is indeed an incredibly beautiful country. (Even in summer, though, do come prepared for a bit of rain too.) Along the less visited eastern shore, where I began my visit after an overnight in Hatgal, hiring a couple of horses and a local herder for a guide was easily arranged – and another Mongolian highlight. I hadn't been on a horse for years and marvelled at mine's ability to stroll so daintily through tangled larch forest, beautifully covered in red needles, along the rocky shore before galloping out onto open grasslands beside a crescent-shaped lagoon.

Travelling back inland on a high ridgeline where trees turn to steppe, the view stretched far and wide with our guide's ger just a tiny dot next to the fish-filled river flowing into our cove. Suddenly, one of the horse's front legs caught in a ground squirrel hole and she stopped, sending me tumbling most gracefully onto the soft ground below, a thankfully short distance on a Mongolian horse. I was still holding the reins but now lying in lush grass and flowers. With all those squirrel holes – as everywhere in this countryside's unpredictable terrain – anticipation helps.

The view of the western mountains across the calm and clear waters of Lake Hovsgol – and its very isolation – makes the eastern side an attractive option. But for those wanting a closer look up into the mountains, the western side is the place to be, although hikes along its shoreline of pebble-covered beaches, lovely coves and flower-covered meadows are very similar. A serious trip up over the mountains and down into the Darhat Valley and back takes 10 days or more on horseback, first up the western shore to **Jitleg Pass** and then along the **Arsaynh Gol** to the town of Renchinlhumbe and back through the dramatic dolomite rock formations of the Horidol Saridag. Another horse trek leads all the way up the west shore to Hanh.

Hiking is another option, but with few bridges, boggy conditions and limited marked trails, guided horse treks are a much wiser option. With the wettest conditions in Mongolia, especially in summer when the weather can change quite dramatically to snow, hail and lightning, mountain climbing requires a lot of caution. The park has no rescue service.

THE OTHER EIGHT MONTHS: WINTER IN MONGOLIA

By *Tjalling Halbertsma*

When I first arrived in Mongolia it was January and Ulaanbaatar – said to be the coldest capital in the world – was covered in a thick layer of ice and snow. I vividly remember trying desperately to keep warm and therefore being amazed to see many Mongolians clutching ice-cream cones in their gloved hands. The 10-cent-a-cone treats were stacked in open fridges – no one bothers to plug in the cord when it is -30°C – or were simply sold from cardboard boxes standing on the pavement along the streets. Then summer came, but only briefly for before I knew it there was snow in the mountains south of Ulaanbaatar... and out came the carton boxes with ice creams again.

Curious and outrageous winter stories abound in Mongolia: thermometers freezing and shattering at -58°C; sudden snows in June; temperature drops of over 30 degrees in a single day and – a practical one, this – construction workers mixing their cement with antifreeze to ensure their buildings dry before they freeze.

Unsurprisingly, city life slows down in winter. Running outdoors is out of the question as rapid breathing freezes the lungs; drivers light a fire under their cars to melt the oil in their engines; and the tarmac on the streets cracks up as it shrinks in temperatures occasionally falling below -50°C. Being located so far from the sea – the nearest harbour is 700 kilometres away in China – this land-locked country truly has a formidable climate.

But don't dismiss a visit to Mongolia in winter out of hand. There are those who might say it's the best time to visit the countryside, for the very reason that because the country is so defined by its climate, experiencing it during the depths of winter will reward you with a perfectly distilled view of life here.

In the countryside the felt *ger* tents face south towards the sun, sheltering themselves from northerly Siberian winds. Piles of frozen dung are gathered to fuel the stoves to melt ice, and animals are brought to their winter shelters, where their legs and backs are covered with cloth blankets to protect them from the cold. Nomadic life slows to a crawl, imitating the hibernating instincts of wild animals. Horses cannot be ridden anymore and the youngest animals are brought indoors. Extra layers of felt are added to ger tent covers, and the winter-chest with thick sheepskin clothing is unpacked to replace lighter garments.

In some respects travel itself is easier in winter, when the swampy northern areas and muddy roads are frozen and metre-thick ice provides shortcuts over lakes and through riverbeds. Car tyres get so stiff they will hardly ever get punctured, though your battery may not work after a night in extreme subzero conditions.

Freak natural phenomena set in at the height of winter. When you carry your thermometer uphill you will see that it actually gets warmer – not colder – as the coldest air flows into the lowest point of the valleys. The atmosphere gets so cold that it holds almost zero water, causing sound to be crystal clear and travel amazing distances. Likewise, views are razor sharp and probably the longest you have ever seen – they are also strikingly beautiful.

Mongolia's winter landscapes of snow and ice may be overwhelmingly picturesque and evocative, but they are also inherently dangerous. As one herder remarked about his newly born animals: "Winter kills first all that is born too late in summer." So come well prepared and fully self-reliant, for winter disasters can see many herds in Mongolia's countryside reduced by two-thirds, leaving herders faced with not only a minimal income but also a dangerously low supply of winter essentials such as wool, dung fuel and food.

If camping, bring a hammer to get your pegs into the frozen ground, and pour water into pots you can heat before it freezes. Bring pencils instead of ballpoint pens for gifts, as pens will freeze while being used, and at night keep torches in your sleeping bag to keep the batteries going. In the depths of winter one sleeping bag may not see you through the night – bring two, or even better, three.

Above all be assured of the unexpected. You'll discover at what temperature toothpaste freezes, how plastic shatters like glass at extremely low temperatures, and return to Ulaanbaatar with your own handful of entertaining winter tales. I have a personal favourite: it concerns a complimentary box of HP sauce (a popular savoury dressing in the United Kingdom) that, after the winter of 2000, made its way from the UK to northern Mongolia. The box was sent by the sauce manufacturer, which had received a letter from two Brits in Hovsgol who had noticed that the condiment was the last thing to freeze in their kitchen during the coldest winter in living memory. They had needed gloves to open the bottle, to prevent their fingers from freezing to the plastic cap. I guess the PR manager in the UK liked the story. I like him for it.

Tjalling Halbertsma, a Dutch lawyer, anthropologist and author, served in Mongolia as adviser to Prime Minister Nambaryn Enkhbayar between 2000 and 2004, then assisted in his successful campaign to become President in 2005. He regularly writes on Chinese and Mongolian history and art.

ADVICE FOR TRAVELLERS

Break Away from the Pack: Many tourists visit Mongolia in groups – but even just hanging out with a driver and guide for 10 days can be a strain. Don't feel like you've got to stick together all the time. If you find yourself with time on your hands in a *sum* or *aimag* centre because of a busted axle or main spring, a spare tyre being fixed or even just fuelling up – all of which can be time-consuming processes – enrich your visit by breaking away for a wander on your own. Catch a museum, hire a sidecar taxi or – once you've mastered a bit of Cyrillic – visit a grocery store, café, bar or pool hall. On the road, call for frequent stops and wander off in any direction. Climbing a mountain revives the soul, Mongolians say.

Taking Photos: Mongolians are shy, even the men, so get their attention and an approving nod before firing away with your camera. Many say no. With digital, especially the kids like seeing the image right away, often with lots of giggles. Mongolians are also very fond of posed group pictures and I'm sure you'll find a way to send them a copy some day. Gobi dust is the biggest threat to camera gear – it gets into everything (worse than

Many hands make light work – erecting a ger is a well-practised and swift affair (Elbegzaya Lhagvasuren).

Horse trekking across open steppe can be an inspirational experience (Leo Murray).

Aussie bulldust, the fine red desert dust of the Outback), so bring large sealable plastic zipper bags from your kitchen. (A small hand-blower is also useful, but be careful not to scratch your lens or filter.) For interior shots, switch manually to a higher ISO speed so that pesky flash doesn't destroy the moment.

Gifts: Those clip-on koalas and kangaroos I took as giveaways sure worked a treat in Mongolia. All those cheap souvenir things made right next door in China are received with glee (I should've brought along key rings and fridge magnets, even though they don't lock their gers or have a fridge.) Other good gifts include pencils (pen ink can freeze in winter), flags, scarves, postcards and small notebooks. You can buy Russian lollies in UB, and packs of (cheap) cigarettes work well. Don't make a ceremony of giving gifts, or expect profuse thanks – but you will have made them very happy. Do indulge in the hospitality offered – and learn the joys of roof-dried cheese curd. Don't forget that drivers and guides expect tips, too.

Can you Play Chess? There's a chess set right under the front seat! I hadn't played for ages but was quickly absorbed by the post-dinner game between driver and guide. They all play – it must be the Russian influence – and if you commit yourself to sharing time with Mongolians in their own favourite pursuits, the rewards are great. Basketball, anyone? Check out the hoops outside many family gers. Join in a quick game if you see one going, though dribbling the ball can be a new experience out in the steppe! Kids also love riding their BMX-style bikes far across the landscape.

Photo opportunities are plentiful when staying with a ger family (Carl Robinson).

Rodeo Skills: Most outsiders don't know that Mongolian nomads switch horses every two or three days. These wiry, wide-shouldered, shaggy-manned horses, squatter than Western horses, run wild most of the time – and it's always an amazing sight bringing on the next shift. For one brief horse trek I took, the guide had chased my very own steed 200 kilometres across the mountain steppe the day before after he'd run off... but "Brown Horse" was as calm as he could possibly be! (Horses don't have names, and are distinguished by colour.) You'll often see little rodeos going on as the replacement horses are brought in. Feel free to join in. Once the horse's front feet are tied, its mouth bridled and the saddle hitched on, someone – often a young kid – jumps on for a wild ride across the steppe. In minutes, the horse is ready for use and rejoins the herd. Mongolian horses are not shod, and the horse riding accoutrements are fascinating: classic wooden Mongolian saddles with beaten-silver medallions; the beloved leather wool-stuffed Russian Cavalry saddle with its distinctive stainless-steel loop; and Russian Cav boots more in use than the traditional Mongolian boot with raised toes.

The Vodka: This is Mongolia's poison of choice. But at the end of a long day's riding, a shot of 37.5% alcohol certainly relaxes the muscles (vodka is also recommended for a wobbly tummy). After that though, all bets are off, with many drinking continuously into the early hours. (Some Germans kept our entire tourist ger camp awake drinking the stuff until 2am, when a blizzard started.) There was a vodka ban in early 2008 after a bad batch killed a few, but the brew is now well monitored. Vodka is available everywhere, along with juices. Relaxing with Mongolians who like a drink, you'll find yourself in

Top: Airag *– fermented mare's milk – is intrinsic to Mongolian life (Leo Murray). Above: A Kazakh family meal , or* dastarkhan *(Elbegzaya Lhagvasuren).*

fascinating conversation; they may ask for entrepreneurial advice, share their hopes and dreams, provide fascinating family tales, and hold forth on politics, religion and customs. You won't need to read yourself to sleep afterwards.

The Women: You'll be falling in love every day in Mongolia! The women are indeed very beautiful; guides have a strict code of ethics and ger camp girls are treated respectfully. Back in UB, where women outnumber men three to one, one can easily find oneself in "deep and meaningful conversation" with any number of lovely women. (No wonder so many marry foreigners.) But a high divorce rate means many single mothers around too. There's a certain feeling of desperation in the ones you meet in bars and clubs. Others, if free for the evening, will certainly join you for dinner. Don't forget, the women really run the country.

The Rock 'n Roll: Let your hosts set the soundtrack for this movie! In fact, especially with your own driver and guide, make sure they're well equipped sounds-wise. The lilting and throatal tones of Mongolian music soon entrance. One particular CD of a popular baritone singer followed me all across the country – and I ended up singing along! Enjoy the silence but share your music too. You must know at least two songs to sing while in Mongolia, and play karaoke star when asked, too.

The Medicine: Don't arrive without travel insurance, including an air evacuation clause if something serious happens. Hospitals in UB are fine but much less so in the provinces. Bring your own prescription medicine. Diarrhoea, rehydration and antibiotic medications are available locally, but bring a "starter pack". Above all, be extra careful and don't take risks. The nearest hospital is often very far away in Mongolia.

Above: A rainbow creates a wonderful sunset backdrop for a tent camp (Leo Murray).
Below: A wolf carcass adorns the spare wheel on a Russian jeep (Carl Robinson).

Other Necessities: A flashlight or two. A lighter. Your favourite mug for tea or coffee. Sunglasses. A good broad-brimmed hat. Sunscreen. Sturdy shoes. A pair of light sandals or thongs (flip-flops). A swimming suit for the hot springs. A washcloth. A blow-up pillow. Camping gear is available but it's cheaper to bring your own along. Film is available but also cheaper purchased overseas.

Left: An archer prepares himself at the Naadam Festival (Graham Taylor).

Below: A Bactrian camel hauls water back to a ger in the Ulz River Valley in the Great Eastern Steppe (Carl Robinson).

The most effective way for a nomad to lasso and capture an errant horse is with a long pole sporting a noose at the end – but expert horsemanship is required (Graham Taylor).

Fly-fishing for taimen in the rivers of northern Mongolia is recognised to be one of the world's great angling experiences (Carl Robinson).

FACTS FOR THE TRAVELLER

GETTING THERE

Mongolia is still relatively unknown as a tourist destination. But from only a handful of carefully chosen, politically correct visitors before the fall of its Communist regime in 1990, Mongolia's tourism industry has grown massively in recent years with an estimated 400,000 visitors in 2008 (this figure is all the more impressive as most tourists visit only in the warm summer months between June and August). In addition to neighbouring countries such as China, Japan and South Korea, most visitors come from Europe, including Britain, Russia and the former Eastern Bloc countries, the United States, Australia and New Zealand. With a still-maturing tourism industry and infrastructure, tourism already contributes 10 percent of Mongolia's GDP. Getting to Mongolia has never been easier – and tourism will inevitably grow in the coming years.

BY AIR

Government-owned **MIAT Mongolian Airlines** (see Airlines, page 496) operates the most extensive international flight network into the capital, Ulaanbaatar (UB), from Berlin, Moscow, Beijing, Seoul, Tokyo, Osaka and Nagoya using a modern fleet of non-Russian

Domestic flights are often the best option when visiting the more remote regions of the country (Leo Murray).

aircraft. In addition, **Air China** flies regularly from Beijing; Russia's **Aeroflot** from Moscow; **ANA** from Japanese cities; and **Korean Air** from Seoul. Mongolia's two privately owned domestic airlines, **Aero Mongolia** and **Eznis**, are experimenting with flights to secondary international destinations such as Hohhot and Hailaar in Inner Mongolia, Urumqi in China's western Xinjiang Uygur Autonomous Region, and Irkutsk and Ulan Ude on Russia's Lake Baikal. For those looking for a more exotic entry into Mongolia, a regular air service connects the Kazakhstan city of Almaty with Olgiy in western Mongolia's Bayan-Olgiy aimag, home to many of the country's Kazakh minority.

International and domestic airlines run winter and summer timetables, increasing flights – and prices – during the busy tourist season. With the growth of business links and tourism, new routes are constantly coming on stream, or at least rumoured so, such as flights into Hong Kong or Bangkok. Even the Internet is confusing, so a well-informed travel agent is strongly recommended for those visiting Mongolia. In general, fares are relatively expensive, and flights need to be booked early.

By Road

Mongolia has numerous border crossing points with China and Russia, but only a few are open to foreigners. Besides the road crossing alongside the Trans-Mongolian rail line at **Erenhot-Zaminn Uud** on the Chinese-Mongolian border, the other crossing points are **Tsagaannuur-Tashant** in western Bayan-Olgiy aimag and **Altanbulag-Naushk Hiagt** north of UB on the Russian border. More may open in coming years but the crossings are notoriously time-consuming and road travel is hardly an attractive option.

By Train

Most visitors arrive in Ulaanbaatar by rail on the **Trans-Mongolian Train** either from Beijing (roughly 30 hours) or from Moscow (five days), spending a couple of days between train services or combining train with air travel for longer stays. (This train is frequently and wrongly referred to as the Trans-Siberian, which actually runs from Moscow to Vladivostok on Russia's Pacific coast.) Direct trains from Beijing to UB run twice a week. With options of two- or four-berth cabins, the cost is reasonable and the trip a wonderful introduction to the country (see Riding the Trans-Mongolian Express, page 166). Daily trains also run from UB to Irkutsk, and there are less regular services to Hohhot in Inner Mongolia. The cheapest alternative is local trains to the Chinese-Mongolian border from either Beijing or UB and then crossing over by taxi.

VISAS

With the exception of those listed below, visitors are required to have a valid passport with at least six months validity remaining and a visa issued by Mongolian diplomatic missions or honorary consuls. Most are issued for 30 days and can be extended for another 30. Citizens of the following countries do not require visas: United States, Hong Kong, Macau, Malaysia, Singapore, Philippines, Kazakhstan, Israel, Cuba, Azerbaijan, Turkmenistan, Ukraine, Georgia, Belarus and Kyrgyzstan. (Visitors in transit via China also need a visa for that country, preferably a double-entry.) Mongolia has numerous diplomatic missions overseas, plus Honorary Consuls, where you can apply for a visa. For a full list check out **www.mongolianconsulate.com.au/mongolia/embassies.shtml**

Visitors are required to fill out a Customs Declaration form, which must be retained until departure. Duty-free allowances include 200 cigarettes, 50 cigars or 250g of tobacco; one litre of vodka, two litres of wine and three litres of beer; goods up to a value of US$1,000 and personal effects. Pornography and publications and other media critical of Mongolia are prohibited. Goods up to a value of Tg20,000 can be exported and official permission is required for antiques and fossils.

GETTING AROUND

Mongolia is not the easiest destination to fly in, rent your own car and drive around the country (although it is possible – **SIXT Rent A Car**, tel: 70110304, info@sixt.mn, www.sixt.mn,

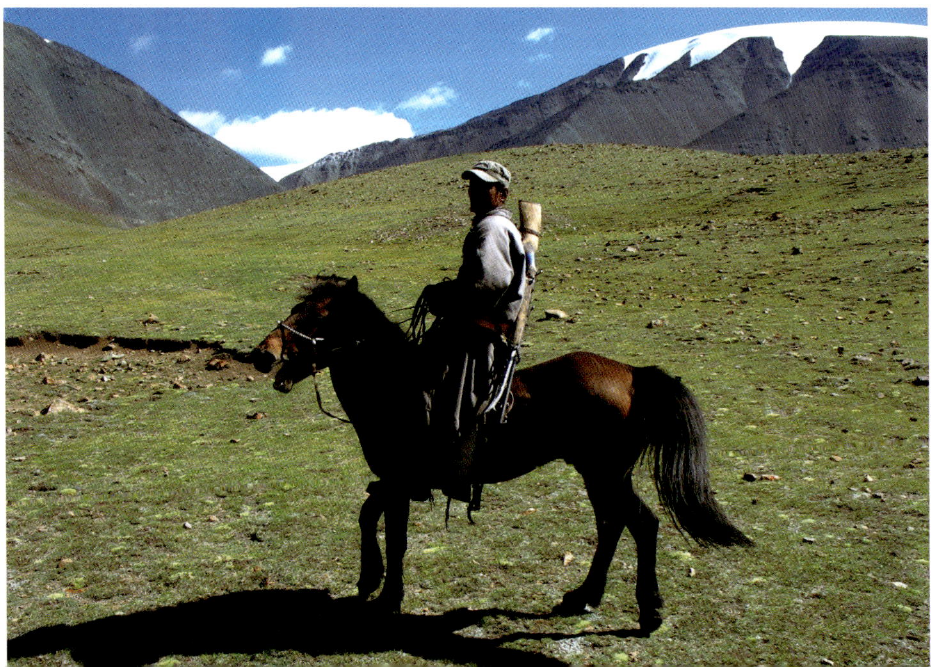

offers short-term and long-term car rental for travel and tour activities, with VIP pick-up/drop-off service). Rail and road transport is still rudimentary and requires a lot of time and patience, especially as foreign languages, other than Russian, are not widely spoken. Hitchhiking is not recommended. Domestic airlines serve many *aimag*, or provincial, centres but getting out into the countryside from them presents the same problems.

Russian vehicles are plentiful in Mongolia – but petrol stations are less so (Carl Robinson).

The best way to travel around Mongolia is with your own driver and guide (roughly US$100 per day) with a tailor-made tour organised beforehand by a local tour company. Many also offer all-inclusive, set-price tours, including catering for special interests such as hunting, fishing and trekking, plus a wide range of adventure tours. Most foreigners arrive on tours organised by overseas-based companies in partnership with locally based providers. Another option is to organise your travel upon arrival with a tailored tour or activity such as horse trekking, or by joining larger tours running set itineraries, a particular favourite among budget travellers. Dropping into Mongolia at the height of the summer tourist season without any preparation, however, can lead to disappointment.

Perhaps the best advice is to study up and then organise your trip well in advance over the Internet with a local operator. Mongolia has an incredible number of tour companies and most offer similar itineraries running the so-called Golden Circuit of the South Gobi, Karakorum (Harhorin) and Lake Hovsgol. Typically lasting from 15 to 21 days, travel is by road with an occasional domestic air flight, such as a flight back to UB at journey's end. Besides sightseeing, tours often offer brief horse, camel and/or yak cart treks and visits with nomad families, sometimes staying overnight. Accommodation is generally at tourist camps, which have a dining and toilet block and neat rows of *gers* with two or three guests sharing each one. (Some camps offer wooden cabins.) Quality and food varies. Less expensive tours offer camping. Tours include all accommodation, entry fees, meals, drivers and guides. Vehicles are a mixture of Japanese, South Korean and Russian 4WDs, with the latter notoriously slow but very reliable. But no matter what you've paid, Mongolia's roads – or lack thereof – are a great leveller. (Just don't be shy about calling a break and insist on a daily rotation of seats.)

Left : Rifle slung over his shoulder, a hunter heads off into the mountain terrain where no motor vehicle can follow (Leo Murray).

While the Golden Circuit certainly gives a good cross-section of Mongolia, my own advice is to find – or create – a tour that goes further off this well-worn trail, such as to the Bayanhongor Gobi, the Altai Mountains or eastern Mongolia; or pursue a special interest such as history, religion or even bird-watching. Distances are always farther than you think – and the pace can be exhausting. It's a lot more rewarding to enjoy one region at a leisurely pace than rushing through a jam-packed itinerary. Make sure your itinerary gives you the odd day of leisure.

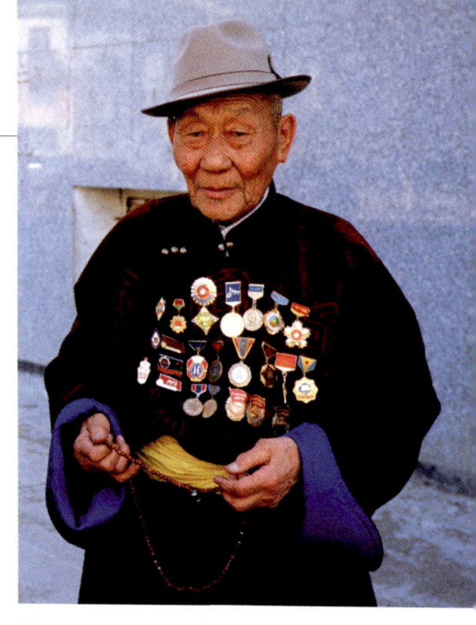

Memories go with the medals for this veteran in UB (Carl Robinson).

Communications

Making international telephone calls, or sending faxes, out of Ulaanbaatar is easy from hotels or the Central Post Office on Suhbaatar Square, but much more difficult outside the capital. IDD Cards, or International Calling Cards, are widely available starting at Tg3,000, as are Globus Card, Smart Card and Micom for use with mobile phones. A cheaper and simpler option is to purchase a prepaid SIM card for your mobile phone from a Mongolian telecom operator – very useful for local calls to your guide and/or tour operator. Internet and even wireless connections are widely available around UB but generally only at post offices in aimag centres. (It's best to advise family and friends by e-mail of your local number in case of emergency. Mongolia's country code is 976.) For those still into "snail mail", you can buy stamps for letters and postcards at hotels, but they're cheaper at the Central Post Office which also sells cards. Parcel post is rather expensive, ranging from US$25 to $40 per kilogramme depending on destination.

Crime

Unfortunately, with Ulaanbaatar's population jump in recent years and the hard-scrabble existence of some, street crime such as aggravated assault has increased and precautions should be taken when walking alone in the city at night. The most common crimes against foreigners are pickpocketing and bag snatching, including slashing victim's clothing to reach wallets, mobile phones and other valuables. Crime rises sharply before, during and after the Naadam Summer Festival in July and throughout the summer tourist season, as well as during and after Tsagaan Sar, the Winter Festival, in January or February. Be especially careful of robbery or pickpockets in crowded areas such as the Chinggis Khan International Airport in UB, the city's State Department Store and Naran Tuul Covered Market. When travelling, don't tempt thieves by leaving valuables out in the open.

CLIMATE & CLOTHING

Mongolia has an extreme climate with temperatures below freezing for most of the year. However in summer, when most tourists visit, temperatures are warm and pleasant in the mid-20s Celsius (70°F), though reaching over 40°C in the Gobi Desert. Spring can be notoriously variable. Even in summer, overnight temperatures can drop dramatically. Depending on what parts of Mongolia you'll visit, a "layered" approach is best with a mix of undergarments such as T-shirts, to sweatshirts or pullovers, a lightweight windbreaker and finally a warm jacket. Don't forget a scarf, gloves and woollen hat. Be practical rather than stylish, although you'll need one or two smart-casual outfits for UB.

CURRENCY

Mongolia's currency is the *tugrug* (also spelled togrog, tughrik or tugrik) and in August 2009 was worth Tg1,443 to US$1. Coins come in 20, 50, 100, 200 and 500 denominations, and banknotes in 10, 20, 50, 100, 500, 1,000, 5,000, 10,000 and 20,000 tugrug. Foreign currency can be exchanged at commercial banks, major hotels and UB's international airport. Stock up before heading out on trips. The US dollar is the preferred currency. Credit cards are also accepted at major hotels, restaurants and tourist shops. UB and major cities also have ATMs. The **Golomt Bank of Mongolia** offers comprehensive financial services for international and domestic businesses as well as individual travellers (e-mail: mail@golomtbank.com, website: www.golomtbank.com).

ELECTRICITY

Mongolia uses 220V/50HZ electricity and a European-style plug, or two widely spaced round pins.

ETIQUETTE

Reference was made earlier to Cultural Taboos (see Special Topic, page 241) and Mongolians appreciate your awareness of and adherence to them. Above all, stay low-key, don't shout or show your anger. When drinking with Mongolians, do "buy a round" or even a bottle or two. In restaurants, the "invitee" usually pays but bill-splitting is also permitted.

HEALTH

Visitors to Mongolia should be in good health and prepared to engage in a reasonable amount of physical activity. Bring your prescription medicine and a batch of anti-diarrhoeal, antacid and antibiotic medications. (Rehydration sachets, sunscreen lotion and lip balm are also useful.) Diarrhoea and altitude sickness are the most common ailments. Medical facilities, including emergency care, are limited or nonexistent, especially outside UB.

A mountain of wool awaits traditional processing either into felt or warm clothing (Leo Murray).

Infectious diseases such as plague, meningococcal meningitis and tuberculosis are present at certain times of the year. Sanitation in some restaurants is poor, particularly outside UB, and stomach illnesses are frequent. Bottled water and other routine precautions are advisable. Travel insurance, including medical evacuation, is imperative. In UB, **Bodi Insurance LLC** (400 Bodi Tower, Jigjidjav St, tel: 70110280, office@bodiinsurance.mn, www.bodiinsurance.mn) is partnered with SOS International and offers emergency evacuation as part of its "Inbound Travel Insurance" policy. **Mongol Daatgal Co Ltd** (Mongol Daatgal Building, Peace Ave-13, tel: 11320524, insurance@mongoldaatgal.mn, www.mongoldaatgal.mn) also offers insurance services.

In the event of serious hospitalisation, ask the doctor or hospital to contact your relevant diplomatic mission for assistance. Even short-term visitors should have up-to-date Tetanus, Diphtheria and Hepatitis A vaccinations. See **www.traveldoctor.info** for more information.

Media

Mongolia has two weekly English-language newspapers, the *UB Post* and *Mongol Messenger*. In summer, a useful publication is the *Mongolian Travel News* with a range of articles on destinations, culture, people and entertainment. Major hotels offer CNN, BBC, CCTV and other news – in addition to quite an eclectic mix of other programmes that are always worth a browse to pick up local colour. Bookstores in UB stock a small number of English-language books, some available only here, such as Baabar's seminal *History of Mongolia* and Don Croner's useful publications.

PUBLIC HOLIDAYS

Mongolia's two main holidays are Tsagaan Sar (Lunar New Year), celebrated in January or February, and National Day on 11 July which is celebrated as the Naadam Festival. Also known as White Month, Tsagaan Sar is a time of family reunions and feasting where blue scarves, or *hadag*, are presented as gifts. The Naadam celebrates the "Three Manly Sports" of Archery, Wrestling and Horse Racing and has become a major tourist attraction in recent years with many itineraries pegged to attending the Festival – or small versions in aimags around the country. Both are marked by three public holidays, although tourism-related facilities remain open. New Year's Day, or Shin Jil, is celebrated with one public holiday while other holidays, such as Constitution Day in January, Mother's and Children's Day in June and Mongolian Republic Day in November take place on normal working days.

SHOPPING

Mongolia is renowned for its top-quality cashmere with boutiques and factory outlets selling sweaters and other knitted products. Other wearable items and decorations are made of camel hair. Other pleasant souvenirs are the traditional silk tunics or *deels*, jackets or *hurrum*, and Mongolian-style boots with uplifted toes. (**Montulga Co Ltd**, PO Box 1135, 3rd Khoroo, Khan-Uul District, tel: 11343445, montulga@mongol.net, www.nomadicart.mn, is a leading producer of leather goods and souvenirs using innovative technology.) Other attractive products are woodcarvings and puzzles, secular and religious paintings, statuary and silver jewellery. Those visiting Bayan-Olgiy in western Mongolia are encouraged to pick up handmade embroidery and other products made by the local Kazakh minority. Finally, don't forget to pick up a few CDs of traditional and modern Mongolian music to bring back pleasant memories of your visit.

The traditonal toe-curling boots of the nomad are a popular memento of the Mongolian experience (Leo Murray).

TIPPING

Like many modern societies, tipping is part of modern life in Mongolia. Leave small amounts with meals and drinks and round off taxi fares. Tip concierges and bellboys for help with luggage, typically Tg1,000 per bag. Most importantly, drivers and tour guides are woefully underpaid and count on tips to supplement their income. Don't forget to do a "whip-round" at journey's end (US$5 per client per day is a good yardstick). However, *do not* "tip" ger families you have visited or stayed with, but do give them a present.

The GREAT KHAANS Theme Park

"Chinggis Khaanii Ongon" LLC

Located in the heart of Chinggis Khaan's homeland, this unique project aims to build a huge theme park on an area covering 3,200 hectares, an expansive historical complex created to pay homage to the Mongolian Great Khaans who ruled vast Nomadic Empires from AD 209 to the 17th century. Set in the picturesque valley of Kherlen River among the foothills of Mount Burkhan Khaldun, the park is a joint-effort initiative by talented artists, Tengri Group and the local community. The Great Khaans Theme Park aims to become a world-class tourist development with museums, monuments, international-standard hotels and related services, serving the needs of connoisseurs of world history and developing into a hot spot for organisers of international conferences. Using a combination of traditional and modern architecture, artistry and oriental hospitality, events and themed performances will be provided throughout the year. The park will be opening its doors in 2011.

PRACTICAL INFORMATION

AIRLINES

MIAT, Mongolian Airlines – www.miat.com – Mongolia's state-owned international carrier no longer flies domestically. MIAT Building, 45 Buyant-Ukhaa, Ulaanbaatar 210134, tel: (976) 11 379935. Ticketing Office, Local Call 1881 or (976) 11 328268 / 11 312423.

EZNIS Airways – www.eznisairways.com – one of Mongolia's two privately owned domestic carriers. 1st floor, 8 Zovkhis Building, Seoul Street, Suhbaatar District, Ulaanbaatar 14251. Reservations, tel: (976) 11 333311, fax: (976) 11 331514.

Aero Mongolia – www.aeromongolia.mn – the second of Mongolia's privately owned domestic carriers. MPRP Central Building, Suhbaatar District, Ulaanbaatar. Reservations, tel: (976) 11 330373, fax: (976) 11 330374.

"Air Trans" Air Ticketing Agency – www.airtrans.mn – USA branch: www.airbridgeusa.com. PO Box 46-274, Suhbaatar St-1, Ulaanbaatar 210646. Tel: (976) 11 303030, fax: (976) 11 311794.

TRAVEL AGENCIES & TOUR OPERATORS

Most itineraries in Mongolia are "land-only". Visitors must make their own way to UB by air or train and obtain their own visas from Mongolian diplomatic missions.

MONGOLIAN TOUR OPERATORS

Mongolia today has dozens of travel companies offering tours from high-end to budget and catering to a wide variety of tastes, including "eco-tours". (Most foreign operators run their tours subcontracting through these local companies.) Many have a solid reputation for reliable service and quality and are easy to deal with over the Internet. With more departures and imaginative destinations, they can be a better option than overseas operators. They also offer tailor-made trips to more off-the-beaten-track destinations and activities to suit any interest. (Costs are not always posted but available on request.) Here is my list of recommendations, in alphabetical order:

Active & Adventure Tours – http://tourmongolia.com – with an emphasis on culture and ecofriendly adventure tours, this innovative company offers a wide range of tours, including winter travel, many in partnership with local communities. Unique family-to-family experiences, plus Music tours. PO Box 166, Ulaanbaatar 13. Tel: (976) 11 354662, fax: (976) 11 354663.

Ashihai Travel – www.ashihai.mn – a good selection of leisurely paced general tours, including the Land of Chinggis Khaan in Hentii, Youth tours and Mountain Climbing.

They own a stunning ger camp on the shore of Lake Hovsgol. PO Box 2738, or 311, State Property Building, 44a Baga Toiruu, Suhbaatar District, Ulaanbaatar. Tel: (976) 11 315459, fax: (976) 11 315459.

Bat Tour Mongolia (Battour Travel Agency) – www.tripsmongolia.com – a well-established company with a rich variety of off-the-shelf tours of varying duration, including day trips out of UB. Bird tours a speciality. Also provides tailor-made tours. PO Box 423, Ulaanbaatar 38. Tel: (976) 11 325677, fax: (976) 11 312617.

Boojum Expeditions – www.boojumexpeditions.com – first renowned for their horse-trekking tours, long-established Boojum provides top adventure trips around Mongolia. Great for personalised tours. Their ecofriendly lodge at Lake Hovsgol is one of the best ger camps. PO Box 902, Central Post Office, Ulaanbaatar. Email: info@boojum.com

Chinggis Toonot – www.chinggistoonot.com – a welcoming tourist camp in the region of the birthplace of Chinggis Khaan. PO Box 676, Ulaanbaatar 210523. Tel: (976) 7733 5588, fax: (976) 7733 5589.

The ETI GROUP – www.eti.mn – "professional and caring service for the discerning traveller". 19/1 Chinggis Avenue, Shine Tugul Complex D-1, Ulaanbaatar. Tel: (976) 7011 1334 or 9911 8959.

Fish Mongolia – www.fishmongolia.com – run as a joint British-Mongolian venture, Andy Parkinson and his hard-working team organise professional guided fly-fishing trips in Mongolia's northern rivers. Extremely knowledgeable, his www.mongolia-travel.mn site also offers planning and organising for canoeing, rafting, trekking and other overland tours around Mongolia, including customised trips to suit any pace or budget. PO Box 1960, Central Post Office, Ulaanbaatar 211213. Tel: (976) 11 311355 or 9977 8354. US toll-free Phone/Voicemail: 1-8660427-9668.

Juulchin Tourism Corporation of Mongolia – www.juulchin.com – established in 1954, this is Mongolia's oldest established travel and tourism company, privatised after 1990. Very professional, it offers a variety of classic cultural tours, adventure and eco-tours, including bird-watching. Tavan Bogd Plaza Building, Prime Minister Amar Street-2, Ulaanbaatar 20-A. Tel: (976) 11 328428 / 11 328455, fax: (976) 11 320246.

Juulchin World Tours Corporation – www.juulchinworld.com – a major operator for both the domestic and international markets, JWTC offers a huge range of tailor-made programmes covering the entire country, and is linked to subsidiary companies in both the US and Germany. Marco Polo Place, Jamyan Gunii Street 5/3, Ulaanbaatar. Tel: (976) 11 319401, fax: (976) 11 319402.

Karakorum Expeditions Mongolia – www.gomongolia.com – operated by long-time expatriate Graham Taylor, this established company offers regularly scheduled, well-paced two-week-minimum adventure and cultural tours. Bike, horse and mountain treks a strength. PO Box 542 or Gangariinn Guray Bldg, 1st Floor, SW side of State Circus, Ulaanbaatar 46. Tel: (976) 11 315655, fax: (976) 11 315655. USA Voicemail/Fax: (212) 658 9938.

Look Mongolia – www.lookmongolia.com – specialising in eco-based adventure tours to more remote parts of Mongolia, this company runs selected well-crafted, high-quality journeys. Discovery tours, Jeep overland tours, horseriding, eco-journeys and cultural expeditions. Excellent short tours include East Gobi, Hovsgol and Amarbayasgalant. Its Terelj Lodge outside UB is renowned for excellent cuisine and accommodation. Look Mongolia Building, Chinggis Khan Avenue 98, Ulaanbaatar 210136. Tel: (976) 11 344488, fax: (976) 11 343757.

Mongol Khan Expeditions – www.mongolkhan.com – imaginative tours and expeditions around Mongolia of 1–2 weeks' duration with visits to more out-of-the-way destinations such as White Cave & Hermen Tsav in Bayanhongor Gobi and western Altai's Lake Uureg and Turgen Mountains. They operate the comfortable and memorable Gobi Camels ger camp south of the Gobi Altai's mighty Ikh Bogd Mountain. PO Box 688, Sky Post or 1st Floor, Building 71, 10th Microdistrict, Bayangol District, Ulaanbaatar. Tel: (976) 11 687122, fax: (976) 11 687122.

Mongolian Travel Corporation – www.mongoliantravelcorporation.com – established in 2002 and including well-reputed German-based Mongolei Reisen GmbH (see International Tour operators below), this pioneering company offers a wide and comprehensive range of tours and products, including hunting and fishing. Constantly innovative, its latest is the Baikal Gobi Express, a luxury train from Russia's Lake Baikal to UB and the Gobi Desert. Juulchnii Street 22A, Ulaanbaatar. Tel: (976) 7013 0695.

Monkhentii LLC – email: undurkhaancamp@yahoo.com – operates the Undurkhaan Tourist Camp and Dadal Tourist Camp in Chinggis Khaan's homeland. House-3, 6th Khoroo, Bayanzurkh District, Ulaanbaatar. Tel: (976) 9888 8897 / 9811 9857, fax: (976) 11 460688.

Nomadic Expeditions – www.nomadicexpeditions.com – pioneers in adventures to all parts of Mongolia and beyond (see International Tour operators below). 76-28, 1-4000, Chingeltei-3, Ulaanbaatar 210644. Tel: (976) 11 313396, fax: (976) 11 320311.

Nomads Tours – www.nomadstours.com – established since 2001, it offers a wide range of tours, including upmarket and cultural offerings all over Mongolia. Trekking and mountaineering a speciality. Stopover tours. German-run with dedicated and highly experienced staff. PO Box 1008 or Peace & Friendship Building, Office 9, Peace Avenue, Ulaanbaatar. Tel: (976) 11 328146 or 7011 9370, fax: (976) 7011 9366.

Three Camel Lodge – www.threecamellodge.com – one of Mongolia's premier expedition eco-lodges. 76-30, 1-4000, Chingeltei-3, Ulaanbaatar 210644. Tel: (976) 11 330998, fax: (976) 11 320311.

Tseren Tours – www.tserentours.com – operated by Dutch-born Rik Idema who famously cycled his way around the world in 1992 and returned to marry Tseren… and start a tour company specialising in active and adventure tours. Offers off-the-map adventures including the Great Eastern Steppe, and suited to various budgets. Jeep tours, hiking, horse and camel treks, fishing, special interest and, of course, cycling. 14/1 Baruun Selbe (near State Dept Store), Ulaanbaatar. Tel: (976) 11 327083, fax: (976) 11 318560.

Tsolmon Travel – www.tsolmontravel.com – one of Mongolia's first post-1990 private tour operators, with a solid reputation. Operates a range of general, jeep safari, horse-riding and fishing tours, plus a range of round-trip fly-drive and special interest trips. Runs ger camps in Terelj and Terhiyn Tsagaan Lake. House C61, Suhbaatar District, Chinggis Ave, Ulaanbaatar 11. Tel: (976) 11 322870 or 9911 4913, fax: (976) 11 310323.

International Tour Operators

In United Kingdom and Europe:

Off the Map Tours – www.mongolia.co.uk – with offices in UK, Germany and Ulaanbaatar, this company offers a wide range of tours, including motorcycle and mountain bike tours. 20 The Meer, Fleckney, Leicester, LE8 8UN, UK. Tel/fax: 012385 643333.

Bales Worldwide – www.balesworldwide.com – group tours of 15 and 19 days, including Naadam Festival in July, with an emphasis on luxury. Bales Worldwide Ltd, Bales House, Junction Road, Dorking, Surrey RH4 3HL, UK. Tel: 0845 0571819.

Mongolei Reisen GmbH – www.mongoliantravelcorporation.com – experienced and well-organised tour company with a wide variety of tours, including hunting trips and luxury trains. Am Spargelfeld 3, 16540 Hohen Neuendorf, (b.Berlin), Germany. Tel: 49 3303 214552,fax: 49 3303 214554. Also with offices in UB (see Mongolian Travel Corporation).

In USA and Canada:

Academic Travel Abroad – www.academic-travel.com – expert-led voyages into Mongolia for National Geographic Expeditions and the Association of Yale Alumni with an emphasis on cultural travel. 1920 N Street NW, Suite 200, Washington, DC, 20036, USA. Tel: (202) 785 9000 or (800) 556 7896, fax: (202) 342 0317.

Boojum Expeditions – www.boojumexpeditions.com – see Mongolian Tour Operators above. 14543 Kelly Canyon Rd, Bozeman, MT 59715, USA. Tel: (800) 287 0125, fax: (406) 585 3474.

Eldertreks – www.eldertreks.com – specialising in adventure tours for older travellers, this Canadian-based company runs several comfortable expert-led expeditions to Mongolia annually. 597 Markham St, Toronto, ON M6G 2L7, Canada. Tel: (416) 588 5000 or (800) 741 7956, fax: (416) 588 9839.

Geographic Expeditions – www.geoex.com – expert-led quality group tours working with a top Mongolian partner. Tours include festivals and cultural events.

1008 General Kennedy Avenue, PO Box 29902, San Francisco, CA 94129 0902, USA. Tel: (415) 922 0448 or (800) 777 8183.

Nomadic Expeditions – www.nomadicexpeditions.com – high-end, well-reputed tour company with long links to Mongolia. Trips to dinosaur and archaeological digs, eagle hunters and cultural centres. Operates the South Gobi's Three Camels Lodge. Group and private tours, some in combination with travel to Siberia and Tibet.

1095 Cranbury-South River Rd, Suite 20A, Jamesburg, NJ 08831, USA. Tel: (609) 860 9008 or (800) 998 6634, fax: (609) 860 9608. Also has an office in UB.

Sweetwater Travel Company – www.sweetwatertravel.com – pioneers of fly-fishing in Mongolia in the early 1990s. Top-quality trips with a strong emphasis on assisting local communities. (Their website will have anglers on the first plane over.)

5082 US Hwy 89 South, PO Box 668, Livingston, MT 59047, USA. Tel: (406) 222 0624 or (888) 347 4286.

In Australia:

Intrepid – www.intrepidtravel.com – with its distinctive style and well-priced tours, this Melbourne-based company offers a 15-day tour, plus others off the Trans-Mongolian Train.

PO Box 2781, Fitzroy, VIC 3065. Tel: (61 3) 9473 2626, fax: (61 3) 9419 4426.

Karakorum Expeditions Mongolia – www.gomongolia.com – see Mongolian Tour Operators above.

Peregrine Adventures – www.peregrineadventures.com – a well-established adventure tour company which offers more unconventional tours to Mongolia, including trekking in the Altai. Well-informed and experienced local guides.

Level 3, 380 Lonsdale St, Melbourne, VIC 3000. Tel: (61 3) 8601 4444, fax: (61 3) 8601 4422.

Wendy Wu Tours – www.wendywutours.com.au – best known for her budget-priced and fully inclusive tours to Asian countries, this Sydney-based company runs a three-week tour coinciding with the annual Naadam Festival in July.

Level 9, 275 George Street, Sydney NSW 2000. Tel: (61 2) 9224 8888 or in-country 1300 727998, fax: (61 2) 9993 0444.

Accommodation

Ulaanbaatar has a wide range of hotels from top-end to budget-priced and the range and quality is also improving in aimag centres. As part of tour packages, overseas and local travel operators arrange hotels, often into those listed below. Higher-end establishments have wireless Internet connection. For independent travellers, contact these hotels directly or go to **www.mongoliahotel-link.com** for a wider choice and the best deals.

Khan Palace Kempinski – www.khanpalace.com (from US$125) – located in East UB, the Kempinski is Mongolia's leading five-star hotel. A "class act" with a variety of restaurants and friendly service. Highly recommended, especially after a long trip out of town. Wireless Internet available. East Cross Road, Peace Avenue, Bayanzurkh District, Ulaanbaatar. Tel: (976) 11 463463, fax: (976) 11 463464.

Chinggis Khaan Hotel – www.chinggis-hotel.com (from US$95) – UB's first post-90s hotel with its glass-fronted design meant to evoke the "steppes" of Mongolia and size to match. A favourite for diplomats. Tokyogiin Gudamj 10, Sansar, Ulaanbaatar. Tel: (976) 11 313788.

Ulaanbaatar Hotel – www.ubhotel.mn (from US$99) – this Grande Dame of Mongolian hotels dates from the Communist period when it hosted visiting comrades and the odd Western journalist. Privatised and revamped, now one of UB's five-star hotels. Close to Suhbaatar Square. 37 Little Ring Road, Ulaanbaatar. Tel: (976) 11 320237/11 325368, fax: (976) 11 324485.

Bayangol Hotel – www.bayangolhotel.mn (from US$80) – this twin-towered landmark hotel is just a quick walk from Central UB and Seoul Street. Rooms with balconies, friendly service and great restaurants – a personal favourite. PO Box 43 or 5 Chinggis Khaan Avenue, Ulaanbaatar. Tel: (976) 11 312255, fax: (976) 11 326880.

Palace Hotel – www.palace.mn (from US$60) – a quick taxi ride from Central UB and right across the roundabout from the Bogd Khaan's Winter Palace. Good restaurants, including a ger-on-wheels beer garden out front. 25 Chinggis Khaan Avenue, Ulaanbaatar 210136. Tel: (976) 11 343565, fax: (976) 11 343001.

Puma-Imperial Hotel – www.pumaimperialhotel.mn (from US$60) -- small, friendly, centrally located hotel just off UB's main square. Great breakfasts, and a café & bar off the lobby. Amar Street-2, Suhbaatar District, Ulaanbaatar 46. Tel: (976) 11 313043, fax: (976) 11 319148.

Tuushin Hotel – www.tuushinhotel.mn (from US$40) – centrally located right off Suhbaatar Square and across from the Culture Palace. Clean and comfortable. 2 Prime Minister Amar's Street, Ulaanbaatar 210620a. Tel: (976) 11 323162, fax: (976) 11 325903.

MTZ
RAILTOUR
Mongolian Railway's Tour Bureau
MONGOLIAN RAILWAY`S TOUR BUREAU
Embark on a TRANS-SIBERIAN RAILWAY
the adventure of a lifetime!
Moscow
Irkutsk
Ulaanbaatar
Zamiin - Uud
Beijing
Tickets available at:
http://eticket.mtz.mn
Tel: 976- 21-244450
976 - 99714320
Fax: 976- 21-244457
mail to: railtoursec@mtz.mn
shagdarsurenamar@yahoo.com
visit us at: www.mongolianrailtour.mn

Kharaa Hotel – www.kharaahotel.mn (from US$40) – located in northwest UB near the Gandan Monastery, this hotel has been tastefully decorated in a Mongolian theme. Pleasant rooms and a good restaurant. 6 Choimbolyn, West UB, Ulaanbaatar. Tel: (976) 11 313717.

RESTAURANTS

While the cuisine outside Ulaanbaatar can be quite basic, even at many ger camps, the capital has quite a variety of restaurants for every taste and budget, including vegetarian. These offer everything from European and American to Chinese, Japanese, Korean, Indian and even modernised Mongolian cuisine. The city has even imported that well-known Western invention, the Mongolian Barbecue. (But after days or weeks of wholesome Mongolian fare outside UB, be extra careful diving into a hot curry or greasy stir-fry. It could upset your stomach!) Here is a selection:

BD's Mongolian Barbeque – imported from the USA, this popular eatery allows guests to choose their own ingredients from a variety of meats, seafood, vegetables, sauces and spices which are then grilled for you on a monster-size grill. Salads too. Frenetic atmosphere. West of Ayanchin Outfitters, 9 Seoul Street, Suhbaatar District. Tel: (976) 11 311191.

Mr Wang Restaurant – a franchise from South Korea specialising in Chinese dumplings, Korean specialities and traditional Mongolian meat dishes. 1st Floor, Chinggis Khan Hotel, Bayan-Zurkh District, UB. Tel: (976) 11 325319.

Pizza Della Casa – started by a Mongolian who studied in Germany and Italy, this is the place to catch up on your pasta cravings, including pizza. Italian and European cuisine. Peace Avenue (West of Palace of Peace & Friendship), Chingeltei Microdistrict, UB. Tel: (976) 11 324114.

UB Delicatessen Restaurant – one of the busiest restaurants in UB, popular with foreign expats, tourists and trendy locals. Great breakfast menu, plus gourmet sandwiches and pizzas, pastas and salads for lunch and dinner. Vegetarian too. 40 Seoul Street, UB. Tel: (976) 11 211213.

Modern Nomads – modern Mongolian cuisine in a relaxing atmosphere. A favourite of locals and tourists alike, with friendly and hospitable service. Centrally located. Amar Street, Suhbaatar District, UB. Tel: (976) 11 318744.

Veranda Terrace Restaurant – located on a side street next to the lovely Choiijin Lama Monastery in central UB, this is one of the city's top restaurants (and a personal favourite). Great international cuisine and wine list; sink into couches inside or at a table on the veranda. **Silk Road** downstairs is another option, with a friendly atmosphere and great service. 5/1 Jamyn Gunii Gudamj, Central UB. Tel: (976) 11 330818.

California – for those hanging out for a hamburger, fries and a milk shake after their travels, this is the place. Also offers some Asian dishes, including Mongolian specialities, and salads and pasta. Pleasant and efficient staff. Seoul Street opposite Aeroflot Office, UB.

Café Amsterdam – operated by a group of Dutch expats, this café offers the best coffee in UB, plus tasty sandwiches and cakes. Airy, smoke-free and comfortable with a small balcony overlooking busy Peace Avenue. There's a library and free wireless Internet connection. My favourite drop-in spot in UB. Peace Ave. Tel: (976) 9578 0057.

Grand Khaan Irish Pub – this imposing establishment at the top end of UB's Seoul Street with its busy bars, restaurants and pleasant outdoor drinking area is a must-see destination. Modern Western and Mongolian food, a great atmosphere for people-watching and drinks. A local favourite – "Le Tout UB" is here! 1 Khoro, Suhbaatar District, UB. Tel: (976) 11 336666/11 330993.

Millie's Café – described by the Shaggy Yak as "routinely excellent" and "one of the best meals you can get", this café offers a pleasant menu of burgers, shakes, sandwiches and salads. A favourite of the local expat community of aid workers, business people and diplomats. Open for lunch and dinner. Marco Polo Building, Seoul Street, UB. Tel: (976) 11 330338.

Useful Websites

With the explosion of the cyber-world, you can find out a lot more about visiting Mongolia simply by surfing the Internet. Any search engine quickly has you in touch with airlines, accommodation, tours, news and current affairs. Here are some useful websites just for starters:

www.mongoliatourism.gov.mn – the official website of the Tourism Department of Ministry of Nature, Environment and Tourism. Updated regularly.

www.mnto.org/index.html – the website of the Mongolian National Tourism Organisation, an industry-based association based in Mongolia.

www.un-mongolia.mn/web – the website for various United Nations activities in Mongolia, with links to other international organisations working in the country.

www.mongolia-web.com – for regular news and feature stories on Mongolia, including many useful links.

www.business-mongolia.com – the best site for business news from Mongolia, including government and legislative activities. Great links too.

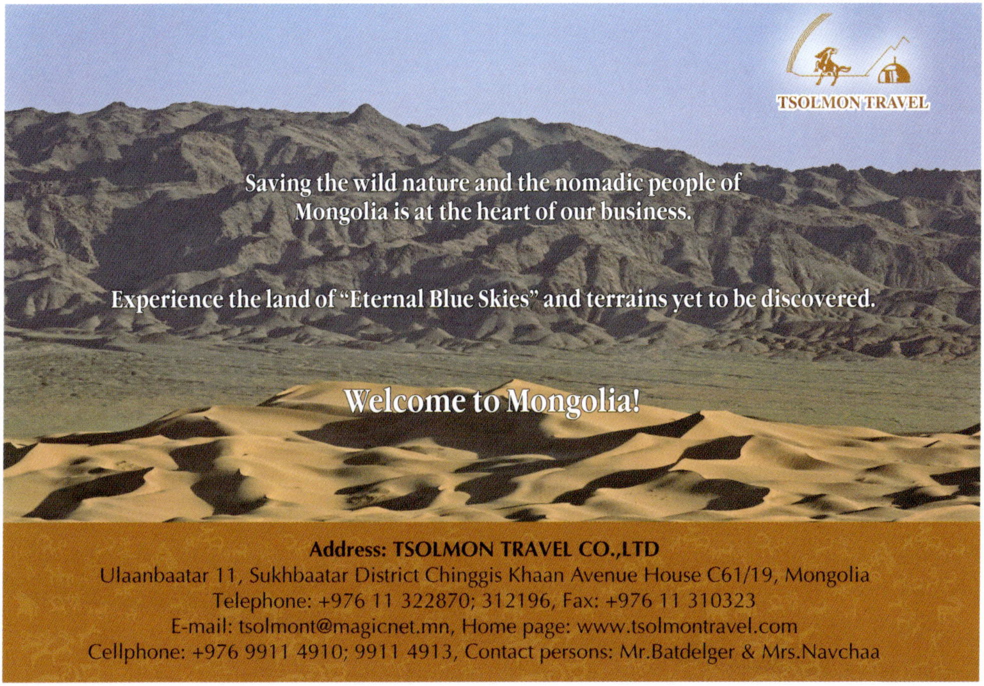
TSOLMON TRAVEL
Saving the wild nature and the nomadic people of Mongolia is at the heart of our business.
Experience the land of "Eternal Blue Skies" and terrains yet to be discovered.
Welcome to Mongolia!
Address: TSOLMON TRAVEL CO.,LTD
Ulaanbaatar 11, Sukhbaatar District Chinggis Khaan Avenue House C61/19, Mongolia
Telephone: +976 11 322870; 312196, Fax: +976 11 310323
E-mail: tsolmont@magicnet.mn, Home page: www.tsolmontravel.com
Cellphone: +976 9911 4910; 9911 4913, Contact persons: Mr.Batdelger & Mrs.Navchaa

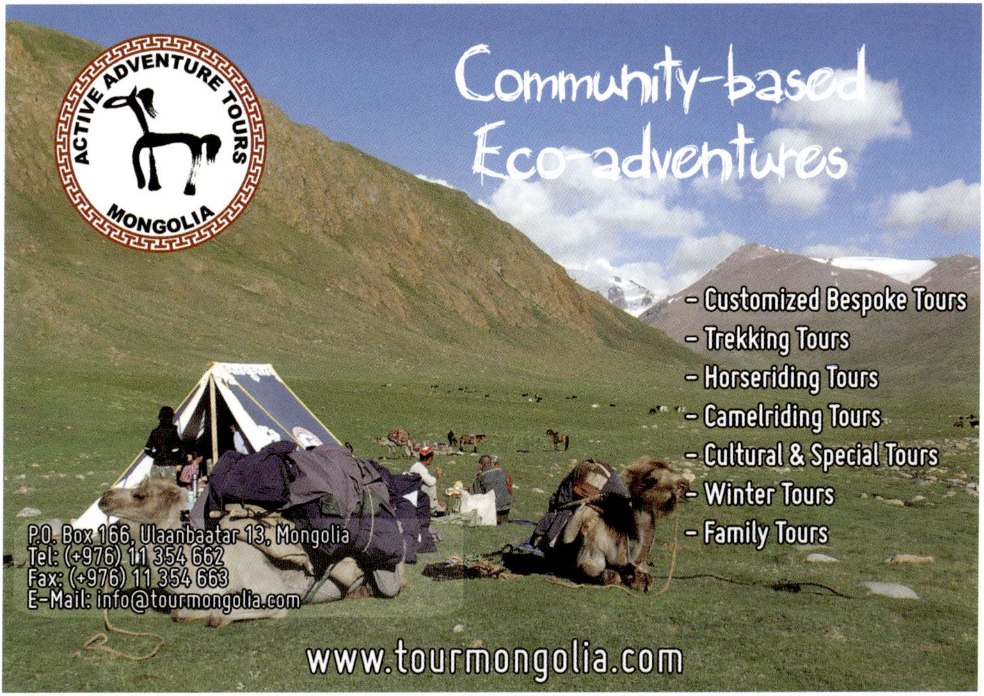
ACTIVE ADVENTURE TOURS MONGOLIA
Community-based Eco-adventures
- Customized Bespoke Tours
- Trekking Tours
- Horseriding Tours
- Camelriding Tours
- Cultural & Special Tours
- Winter Tours
- Family Tours
P.O. Box 166, Ulaanbaatar 13, Mongolia
Tel: (+976) 11 354 662
Fax: (+976) 11 354 663
E-Mail: info@tourmongolia.com
www.tourmongolia.com

FAVOURITE WEBSITES

During the course of researching and writing this guidebook, I've stumbled onto a handful of wonderful websites on Mongolia. Mostly blogs, they provide great insights into the country and its culture:

www.doncroner.net/blog.html: An expatriate American so deep into Mongolia and Buddhism – especially anything to do with Shambhala and Dambijantsan – you can't help but be drawn into his slightly eccentric life, travels... and love of tea. Visit the blog's lengthy archives and follow the links – his stories are impossible to find anywhere else.

www.chriskaplonski.com/index.html: Another American expat, this one at Cambridge University's Mongolia and Inner Asia Studies Unit and one of the world's leading and most widely published Mongolists. There are excerpts from his articles and latest research projects. Follow the fascinating links too.

http://mongolianhistory.blogspot.com: For history buffs on the prowl for yet another angle on Mongolia's long and fascinating history. Fascinating articles, literary excerpts and archival photos. And don't neglect "older posts" for even more. See also **http://mongolculture.blogspot.com** – these sites deserve a much wider readership.

www.mongolianculture.com: Operated by the Indo-Mongolian Society and slightly out of date, this site's still-live links to online historic, cultural and other resources are absolutely encyclopaedic.

http://mongolianstudies.blogspot.com: "This Month in Mongolian Studies" is run by the American Centre for Mongolian Studies (ACMS). Latest research projects and seminars, such as its 2008 conference on Owen Lattimore. Keep an eye out for special events. With time on your hands in UB, drop in for a visit at Building No. 5, Room 304, National University of Mongolia, tel: (976) 11 350486.

http://mongolianmusic.blogspot.com: A great introduction to the wide spectrum of Mongolian music, traditional to modern, including downloads. Click onto Bat-Ochir Araanz for a soundtrack for the journey ahead.

Glossary of Terms

Mongolian words and phrases are not always easy to translate into English. Here is a selection of everyday words you'll find useful during your visit:

Aimag – a province. Capitals are called aimag centres.

Bag – a smaller administrative centre, usually a former collective farm.

Davaa – Mountain Pass.

Deel – Traditional garment worn by men and women.

Els – Sand dunes.

Erdene – Jewel.

Ger – The traditional Mongolian dwelling, called yurts in other countries.

Gol – River.

Govi – Desert or Gobi.

Hiid – Monastery.

Hoomii – Throat singing.

Morin Huur – Horse fiddle, Mongolia's most renowned musical instrument.

Naadam – Mongolia's biggest holiday, celebrating the "Three Manly Sports" of wrestling, archery and horse racing.

Nuruu – Mountain Range.

Nuur – Lake.

Ovoo – Piles of stones at auspicious places, usually mountain passes or crests, with deep religious significance.

State Great Hural – Mongolia's parliament.

Sum – a district. Capitals are called sum centres.

Tal – Steppe.

Tsagaan Sar – the Mongolian Lunar New Year, or White Month.

Tsam – Distinctive religious dance with characters in large and colourful masks.

Uul – Mountain, usually following the name.

LANGUAGE

To get you started, here are a few greetings and expressions given as phonetic translations of spoken Mongolian. Vowel sounds and consonants are pronounced as follows:

aa	ar as in "car"	o	o as in "honey"
ai	i as in "live"	oi	oy as in "boy"
e	e as in "get"	oo	o as in "shown"
ee	ei as in "reign"	oo	or as in "corn"
ei	ay as in "say"	u	ou as in "course"
ii	ee as in "been"	u	ew as in "new"
iu	yu as in "you"	uu	oo as in "soon"
kh/h	an aspirated sound like "loch"	z	dz
o	o as in "got"		

WORDS & PHRASES

How are you? – *Saim bainuu?* (A typical form of "hello", usually followed by questions on health, family, cattle, etc)

Fine. How are you? – *Saing, ta saim bainuu?*

What's up? – *Soning yuu wain?*

Nothing new – *Soning yumyui*

Goodbye, or **Stay Well** (by one leaving) – *Saing suuyaarai*

Goodbye, or **Go Well** (by one staying) – *Saing yawaarai*

Goodbye (another form) – *Bayartai*

Thank you – *Bayarlalaa* (use sparingly)

Yes – *Tiim*

No – *Uu-gui*

Excuse me – *Uuch laa rai*

What is your name? – *Tanii ner hen be?*

My name is… – *Minii ner*…

Where are you from? – *Ta haanaas irsen be?*

I am from... – *Bi... aas irsen*

America – *Amerik*

Germany – *German*

Japan – *Yapon*

England – *Angli*

France – *Frants*

I understand – *Bi oilgoj baina*

I don't understand – *Bi oilgohgui baina*

I'm hungry – *Bi olsoj baina*

I'm thirsty – *Bi tsangaj baina*

I'm tired – *Bi yadarch baina*

I'm sick – *Bi ovdoj baina*

I'm lost – *Bi toorchihloo*

How much does it cost? – *Ene yamar unetei ve?*

Do you have a single/double room? – *Tainaid neg/hoyor ortoi oroo baina uu?*

Where is the...? – *Haana baodag ve...?*

Bank – *Bank*

Post Office – *Shuudan*

Hospital – *Emneleg*

Temple – *Hiid*

Museum – *Muzei*

Toilet – *Jorlon*

Shop – *Delguur*

Market – *Zakh*

Hotel – *Zochid buudal*

Hospital – *Emnelgiin gazar*

Food – *Hool*

Drink – *Undaa*

Water – *Us*

Beer – *Pivo*

Soap – *Savan*

Medicine – *Em*

Doctor – *Emch*

Police – *Tsagdaa*

Telephone – *Utas*

NUMBERS

1	*neg*
2	*hoyor*
3	*gurav*
4	*duruv*
5	*tav*
6	*zurgaa*
7	*doloo*
8	*naim*
9	*yus*
10	*arav*
11	*arvan neg*
12	*arvan hoyor*
20	*hori*
21	*horin neg*
22	*horin hoyor*
30	*guch*
31	*guchin neg*
40	*duch*
50	*tavi*
100	*zuu*
1,000	*myanga*

Following spread: Early morning light casts heavy shadow across the cliffs at Hermen Tsav in Bayanhongor Gobi (Carl Robinson).

RECOMMENDED READING

As a relatively unknown travel destination, it is certainly worthwhile reading a cross-section of books before your arrival, even bringing a couple along as travelling companions. Books on Mongolia fall into distinctive genres such as history, exploration, personal journeys and even fiction. With history in particular, there are glaring gaps with an overemphasis on the Mongol Empire period yet virtually nothing on the Manchu (Qing) and mostly Communist modern period.

The most detailed and comprehensive history is Baabar's *From World Power to Soviet Satellite: History of Mongolia* (University of Cambridge Press, 1999). Very expensive outside the country, the book is best purchased in UB. (The second volume up to 1990 is not yet translated.) More easily available is Paula L.W. Sabloff's large-format but paperback *Modern Mongolia: Reclaiming Genghis Khan* (University of Pennsylvania, 2001), which provides a well-illustrated look at the entire sweep of Mongolian history and culture, including the Communist period and afterwards. A great introduction.

On the Mongol Empire period, the best comes from John Man's *Genghis Khan, Life, Death and Resurrection* (St Martin's Press, 2004) and *Kublai Khan, the Mongol King Who Remade China* (Bantam, 2006), all the better for his taking readers to modern locales. Annoyingly revisionist but very readable is Jack Weatherford's bestseller *Genghis Khan and the Making of the Modern World* (Crown 2006). Others of interest are Tim Severin's *In Search of Genghis Khan* (Atheneum, 1991), written in the early post-Communist period, and Stanley Stewart's *In the Empire of Genghis Khan, A Journey Among Nomads* (Harper-Collins, 2000), which retraces the steps of an early Roman Catholic friar to the Mongol court. *The Secret History of the Mongols: The Origin of Chingis Khan* (Cheung & Tsui Company, 1998) is a translation of this famous book but is hard going, especially without more background knowledge of Mongolian locations. (A copy will definitely impress your hosts, however.) Although an odd recommendation, historical fiction writer Conn Iggulden is creating a six-book Conqueror Series on Genghis and Kublai Khan, starting with his *Wolf of the Plains* (*Genghis: Birth of an Empire* in the US) (Harper-Collins, 2007), which is racy and readable. (He also honestly explains his "literary licence" in the Afterword.)

Entering the more modern period, Martha Avery's excellent but not-easy-to-find *The Tea Road: China and Russia Meet Across the Steppe* (China Intercontinental Press, 2003) is one of the rare books on the Qing period and how tea became Mongolia's currency of trade. (Look out also for translated works of early Russian and other explorers.) Although more descriptive of Inner Mongolia and Xinjiang, Owen Lattimore's *The Desert Road to Turkestan* (Kodansha International, 1995) and his hard-to-get other publications on early Communist

Mongolia are absolute classics. Roy Chapman Andrews' reprinted *Across Mongolian Plains* (Fredonia Books, 2001) shows another face to the dinosaur-seeker of Charles Gallenkamp's well-written *Dragon Hunter: Roy Chapman Andrews and the Central Asiatic Expeditions* (Penguin, 2001). For the post-1990 period, Morris Rossabi's *Modern Mongolia: From Khans to Commissars to Capitalism* (University of California Press, 2005) is an essential, if slightly depressing, examination of where Mongolia's economy and politics are today.

Another genre are memoirs of travel and, more rarely, of living there, the best of which is Louisa Waugh's great *Hearing Birds Fly: A Nomadic Year in Mongolia* (Abacus, 2003) about her year in western Mongolia's Bayan-Olgiy aimag. Written still early in the post-Communist period, Beijing-based foreign correspondent Jasper Becker's *The Lost Country* (Sceptre, 1993) brings a journalist's eye to widest Mongolia, including Buryatia and Tuva, and explores multiple aspects of its culture. Less attractive are self-indulgencies such as Nick Middleton's *The Last Disco in Outer Mongolia* and Tim Cahill's Mongolian entry in *Remote Journeys Oddly Rendered*, which poke unnecessary fun at Mongolia. While we have excerpted Ewan McGregor and Charley Boorman's *Long Way Round* and Ben Kozel's *Five Months in a Leaky Boat*, their passages through Mongolia were only brief.

Other books of particular interest, available either online or in UB, are Don Croner's *Travels in Northern Mongolia* and *Guidebook to Locales Connected with the Life of Zanabazar*, both great travel companions. Also available locally is Gaby Bamana's *On the Tea Road: A Journey into Mongolian Life and Culture*. Keep an eye out for T*he Sun Eater & Almas, 12 Amazing Snowman Legends*, by Battulga Tumurdash (edited by Louisa Waugh, Ulaanbaatar, 2009).

With maps, I'd strongly recommend the excellently detailed *Mongolia Road Map* by Gazryn Zurag, whose assistance we enlisted in creating our own maps. Although difficult to find outside Mongolia, do purchase one upon your arrival (Cafe Amsterdam in Peace Avenue stocks them). Canadian-based International Travel Maps (www.itmb.com) produces a topographical map of Mongolia highlighting important sites, including tourist camps, but is not as accurate or comprehensive. The locally available *Tourist Map of Mongolia* produced by MPM includes tourist camps, historic sites and national parks – and a reverse full of facts and information. For specific destinations in Mongolia, especially its national parks, the best and most comprehensive are the "maps and guides" produced by Conservation Ink in Wyoming, USA (www.conservationink.org). Among their titles are the national parks of: Terelj and Hustai outside UB; the Gobi's Gurvan Saihan; Tavan Bogd in the Altai; and Lake Hovsgol. Order online or visit UB's Xanadu Bookshop.

DVDs always provide another insight with Mongolian feature films *The Song of the Weeping Camel*, *Cave of the Yellow Dog* and *My Beautiful Jinjiimaa* available online.

Above: The statue of Mongolian revolutionary Suhbaatar in Ulaanbaatar's central square.
Left: Bronze Age petroglyphs in Bichigt Khad, the Valley of Writings in the Gobi (Carl Robinson x2).

INDEX

User's Note: Mongolian names of individuals in the early historical period that have two elements are indexed under the first name (eg "Kutlug Tigin" is entered under "Kutlug"). Mongolian names from the modern era are indexed under the last name (eg "Horoloogiin Choibalsan" is entered under "Choibalsan").

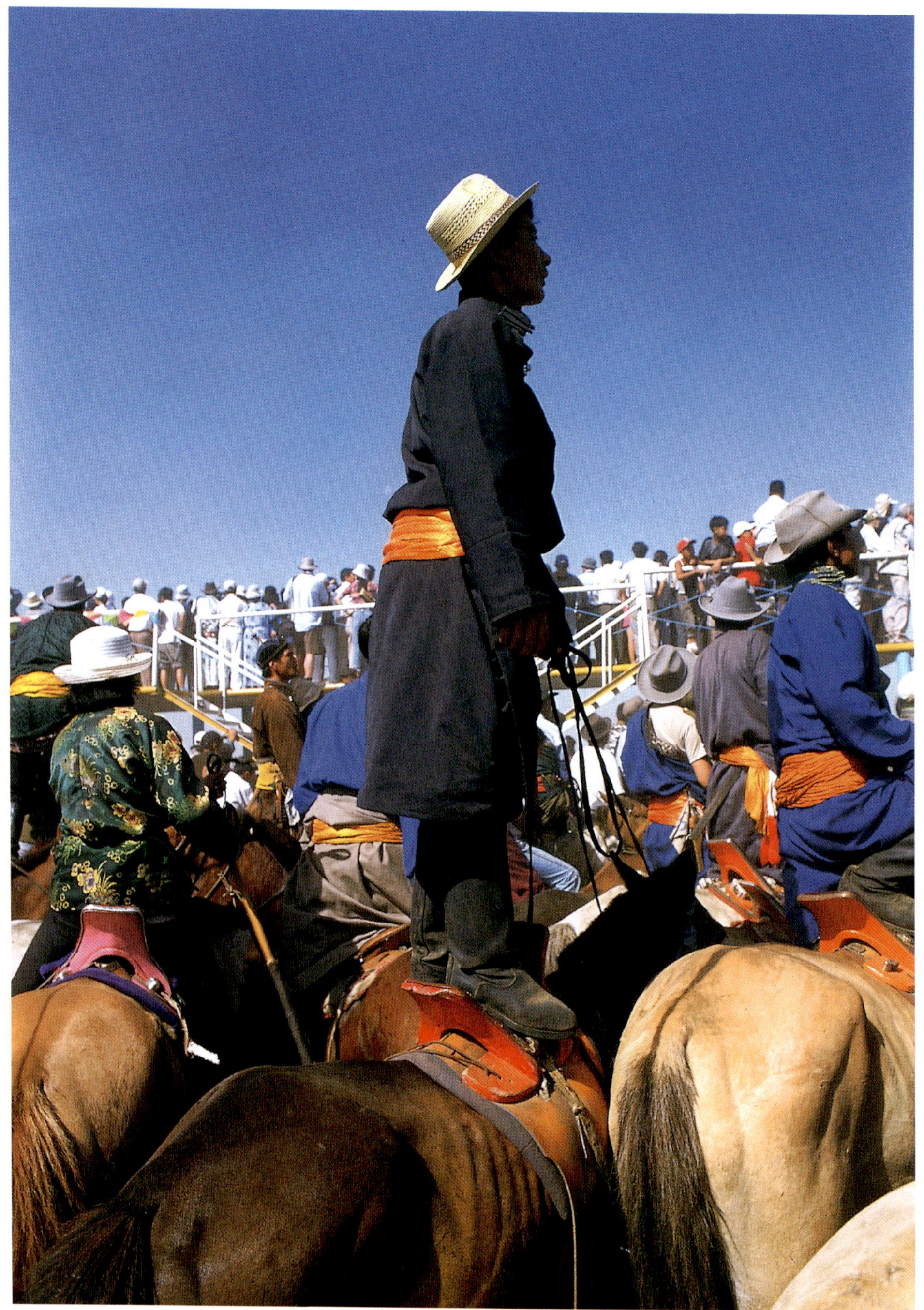

Above: Even the spectators at a Naadam festival can demonstrate skill on horseback (Graham Taylor). Right: Two young nomad children keep tight rein on their family's guard dog (Carl Robinson).

68

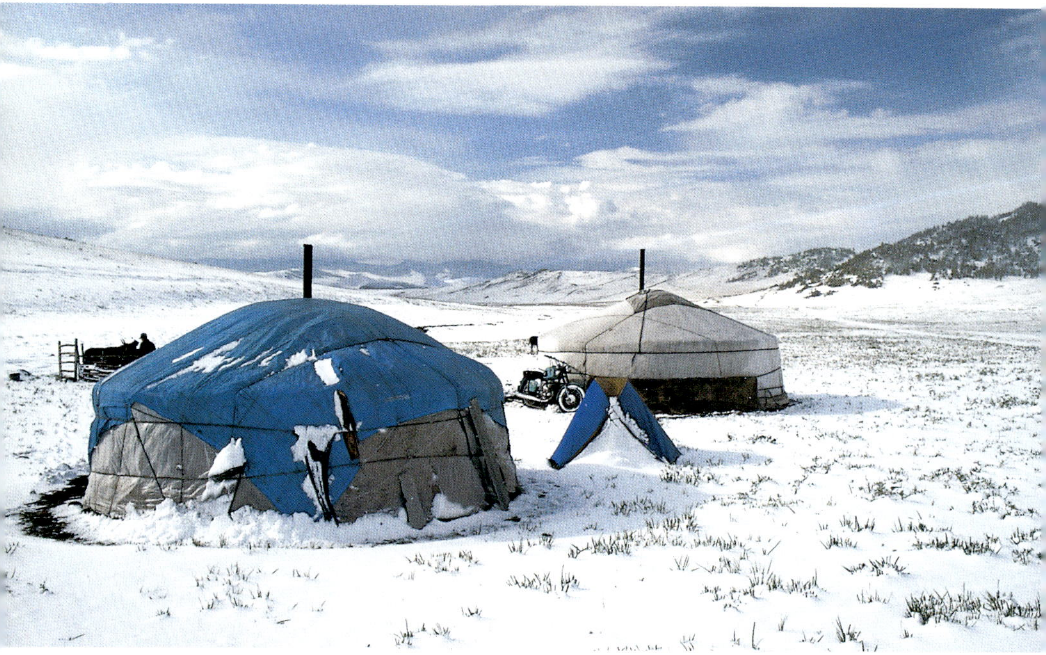

Top: A girl and her mother draw water for their cashmere goats from a well in the Bayanhongor Gobi (Carl Robinson). Above: Winter snowfall is rarely heavy, but can still cut nomadic encampments off from the outside world (Graham Taylor).

Make the most of your journey with ODYSSEY books, guides and maps

The Odyssey imprint ISBN prefix is 978-962-217

The Silk Road—Xi'an to Kashgar, Judy Bonavia, paperback, 8th ed, -761-1, © 2008

Russia and Asia, Edgar Knobloch, paperback, 1st ed, -785-7, © 2007

Silk Road—Monks, Warriors & Merchants, Luce Boulnois, paperback, Revised 1st ed, -721-5, © 2008

Afghanistan, Omrani & Leeming, paperback, Revised 1st ed, -746-8, © 2007

Moscow & St Petersburg, Masha Nordbye, paperback, 3rd ed, -771-0, © 2007

Kyrgyz Republic, Rowan Stewart & Susie Weldon, paperback, 3rd ed, -791-8, © 2008

Tajikistan, Robert Middleton & Huw Thomas, paperback, 1st ed, -773-4, © 2008

Ancient Silk Road Map, Tucker & Tozer, paperback, 1st ed, -788-8, © 2007

Land of the High Flags, Rosanne Klass, paperback, 1st ed, -786-4, © 2007

Uzbekistan, Calum MacLeod & Bradley Mayhew, paperback, 6th ed, -795-6, © 2008

Distributed in the United Kingdom and Europe by:
Cordee Ltd
11 Jacknell Road, Dodwells Bridge Industrial Estate
Hinckley, Leicestershire, UK, LE10 3BS
Tel: 01455 611185 Fax: 01455 635687
www.cordee.co.uk

Distributed in the United States of America by:
W.W. Norton & Company, Inc.
500 Fifth Avenue, New York, NY 10110
Tel: 800-233-4830 Fax: 800-458-6515
www.wwnorton.com

For more information, please visit: www.odysseypublications.com

RUSSIA
KYZYL
ULAANGOM
OLGIY
HOVD
ULIASTAI
ALTAI
MORON
TSETSERLEG
BAYANHONGOR
ARVAYHEER
Uvs
Hovsgol
Har Us
Hyargas
LEGEND
Road
Railway
ULAANBAATAR Capital of Mongolia
OLGIY Centre of aimag
Altay Centre of sum
National boundary of Mongolia
Boundary of the aimag
Pass
Bridge
Border exits
Mine
78.6 0 78.6 157km
© "GAZRYN ZURAG"Co.,Ltd